Social Security Law in Ireland

Social Security Law in Ireland

Fourth Edition

Mel Cousins

Gerry Whyte

This book was originally published as a monograph in the International Encyclopaedia of Laws/Social Security Law.

Founding Editor: Roger Blanpain
General Editor: Frank Hendrickx
Volume Editor: Willy van Eeckhoutte

Wolters Kluwer

Published by:
Kluwer Law International B.V.
PO Box 316
2400 AH Alphen aan den Rijn
The Netherlands
E-mail: lrs-sales@wolterskluwer.com
Website: www.wolterskluwer.com/en/solutions/kluwerlawinternational

Sold and distributed by:
Wolters Kluwer Legal & Regulatory U.S.
920 Links Avenue
Landisville, PA 17538
United States of America
E-mail: customer.service@wolterskluwer.com

ISBN 978-94-035-1818-3

e-Book: ISBN 978-94-035-1828-2
web-PDF: ISBN 978-94-035-1838-1

The Authors

Mel Cousins qualified as a barrister-at-law at the King's Inns, Dublin and has a PhD from the School of Law and Social Sciences, Glasgow Caledonian University. He has worked as a social policy and legal adviser to a wide range of organizations, including the Asian Development Bank, the European Commission, and United Nations agencies, including the International Labour Organization, the United Nations Children's Fund, and the United Nations Development Programme, the World Bank and social security authorities in a number of countries. Dr Cousins has written extensively on Irish social security and social policy issues from both a legal and political perspective and is a research fellow at the School of Social Work and Social Policy, Trinity College, Dublin.

Gerry Whyte lectures in Public Interest Law, Constitutional Law, and Collective Labour Law at the School of Law, Trinity College Dublin. The second edition of his book, 'Social Inclusion and the Legal System: Public Interest Law in Ireland' was published in 2015, and he is also a co-author of Kelly, The Irish Constitution (5th ed., 2018). He is a former director of two law centres, Community Law and Mediation and Mercy Law Resource Centre.

The Authors

Table of Contents

Table of Cont

Chapter 2

Table of Contents

List of Abbreviations

BP	Blind Pension
BTWFD	Back-to-Work Family Dividend
BWA	Blind Welfare Allowance
CA	Carer's Allowance
CB	Child Benefit
CPCROCA	Civil Partnership and Certain Rights and Obligations of Cohabitants Act
CSG	Carer's Support Grant
CSW	Commission on Social Welfare
DA	Disability Allowance
DCA	Domiciliary Care Allowance
DSP	Department of Social Protection
EAT	Employment Appeals Tribunal
ECHR	European Convention on Human Rights
ECtHR	European Court of Human Rights
EEA	European Economic Area
ENP	Exceptional Needs Payment
ESB	Electricity Supply Board
EU	European Union
FA	Farm Assist
FIS	Family Income Supplement
FLMPA	Family Leave and Miscellaneous Provisions Act 2021
GDP	Gross Domestic Product
GNP	Gross National Product
GP	General Practitioner
HA (with year)	Health Act
HA(No. 2)A	Health (Amendment) (No. 2) Act
HAA	Health (Amendment) Act
HACEA	Health (Alteration of Criteria for Eligibility) Act
HACE(No. 2)A	Health (Alteration of Criteria for Eligibility) (No. 2) Act

List of Abbreviations

HAP	Housing Assistance Payment
HGPSA	Health (General Practitioner Service) Act
HMPA	Health (Miscellaneous Provisions) Act
HMP(No. 2)A	Health (Miscellaneous Provisions) (No. 2) Act
H(PPEMPI)A	Health (Preservation and Protection and other Emergency Measures in the Public Interest) Act
HPSMGA	Health (Pricing and Supply of Medical Goods) Act
HRC	Habitual Residence Condition
HRTPA	Health (Regulation of Termination of Pregnancy) Act
HSE	Health Services Executive
IB	Illness Benefit
IP	Invalidity Pension
IQA	Increase with Respect to a Qualified Adult
IQC	Increase with Respect to a Qualified Child
ISI	Import Substitution Industrialization
JB	Jobseeker's Benefit
LTRCS	Long-Term Residential Care Services
NHSS	Nursing Home Support Scheme
NHSSA	Nursing Homes Support Scheme Act 2009
OFP	One-Parent Family Payment
OIB	Occupational Injuries Benefit
P	President
PAYE	Pay As You Earn
PCB	Partial Capacity Benefit
PRETA	Pre-retirement Allowance
PRSI	Pay-Related Social Insurance
PUP	Pandemic Unemployment Payment
SCP	Surviving Civil Partner
SW Acts	Social Welfare Acts
SW(CCI)R	Social Welfare (Consolidated Contributions and Insurability) Regulations of 1996
SW(CCP&C)R	Social Welfare (Consolidated Claims, Payments and Control) Regulations of 2007
SW(COI)R	Social Welfare (Consolidated Occupational Injuries) Regulations of 2007
SW(CSWA)R	Social Welfare (Consolidated Supplementary Welfare Allowance) Regulations of 2007
SWA	Supplementary Welfare Allowance
SWA (with year)	Social Welfare Act (of that year)
SWAO	Social Welfare Appeals Office

SWLRPA	Social Welfare Law Reform and Pensions Act
SWMPA	Social Welfare Miscellaneous Provisions Act
SWP(MP)A	Social Welfare and Pensions (Miscellaneous Provisions) Act
SWP(No.2)A	Social Welfare and Pensions (No.2) Act
SWPA	Social Welfare and Pensions Act
SWPCRA	Social Welfare, Pensions and Civil Registration Act
TCA	Trade and Cooperation Agreement
TD	Teachta Dála
TFEU	Treaty on the Functioning of the European Union
UCD	University College Dublin
UK	United Kingdom
UN	United Nations
US	United States
VTOS	Vocational Training Opportunities Scheme
WFP	Working Family Payment
WNCP	Widow(er)'s (Non-contributory) Pension
WUKEU(CP)A	Withdrawal of the United Kingdom from the European Union (Consequential Provisions) Act 2020

List of Abbreviations

Preface

This latest edition of this book updates the position from September 2020. At that time, we were in the middle of the COVID-19 epidemic (and its very significant social protection response), but the disease has now receded, if not disappeared, and the response has also been substantially scaled back with the specific COVID-19 schemes (including the Pandemic Unemployment Payment (PUP)) now closed to new applications.

The number of court judgments concerning social welfare law has increased in recent years, but there remain many areas of law untouched by the higher courts. The recent Irish cases mentioned in this book are, in general, discussed in more detail in our joint contribution to the *Annual Review of Irish Law*.

While the Social Welfare Appeals Office (SWAO) publishes detailed 'case studies' of its decisions, this does not yet provide a real system of precedent, although (from 2012) both the quantity and quality of reports have improved significantly.[1] This is in contrast to the extensive case law both before the courts and the specialist Upper Tribunal in the United Kingdom (UK).[2] Accordingly, we have, when it appeared relevant, made reference to UK case law and also to case law from Australia, Canada, New Zealand and the United States.

The number of Irish court decisions in relation to access to healthcare law is even smaller, while, unfortunately, as a result of the different statutory language, one does not even have the benefit of being able to draw on comparable decisions from other jurisdictions.

We have, of course, cited relevant decisions of the Court of Justice of the EU and, in light of the European Convention on Human Rights Act 2003, those of the European Court of Human Rights.

The usual disclaimers apply, and the views expressed and any remaining errors are entirely the responsibility of the authors.

The law is stated as we understand it to be on 11 September 2023.

1. These are available in the annual reports on the SWAO Website https://www.gov.ie/en/campaigns/031734-the-social-welfare-appeals-office/.
2. In Northern Ireland, the title of Social Security Commissioners remains.

General Introduction

§1. General Background

1. The Republic of Ireland (hereinafter, 'Ireland') is a small country of over 5 million people. The island of Ireland is located in the North Atlantic to the west of Great Britain. The northern part of the island of Ireland forms part of the United Kingdom (UK). Until 1922, all of Ireland was part of the UK, and the basis of the Irish social security system was established at that time. Accordingly, there remain many similarities today between the Irish and British systems, although these are decreasing over time.

2. The country is a unitary one from a social welfare perspective, and the same laws apply throughout the country.

§2. Historical Background

3. The basis of the Irish welfare system was established primarily in the period from the 1830s to 1911 when Ireland was a part of the UK.[3] Unlike England and Wales, which had had a national Poor Law since the 1600s, Ireland had no national Poor Law before 1838. The lead-up to the reform of the 'old' English Poor Law in 1834 led to considerable debate about the appropriate policy in an Irish context, and a number of public commissions were established to report on the issue. Perhaps the most important was the Whately Commission, reported in 1836, which called for a scheme of national development rather than a general Poor Law. However, the Whig government rejected these proposals and opted instead to apply the Poor Law to Ireland broadly along the lines of the reformed New Poor Law in England and Wales. This was to be based solely on 'indoor relief' in a network of workhouses that were quickly built across Ireland. However, the advent of the Great Famine in the 1840s and the ultimate decision to make the Poor Law (funded primarily by Irish property) the main mechanism to combat the Famine led to the extension of the system to 'outdoor relief' in 1847. Over the remainder of the century, the Poor Law was broadened to provide a range of other services, including medical treatment.

3. This section draws on M. Cousins, *Explaining the Irish Welfare System* (Lewiston: Edwin Mellen, 2005).

4. The next major welfare reform, that of workmen's compensation, came from quite a different perspective. The intention was to replace an increasingly unsatisfactory legal position whereby 'workmen' injured in the course of employment often received no compensation under the existing legal rules. The proposals, introduced by the Conservative government, put the responsibility on employers to compensate employees injured in the course of employment. Employers could, but were not obliged to, insure against such a contingency. The State played a supervisory role only and did not directly fund the workmen's compensation scheme. However, the Conservatives were unable or unwilling to develop similar proposals for old-age pensions.

5. The first great 'New Liberal' reform was the Old Age Pension Act of 1908. This significantly increased public expenditure and gave support as a right to people over seventy for the first time. The 1908 legislation marked the first major shift away from the Poor Law as the main instrument of relief. It was followed soon after by further New Liberal reforms in the areas of unemployment and national health insurance. Unlike the old-age pension, which was means-tested, both schemes were insurance-based (influenced by German practice). In the rest of the UK, the national health insurance measure also included medical benefits (i.e., the services of a general practitioner (GP)), but this part of the scheme was not applied to Ireland because of the opposition of the Catholic Church and sections of the medical profession. Both schemes were significantly extended during and after World War I.

6. These schemes were inherited by the Irish State upon independence. The only significant reform that took place in the period up to independence was that of the Poor Law. This became an instrument in the struggle for control of local government between Sinn Fein and the British. Sinn Fein-controlled local authorities had funding withdrawn by the British State and were forced to seek economies in the running of local government generally. This led to significant reform of the Poor Law, including the closing of many workhouses and a general shift to outdoor relief. At this time, Ireland, because it was part of the UK, had one of the most advanced welfare systems in Europe. Because Irish wages and costs of living were generally lower than those in England, whereas benefits were normally set at a standard UK level, these were relatively more generous in an Irish context. However, because of Ireland's radically different occupational structure, with over half the workforce still engaged in agriculture, coverage for sickness and unemployment did not extend to wide groups of the population. Thus, other than in relation to old-age pensions, which applied to all classes, Ireland was left with comparatively generous but narrowly focused coverage.

7. Ireland achieved independence from the UK in late 1921, which was followed by a brief civil war. At the time of independence, Ireland was a highly agricultural country with a population of 3 million. Over half the working population was engaged in agriculture in 1926, with only 13% engaged in industry. The level of reliance on agriculture was increased by the partition of Ireland with the more industrialized north-eastern remaining part of the UK. However, Ireland's level of economic development was quite high at this time, with per capita income at about

60% of that of the UK, the then-European leader. It had a comparatively high level of trade, but overwhelmingly, this was conducted with the UK. Politically, Ireland had, in comparative terms, one of the more democratic electoral systems. Full adult male suffrage and the right to vote for women over age 30 was introduced in 1918 and extended to all adult women in 1923.

8. The country was ruled by the socially conservative and fiscally liberal Cumann na nGaedheal government for almost all of the next decade. Cumann na nGaedheal introduced few reforms in the area of social welfare – other than an infamous cut in the old-age pension in 1924. The Democratic Programme of the First Dáil had called for the abolition of the 'odious, degrading and foreign Poor Law system', but it was largely retained, albeit indoor relief was significantly reduced and outdoor relief was renamed as 'home assistance'. From a gender perspective, there was little difference between the parties, and the main development in this area was the effective exclusion of married women from insurance upon marriage in 1929 – a development that was not opposed by any of the major parties.

9. Following a decade of Cumann na nGaedheal rule, Fianna Fáil won the 1932 election and remained continuously in power until 1948. The advent of Fianna Fáil marked a significant shift in public policy away from the liberal, low-spending, free-trade approach of its predecessors to a more interventionist and protectionist approach to policy, including a strategy of import substitution industrialization (ISI). The policy of ISI saw a significant increase in employment in the 1930s. Over the period from 1932 to 1948, the overall population remained at just under 3 million. Reflecting the policy of ISI, there was a slow shift in the constitution of the workforce with an increase in industry (to 23%) and a decline in agriculture to 41% (1951 data). Trade fell sharply, first, as a result of Fianna Fáil's shift to protectionism in the 1930s and the subsequent 'economic war' with the UK, and second, as a result of the impact of World War II (or the 'Emergency', as the period was known in Ireland). Part of Fianna Fáil's interventionist policy involved a significant expansion of welfare schemes with the introduction of unemployment assistance (1933), the unification of national health insurance (1933), a new widow's pension scheme (1936), and children's allowances, initially for larger families (1944). Fianna Fáil also oversaw an expansion in other areas of social policy, such as health and public housing. In 1947, the Fianna Fáil government established new departments of social welfare and health – clearly as a prelude to further policy developments in both areas.

10. Fianna Fáil's first period of hegemony ended in 1948 with the election of a coalition (or inter-party) government drawn from a very wide range of political perspectives. It was led by the conservative Fine Gael party (the successor party to Cumann na nGaedheal) and also included the Labour party, whose leader, William Norton, a Teachta Dála (or TD, meaning 'Member of Parliament'), became Tánaiste (Deputy Prime Minister) and Minister for Social Welfare. Following the publication of a White Paper on Social Security by the inter-party government in 1949, the government published a Social Welfare Bill to provide for the unification of the existing social insurance systems and to introduce a number of new benefits, including a contributory retirement pension. However, the government fell before the Bill could be enacted. Fianna Fáil returned to power and enacted a watered-down version of the reforms, dropping a number of new measures, including the retirement pension. While Norton had originally proposed to extend social insurance to all employees, resistance from public servants already covered by occupational schemes had led to their exclusion from full insurance, and Fianna Fáil also subsequently excluded higher-paid workers. In a classic statement of its non-solidaristic approach, Fianna Fáil's Minister for Social Welfare, James Ryan TD, stated that he could not see 'either the justice or necessity for the inclusion of classes that can never benefit' in the social insurance scheme and that he could not approve of 'hidden' taxation on such classes by the imposition of social insurance contributions.[4] The legislation did provide for equal rates of benefits for single men and women, but married women continued to receive lower rates of benefits, and many other areas of gender discrimination also remained. Children's allowances were extended to the second child in 1952, but this was a compensatory measure for the reduction in food subsidization at that time. Healthcare also saw major reforms at that time with the publication of a White Paper on health policy and the subsequent enactment of health legislation. Health was to prove a controversial policy area in the late 1940s and early 1950s, contributing to the fall of the first inter-party government following a dispute between (and within) government, the Catholic hierarchy, and the medical profession on proposals to extend universal healthcare to mothers and children.

11. The 1950s was a period of economic stagnation in Ireland. In contrast to most European countries, economic growth was slow, and exports did not return to pre-war levels until about 1960. While there was a further slow shift from employment in agriculture to industry and services, the main feature of the 1950s was the significant fall in the number of working people, a rise in unemployment, and massive emigration (primarily to the UK). Developments in the social sphere mirrored the decline in economic fortunes. Unsurprisingly, there were few major welfare reforms other than the introduction of a contributory old-age pension in 1961. Politically, also, the period was one of instability, with Fianna Fáil and inter-party governments alternating in the 1950s without either one showing any clear policy direction. It was not until Sean Lemass took over the leadership of the Fianna Fáil party in 1959 that a clearer economic and social policy direction emerged, leading to the second period of Fianna Fáil hegemony lasting until 1973.

12. The period from the early 1960s saw record economic growth in Ireland, with the policy of protectionism being abandoned and replaced by a move towards export-led industrialization. This tendency was increased by Ireland's membership in the European Economic Community beginning in 1973. In the period from 1961 to 1973, the economy grew at an average of 4.2% of the gross national product (GNP) per annum. While the first oil shock led to major unemployment, an (unsuccessful) counter-cyclical policy of reflation kept the Irish economy growing until the late 1970s at the cost of rising national debt. There was a significant shift in the

4. *Dáil Debates*, vol. 130, col. 633, 27 Mar. 1952.

composition of the labour force. Over the period from 196 the workforce engaged in agriculture halved, while that in indu increased.

13. In the 1960s, the UK started to move towards a more Bismarckian related approach with the introduction of pay-related benefits and (in the 1970s, State earnings-related pension. Fianna Fáil, in government continuously up to 1973, and the Fine Gael-Labour coalition (1973–1977) followed these trends with a pay-related benefit of short-term payments (1974), the replacement of the old workmen's compensation scheme with a new occupational injuries benefit (OIB) (1966), the reduction in pension age from 70 to 66 (1973–1977), the replacement of the remains of the old Poor Law with supplementary welfare allowance (SWA) (1975), the extension of social insurance to all full-time private-sector employees (1974), the introduction of pay-related (rather than flat rate) social insurance contributions (1979), and a range of new benefits, including invalidity and retirement pensions (1970), a death benefit (1970), and a number of insurance and means-tested schemes for deserted wives and unmarried mothers (1970–1973). Similar reforms were seen in the areas of education and health, with the introduction of free second-level education (1967–1968) and a major reform of healthcare structures, eligibility, and funding in the 1970s. The expansionary approach to social welfare policy continued into the late 1970s with the publication of Green Papers on the extension of social insurance to the self-employed (1978) and on the introduction of earnings-related pensions (1976). However, over this period, expenditure on children's allowances did not increase as a percentage of gross domestic product (GDP), and while allowances were extended to the first child in 1963, there was a significant fall in the relative value of the payments.

14. Economic growth in the 1980s was effectively stagnant in the period up to 1986, and the national debt increased significantly. While the economy began to improve from about 1987, with economic growth up to 1993 averaging 3.6% of GNP per annum, economic recovery was initially somewhat erratic. Unemployment rose significantly in the 1980s and 1990s, peaking in 1993 at a level of 294,000. This economic crisis was reflected in political instability up to 1986. Fianna Fáil returned to power in 1987 and established a new system of social partnership involving employers, trade unions, farming organizations, and, from 1996, community and voluntary organizations, which lasted until the Great Recession in 2008. Over one-quarter of the working-age population was reliant on social welfare payments in the mid-1980s. Welfare spending rose significantly in this period, driven by rising unemployment (and non-employment). However, there was no concerted retrenchment drive, as was seen during the same period in the UK. This is exemplified by the reform processes in the two countries. In the UK, the government established the Fowler Review (1985), which had a clear remit to reduce and refocus the level of spending. In contrast, in Ireland, the Fine Gael-led coalition government (with Labour TD Barry Desmond as Minister for Social Welfare) established a broadly based Commission on Social Welfare (CSW), which was reported in 1986. The Commission included Labour party advisers, social policy academics, and representatives of trade unions and employers.

...on set out four priority recommendations: to achieve imme-...nts in the lowest social welfare rates, to reform support for chil-...improving children's allowances and reforming child-dependent ..., to broaden social insurance to cover the self-employed and to improve ... delivery. The approach of the CSW can, in many ways, be seen as 'back to Beveridge'. The emphasis was on a flat rate and adequate benefits, and the Commission gave no support for a shift to a more earnings-related system. Although the government did not give any commitment to implement the CSW recommendations, in practice, policy tended to follow the main lines recommended. The focus over the next decade was on reaching the social welfare 'adequacy' rate set by the CSW (this was not finally achieved until 1999). As part of this process (and as recommended by the CSW), pay-related benefits were reduced and eventually abolished in 1994. Social insurance was extended to the self-employed in 1988, and a range of service-delivery improvements were implemented. Only in relation to child support were the key recommendations of the CSW not broadly implemented.

16. Unsurprisingly, there were relatively few new developments in the social welfare system in the early part of this period. Contribution conditions were tightened up for a number of schemes, and limited 'job search' schemes were introduced. One of the most important developments was the implementation of the European Union (EU) directive on equal treatment for men and women in social security (79/7/EEC), agreed on in 1979. This required the introduction of equal rates of unemployment and disability benefits and the replacement of the existing discriminatory system of dependency payments with a more factually based approach. Subsequently, a number of means-tested payments were introduced, building on the existing scheme, for persons (mainly women) with caring responsibilities. These included carer's allowance (CA) (1991) and lone parent's allowance (1990) – subsequently restructured as one-parent family payment (OFP) in 1996.

17. The Irish economy recovered somewhat sporadically in the early 1990s, but by the mid-1990s, the economy was growing at rates never before experienced. The openness of the Irish economy increased even further, and employment grew dramatically. This had many positive impacts, including a sharp fall in unemployment, improved real living standards, substantial upgrading of the class structure, and increased levels of social mobility. The rapid economic growth has had major implications for the social welfare system, although there have been relatively few changes in the structure of the system in the recent period. Reflecting the growth in employment, there has been a striking increase in the numbers insured under the social insurance scheme. As a result of the significant growth in social insurance contributions, the Social Insurance Fund has become self-financing for the first time since it was established.

18. The level of unemployment fell sharply, and the proportion of the working-age population dependent on welfare also fell rapidly from one in four in 1997 to one in five by 2000. There was a much greater emphasis on an active role in social welfare policy in relation to people of working age. This was particularly apparent in relation to those on unemployment payments, whereby the Employment Action

Plan (1998) required that unemployed people passing a certain duration of employment be referred to the public employment service. Related measures were also gradually introduced on a pilot basis in relation to lone parents and people with disabilities, although, unlike in the UK, government policy did not adopt a clear policy of activation of the broader working-age population. In the early years of the Fianna Fáil-led government, beginning in 1997, welfare rates for those of working age were increased less rapidly than take-home pay (although they were well ahead of inflation), leading to a fall in replacement ratios. Thus, the emphasis for those of working age was heavily on incentivization. Subsequently, in the context of the significant fall in unemployment levels and having regard to the recommendations of the Social Welfare Benchmarking group (2001) established under the Scheme for Prosperity and Fairness, the government gave a commitment to raise social welfare levels to a benchmark of EUR 150 in 2002 terms to be met by 2007. In relation to pensions, significantly higher increases were given to pensioners in the period from 1997 to 2003, with the old-age pension increasing as a percentage of gross average industrial earnings towards the target of 34% set in 1998 by the National Pensions Policy Initiative. In addition, the working population was further incentivized to build on the base of the social welfare pension by providing personal pension coverage with the introduction in 2002 of the new personal retirement savings account, to which significant tax incentives apply. A National Pensions Reserve Fund was established to fund future pensions with a legal commitment to put aside 1% of GNP per annum.

19. In the area of child support, the 1994–1997 government adopted a policy of freezing child-dependent allowances and putting any available resources into child benefit (CB) increases. This was continued by the Fianna Fáil-led coalition, but in the early years of that government, the level of resources invested was very low. However, in 2000–2001, the government provided major increases in the CB scheme, and the rates of payment almost tripled. In 2006, an early childcare allowance was introduced to assist with childcare costs for younger children. One other area in which there has been significant development in recent years is support for carers. The CA scheme was broadened with the take-up of the scheme more than doubling in the period from 1997. In addition, a new carer's leave and benefits were introduced to allow workers to take up to two years off to care for a person in need of full-time care and attention while receiving a social welfare payment. There was also a range of other improvements in schemes, including the extension of the period of maternity leave and benefit, the introduction of a new increased bereavement grant (later abolished in 2014), the establishment of a widowed parent's grant to benefit widow(er)s with children on bereavement, and the transformation of the smallholders' unemployment scheme into a reformed farm assist (FA) scheme.

20. The impact of the great recession in 2008 and after led to a significant increase in spending on social welfare (as a percentage of GDP) and to major growth in the proportion of the working-age population on welfare payments. The ratio of the average payment per beneficiary to national income per capita *rose* in the case of both working age and older persons and fell only in the case of child-related payments.[5] Since 2008, there has been an increased emphasis on the use of policy measures intended to encourage persons to seek employment (or other supports) rather than welfare payments.[6] However, there have also been positive changes in the social security system, including the introduction of the nursing home support scheme (NHSS), the amendment of the social welfare code to reflect the introduction of civil partnership in Ireland and the introduction of paternity and parental benefits. Overall, however, the period saw a limited change in the overall structure of the social welfare system.

21. Most recently, the COVID-19 pandemic (2020–2021) saw a major social welfare response with the introduction of a Pandemic Unemployment Payment and the amendment of the Social Welfare Acts (SW Acts) to provide illness benefits to those who are incapable of work due to COVID-19 or who are advised to self-isolate for health reasons. With the removal of most COVID-19 restrictions, these payments, including PUP, have been phased out.

§3. Sources of Social Security Law

I. General

22. The basic source of Irish social security law (or social welfare law, as it is known) is legislation.[7] This is subject to compatibility with the terms of the Irish Constitution (and, of course, with legislation arising from Ireland's membership in the EU).

II. Legislation

23. The vast majority of social welfare payments are based on statutory entitlement as set out in the SW Acts and Regulations. The current primary legislation is the Social Welfare (Consolidation) Act of 2005 (hereinafter, 'the Act'), which is amended on at least an annual basis.[8] In general, the Act sets out the main features of the particular payment. Eligibility for and entitlement to health services is set out in the Health Acts (HA), which have not, to date, been consolidated, although an administrative consolidation by the Law Reform Commission is now available.

5. M. Cousins, 'The Irish Social Protection System: Change in Comparative Context' in M.P. Murphy & F. Dukelow eds, *The Irish Welfare State in the Twenty-First Century: Challenges and Change*, London: Palgarve Macmillan, 2016.
6. M. Cousins, 'Welfare Conditionality in the Republic of Ireland after the Great Recession', JSSL 26(1) (2019): 30–40.
7. The terms 'social security' and 'social welfare' are used interchangeably throughout this book.
8. In practice, DSP maintain a rolling administrative consolidation of the Acts which has been used in this book, and it is understood that a quasi-official administrative consolidation is being finalised by the Law Reform Commission which will replace the periodic consolidation of the Acts.

III. Regulations and Guidelines

24. Further details in relation to, for example, claims and payments, specific definitions, transitional provisions, and so on are set out in Ministerial Regulations. Obviously, these Regulations must be constitutional, must be *intra vires* the Minister in terms of the powers given in primary legislation, and, in particular, must not be so unreasonable as to be *ultra vires* the Minister.[9] In addition, as we will see throughout this book, the Department of Social Protection (DSP) issues a very large number of guidelines to its staff (most of which are available on the Departmental Website).[10] These largely explain the Acts and Regulations in non-legalistic terms. However, in a number of cases, issues that have not been addressed in legislation are provided for in the guidelines. Obviously, again, such guidelines must be consistent with the primary and secondary legislation.[11] In addition, in a number of cases – including the Household Benefit schemes and the Back-to-Work and Back-to-Education allowances – entitlement is not provided for in the SW Acts, and the details of the schemes are entirely set out in administrative guidelines. The legal status of such guidelines is considered in more detail below.

IV. Adjudication

25. Most disputes in relation to social welfare are adjudicated by the social welfare appeals officers (*see* Part XII). Their decisions are not published in any structured manner and do not form a system of precedent.[12] A very limited number of cases do go before the general courts, and the decisions of such courts (which are normally in writing) do provide binding legal guidance as to the interpretation of specific provisions. There is no general appeal system in relation to healthcare, and the appeals mechanisms that do exist are discussed in Part III.

V. Labour Agreements

26. Labour agreements are not generally relevant to Irish social security and health law.

---

9. *See McHugh v. Minister for Social Welfare* [1994] 2 IR 139; *State (McLoughlin) v. Eastern Health Board* [1986] IR 416. The general power to make regulations is set out in s. 4 of the Act.
10. *See* https://www.gov.ie/en/collection/ff767-social-welfare-schemes-and-services/#operational-guidelines.
11. *See*, e.g., *State (Kershaw) v. Eastern Health Board* [1985] ILRM 235; *State (McLoughlin) v. Eastern Health Board* [1986] IR 416. *See also Green v. Daniels* (1977) 51 ALJR 463 where guidelines involved an attempted substitution of inconsistent criteria for those set out in law.
12. Although ‘case studies’ of decisions are published in the annual reports of the Social Welfare Appeals Office (SWAO) and on its Website https://www.gov.ie/en/campaigns/031734-the-social-welfare-appeals-office/.

VI. EU Law and Bilateral Agreements

27. EU law is, of course, relevant in a number of areas of social welfare law.[13] In particular, Directive 79/7/EEC on equal treatment in matters of social security led to a number of cases in the 1980s and 1990s, and its current implications are discussed at a number of points below.[14] Regulation 883/2004 (and its implementing Regulation) concerning the coordination of social security for EU citizens is directly effective.[15] These Regulations also apply to the European Economic Area (EEA) countries. For countries outside the EEA, Ireland has agreed on a number of bilateral conventions on social security rights. These currently cover Australia,[16] Austria,[17] Canada,[18] Japan,[19] the Republic of Korea,[20] New Zealand,[21] Switzerland,[22] the UK,[23] and the United States (US).[24] The main purpose of the bilateral agreements on social security is to protect the pension rights of persons who have paid social insurance contributions in Ireland and have periods of insurance or of residence (depending on the social security system) in the other country. The Agreements protect pension rights by allowing reckonable periods in each country to be taken into account in either country in determining entitlement to certain benefits where there would be no entitlement if national legislation only applied. The Agreements contain provisions to determine the correct legislation applicable in situations where double liability for social insurance contributions might exist. The details of the agreements vary somewhat from one country to another. While the

---

13. In C-378/17, *Minister for Justice and Equality and Commissioner of An Garda Síochána v. Workplace Relations Commission*, EU:C:2018:979 the EU Court of Justice held that 'bodies called upon, within the exercise of their respective powers, to apply EU law are obliged to adopt all the measures necessary to ensure that EU law is fully effective, disapplying if need be any national provisions or national case-law that are contrary to EU law'. This would appear to include social welfare appeals officers.
14. For the legal history, *see* G. Whyte, *Social Inclusion and the Law: Public Interest Law in Ireland*, 2nd ed. (Dublin: IPA, 2015), 236–247.
15. *See*, generally, F. Pennings, *European Social Security Law* (Antwerp: Intersentia, 2022). Regulation 492/2011 may also be relevant in this area: *see* Pennings, Chapter 9.
16. Social Welfare (Agreement with Australia on Social Security) Order, 1992 [S.I. No. 84 of 1992] and Social Welfare (Revised Agreement with Australia on Social Security) Order 2005 [S.I. No. 799 of 2005].
17. Social Welfare (Agreement with Republic of Austria on Social Security) Order 1989 [S.I. No. 307 of 1989]. This, of course, predates Austria's accession to the EU and Regulation 883 would now generally apply.
18. Social Welfare (Agreement with Canada on Social Security) Order 1991 [S.I. No. 317 of 1991]. *See also* Social Welfare (Understanding with Québec on Social Security) Order 1995 [S.I. No. 120 of 1995].
19. Social Welfare (Agreement with the Government of Japan on Social Security) Order, 2011 [S.I. No. 527 of 2010].
20. Social Welfare (Agreement with Republic of Korea on Social Security) Order, 2008 [S.I. No. 552 of 2008].
21. Social Welfare (Agreement with New Zealand on Social Security) Order 1994 [S.I. No. 57 of 1994].
22. Social Welfare (Agreement with Switzerland on Social Security) Order 1999 [S.I. No. 206 of 1999].
23. Social Welfare (Convention on Social Security between the Government of Ireland and the Government of the United Kingdom of Great Britain and Northern Ireland) Order 2020 [S.I. No. 746 of 2020].
24. Social Welfare (Agreement with the United States of America on Social Security) Order 1993 [S.I. No. 243 of 1993].

variations between the agreements and – more significantly – the non-agreement of conventions with other countries might be suggested to give rise to discrimination on the grounds of nationality and/or residence, it seems unlikely that the courts would interfere with the government's discretion in this area.[25]

28. The UK left the EU on 31 January 2020, but a transition period was in place, lasting until 31 December 2020. During this time, all the existing EU social security regulations continued to apply to the UK. A new agreement between Ireland and the UK has been agreed to cover arrangements subsequent to the transition period.[26] The main purpose of the Agreement is to ensure that all the existing arrangements with regard to the recognition of and access to social insurance entitlements will be maintained in both jurisdictions. The Agreement provides that periods of insurance or residence in one State may be taken into account, where necessary, by the other State in order to qualify for certain benefits and pensions. In the case of Ireland, the Agreement covers illness benefit, health and safety benefit, carers benefit, treatment benefit, maternity benefit, adoptive benefit, paternity benefit, partial capacity benefit, invalidity pension, State pension (contributory), widow's, widower's or surviving civil partners (contributory) pension, guardian's payment (contributory), occupational injuries benefit, widowed or surviving civil partners grant, jobseeker's benefit, guardian's payment (non-contributory), one parent family payment, domiciliary care allowance, child benefit, back to work family dividend, working family payment. In relation to healthcare, Health Act 1970 (Section 75A) Order 2020 sets out reciprocal healthcare provision between the United Kingdom and Ireland, recognising that both countries operate residency-based systems. However, these overlap with the reciprocal healthcare arrangements agreed in the UK/EU and EAEC: Trade and Cooperation Agreement (TCA)[27] and following an exchange of letters between the UK and Ireland, only certain parts of this memorandum of understanding currently apply and in most areas the TCA takes precedence.[28]

VII. International Conventions

29. The Irish legal system adopts a 'dualist' approach in terms of international conventions. In other words, such conventions do not form part of national law unless and until they have been incorporated into national law.[29] This applied to the European Convention on Human Rights (ECHR) until it was (in a certain way)

---

25. *Carson v. United Kingdom* (2009) 48 EHRR 41.
26. Social Welfare (Convention on Social Security between the Government of Ireland and the Government of the United Kingdom of Great Britain and Northern Ireland) Order 2020 [S.I. No. 746/2020].
27. *See* https://www.gov.uk/government/publications/ukeu-and-eaec-trade-and-cooperation-agreement-ts-no82021.
28. https://www.gov.uk/government/publications/exchange-of-letters-on-uk-ireland-reciprocal-health care-arrangements.
29. Article 29.6 of the Irish Constitution states that 'No international agreement shall be part of the domestic law save as may be determined by the Oireachtas.' *See Kavanagh v. Governor of Mountjoy Prison* [2002] IESC 13.

incorporated into national law (though without direct effect) by the ECHR Act of 2003. Thus, other international conventions ratified by Ireland which may have some relevance to social security (such as the European Social Charter, European Agreement on Social Security, or the United Nations (UN) Convention on the Rights of the Child) are not binding in Irish law and we do not generally refer here to their provisions or to the 'case law' of implementing bodies.[30] At best, such agreements may be taken into account as an aid to interpretation if and when there is an ambiguity in the Irish law, e.g., where the law is reasonably capable of more than one meaning.[31] Therefore, even if the Irish provision happens to be in breach of such agreements, this has no legal effect in Irish law.

30. However, it is arguable that, in a limited way, such agreements might be incorporated into Irish law by way of the ECHR. In *Demir*, the Grand Chamber of the European Court of Human Rights (ECtHR) stated that:

> The Court, in defining the meaning of terms and notions in the text of the Convention, can and must take into account elements of international law other than the Convention, the interpretation of such elements by competent organs, and the practice of European States reflecting their common values.[32]

In *Demir*, this meant that the Court had regard to the European Social Charter (even though the specific provisions had not been ratified by Turkey). The Court has not, to date, relied greatly on such instruments in the area of social security.[33]

§4. Legal Status of Social Security Benefits

I. A Constitutional Right to Social Welfare

31. The Irish Constitution contains no explicit reference to social welfare payments. Article 45 might be considered to be relevant insofar as it states that:

> The State pledges itself to safeguard with especial care the economic interests of the weaker sections of the community and, where necessary, to contribute to the support of the infirm, the widow, the orphan and the aged.

30. *See*, for example, *International Federation of Human Rights Leagues (IFHR) v. Ireland*, 42/2007, 3 Jun. 2008 (where a complaint concerning the European Social Charter was rejected).
31. *Abdirahman v. Secretary of State for Work and Pensions* [2007] EWCA Civ 657 at 35–40.
32. *Demir and Baykara v. Turkey* [2009] IRLR 7 (2009) 48 EHRR 54. *See also Opuz v. Turkey* (2010) 50 EHRR 28.
33. *See*, for example, *Weller v. Hungary*, App. 44399/05, 31 Mar. 2009 in which Judge Tulkens (in a 'concurring' judgment) suggested that Art. 14 should be construed in light of Art. 12.4 of the European Social Charter, which provides that domestic law cannot reserve social security rights to their own nationals (although this was strictly *obiter*).

However, Article 45 specifically provides that the 'directive principles of social policy' that it sets out are not cognizable by the courts, at least in the context of the judicial review of legislation.

32. It might, however, be argued that entitlement to social welfare could constitute a 'property right' under Article 43, which provides that:

(1) The State acknowledges that man, by virtue of his rational being, has the natural right, antecedent to positive law, to the private ownership of external goods.
(2) The State accordingly guarantees to pass no law attempting to abolish the right of private ownership or the general right to transfer, bequeath, and inherit property.

33. Given the status that has been attached to property rights in Irish constitutional jurisprudence, this could provide important additional weight to the rights of social welfare claimants. However, the very wording of the Article and the philosophical approach underlying it would argue against a statutory right to a welfare payment being elevated to a 'natural right, antecedent to positive law'. Insofar as this issue was considered by the Supreme Court, it appeared that the Court did not see entitlement to social welfare itself as being a property right within the meaning of Article 43. *Minister for Social, Community and Family Affairs v. Scanlon* involved the retrospective application of legislation concerning the recovery of overpaid benefits.[34] It was argued that the claimant enjoyed a property right in the benefits that he had received and that, accordingly, a retrospective reading of the legislation should not be adopted. However, Judge Fennelly (with whom the other judges agreed) stated that the entitlement was created by statute and that he could not identify any constitutional right to retain benefits that had been wrongly paid. In a second case, *PC v. Minister for Social Protection*,[35] the Supreme Court, per Judge MacMenamin, took the view that a statutory welfare entitlement was not a property right within the meaning of the Constitution as the entitlement could be varied by the Oireachtas. Instead, he referred to the entitlement variously as 'a qualified entitlement derived from statute' – paragraph 33 – and 'a justiciable, if conditional, legal entitlement' – paragraph 47. These decisions appear unexceptional insofar as they relate to a claimant's contingent right, subject to complying with statutory conditions, to claim or retain a welfare payment.

34. However, it is arguable that where a claimant satisfies the various statutory conditions of eligibility for a welfare payment and where any statutory grounds of disqualification do not apply, s/he has a vested right to the relevant welfare payment that could be regarded as a property right. In *In re Article 26 of the Constitution and*

34. [2001] IESC 1 [2001] 1 IR 64. *See* paras 816–818.
35. [2017] IESC 63 [2017] 2 ILRM 369.

the Health (Amendment) (No. 2) Bill 2004,[36] the Supreme Court considered the constitutionality of legislation purporting retrospectively to legalize the imposition of charges for hospital services on persons who were statutorily entitled to such services without charge. The Court held that such persons were entitled to recover those charges as a right (subject to any normal defences) and that this right was to a type of personal property known as a chose in action. The Court went on to hold that this was a property right protected by the Constitution and that, under the circumstances, the proposed legislation, which sought to 'abrogate … in their entirety' the property rights of 'the most vulnerable members of society' constituted an unjust attack on those rights and was therefore unconstitutional. The State sought to argue that the right was a 'mere statutory right', but the Court somewhat obscurely dismissed this argument as 'not address[ing] the nature of the property right'. Clearly, the rights disputed in *Scanlon* (a statutory right to benefits) and those in the *Health (Amendment) Bill* (charges unlawfully imposed with respect to a statutory right to a free service) are different.[37] However, following the latter decision, it is arguable that where a person was unlawfully refused a benefit to which s/he had a statutory entitlement, s/he would be entitled subsequently to recover those benefits from the state and that this is a type of personal property known as a chose in action, arguably protected by the Constitution.

35. It is worth digressing to consider the position under US Constitutional law – albeit the approach to property rights is substantially different from that in Irish law. The Due Process Clause of the Fifth Amendment to the US Constitution provides that:

> No person shall … be deprived of life, liberty, or property, without due process of law; nor shall private property be taken for public use, without just compensation.

The US Supreme Court has held that:

> Procedural due process imposes constraints on governmental decisions which deprive individuals of 'liberty' or 'property' interests within the meaning of the Due Process Clause of the Fifth or Fourteenth Amendment.

The Court held that the interest of an individual in continued receipt of Social Security benefits is a statutorily created 'property' interest protected by the Fifth Amendment so as to bring into play the right to procedural due process and protection against 'arbitrary governmental action'.[38] The Court has *not* gone further to hold that interest in Social Security gave rise to strong substantive constitutional

36. [2005] IESC 7 [2005] 1 IR 105. *See* E. O'Dell & G. Whyte, 'Is This a Country for Old Men and Women? In Re Article 26 and the Health (Amendment) (No. 2) Bill 2004', DULJ 27 (2005): 368.
37. The 'moral' circumstances also differed. The Court appears to have been influenced by the fact that in *Scanlon*, the claimant, while not found to be fraudulent, had no entitlement to the benefits reclaimed from him, whereas in the latter case, the State was clearly culpable of making charges directly contrary to the original legislative intention.
38. *Mathews v. Eldridge*, 424 US 319.

property rights. In *Flemming v. Nestor*[39] – a case involving the termination of old-age benefits payable to a person who was deported from the US – the Court held that a person covered by the Social Security Act did not have such a right in old-age benefit payments as would make every defeasance of 'accrued' interests violative of the Due Process Clause of the Fifth Amendment. The Court took the view that the non-contractual interest of an employee covered by the Social Security Act could not be soundly analogized to that of the holder of an annuity, whose right to benefits was based on his or her contractual premium payments and that 'to engraft upon the Social Security System a concept of "accrued property rights" would deprive it of the flexibility and boldness in the adjustment to ever-changing conditions that it demands and that Congress probably had in mind when it expressly reserved the right to alter, amend, or repeal any provision of the Act'.[40]

36. The status of social welfare entitlements has also been considered under both the ECHR and EU law. Article 1 of the First Protocol to the ECHR provides that:

> Every natural or legal person is entitled to the peaceful enjoyment of his possessions. No one shall be deprived of his possessions except in the public interest and subject to the conditions provided for by the law and by the general principles of international law.
>
> The preceding provision shall not, however, in any way impair the right of a state to enforce such laws as it deems necessary to control the use of property in accordance with the general interest or to secure the payment of taxes or other contributions or penalties.

The ECtHR has ruled that social welfare payments, whether contributory or non-contributory, constitute 'possessions' within the meaning of Article 1.[41] The Court has also held that payment of social insurance contributions falls within Article 1.[42]

37. In the case of EU law, in *Testa*,[43] the Court of Justice of the EU considered an argument that a provision of Regulation 1408/71 (now replaced by Regulation 883/2004), which deprived a person of entitlement to unemployment benefit under national law, might be regarded as being incompatible with the German constitutional protection of the right to property. The Court held that:

> The question of a possible infringement of fundamental rights … can only be judged in the light of Community law itself, since fundamental rights form an integral part of the general principles of the law, the observance of which it

39. (1960) 363, US 603. Affirmed in *Richardson v. Belcher*, 404, US 78.
40. *Ibid.*, at 608–611. Although the decision was by a five to four majority, only Black J dissented on the question of accrued property rights. The case concerned a Bulgarian who had lived in the United States for forty-three years and was deported in 1956 for having been a member of the Communist party between 1933 and 1939, at a time when this was not illegal nor grounds for deportation.
41. *Stec v. United Kingdom* (2005) 41 EHRR SE 295.
42. *Van Raalte v. Netherlands* (1997) 24 EHRR 503.
43. Joined Cases 41/79, 121/79 and 796/79 *Testa, Maggio and Vitale* [1980] ECR 1979.

ensures. One of the fundamental rights which is accordingly protected under Community law in accordance with the constitutional concepts common to the Member States and in the light of international treaties for the protection of human rights on which Member States have collaborated or to which they are signatories is the right to property.

However, on the facts of the case, the Court concluded that it was not necessary to decide whether or not the entitlement to the social security benefits in question might be held to be covered by the protection of the right to property, as guaranteed by Community law.

II. A Contractual Right to Benefits

38. The notion of social insurance is, to some extent, presented as being analogous with commercial insurance. Contributions are paid in relation to a specific risk, and, on the occurrence of that risk, compensation is payable to the insured person. However, as Freud wrote, analogies 'decide nothing but they can make one feel more at home'.[44] In the case of the introduction of social insurance, this was clearly the intended purpose of the analogy with commercial insurance. It helped to portray a new type of 'social welfare' payment in a manner with which the general public and legislators were familiar. However, there are very significant differences between social and commercial insurance. Unlike commercial insurance, social insurance is generally made compulsory by law; there is often no actuarial relationship between the level of contribution and likely risk, nor between contribution and benefits. It is clear from the Irish case law that entitlements to social insurance payments are entirely on a statutory basis and that there is no element of a contractual relationship between the citizen and the state in this regard.[45] Thus, there is no *contractual* reason why the Oireachtas cannot modify (or even abolish) entitlement by legislation – as has been done, for example, in relation to pay-related benefits.

---

44. S. Freud, 'The Dissection of the Psychical Personality' in Anna Freud ed., *The Essentials of Psychoanalysis,* Harmondsworth: Penguin, 1986.

45. *P.C. v. Minister for Social Protection* [2017] IESC 63 at 34; *Sobhy v. Chief Appeals Officer* [2021] IESC 81 at 71–77. The US position is outlined in *Flemming v. Nestor* (1960) 363 US 603; *Richardson v. Belcher*, 404, US 78. Although *see contra.* Marshall J dissenting in *Belcher* (with whom Brennan J joined) who opined that 'Surely a worker who is forced to pay a social security tax on his earnings has a clearly cognizable contract interest in the benefits that justify the tax. The characterization of this interest as "non-contractual" in *Flemming v. Nestor*, 363, US 603, 611 (1960), is, in my view, incorrect. The analogy to an annuity or insurance contract, rejected there, seems apt … Of course, as the Court says, Congress may "fix the levels of benefits under the Act or the conditions upon which they may be paid". But once Congress has fixed that level and those conditions, and a worker has contributed his tax in accord with the law, may Congress unilaterally modify the benefits in a way that defeats the expectations of beneficiaries and prospective beneficiaries? At the least, it would seem that after a worker has contributed … and his interest in the benefits has fully accrued, Congress may not unilaterally qualify that interest by introducing an offset provision not previously contemplated by the parties.' *Richardson v. Belcher*, 404, US 78 at 97, fn. 10.

III. Legitimate Expectation

39. If an insured person cannot rely on any contractual right to benefit, is there any situation in which he or she could rely on a legitimate expectation of entitlement against the State? Legitimate expectation is a developing area in Irish administrative law, and its boundaries are as yet ill-defined.[46] Its operation has, to date, received only limited judicial consideration in the area of social welfare law. In the words of Hogan, Morgan and Daly, 'Legitimate expectations are protected in the interests of safeguarding the citizen against haphazard and unfair changes in administrative policy and practice.'[47] However, how does this principle fit in with the important principle of administrative law that a public body cannot act *ultra vires*, that is, outside its legal powers? Traditionally, it has been held that a statutory authority cannot extend its powers by creating an estoppel – a concept similar to but not the same as legitimate expectation.[48]

40. In *Galvin v. Minister for Social Welfare*,[49] Costello P considered a claim that the applicant was entitled to a pension based either on the doctrine of estoppel or legitimate expectation. It was alleged that the applicant had been assured both verbally and in writing by an official of the Department that his social insurance record was such that he would qualify for a contributory pension at retirement. However, the Department, while accepting that the applicant was given incorrect information, argued that the doctrine of estoppel did not apply because the applicant suffered no detriment as a result (as he could not have improved his contribution record in any case) and the doctrine could not confer a right on the applicant to which he was not statutorily entitled. Costello P accepted these submissions and held that the doctrine of estoppel had no application where the applicant was not entitled by statute to the benefit claimed. He also held, albeit without detailed discussion, that the doctrine of legitimate expectation could not be relied upon to support a claim that the Department could not be heard to submit that the law does not permit the payment of the benefit claimed.

41. However, in *Power v. Minister for Social and Family Affairs*,[50] the High Court considered the implications of the doctrine of legitimate expectations in the area of non-statutory benefits. The applicant was in receipt of a back-to-education allowance, a non-statutory payment to persons in receipt of social welfare payments who return to education and designed to promote second-chance education. The terms and conditions of the scheme were set out in general terms in a booklet published by the Department. This stated that the allowance was payable for the duration of the course, including all holiday periods. The applicant argued that, but for the operation of the scheme and the payment of the allowance, he would have been

46. For an extensive discussion, *see* Gerard Hogan, David Gwynn Morgan & Paul Daly, *Administrative Law in Ireland*, 5th ed. (Dublin: Round Hall Sweet & Maxwell, 2019), Ch. 21.
47. *Ibid.*, 21.08.
48. *Power v. Minister for Social Welfare* [1987] IR 307 at 308.
49. [1997] 3 IR 240.
50. [2006] IEHC 170.

unable to go to university for financial reasons. In particular, he said that the provisions concerning payments during the summer vacations and the entitlement to obtain supplementary income from work during that period had a large influence on his decision to return to college. However, in March 2003, he was notified that changes had been made in terms of the scheme and that, in particular, the allowance would not be payable for the summer holiday period. The applicant and others brought judicial review proceedings asserting a legitimate expectation that the scheme as constituted when they were admitted thereto would continue for the duration of their time in college and, in particular, that they would continue to receive payment during college vacations. They did not dispute that the scheme could be amended for future entrants but argued that they reasonably and legitimately expected that the terms and conditions of the scheme would remain akin to those extant on their entry into the scheme for the duration of their entitlement and that it would be unjust for the respondent to resile from the representation that they claimed had been made through the Departmental booklet.

42. The High Court, following the judgment of Fennelly J in *Glencar Exploration plc. v. Mayo County Council*,[51] considered that to succeed in a claim based on legitimate expectations, three matters must be established. First, the public authority must have made a statement or adopted a position amounting to a promise or representation, express or implied, as to how it would act with respect to an identifiable area of its activity. Second, the representation must be addressed or conveyed either directly or indirectly to an identifiable person or group of persons, affected actually or potentially, in such a way that it forms part of a transaction definitively entered into or a relationship between that person and group and the public authority or that the person or group has acted on the faith of the representation. Third, it must be such as to create an expectation, reasonably entertained by the person or group, that the public authority will abide by the representation to the extent that it would be unjust to permit the public authority to resile from it.[52] In considering whether these conditions were met in the case at hand, the Court emphasized the fact that the scheme in question was not a statutory one but rather an administrative scheme approved by government decision only.

43. MacMenamin J took the view that the Departmental booklet amounted to a representation to the applicant (thus satisfying the first two legs of the test). He stated that the booklet could not be seen as 'a mere general statement of policy particularly so when taken in conjunction with the application form which creates an individualized clear and unequivocal relationship between the applicant and the respondent'. Thus, he held that having regard for the circumstances, the relationship created 'was more akin to an individualized promise and representation rather than the mere enunciation of a general policy'. The Court held that it was reasonable for Mr Power to conclude that the respondent would abide by the representation to the extent that it

51. [2002] 1 IR 84, [2002] 1 ILRM 481.
52. [2001] IESC 64 at para. 168.

would be unjust to permit the respondent to resile therefrom. The Court did not consider that the evidence was sufficient to justify removing the benefit of the scheme from him. While the change took place as a result of a budgetary constraint, no 'sufficient overriding interest' had been established. On the evidence, 'The respondent has not demonstrated the existence of any overriding public interest … to justify the change in the application of the scheme to … a person who, on specific representations, had been admitted to third level education and who was participating in the scheme; as opposed to any person seeking to benefit from the modified scheme in the future.' In this particular case, one might certainly have considerable sympathy for the applicant. However, the question arises as to whether the tests set out in *Glencar Exploration* were, in fact, satisfied. It may perhaps be placing too much weight on a simple informational booklet published by the Department to describe it as containing a representation addressed to an identifiable person or group of persons. At best, this decision should, perhaps, be confined to its own facts, whereby, unlike most social welfare schemes, a very specific action, that is, returning to education, was required by the applicant for benefits.

44. Hogan, Morgan and Daly have argued that while the doctrine of legitimate expectation cannot be relied on to prevent a change in the law, it can be invoked to require the observance of procedural rights, and it may be that this and the issue of the creation of legitimate expectation by administrative circulars are the main areas in which it may have implications in relation to social welfare law.[53]

IV. The Legal Status of Administrative Guidelines

45. As has been outlined above, the Department of Social Protection relies heavily on the issue of administrative guidelines for its staff.[54] These are used both to explain statutory provisions to its staff (including deciding officers) in readable English and to fill in lacunae that are not covered by legislation (e.g., the precise operation of the 'benefit and privilege' rule)[55] or to expand on statutory provisions (e.g., to discuss in more detail the definition of *farmer*).[56] In addition, administrative guidelines are utilized to suggest how discretion might be exercised in the limited number of areas in which discretionary social welfare payments arise (e.g., in relation to exceptional needs payments under the SWA Code).[57] Administrative guidelines are also used to set out the detailed rules of non-statutory schemes, such as Household Benefits, Back-to-Work, and Back-to-Education schemes. The High

53. Hogan, Morgan & Daly, *Administrative Law in Ireland* (Dublin: Round Hall Sweet & Maxwell, 2019), Ch. 21 passim.
54. *See ibid.*, 41–57 and G. Hogan, 'The Legal Status of Administrative Rules and Circulars', Ir. Jur. 22 (1987): 194.
55. *See* Part XI.
56. *See* Part VII, Ch. 4.
57. *See* Part X.

Court has held that the issue of administrative guidelines concerning the operation of a particular social welfare scheme was, in itself, 'clearly a proper and valid administrative act'.[58]

46. Insofar as they purport to explain or interpret legislation or indicate in what manner discretion might be exercised, guidelines must be consistent with the relevant primary and secondary legislation (and, of course, with the Constitution and EU law) and, in particular, they must not fetter the discretion of adjudicating officers. Hogan, Morgan and Daly state that the fundamental principles of common law indicate that administrative guidelines 'are not law'.[59] Indeed, if they were, this would raise the issue of the compatibility of the use of circulars with Article 15.2 of the Constitution, which provides that:

> The sole and exclusive power of making laws for the State is hereby vested in the Oireachtas: no other legislative authority has power to make laws for the State.[60]

Thus, a public body cannot rely on guidelines against an individual to affect or prejudice his or her legal rights. However, the Irish courts have held that an administrative guideline can create legally binding entitlements against a public body and may be subject to judicial review.[61]

V. What Is the Law?

47. Finally, we will consider the broader question as to the definition of *the law*. From a legal positivist point of view, 'law consists of data – primarily rules – which can be recognized by relatively simple tests or "rules of recognition"'.[62] The principal test is that the rules have gone through the formal stages of a legislative procedure; that is, they have been properly adopted by Parliament or by a subordinate authority. Thus, for example, it is said that social welfare law 'is an exclusively twentieth century phenomenon and as such is almost exclusively derived from Acts of the Oireachtas and delegated legislation'.

48. Others, however, have put forward a much broader view of the law. Ehrlich, for example, sees the law as involving not just the norms created and applied by the

58. *State (Kershaw) v. Eastern Health Board* [1985] ILRM 235 at 239. The case involved the operation of the fuel scheme under the Social Welfare (Consolidation) Act, 1981. In the particular circumstances, Finlay P held that the guidelines could not operate to bind the discretion of the adjudicating authorities.

59. *Ibid.*, para. 2.165.

60. *See* G. Hogan, 'The Legal Status of Administrative Rules and Circulars', Ir. Jur. 22 (1987): 211.

61. *Latchford v. Minister for Industry and Commerce* [1950] IR 33. As Hogan & Morgan point out, this result could be arrived at on the basis of the doctrine of legitimate expectations although Latchford long predates this concept. *See also Power v. Minister for Social and Family Affairs* [2006] IEHC 164 discussed above.

62. R. Cotterrell, *Sociology of the Law* (London: Butterworths, 1992), 9.

State but also including what he calls 'social order', that is, the rules that are actually followed in social life – the real 'living law'. Cotterrell, for the purposes of his study of the sociology of the law, steers a path between these two approaches and refers to the *law* as:

> the social rules and related doctrine created, adopted, interpreted and enforced by state agencies as a framework of general regulation within a politically organized society.[63]

49. Studies show that bureaucracies – from time to time – have adopted official practices that are not fully in line with the legal rules. Sometimes, these 'official practices' operate to the advantage of individuals but, on other occasions, to their disadvantage.[64] The legal positivist viewpoint would see the law as consisting solely of the legal rules, and any discordant 'official practice' would be seen to be in breach of the law. However, in the broader sense, discussed above, the 'official practice' could certainly be seen as being 'the law' in a situation where sections of the state create and adopt a practice that is implemented by a state agency that is also able to enforce its decisions by awarding or falling to award welfare payments to those affected.

50. The usefulness of definitions depends, of course, on the purpose for which the definitions are required. For the purposes of this legal study of the operation of the social welfare system, we will, in general, confine ourselves to the narrower 'legal' understanding of the law. However, for those who wish to understand the practical operation of the social welfare system, it may be that a broader definition of the law is more helpful to a practical and theoretical understanding. For example, if one wishes to consider the development of public interest litigation to establish socio-economic rights, it is well to be aware that welfare law involves much more than the legal rules contained in the relevant statutes and statutory instruments.[65]

63. *Ibid.*, at 43.
64. *See*, e.g., several examples of such a divergence between the 'law' and 'official practice' in the area of health services in Part III.
65. On public interest litigation, *see* G. Whyte, *Social Inclusion and the Law: Public Interest Law in Ireland,* 2nd ed. (Dublin: IPA, 2015).

Part I. The Institutions

Introduction

51. The social welfare and healthcare systems outlined in this book operate almost entirely separately. The DSP is responsible for the planning and delivery of the social welfare system. In the area of healthcare, planning and oversight is the responsibility of the Department of Health, while services are delivered by the Health Services Executive (HSE) in conjunction with a range of publicly and privately owned hospitals and institutions and staff who are employed by the HSE, and by private bodies and private doctors who have a contractual relationship with the HSE to provide public healthcare.

..ERIAL DEPARTMENTS

52. As outlined above, two Departments – Social Protection and Health – are involved in the provision of social welfare and healthcare, respectively. The same legal principles apply to both.[66] The head of each department is, in principle, the Minister, who is a member of the Executive (government). Ministers are appointed by the Taoiseach (Prime Minister), subject to the approval of the Oireachtas (Parliament). In practice, Ministers are almost invariably elected members of the Dáil (the lower house of Parliament).[67]

53. The role of Ministers is set out in the Ministers and Secretaries Act of 1924 as amended. In recent years, the fictive nature of the role of the Minister as responsible for all activities of his or her department has become increasingly apparent, and legislation has begun to specify the role and responsibilities of the 'permanent' civil service head of the department (the Secretary-General).[68]

54. The Minister, in his or her role as the head of the department, is a *corporation sole*.[69] In law, many of the activities of the department are attributed to the Minister,[70] but, in practice, these are delegated to departmental officials who are civil servants. One potentially important issue is the extent to which such delegation is allowed by law. Irish law, following English common law in this regard, takes the position that the powers vested in a Minister may be exercised *without any express act of delegation* by responsible officials on behalf of the Minister.[71] The Irish courts have taken a particularly broad approach to allowing such implied delegation.[72] In the social welfare area, the functions that are normally delegated, such as the receipt of claims, are particularly of a mass and administrative nature, and it seems unlikely that issues would generally arise as to whether such delegation is allowed by law. Ultimately, however, as Hogan, Morgan and Daly point out, whether or not delegation is allowed is a matter of statutory interpretation; that is, one must establish whether, in relation to the particular function, the law intended it to be carried out personally by the Minister.

66. The leading Irish text on administrative law is Hogan, Morgan & Daly, *Administrative Law in Ireland*, 5th ed. (Round Hall: Sweet & Maxwell, 2019).
67. Although, legally, it is possible for a Minister to be a member of the Seanad (upper house) and a small number of members of this body are appointed by the Taoiseach rather than elected.
68. In fact, secretaries-general now serve as such for a maximum of seven years.
69. *See* Hogan, Morgan & Daly, *Administrative Law in Ireland* (Dublin: Round Hall), 3.39.
70. Such as, e.g., receipt of claims for social welfare payments.
71. *See* Hogan, Morgan & Daly, *Administrative Law in Ireland* (Dublin: Round Hall), 11.83 et seq.
72. *See*, e.g., *Tang v. Minister for Justice* [1996] 2 ILRM 46; *Devanny v. Minister for Justice* [1998] 1 ILRM 81.

§2. Public Institutions

55. The other main public body involved in the provision of health and, to a much lesser extent, social welfare services is the HSE. The HSE is a relatively recent creation, established by the HA of 2004, replacing the previous regional health boards. The object and functions of the HSE are set out in section 7 of the 2004 Act. This provides that the objective of the HSE is 'to use the resources available to it in the most beneficial, effective and efficient manner to improve, promote and protect the health and welfare of the public'.[73] Section 7(4) provides, in particular, that the HSE shall manage and shall deliver, or arrange to be delivered on its behalf, health and personal social services. The Board of the HSE is appointed by the Minister for Health.[74]

73. Section 7(1) of the Health Act of 2004.
74. Section 11 of the 2004 Act.

Chapter 2. Position and Competence of the Public Institutions

56. The DSP has responsibility for both the planning and delivery of social welfare systems. In 2010, the Department was also given responsibility for the provision of employment schemes, assistance in obtaining employment and/or work experience and job placement schemes.[75]

57. The Department of Health is responsible for policy and budgetary issues concerning health services. The objective and main functions of the HSE have been set out above. The HA of 2004 provides the Executive with 'all powers necessary or expedient for it to perform its functions'.[76]

58. The Departments and the HSE as public bodies are subject to the general principles of administrative law.[77]

75. Part 3 of the SWPA 2010.
76. Section 7(8) of the Health Act of 2004.
77. These are discussed in Hogan, Morgan & Daly, *Administrative Law in Ireland* (Dublin: Round Hall).

Chapter 3. Private Institutions

59. The public social welfare system outlined in this monograph operates entirely through public institutions. Private institutions are not directly involved, although such bodies – including pension trust funds and pension consultancy firms – are heavily involved in the provision of private occupational pensions.

60. The healthcare system involves much more of a public-private mix in that many of the public healthcare services are provided in hospitals and other institutions owned and managed by 'private' bodies (including 'voluntary' organizations). However, decision-making in relation to entitlement to healthcare (other than in relation to clinical aspects) is entirely a matter for the public bodies (currently the HSE).

Part II. Contribution and Financing

Introduction

61. There are effectively five main legal categories of social insurance contributors: employed contributors, occupational injuries contributors, self-employed contributors, optional contributors, and voluntary contributors. However, in practice, the two latter categories apply only to very small groups of people. Conversely, the category of employed contributors is broken down into employed contributors who are fully insured for all contingencies (known as Class A contributors)[78] and 'modified' contributors (mainly civil and public servants) who are covered for only a limited range of benefits. Many of these modified groups have been closed to new entrants since April 1995, as civil and public servants recruited after that date are in Class A.

62. There are currently five modified categories, including permanent and pensionable civil servants, registered doctors and dentists employed in the civil service, and Gardaí (police), all of whom were recruited prior to 6 April 1995 (Class B); commissioned Defence Forces Officers and members of the Army Nursing Service, again, recruited prior to 6 April 1995 (Class C); permanent and pensionable employees in the public service other than those mentioned in Classes B and C, recruited prior to 6 April 1995 (Class D); Ministers of Religion, employed by the Church of Ireland Representative Body (Class E); and non-commissioned officers and enlisted personnel of the Defence Forces (Class H). Persons insured for OIBs only (e.g., persons earning less than EUR 38 per week, employees over age 66, and people in subsidiary employment) are categorized as Class J. Class K covers public office holders who, from 2011, are liable to social insurance. Self-employed contributors are categorized as Class S. Persons who were formerly insured can continue to pay contributions as voluntary contributors (not assigned any class letter for no apparent reason). Finally, optional contributors (i.e., share fishermen or women who are classified as self-employed and are already paying Class S contributions) are also allowed to pay optional Class P contributions for additional benefits.

63. The scope of social insurance in Ireland is now quite extensive. In contrast to the position at the time of the CSW in 1986, self-employed persons are covered

78. It should be noted that the terminology of the various 'classes', although widely used in social welfare literature, has no specific legal basis.

(albeit for a restricted range of benefits), as are the vast majority of part-time workers and persons employed for 'community employment' types of work. Only employees earning less than EUR 38 per week or self-employed persons earning below EUR 5,000 per annum are excluded, and at these earning levels, occupational income is clearly not the person's main source of income. In addition, some assisting spouses and relatives are excluded, but this group continues to fall in size, and such persons can be employed in such a manner as to be insurable if this is so desired.

64. As will be seen, the question of whether and how a person is insured under the SW Acts is, in general, reasonably clear, although there are complicated legal issues in relation to some cases – particularly those at the margins between employment and self-employment (or partnership). Indeed, this has always been the case, and the law reports since the establishment of the precursor schemes are full of cases involving disputes as to whether or not particular types of employment fell within the scope of insurance (or, indeed, of the workmen's compensation scheme). Those employed under a 'contract of service' are fully insured, and the legislative tendency has been to add specific groups of workers who were not so employed rather than to attempt to broaden the general definition of insurability. Indeed, it is difficult to see that any one definition could cover the full range of employment currently within the scope of the Acts. However, consideration might be given to a general statutory broadening of the 'contract of service' test – as applies in the case of a number of employment protection statutes. This might assist in including workers who are, in economic reality, dependent on the 'employer', although they may, according to a strict interpretation of the law, be employed under a contract for services.

Chapter 1. Contribution Regulation for Employees

§1. Field of Application

I. Territorial Field of Application

65. As set out below in relation to the individual categories of insurance, the Irish Social Security Code generally requires that a person be employed within the State, that is, in the territory of the Republic of Ireland.[79] This condition is, however, overruled in certain cases by EU law whereby persons insured under Irish law can be posted abroad and remain insured under the Irish Social Welfare Code.[80] In addition, in relation to countries outside the EU or EEA and those covered by bilateral agreements, Article 98 of the Social Welfare Regulations (S.I.) No. 312 of 1996, in accordance with the powers provided under section 31 of the Act, provides that when an insured person who is ordinarily resident in the State is temporarily employed outside the State in the service of an employer who is resident or has a place of business in the State in employment that would otherwise be employment within the meaning of paragraph 1, that paragraph is to be construed as if the words 'in the State' were deleted. However, a person shall cease to be treated as temporarily employed outside the State when the period of absence exceeds fifty-two contribution weeks unless the Minister otherwise decides in any particular case.[81]

II. Personal Field of Application

66. *Insured Employments:* section 12(1) provides that:

(a) subject to paragraph (b), every person who, being over the age of 16 years and under pensionable age (*see* paragraph 545), is employed in any of the employments specified in Part 1 of Schedule 1, not being an employment specified in Part 2 of that Schedule, shall be an employed contributor for the purposes of this Act; and
(b) every person, irrespective of age, who is employed in insurable (occupational injuries) employment shall be an employed contributor, and references in this Act to an employed contributor shall be read accordingly.

Section 12(1)(c) provides that every person becoming for the first time an employed contributor thereby becomes insured under the Act and continues throughout his or her life to be so insured.

79. Republic of Ireland Act of 1948.
80. F. Pennings, *European Social Security Law*, 5th ed. (Antwerp: Intersentia, 2010), Ch. 7. *See* Case C-202/97, *Fitzwilliam Executive Search* [2000] ECR I-883.
81. *See Kenny v. Minister for Trade and Employment* [1999] IEHC 110, in which the Court ruled that a person who was employed outside the State for four years (without a specific authorization by the Minister) ceased to be in insurable employment after fifty-two weeks.

67. Part 1 of Schedule 1 to the Act lists those types of employment fully covered by the Act. Paragraph 1, the wording of which dates back to the original National Insurance Act of 1911, is the principal provision:

> Employment in the State under a contract of service or apprenticeship, written or oral, whether expressed or implied, and whether the employed person is paid by the employer or some other person, and whether under one or more employers, and whether paid by time or by the piece or partly by time and partly by the piece, or otherwise, or without any money payment.

68. Thus, insurability as an employed contributor requires a person to be: (i) employed under a contract of service or apprenticeship, and (ii) in the State. There is no statutory definition of 'contract of service', and the general case law in relation to the distinction between a 'contract of service' and a 'contract for services' is relevant to insurability under the Social Welfare Code. As is well known, a range of different tests has been applied to distinguish between the two categories of contact, including the degree of control exercised over the work of the person concerned,[82] the extent to which he or she is engaged in business of his or her own account,[83] whether the person is an integral part of the business,[84] and whether 'mutuality of obligation' exists.[85]

69. In *Henry Denny v. Minister for Social Welfare*,[86] the Supreme Court considered whether a supermarket demonstrator was employed under a contract of service and thus fully insurable under the SW Acts or whether she was employed under a contract for services. The person concerned was recruited by the company and signed a twelve-month contract that was renewed over a number of years from 1991 to 1993. The 1993 contract described her as an independent contractor and purported to make her responsible for any liability to taxes. When a store requested a demonstration of a product, she was contacted by the company, sent to the store, and carried out a demonstration. She then submitted an invoice to the company signed by the store manager and was paid at a daily rate and given a mileage allowance. She worked an average of twenty-eight hours per week for forty-eight to fifty weeks per year. The demonstrations were not carried out under the direct supervision of the company, but she was provided with written instructions as to how to carry out the work and the relevant materials. She required the consent of the company to subcontract out any of the work assigned to her.

70. A question had arisen as to whether this supermarket demonstrator was an insured person under the Acts, and an appeals officer had held that she was employed under a contract of service. Having reviewed the extensive case law in

---

82. *Roche v. P. Kelly & Co.* [1969] IR 100.
83. *Ó Coinealbhain v. Mooney* [1990] 1 IR 422, and *see Graham v. Minister for Industry and Commerce* [1933] IR 156.
84. *Stephenson, Jordan and Harris Ltd v. McDonald and Evans* 1952 ITR 191.
85. *Brightwater Selection v. Minister for Social and Family Affairs* [2011] IEHC 510; *Revenue Commissioners v. Karshan Midlands Ltd T/A Domino's Pizza* [2023] IESC 24.
86. [1988] 1 IR 34.

this area, the Supreme Court held that in deciding whether a person was employed under a contract of service or under a contract for services, each case must be considered in light of its particular facts and in light of the general principles that the courts have developed. In general, the Court held that a person would be regarded as being employed under a contract of service when he or she is performing services for another person and not for himself or herself; that is, when the person is not in business on his or her own account. The inference that a person is engaged in his or her own business will more readily be drawn when he or she provides the necessary premises or equipment or some other form of investment, when he or she employs others to assist in the business, and when the profit that he or she derives from the business is dependent on the efficiency with which it is conducted. The Court further held that the degree of control exercised over how the work was to be carried out was a factor to be taken into account but was not decisive. On the basis of the facts, in this case, the Court held that the appeals officer was entitled to arrive at the conclusion that he did.

71. As is clear from *Henry Denny*, the question of whether or not a particular type of employment is or is not within the scope of the social insurance scheme can, in general, only be decided on the particular facts, although the Department obviously tries to ensure that all cases of similar types of employment are treated in a similar way from a social insurance point of view. The US approach, whereby the courts consider whether a person is an employee 'as a matter of economic reality', is not in accordance with Irish law.[87]

72. The Irish courts have held that persons delivering newspapers who owned their own delivery vehicles and were responsible for all journeys in them were self-employed rather than employees of the newspaper distributor,[88] that cattle inseminators were self-employed,[89] that certain contract cleaners were self-employed,[90] and that share fishers paid by way of a share of the profits of any catch were partners with, rather than employees of, the boat owners.[91] Conversely, the High Court upheld an appeals officer's decision that Electricity Supply Board (ESB) meter readers were employees of the company.[92] The High Court also upheld an appeals

87. *Griffin v. Minister for Social, Community and Family Affairs*, High Court, unreported 2 Oct. 2001 refusing to apply *US v. Silk*, 331, US 704.
88. *McAuliffe v. Minister for Social Welfare* [1995] 2 IR 238. And *see Hogan v. United Beverage* [2006] ELR 267 and *McArthur v. Minister for Industry and Commerce* [1928] IR 555 for similar conclusions. An appeals officer ruled that motor-cycle couriers were also self-employed: *Social Welfare Appeals Office Report 1998*, 24–25.
89. *Castleisland Cattle Breeding Society Ltd v. Minister for Social and Family Affairs* [2004] IESC 40.
90. When the person was free to send a substitute to do the work, had to indemnify the company against public liability risks, and there was no entitlement to holiday or sick pay. There does not appear to be a written report of this judgment, but *see Social Welfare Appeals Office Report 2003*, 14.
91. *Griffin v. Minister for Social, Community and Family Affairs*, High Court, unreported 2 Oct. 2001 following *DPP v. McLoughlin* [1986] 1 IR 355.
92. *ESB v. Minister for Social, Community and Family Affairs* [2006] IEHC 59. Appeals officers have also ruled that market research interviewers are employees. *See also Kirwan v. Technical Engineering & Electrical Union* [2005] IEHC 5 ruling that a trade union branch secretary was an employee on the facts of that case.

officer's decision that a company director with a minority shareholding was an employee of the company (rather than self-employed).[93]

73. These cases are not always easy to reconcile. In *Castleisland*, the Supreme Court, while purporting to follow *Henry Denny*, held that the case for cattle inseminators being self-employed was 'overwhelming', referring, in particular, to: (i) the fact that the persons who had previously been employed by the same company as employees and made redundant, were fully aware that they were to work under a contract for services, as this had been reflected in their redundancy package,[94] and that they, for example, paid taxes as self-employed persons; and (ii) 'even more important', that the persons concerned had to carry their own insurance. With respect, the Court seems to have focused on the incidentals of the employment relationship, which, of course, reflected the purported contract for services relationship, rather than looking at the test emphasized in *Henry Denny* as to whether they were performing the services for another person and not for themselves.[95] From that perspective, the outcome looks much less clear. The evidence appears to have been that inseminators *could* influence their level of profits, but it is unclear whether this occurred in practice. While the inseminators did have to provide their own transportation, it appears that this had also been the case when they worked as employees. The Court attached no importance to 'strict requirements regarding replacements, time of holidays, [and] on-call availability', reading these as 'natural terms' of such a contract.[96] The Court was quite ready to substitute its views for those of the appeals officer (as, of course, it was entitled to do if the appeals officer had erred in law).[97]

74. In contrast, *ESB v. Minister for Social, Community and Family Affairs*[98] concerned contract meter readers working for the ESB. Their contract specifically stated that they were independent contractors, and previously, such workers had been considered to be self-employed. However, an appeals officer held that the workers were employed under a contract of service. She drew attention to two fundamental changes that had occurred. The first was that to employ a relevant substitute, a meter reader had to seek ESB approval, and the person concerned had to

93. *Neenan Travel v. Minister for Social and Family Affairs* [2011] IEHC 458. The Court left open the issue as to the point at which, or the circumstances in which, a substantial shareholding and the top management role in a company may be indicative of the fact that the person in that position is acting on his own account and not as an employee of the company (though *see* below para. 98 for a legislative response). *See also Secretary of State for Trade & Industry v. Bottrill* [1999] EWCA Civ 781.
94. The Canadian Federal Court of Appeal has reviewed Canadian law as to the distinction between employment and self-employment (in the context of an insurability decision) with particular emphasis on the relevance of the intention of the parties: *1392644 Ontario Inc. (Connor Homes) v. Minister of National Revenue*, 2013 FCA 85.
95. *See also* the discussion of this aspect in *Tierney v. An Post* [1999] IESC 66.
96. In contrast, in *Henry Denny*, the Court had considered that the fact that the person in that case was not allowed to provide a replacement without authorization of the company as significant.
97. Unfortunately, neither High Court nor Supreme Court judgments reproduce the appeals officer's actual decision, so it is somewhat difficult to establish what facts had been found and the extent to which the appeals officer had or had not taken different factors into account.
98. [2006] IEHC 59.

obtain an ESB ID card. The second was that the meter readers had been by the ESB with a hand-held terminal in which they recorded the meter re which were downloaded daily to the ESB records. In relation to the 'entreprene test', the appeals officer noted that the meter readers did not ply for hire, nor did they take financial risk, nor did they stand to make a profit other than their earnings. Having considered the overall picture, she concluded that the meter readers were employed under a contract of service. On appeal, Gilligan J expressed the view that the written agreement existing between the parties is of considerable importance and has to be given due consideration but is not conclusive in its own right and that, therefore, following the judgment of Keane J in *Henry Denny*, the particular facts and circumstances of the case had to be considered. These included whether the person was performing the services for another person and not for himself or herself, the degree of control exercised over how work is to be performed, who provides the necessary premises and equipment or other forms of investment, whether others are employed to assist in the business, and whether the profit derived is dependent on the efficiency of the person concerned. He held that the appeals officer had adopted a reasoned approach in deciding the issue before her and that it was open to her to have come to the conclusion that there had been a change in the level of control exercised through the introduction of the data logger and that the freedom of the meter reader in relation to the use of the substitute had been limited. The Court was satisfied that the appeals officer was entitled to conclude that the meter readers were employed under a contract of service.

75. Mutuality of obligation is a key factor in any contract, including a contract of service.[99] In recent case law (particularly cases involving casual employment), it has sometimes been referred to as a '*sine qua non*' or 'the irreducible minimum' necessary to show a contract. It is clear from the UK case law that there is a difference between the situation where a person is trying to show an ongoing contract of employment (where the question of the obligation to offer and accept employment is relevant) and the case where a person has actually worked in specific employment where the obligations to actually work and to pay for that work satisfy the mutuality of obligation test.[100]

76. The leading Irish case on mutuality of obligation is *Minister for Agriculture v. Barry*, which concerned temporary veterinary inspectors who claimed under the Redundancy Payments Acts and the Minimum Notice and Terms of Employment

99. *Sister Dolores v. Minister for Social Welfare* [1962] IR 77 can be seen as an example of a lack of mutual obligations (in that case in relation to a contract of apprenticeship). *See* Maguire CJ at 92–94.
100. *Stephenson v. Delphi Systems* [2003] ICR 471; *Cornwall County Council v. Prater* [2006] EWCA Civ 102. Cases in which the UK courts have held that mutuality of obligation did not exist in relation to casual employment are distinguishable from the above decisions as they involved claims that an umbrella or ongoing contract existed, as, for example, in *Clark v. Oxfordshire Health Authority* [1998] IRLR 125; or *Carmichael v. National Power plc* [1999] ICR 1226.

the High Court (Edwards J.) put it, 'entitlement to the payments claimed ntingent on them having been employees who were employed at all material s by the appellant under a contract of service'. Given this, the issue of mutuality of obligation focused on whether there were mutual obligations on the employer to provide work for the employee and on the employee to perform work for the employer. The Employment Appeals Tribunal (EAT) had found that there was an 'implied agreement' between the parties to carry out work on an ongoing basis from which it found a mutuality of obligation. In short, the High Court found that on the facts of the case, this finding of an implied agreement was 'untenable'. However, this case did not address the issue of whether there was a contract of service in relation to each of the individual periods of employment.[102]

77. In the *Brightwater* decision, Gilligan J stated that:

> Mutuality of obligation exists where there is an obligation on a body to provide work to an individual and a corresponding obligation on the individual to perform that work.[103]

The Court did not, however, refer to the situation where work has already been performed and remuneration provided in return.

The High Court in *Domino's Pizza* (involving pizza delivery drivers) ruled that mutuality of obligations did not always require an obligation to provide work and to complete that work on an *ongoing* basis.[104] However, on appeal to the Court of Appeal, a majority of the court held that there was no mutuality of obligation.[105] Costello J. stated that 'Irish authorities on mutuality of obligation are unambiguous in requiring an ongoing reciprocal commitment to provide and perform work on the part of the employer and the employee respectively'.[106]

78. In *FÁS v. Minister for Social Welfare*, the Supreme Court considered the effect of an illegal or *ultra vires* contract.[107] The Court held that an illegal contract would not be enforced by the courts and could not be regarded as coming within

101. [2008] IEHC 216, *see also McGurk v. Department for Social Development* [2006] NICA 20; *Mansoor v. Minister for Justice, Equality and Law Reform* [2010] IEHC 389; *McKayed v. Forbidden City Ltd* [2016] IEHC 722.
102. The case was remitted to the EAT which seems to have considered itself bound to reverse its earlier ruling but this was overturned on appeal by the Supreme Court which again remitted the case to the EAT (but without considering in detail the substantive issues involved): *Barry v. Minister for Agriculture & Food* [2015] IESC 63.
103. *Brightwater Selection v. Minister for Social and Family Affairs* [2011] IEHC 510 at para. 48.
104. *Karshan Ltd. (t/a Domino's Pizza) v. Revenue Commissioners* [2019] IEHC 894 at 50–57 citing *Weight Watchers (UK) Ltd v. Revenue and Customs Commissioners* [2011] UKUT 433.
105. *See* now *Revenue Commissioners v. Karshan Midlands Ltd T/A Domino's Pizza* [2023] IESC 24.
106. At 110.
107. Unreported, Supreme Court, 23 May 1995. *See* below para. 107 for a specific provision in relation to occupational injuries employment.

the definition of 'contract of service' under the SW Acts.[108] Egan J ruled that if the Oireachtas had decided to prohibit a particular type of contract, it would be anomalous if reliance were to be placed on it for the purpose of social welfare contributions and benefits. Accordingly, when a contract is found to be illegal, whether because its object was the committing of an illegal act or because it was expressly or implicitly prohibited by statute, it will not be recognized by law. In the case of *ultra vires* contracts, although they are void *ab initio*, it might happen in practice that the validity of the void act becomes immune from challenge. The element of uncertainty, said the Court, means that an appeals officer should not rely on the *ultra vires* nature of a contract. It would be anomalous were the appeals officer to treat as invalid a contract that a court in its discretion might refuse to invalidate. This decision appeared to mean that foreign nationals who required an employment permit under the Employment Permits Act of 2003 (as amended) but who were in employment without such a permit were *not* insurable.[109]

79. This view was confirmed by the Supreme Court in *Sobhy v. Chief Appeals Officer*.[110] This case involved the question as to whether a person employed under an illegal contract was insurable under the Social Welfare Acts (and, therefore, entitled to maternity benefit). In this case, the non-EU national worker did not have a work permit as required by the Employment Permits Act 2003 (as amended). The appeals officer in this case adopted the long-standing view that such persons were not insurable. However, the High Court applied the apparent logic of the Supreme Court decision in *Quinn v. IBRC*[111] and quashed the appeals officer's decision.[112] In *Quinn*, the Supreme Court had considered the appropriate modern approach to be applied when determining whether to enforce a contract, notwithstanding that it had been tainted by illegality.

80. On appeal, the Supreme Court upheld the appeals officer's decision. The Court (Baker J.) pointed out that the case did not directly concern the enforcement of a contract of employment. Nor was the Court convinced by the argument that there was such a contractual nexus between the employee, the employer and the

108. *Ibid.*, at 8–9 of the judgment, albeit that this was strictly *obiter* as the Court found that neither an illegal nor *ultra vires* contract arose on the facts. *See also McHugh v. Ministry of Labour for Northern Ireland* [1940] NI 174, in which the Court held that the employment of a bookmaker's clerk in both legal and illegal betting was not insurable employment. *See*, however, *Still v. M.N.R.*, 1997 CanLII 6379 (FCA) in which the Canadian Federal Court of Appeal held that this approach no longer reflected reality and that when a person had acted in good faith, he or she should not be denied benefits.

109. Section 2 of the 2003 Act (as amended by s. 2 of the Employment Permits Act of 2006) provides that a foreign national 'shall not' enter the service of an employer or be in employment in the State except in accordance with an employment permit and makes it a criminal offence to do so. It is understood that it is the practice of the Department to return contributions paid under such circumstances. *See*, in relation to Bulgarian and Romanian nationals employed between 2007 and 2011, para. 2A of Part 1 of Sch. 1 inserted by s. 20 SWA 2016.

110. [2021] IESC 81.

111. [2015] IESC 29.

112. [2021] IEHC 93.

State that the approach in Quinn should be applied. Rather – following *P.C. v. Minister for Social Protection*[113] – Baker J. held that 'the social welfare code created a statutory entitlement and not a contractual right'.[114] The Court concluded that the contract of employment in question was one prohibited by statute, even though it did not have an inherently unlawful subject matter. The Court found that 'the decision in *FÁS v. Abbott* is correct and that a person without a work permit is excluded from the social welfare code, both as regards the obligation to pay PRSI or other social contributions, and any entitlement that might arise therefrom'.[115]

81. Therefore, the Court held that the Oireachtas intended to designate a contract of employment entered into without a work permit by a person unlawfully in the State as illegal for all practical purposes, save as expressly provided by statute. The contract of employment cannot therefore be a qualifying 'contract of service' for the purpose of the entitlement to maternity benefit. The Oireachtas intended that only contributions made by persons in employment whose contracts are made or to be performed in a legal manner could obtain benefit under the code.[116]

82. Baker J ruled that 'the policy of the [employment permit] legislation would be frustrated if a person, having failed to obtain a [work] permit … could still obtain the benefit of social welfare payments or entitlements derived from working in the State … '. Although the Supreme Court held that *Quinn* was 'irrelevant' in this case as the issue related to statutory entitlement and not contract, Baker J. went on to say (albeit *obiter*) that 'even on the nuanced approach adopted by this Court in *Quinn v. IBRC*' the appeal must be allowed.[117]

83. Schedule 1 also refers to a number of other types of private-sector employment that are also fully insurable. Listing them with the paragraph numbers they have in the Schedule, these are:[118]

2. Employment under such a contract of service referred to in paragraph 1:
   - (a) as master or a member of the crew of:
     - (i) any ship registered in the State; or
     - (ii) any other ship or vessel of which the owner, or, where there is more than one owner, the managing owner or manager, resides or has his or her principal place of business in the State; or
   - (b) as captain or a member of the crew of:
     - (i) any aircraft registered in the State; or
     - (ii) any other aircraft of which the owner, or, where there is more than one owner, the managing owner or manager, resides or has his or her principal place of business in the State.

113. [2017] IESC 63.
114. *Sobhy* at 71.
115. At 81.
116. At 92.
117. At 123.
118. Paragraphs 3, 4, 5, 6, and 9 refer to public sector employments and are outlined below.

7. Employment as a trainee midwife, student midwife, pupil midwife, probationary midwife, trainee nurse, student nurse, pupil nurse or probationary nurse. In this paragraph 'nurse' includes a nursery or children's nurse.

84. This paragraph was inserted as a result of the High Court and Supreme Court decisions in *National Maternity Hospital v. Minister for Social Welfare*[119] and *Sister Dolores v. Minister for Social Welfare,*[120] in which it was held that the relationship between a trainee nurse and a hospital was fundamentally that of pupil and teacher and not that of master and servant, nor of apprenticeship, and consequently, that such employment was not insurable under the SW Acts:

8. Employment by the Minister as manager of an employment office.

85. This paragraph was inserted as a result of the High Court decision in *Ó Coindealbhain v. Mooney,*[121] a tax case in which it was held that a branch manager of an employment office was employed under a contract for services:

9. Employment as a member of the Garda Síochána (police force).
10. Employment where the employed person is a person in Holy Orders or other ministers of religion or a person living in a religious community as a member of that community.[122]

86. Traditionally, the courts have held that a member of the clergy is not employed under a contract of service,[123] and that approach has been followed in unfair dismissal cases by the Irish courts and tribunals.[124] However, more recently, the UK courts have held that clergy may be employed under a contract of service, and it remains to be seen whether this approach will be followed in Ireland:[125]

11. Employment by An Post as a sub-postmaster remunerated by scale payment.

119. [1960] IR 74.
120. [1962] IR 77 (but decided in 1957).
121. [1990] I IR 422.
122. The Oxford Dictionary on the Christian Church indicates that the reference to 'Holy Orders' covers deacons, priests and bishops. The reference to 'other minister of religion' probably covers denominations that do not have these clerical ranks, such as Presbyterianism. 'Person living in a religious community' could include nuns and brothers.
123. *Davies v. Presbyterian Church of Wales* [1986] 1 All ER 705. *See also* the early case of *In re National Insurance Act* 1911 [1912] 2 Ch. 563 to the same effect.
124. *Millen v. Presbyterian Church in Ireland* [2000] ELR 292; *Representative Church Body v. Frazer* [2005] ELR 292. However, a cleric may be employed as, for example, a teacher: *Dolan v. K.* [1944] IR 460.
125. *New Testament Church of God v. Stewart* [2007] EWCA Civ 1004; *Percy v. Church of Scotland Board of National Mission* [2005] UKHL 73 (although the definition at issue in *Percy* was broader than a contract of service) and the UK courts have ruled that other clergy are not employees on different facts: *Sharpe v. The Bishop of Worcester* [2015] EWCA Civ 399.

87. Such persons would otherwise be considered to be self-employed. See the Supreme Court decision in *Tierney v. An Post* (although the statutory provision predates the judgment):[126]

12. Employment under a scheme known as Community Employment or employment under a scheme known as the Part-Time Job Opportunities Scheme administered by or on behalf of the Conference of Religious of Ireland, where:
    (a) the said employment commences on or after the 6 April 1996; or
    (b) in any other case, where, subject to such conditions and in such circumstances as may be prescribed, the person employed in either of the said employments elects to be an employed contributor within the meaning of section 12(1)(*a*).
13. Employment whereby an individual agrees with another person who is carrying on the business of an employment agency within the meaning of the Employment Agency Act of 1971 and is acting in the course of that business, to do or perform personally any work or service for a third person (whether or not the third person is a party to the contract and whether or not the third person pays the wages or salary of the individual with respect to the work or service).

88. This paragraph was inserted in 2003 to clarify the position of agency workers under the Acts.[127] Social welfare law did not originally provide specifically for the situation of agency workers. However, in the 1970s, the English courts ruled that agency workers provided to the construction industry were not employed under a contract of service by the agency (but rather under a contract for services or a contract sui generis (of its own kind)).[128] A rather similar approach was taken by the Irish courts in 1986 when the High Court ruled that a typist provided to the PMPA by an employment agency was not employed by PMPA.[129] This decision was followed by an appeals officer in the PARC Aviation case, which eventually led to this amendment.[130] Despite the 2003 change, it may still be relevant to establish whether an agency worker is employed under a contract of service (particularly in pre-2003 cases).

89. Each agency worker case must be approached on its own facts. However, in the majority of cases, the worker will have a contract with the employment agency (the agency) and no written contract with the end-user (the company). The English Court of Appeal has ruled that a contract should only be implied where it is necessary to do so to give business effect to the relationship.[131] It is not sufficient that the conduct of the parties is more consistent with an intention to form a contract

126. [1999] IESC 66.
127. *See* Robert Clark's excellent note: 'Agency Workers and Social Insurance', DULJ 23 (2003): 198.
128. *Construction Industry Training Board v. Labour Force* [1970] 3 All ER 220.
129. *Minister for Labour v. PMPA* [1986] JISLL 215. There was a contract between the worker and the agency, but the court did not comment on the nature of that contract.
130. The appeals officer's decision is discussed by Robert Clark, *Annotated Guide to Social Welfare Law* (London: Sweet & Maxwell, 1995).
131. *James v. Greenwich* [2008] EWCA Civ 35; *Tilson v. Alstom Transport* [2011] EWCA Civ 1308.

than not to do so, nor should a contract be implied just because a worker does the same kind of work that an employee in the same company does or because the court (or tribunal) wishes to extend the protection enjoyed by employees to agency workers. The fact that the worker is integrated into the overall work of the company is not sufficient to require the implication of a contract of service. Therefore, it will only be exceptional that a contract of any type and, *a fortiori*, a contract of service will be implied between the worker and the company. While the text of necessity is based on the English law of contract, it would seem to be similar to the approach adopted by the Irish courts.[132]

90. In *Brightwater*, the facts of which predated the 2003 change, an agency worker was supplied to University College Dublin (UCD). An appeals officer took the view that the agreement between Brightwater (the agency) and the worker established sufficient control (particularly with regard to terms of engagement, the requirement for her to notify them of any changes in relation to responsibility, hours worked, pay, grievances, sickness, permanent employment, to produce a time sheet, and to follow various other instructions) to establish a contract of service. However, Gilligan J in the High Court held that the appeals officer should have directed his mind to whether the agency 'possessed the power to direct the manner in which work was to be done by [the worker]'.[133] He ruled that the correct test was 'whether the body in question possessed or exercised the right to control the individual both as regards the work to be done and also as regards the manner in which the work is to be done'. Gilligan J also pointed out that the appeals officer erred in law in failing to consider whether mutuality of obligations existed.[134] The Court remitted the matter for a decision in line with its judgment and did not come to any specific conclusion as to the type of relationship involved.

91. Clark has argued that before establishing whether paragraph 13 applies, it should be necessary to consider whether an agency worker is an employee (under paragraph 1) or is genuinely self-employed. However, it is not clear that this is, in fact, required by the statutory language.[135] Rather, in the case of an agency worker who is also employed under a contract of service within the meaning of paragraph 1, one might argue on the basis of the general rules of statutory interpretation that the more specific provision concerning agency workers in paragraph 13 overrides the general provision and the person is insured under paragraph 13.[136] In the case of

132. *See Sweeney v. Duggan* [1997] 2 IR 531.
133. *Brightwater Selection v. Minister for Social and Family Affairs* [2011] IEHC 510 at para. 23.
134. However, in that case, it would appear that there was mutuality in the sense that, having accepted the assignment with UCD, the worker was obliged to and did carry out the work and the agency was obliged to (and did) pay her for that work.
135. Although the intention does appear to have been to provide for insurability of workers who were neither employees under a contract of service nor self-employed. *See* the comments of the Minister at *Seanad Debates*, vol. 172, col. 272, 25 Mar. 2003.
136. This makes no difference to the person's insurability but might make a difference as to the person considered to be the employer. Under s. 12(4), the person liable to pay the wages or salary is deemed to be the employer.

a self-employed agency worker, as self-employment is effectively a residual category, the effect of paragraph 13 might appear to bring such workers (who fall within the terms of paragraph 13) fully within the social insurance net.[137] However, it appears that this is not how the provision is interpreted in practice, and 'genuinely' self-employed agency workers remain insured under Class S.

92. Schedule 1 covers persons employed under a contract of service in (or linked to) the State (paragraphs 1 & 2), civil and public servants who might not be considered to be legally employed under a contract of service but are for all practical purposes 'employees' (e.g., paragraphs 3, 4, 5, and 9), and a range of persons who are (probably) not employed under a contract of service at all but when it has been felt appropriate from a policy perspective to specifically include them within the scope of social insurance. In a number of these cases – including the trainee nurses and branch employment office manager – the courts have specifically held that these persons are not employed under a contract of service. This category of cases might be under some legal doubt as a result of the decision of Blayney J in *Griffiths v. Minister for Social Welfare*.[138] That case concerned share fishers who were, at that time, also included in a specific paragraph of the Schedule. As a result of the finding that share fishers were not employees in *D.P.P. v. McLoughlin*,[139] the Minister promulgated regulations specifying the person deemed to be the employer for the purposes of the Act. However, in *Griffiths*, Blayney J held that in enacting the relevant legislation, the Oireachtas did not intend to alter the traditional meaning given to the term 'employment', which term necessarily implied that there be a relationship between employer and employee. Accordingly, he held that to be an employed contributor under the Act, a person had to be employed by another person. In that case, he also held that as the relationship between the share fishers and the boat owner was one of partnership, not employment, accordingly, the share fishers were not employed contributors within the meaning of the Act. Although the case concerned only share fishers and the specific provisions concerning them, the logic of this decision could also apply to a number of the other paragraphs of Schedule 1, whereby an employment relationship also does not exist. The counter-argument to this is quite simply that the decision in *Griffiths* is incorrect. The Oireachtas clearly did mean to alter the traditional meaning given to the term 'employment' both in relation to the share fishers and in relation to the other non-employee groups specifically brought into insurance in Schedule 1. If the Oireachtas did not wish to do so, then its actions would be meaningless, as the relevant paragraphs of the Schedule have no purpose if they are considered not to alter the meaning of the term 'employment'.[140]

137. As we have seen, many of the provisions of the Schedule are intended precisely to ensure that self-employed persons are fully insurable.
138. [1992] 1 IR 103.
139. [1986] 1 IR 355. *See* M. Cousins, 'Social Welfare: Persons Engaged in Sharefishing – Employees or Self-Employed', DULJ 16 (1994): 207.
140. This is shown by the fact that the relevant paragraph covering sharefishers was dropped from the 1993 Consolidation Act following the *Griffiths* decision as it was now otiose.

93. Part 2 of Schedule 1 sets out a range of employments that, while they would otherwise be within the scope of the Act, are deemed to be excepted from insurability. Such persons are, in general, insurable for OIBs only (Class J). The excepted employments are:

1. Employment in the service of the spouse[141] or civil partner[142] of the employed person.

94. The purpose of the exception appears to be to prevent the insurability of 'collusive' employment relationships whereby a person employs his or her spouse or civil partner at the minimum rate of pay sufficient to qualify the person for benefits. However, given that this is likely to impact disproportionately on women, it might be open to question whether this is justified under EU law. When a spouse is employed under a contract of service by a partnership consisting of the spouse and another person or persons, he or she will ordinarily be regarded as employed by the partnership and not by the spouse. This will also apply when he or she is employed by a limited company in which either member of the couple is a director:

2. Employment of a casual nature otherwise than for the purposes of the employer's trade or business, and otherwise than for the purposes of any game or recreation where the persons employed are engaged or paid through a club.
3. Employment by a prescribed relative of the employed person, being either employment in the common home of the employer and the employed person or employment specified by regulations as corresponding to employment in the common home of the employer and the employed person.

95. Article 93 of S.I. No. 312 of 1996 defines this as employment, other than employment under a written contract of service or apprenticeship, by the father, mother, grandfather, grandmother, stepfather, stepmother, son, daughter, grandson, granddaughter, stepson, stepdaughter, brother, sister, half-brother, or half-sister of the employed person (other than in a case in which any such relative is a ward of court), when the employed person is a member of the employer's household and the employment is related to a private dwelling house or a farm in or on which both the employer and the employed person reside. Again, the purpose appears to be to exclude 'collusive' employment relationships:[143]

4. Employment specified in the Regulations as being of such a nature that it is ordinarily adopted as subsidiary employment only and not as the principal means of livelihood.

141. Substituted by s. 17(a) SW&PA 2015.
142. Substituted by s. 26 and Sch. 3 SW&PA 2010.
143. In *Tyson v. Heckler* (1984) 727 F2d 1029, the US Circuit Court of Appeal held that a similar exclusion furthered the government's legitimate goal of preventing social security fraud by excluding a class of persons whose situation suggested a high potential for collusion and therefore had a rational basis and was not over-inclusive.

96. A list of subsidiary types of employment is specified in Schedule C of S.I. No. 312 of 1996 as:

(1) Any employment adopted by a person who is ordinarily and mainly dependent for his or her livelihood on another employment which is:
   (a) an excepted employment by virtue of paragraph 1 [employment by spouse or civil partner] or paragraph 3 [employment by prescribed relative] of Part 2 of Schedule 1 to the Act; or
   (b) a [modified] employment[144] ... where the person is liable to pay employment contributions at a [reduced] rate.

(2) Employment as attendant at or in connection with examinations held by the Department of Education.

(3) Employment involving occasional service only, as presiding officer or as poll clerk at Presidential elections, elections to the European Parliament, general elections, by-elections, local elections, or at referenda.

(4) Employment as a member of the Defence Forces involving service in either An Foras Cosanta Áitiúil (now the Army Reserve) or An Slua Muirí (now the Naval Service Reserve) for any period not in excess of twenty-one consecutive days.

5. Employment specified in regulations as being of inconsiderable extent.

97. Prior to 1991, employment of less than eighteen hours per week was generally excluded under this heading. This excluded a significant number of part-time workers – mainly women. However, this is now defined as employment in any contribution week in one or more employments (other than systematic short-time employment) where the total amount of reckonable earnings payable to or with respect to an employee from such employment or employments is less than EUR 38 in or with respect to that contribution week.

98. Prima facie, the pre-1991 situation might appear to be contrary to EU law, as the majority of part-time workers were women. In a number of cases, appeals officers upheld the pre-1991 law.[145] The subsequent jurisprudence of the EU Court held that discrimination against part-time workers is not necessarily in breach of EU law and appears to have confirmed the Irish decisions. In the *Nolte* case – a case involving the exclusion of persons working less than fifteen hours from German social insurance – it was accepted that the exclusion of such workers disproportionately affected women.[146] However, the German government – supported by the UK and Ireland – argued that the exclusion of part-time workers corresponded to a structural principle of the German social security scheme. It was stressed that in contributory social security schemes, equivalence must be maintained between the

144. Mentioned in Arts 81(1), 82(1), 83(1), or 87(1) of S.I. No. 312 of 1996.

145. M. Cousins, 'Indirect Discrimination in Social Welfare', ILT 11 (1993): 147–151.

146. Case C-317/93, *Nolte v. Landesversicherungsanstalt Hannover* [1995] ECR I-4625; Case C-444/1993, *Megner v. Innungskrankenkasse Vorderpfalz* [1995] ECR I-4741. *See also Canada (AG) v. Lesiuk*, 2003 FCA 3 in which the Canadian Court of Appeal ruled that the Canadian provisions that required a minimum number of hours worked to qualify for benefit was not in breach of the equality provisions of the Canadian Charter of Rights.

contributions paid by employees and employers and the benefits paid. It was argued that the structure of the scheme could not be maintained in its present form if the provisions excluding part-time workers had to be abolished. The German government further argued that it was responding to the social demand for part-time employment by fostering the supply of such employment and that the only way of doing so was to exclude part-time employment from social insurance. The Court, in response, noted that, in the current state of EU law, social policy is a matter for the Member States and, consequently, it is for the Member States to choose the measures capable of achieving the aim of their social and employment policy. In exercising that competence, the Court held, Member States have a broad margin of discretion. In a somewhat tautologous construction, the Court noted that the social and employment policy relied on by Germany was objectively unrelated to any discrimination on the grounds of gender and that, in exercising its competence, the national legislature was reasonably entitled to consider that the legislation in question was necessary to achieve that aim. Accordingly, the Court held that the legislation could not be described as indirect discrimination. While the Court held that to justify disproportionate treatment, it must be shown that the measures reflect a legitimate social policy aim of the Member State, are appropriate to achieve that aim, and are necessary to do so, in *Nolte*, it simply accepted that the social policy aim claimed by the German government of encouraging part-time employment was legitimate. It does not seem to have given any consideration as to whether the exclusion of part-time workers was appropriate to achieve that aim unless its unsupported statement that the policy was 'objectively unrelated' to discrimination on the grounds of gender is supposed to do so. The Court simply accepted that the national legislature was 'reasonably entitled to consider' that it was necessary:

6. Employment under a scheme known as Community Employment where the employment commenced before 6 April 1996.
7. Employment in the State in a company under a written or an oral contract of service, whether expressed or implied, where the employed person is (a) the beneficial owner of that company, or (b) able to control 50% or more of the ordinary share capital of that company, either directly or through the medium of other companies or by any indirect means.[147]

99. The combined effect of the inclusion of employments in Part 1 of Schedule 1, the exception of employments in Part 2, and the modification of entitlements discussed below is to leave full-time private-sector employees (under age 66) (paragraph 1), civil and public service employees first employed after April 1995, and the employments listed in paragraphs 2, 6, 7, 8, 10, 11, 12, and 13 of Part 1 of Schedule 1 (insofar as they are not excepted by Part 2) as being fully insured for all contingencies and designated administratively as Class A.

147. Inserted by s. 16 SW&P(MP)A 2013. Thus, directors who own or control 50% or more of the shareholding of the company are excluded from insurance as employed contributors of that company and are treated as self-employed contributors. This would appear to be a response to *Neenan Travel v. Minister for Social and Family Affairs* [2011] IEHC 458 which had left open the issue of the insurability of 'controlling' directors.

100. Insurable (Occupational Injuries) Employment: The scope of insurable (occupational injuries) employment is set out in sections 70 and 71. Generally speaking, the scope of occupational injuries employment is broadly similar to that of Class A except that there are no age limits. The slightly different scope of insurance is largely a result of the fact that the scheme came from different origins (originally the Workmen's Compensation legislation and then the 1996 Occupational Injuries legislation) and that it has never been fully integrated into the general social insurance scheme. As we have seen, all persons insured in Class A and a number of persons in modified categories have entitlement to occupational injuries employment. In addition, there are a number of people who are insured only for OIBs (e.g., people over age 66). However, the self-employed are not insured for occupational injuries.[148]

101. Section 70 provides that every person, irrespective of age, who is employed in insurable (occupational injuries) employment is insured against personal injury caused by an accident arising out of and in the course of that employment. Insurable (occupational injuries) employment is construed to be any employment specified in Part 1 of Schedule 1, not being an employment specified in Part 2 of that Schedule (*see* above).[149] In addition, the following employments are added by section 71(1):

(i) employment in the State in plying for hire with any vehicle, vessel, aircraft, machine or animal, the use of which is obtained under any contract of bailment (other than a hire purchase agreement) in consideration of the payment of a fixed sum or a share in the earnings or otherwise;
(ii) employment under any contract of service or apprenticeship entered into in the State (otherwise than as captain, master, or a member of the crew) on board a ship or aircraft, being employment for the purpose of the ship or aircraft or of any passengers or cargo or mails carried by ship or aircraft;[150] and
(iii) employment in the State as a member or as a person training to become a member of any such fire brigade, rescue brigade, first-aid party, or salvage party at a factory, mine or works, as may be prescribed, or of any such similar organization as may be prescribed.

102. Conversely, the following employments are added to the excepted employments specified in Part 2 of Schedule 1:

(a) employment as a member of the Defence Forces;

148. *See* J. Brown, *A Policy Vacuum: Social Security for the Self-Employed* (Joseph Rowntree Foundation, 1992).
149. Section 71(1).
150. In addition, a pilot to whom the Pilotage Act of 1913 applies, when employed on any ship, is deemed to be a member of the crew of that ship, s. 50(5).

(b) employment, which is neither whole time as may be defined in regulations nor under contract of service, as a member of the crew of a fishing vessel where the employed person is wholly remunerated by a share in the profits or the gross earnings of the working of the vessel;
(c) employment under any local or other public authority in the execution of any contract for services;
(d) employment, otherwise than under contract of service, specified in paragraph 10 of Part 1 of Schedule 1 (i.e., persons in Holy Orders, Ministers of religion, and members of a religious community).

For the purposes of section 71, paragraph 2 of Part 2 of Schedule 1 is not to be taken as including employment of a casual nature for the purposes of any work in or about the residence of the employer.

103. Section 71(6) provides that the Minister may, in relation to paragraphs 4 and 5 of Part 2 of Schedule 1, by Regulations, provide that an employment specified as being subsidiary employment or an employment specified as being of inconsiderable extent shall be taken for the purposes of this section as not being so specified. Section 71(7) further provides that the Minister may, by Regulations, provide that any specified employment under any local or other public authority shall be taken for the purposes of this section as being added to Part 2 of Schedule 1.

104. Section 71(8) gives power to the Minister when it appears to him or her that the nature or other circumstances of the service rendered or the work performed in any employment, which, apart from this Subsection, is insurable (occupational injuries) employment and in any employment which, apart from this Subsection, is not such employment are so similar as to result in anomalies in the operation of this Part, and that when either:

(i) the first-mentioned employment can conveniently be included among the excepted employments; or
(ii) the second-mentioned employment can conveniently be included among the insurable (occupational injuries) employments; the Minister may, by Regulations, provide that the employment shall be so included.

105. Section 71(10) provides that a person who is unemployed shall, while in attendance at prescribed courses, be deemed to be in insurable (occupational injuries) employment and to be employed by the person by whom the course is being provided. Likewise, a person employed under a community employment scheme is deemed to be in insurable (occupational injuries) employment where the person's employment under that scheme began before 6 April 1996.[151]

151. Section 71(11) as substituted by s. 29(2) SW&PA 2010.

106. It is worth noting that the Minister is empowered to provide in any given case that employment should be treated as insurable (occupational injuries) employment notwithstanding that, by reason of a contravention of or non-compliance with a statutory provision *passed for the protection of employed persons*, the contract of employment is void, or the insured person is not lawfully employed in that employment.[152] However, the general law of contract would normally mean that a person would not be entitled to OIBs with respect to an illegal contract of employment (*see* above paragraph 78).

§2. Calculation of Contributions

107. This section examines the rules concerning the payment of social insurance contributions under the SW Acts.

I. Calculation Base

108. Section 13 sets out the rules in relation to the payment of contributions by employed contributors (as defined in section 12(1)) and their employers.[153] Calculations of contributions are on the basis of (i) 'payment',[154] (ii) 'in any contribution week', (iii) being 'made to or for the benefit of an employed contributor', (iv) with respect to employees' 'reckonable earnings'.[155]

109. The term 'payment' is not statutorily defined, but its scope is limited by the subsequent reference to 'reckonable earnings ... relating to an employment'. It would appear that the main relevance of the term is to require an actual payment (or transfer of monies), thereby defining the temporal rather than the material scope of the obligation to pay contributions. In the absence of actual payment, although earnings may be due, it would appear that no obligation arises. The payment must be made to or for the benefit of the employed contributor. 'Contribution week' is defined in section 2 as:

> one of the successive periods of 7 consecutive days in a contribution year beginning on the first day of that contribution year [i.e., a year of assessment within the meaning of the Income Tax Acts], or on any seventh day after that day, the last day of a contribution year (or the last two days of a contribution year ending in a leap year) being taken as included in the last contribution week of that contribution year.

---

152. Section 73(1).
153. *See also* the specific provisions in the Social Welfare (Contributions and Insurability) Regulations of 1996 (SW(CI)R) as amended.
154. Including a notional payment as defined in s. 985A of the Taxes Consolidation Act of 1997: s. 13(2)(e).
155. Section 13(2).

110. 'Reckonable earnings'[156] is defined as meaning, subject to section 13(2)(da):[157]

(i) in the case of an employed contributor, not being a special contributor, emoluments derived from insurable employment or insurable (occupational injuries) employment, to which the Pay as You Earn (PAYE) system applies,[158] but without regard to the provisions concerning married, divorced, and separated persons,[159] and

(ii) in the case of a special contributor (a) salaries, wages, or other remuneration including non-pecuniary remuneration derived from insurable employment or insurable (occupational injuries) employment to which the Taxes Consolidation Act of 1997 (other than the PAYE system) applies or would apply if the employed contributor in receipt of the remuneration were resident in the State but without regard to the provisions concerning married, divorced, and separated persons; (b) payments to persons attending courses of training; and (iii) payments to persons attending or engaged in courses or schemes provided or approved by (i) Teagasc, or (ii) the National Tourism Development Authority.[160]

Section 13(2)(da) provides that for the purposes of calculating the employer's contribution, reckonable earnings shall be reduced by superannuation contributions[161] and any share-based remuneration.[162]

II. Contribution Amount

111. Employed Contributor: When the payment is not more than a set minimum (currently EUR 441 per week or equivalent in the case of a person remunerated other than on a weekly basis), no contribution is payable by the employed contributor.[163] When payment exceeds this amount, contributions are payable by the employed contributor generally at a set rate (currently 4%).[164] The employer is, in

---

156. This includes share-based remuneration realized, acquired or appropriated, as the case may be on or after 1 Jan. 2011, and the 'specified amount' within the meaning of s. 825C of the Taxes Consolidation Act of 1997. The later concerns the 'Special Assignee Relief Programme' which provides tax relief to employees who are assigned to work in Ireland from abroad.
157. Section 2(1) as substituted by s. 8(a) SWA 2010 and amended by s. 3(1)(a) SW&P(MP)A 2013.
158. Chapter 4 of Part 42 of the Taxes Consolidation Act of 1997.
159. Set out in Ch. 1 of Part 44 of that Act.
160. SW(CCI)R, Art. 3 as substituted by S.I. No. 684 of 2011 which also includes income from (a) approved profit sharing schemes, (b) approved Save-As-You-Earn schemes, (c) share awards, and (d) unapproved share option gains. Obviously, the definition in the Regulation is confined by that in the Act and can specify more precisely the meaning of the term but could not go beyond earnings derived from insurable employment.
161. As allowed by Regulation 31(1) of the Income Tax (Employments) Regulations 2018.
162. As inserted by s. 13(b) SWA 2010 and amended by ss 13 & 14 SWA 2011 and s. 3(1)(b) SWPCRA 2018.
163. Section 13(2) as amended by s. 2 of SWA 2021.
164. Section 13(2). Income ceilings were abolished by SWA 2010, s. 11.

the first instance, liable to pay both the employed contributor's and the employer's contribution.[165] The employer is entitled to recover the employee's contribution – but *not* the employer's contributions – from the employee by deduction from remuneration.[166]

112. *Employer:* Contributions are payable by the employer with respect to payments generally at a set rate (currently 7.8%) when earnings do not exceed a set amount (currently EUR 441 per week) and at a higher rate (currently 10.05%) when this threshold is exceeded.[167]

§3. Reductions and Exemptions

113. Section 13(9) allows for the exemption of employers from the payment of employer's contributions when they employ a person under the Pay-Related Social Insurance (PRSI) exemption scheme (intended to encourage the employment of unemployed or disadvantaged persons).[168] In addition, social insurance refunds are paid to employers with respect to seagoing employees on wholly Irish-owned and registered ships, ships leased in the State, or any EU-registered vessel.[169]

§4. 'Temporary' New Contributions

114. This does not appear to be relevant to the Irish system.

§5. Contributions on Benefits

115. Social insurance contributions are not payable on benefits, as these do not fall within the definition of 'payment' as set out above.

§6. Administration

116. Administration of social insurance contributions is largely integrated into the general income tax system, and many of the functions of collection and related issues are carried out by the Revenue Commissioners on behalf of the DSP.

165. Section 13(4) as amended by s. 13 SWA 2011 and s. 9 SW&PA 2012.
166. Section 13(5)–(7).
167. Section 13(2)(d) as amended by s. 3 SWA 2021. An additional 1% is payable as a National Training Fund Levy.
168. However, no such scheme is currently in force.
169. Section 36 as substituted by s. 6 SW&PA 2014. And *see* Social Welfare (Consolidated Contributions and Insurability) (Amendment) (No. 1) (Return of Contributions) Regulations 2018 [S.I. No. 105/2018], as amended by S.I. No. 515/2022.

Chapter 2. Contributions for Public Sector Workers and Public Office Holders

§1. Field of Application

117. Schedule 1 also refers to a number of public sector employments that are also insurable. Listing them with the paragraph numbers that they have in the Schedule, these are:

3. Employment in the civil service of the government or the civil service of the State and employment such that the service therein of the employed person is, or is capable of being, deemed under section 24 of the Superannuation Act of 1936, to be service in the civil service of the government or the civil service of the State.

118. The Supreme Court held in *McLoughlin v. Minister for Social Welfare*[170] that a temporary assistant solicitor employed in the Chief State Solicitor's office was employed in the civil service of the State and not that of the government and so was not insurable under the then-provisions of the SW Acts. The legislation was subsequently amended to include a reference to employment in the civil service of the State. In *Murphy v. Minister for Social Welfare*,[171] the High Court, applying *McLoughlin*, held that an ordinary member of the Labour Court was engaged in the civil service of the State:[172]

4. Employment as a member of the Defence Forces.
5. Employment under any local or other public authority.

119. In *General Medical Services (Payments) Board v. Minister for Social Welfare*,[173] the High Court held that a public authority was a board that has public or statutory duties to perform for the benefit of the public, and not for private profit:

6. Employment as a court messenger under section 4 of the Enforcement of Court Orders Act of 1926.

120. Modified Employed Contributors: This group covers persons who are included in the definition of 'employed contributors' outlined above (mainly public sector employments) but whose entitlements and rate of social insurance contribution are modified – generally by regulation.

170. [1958] IR 1.
171. [1987] I IR 295.
172. *See also Walker v. Department of Social, Community and Family Affairs* [1999] 10 E.L.R. 260 (a rare report of an appeals officer's decision).
173. [1976–1977] ILRM 210.

121. Section 14 provides that regulations may modify the insurability provisions in their application in cases of:

(a) persons employed in any of the employments specified in paragraphs 2, 3, 4, 5, 9, and 10 of Part 1 of Schedule 1;
(b) in such cases, as may be prescribed, persons employed by Eircom PLC; or
(c) in prescribed cases, persons who on 5 April 1995 (when new entrants to the public service became fully insurable) were employed at (a) or (b) above and who transfer to non-public sector employment under terms and conditions allowing them to continue in a permanent and pensionable capacity and that provide for illness payments;[174]
(d) persons employed in a statutory transport undertaking;
(e) persons employed as teachers in primary schools that are recognized schools within the meaning of the Education Act of 1988;
(f) persons employed as teachers in training colleges recognized by the Minister for Education for teachers in primary schools;
(g) persons employed as teachers in post-primary schools that are recognized schools within the meaning of the Education Act of 1988;
(h) persons employed as teachers in domestic science training colleges funded by money voted by the Oireachtas for that purpose;
(i) persons employed as members of the Army Nursing Service;
(j) persons employed in voluntary hospitals to which grants are paid from money provided by the Oireachtas in the recoupment of revenue deficits;
(k) persons employed by voluntary organizations that are providing district nursing services; or
(l) persons employed in employment that is an insurable (occupational injuries) employment pursuant to section 71.

122. As we have seen, there are five classes of modified contributors:

> Class B – Permanent and pensionable civil servants, registered doctors and dentists employed in the civil service and Gardaí, all of whom were recruited prior to 6 April 1995. This group are brought within the definition of employed contributor by paragraphs 3 and 9 of Part 1 of Schedule 1, and their position is modified by S.I. No. 312 of 1996.[175] As a result, they pay a reduced rate of social insurance contribution and are only entitled to a widow(er)'s and surviving civil partner's (contributory) pension, guardian's payment (contributory), limited OIB,[176] carer's benefit and parental benefit.

174. The purpose is to allow modified contributions to continue to apply to former public sector employees in privatized employment who continue to have job security and illness and pension provisions.
175. SW(CCI)R, Art. 81 as amended by S.I. No. 85 of 1999, S.I. No. 338 of 2000, S.I. No. 602 of 2011 and S.I. No. 591 of 2019.
176. On the basis that these groups have occupational protection against such risks, their OIB entitlements are limited. Injury benefit is not payable and they receive half-rate disablement benefit starting twenty-six weeks after the occupational accident or disease.

Class C – Commissioned Defence Forces Officers and member of the Army Nursing Service again recruited prior to 6 April 1995. This group are brought within the definition of employed contributor by paragraph 4 of Part 1 of Schedule 1, and their position is modified by S.I. No. 312 of 1996.[177] As a result, they pay a reduced rate of social insurance contribution and are only entitled to widow(er)'s and surviving civil partner's (contributory) pension, guardian's payment (contributory), carer's benefit and parental benefit.

Class D – Permanent and pensionable employees in the public service other than those mentioned in Classes B and C recruited prior to 6 April 1995.[178] In addition to persons employed (in a permanent and pensionable capacity) by local and public authorities per se, this group also includes persons employed (in a permanent and/or pensionable capacity) in a statutory transport undertaking; as a teacher in a national, comprehensive, community or secondary school, a domestic science training college, or in a teacher training college; as registered medical practitioners[179] employed in a voluntary hospital, or, persons employed in Eircom PLC.[180] This group are brought within the definition of employed contributor by paragraph 5 of Part 1 of Schedule 1, and their position is modified by S.I. No. 312 of 1996.[181] As a result, they pay a reduced rate of social insurance contribution and are only entitled to a widow(er)'s (contributory) and surviving civil partner's pension, guardian's payment (contributory), OIB, carer's benefit and parental benefit.

Class E – Ministers of Religion employed by the Church of Ireland Representative Body. This group are brought within the definition of employed contributor by paragraph 10 of Part 1 of Schedule 1, and their position is modified by S.I. No. 312 of 1996.[182] As a result, they pay a slightly reduced rate of social insurance contribution and are entitled to all social insurance benefits other than jobseeker's benefit (JB) and OIB. This treatment of one group of about 200 clergy in this way appears to arise from historical circumstances, although the legal basis for singling out one particular group of the clergy must be somewhat doubtful.[183] The ECtHR ruled that a difference in treatment between Roman Catholic priests and Evangelical pastors as regards social insurance coverage was a breach of Article 14 of the

177. Article 82 as amended by S.I. No. 602 of 2011 and S.I. No. 591 of 2019.
178. S.I. No. 512 of 2014 (inserting Art. 83A) provides for the continuation of the payment of the existing modified rate of PRSI contributions by employees of An Post who transfer to the new National Lottery company on the transfer of the National Lottery licence to Premier Lotteries Ireland Ltd.
179. Registered medical practitioner has the meaning assigned to it by the Medical Practitioners Act 2007: s. 2 as amended by SWMPA 2010, s. 24.
180. Article 83(1) and 83A.
181. Article 83 as amended by S.I. No. 602 of 2011 and S.I. No. 591 of 2019 and Art. 83A as amended by S.I. No. 591 of 2019.
182. Article 86 as amended by S.I. No. 600 of 2015.
183. On the historical context, *see* the Dáil Debates at https://www.oireachtas.ie/en/debates/question/2018-01-16/1661/.

ECHR.[184] However, although superficially similar, the details of the case are very different from the Irish situation, and the ruling does not greatly clarify the legality of Irish law.

Class H – Non-commissioned officers and enlisted personnel of the Defence Forces. This group are brought within the definition of employed contributor by paragraph 4 of Part 1 of Schedule 1, and their position is modified by S.I. No. 312 of 1996.[185] As a result, they pay a slightly reduced rate of social insurance contribution and are entitled to all social insurance benefits. However, benefits (other than carer's benefit and treatment benefit, to such extent as may be provided for in regulations, and widow's (contributory) pension, widower's (contributory) pension, surviving civil partner's (contributory) pension or deserted wife's benefit where such pension or benefit is granted in respect of death or desertion arising before the current period of employment commenced) shall not be granted while the person is serving as a member of the Defence Forces.[186]

123. The Social Welfare and Pensions Act (SWPA) 2010 introduced social insurance contribution liability for a group of 'public office holders' (Class K).[187] However, this group has no entitlement to social insurance benefits.

§2. Basis and Amount of Contribution

124. The basis of contribution for public sector workers is, in general, the same as for private-sector employees, as outlined above. However, given that public sectorcontributors are entitled to reduced benefits, they pay reduced contributions, which vary from class to class.[188]

125. Public office holders pay social insurance at a rate of 4% of the total remuneration paid in respect of the office. However, where in any contribution week, payment is not more than EUR 100 per week, no contribution is payable, and where

184. In *Manzanas Martin v. Spain*, App. 17966/10, 3 Apr. 2012. In 1977 Spanish law provided that, in principle, religious should be insurable. This was implemented immediately in the case of Catholic priests but only twenty-five years later in the case of Evangelical pastors. The Government explained that this was due to the existing relationship between the state and the Catholic Church, whereas, in contrast, lengthy negotiations were required with the Evangelical church. In fact, the Court of Human Rights accepted the Government's justification on this point, referring to the state's margin of appreciation in progressively introducing full equality having regard to the social and economic implications of social insurance cover. However, the Court went on to rule that the remaining differences between the treatment of both religions – Catholic priests were, in certain cases, allowed to 'backdate' contributions to qualify for pension – were in breach of Art. 14.
185. Article 87 as amended by S.I. No. 600 of 2015.
186. Article 87 as amended by S.I. No. 602 of 2011.
187. Chapter 5A of the Act as inserted by SWPA 2010, s. 14 as amended by SWA 2016, s. 10. The concept of public office holders is defined in s. 30A and includes, for example, members of either House of the Oireachtas and members of the judiciary.
188. For the updated position *see* the annual guide to PRSI contribution rates published by the Department of Social Protection.

the total amount of remuneration from the holding of a public office does not exceed EUR 5,200 in any contribution year, any contributions paid will be repaid to the public office holder.[189]

189. Section 30B as inserted by SWPA 2010, s. 14.

Chapter 3. Contributions for the Self-Employed

§1. Field of Application

I. Territorial Field of Application

126. Arising from the definition of the basis for the calculation of contributions (*see* below), a person is effectively subject to Irish social insurance contributions as a self-employed person on the basis that his or her income is subject to Irish income tax rather than (directly) that the activity is carried out in the State. However, in general, most self-employed persons are subject to income tax in the State on the basis that they are 'ordinarily resident' there.[190]

II. Personal Field of Application

127. The category of self-employed contributors (Class S) is really a residual category and is defined on the basis of income received rather than economic activity. Thus, it is not necessary for a person to be categorized as self-employed under employment law to be a self-employed contributor under the Act.

128. Section 20(1)(*a*) provides that:

> Every person who, being over the age of 16 years and under pensionable age (not being a person included in any of the classes of person specified in Part 3 of Schedule 1) who has reckonable income or reckonable emoluments shall be a self-employed contributor for the purposes of this Act, regardless of whether he is also an employed contributor.

129. Section 20 goes on to provide that every person becoming for the first time a self-employed contributor thereby becomes insured under the Act and continues throughout his or her life to be so insured, and that, in the case of a person who, not having been an employed contributor at any time, becomes for the first time a self-employed contributor, the first day of the contribution year in which he or she becomes a self-employed contributor is to be regarded as the date of entry into insurance.

130. Excepted Self-Employed Contributors: Part 3 of Schedule 1 lists the excepted self-employed contributors, which, listed with the paragraph numbers they have in the Schedule, are:

1. A prescribed relative of a self-employed contributor who:
   (a) participates in the business of the self-employed contributor, and

190. It should be noted that specific rules in relation to residence are set out in the Income Tax legislation and the concept of residence for tax purposes is not necessarily the same as the concept(s) of residence for social welfare purposes discussed at Part XII, Ch. 3.

(b) performs the same tasks or ancillary tasks to those performed by the self-employed contributor, other than a person (i) who is a partner in the business of the self-employed contributor, or (ii) who is the spouse or civil partner of the self-employed contributor.[191]

131. The following are prescribed as relatives for these purposes: father, mother, grandfather, grandmother, stepfather, stepmother, son, daughter, grandson, granddaughter, stepson, stepdaughter, brother, sister, half-brother, or half-sister, where that relative (i) participates in the business of the self-employed contributor, (ii) performs the same tasks or ancillary tasks to those performed by the self-employed contributor, and (iii) is not a partner in the business of the self-employed contributor:[192]

2. A self-employed contributor who is in receipt of pre-retirement allowance (PRETA).[193]
3. A person, the aggregate of whose total reckonable income, reckonable emoluments, or reckonable earnings (if any) before allowable deductions under the Finance Acts is below a prescribed amount (currently EUR 5,000).[194]
4. An employed contributor or a person who is in receipt of a pension arising from previous employment of his or hers or of his or her spouse or civil partner,[195] in the case of either of whom the income for the contribution year does not include reckonable emoluments or in the case of reckonable income, income to which Chapter 3 of Part 4 or Part 43 of the Taxes Consolidation Act of 1997, applies.
5. A person employed in any one or more of the 'modified' employments specified in Article 81 (civil servants and members of Garda Síochána), 82 (commissioned army officers and members of army nursing service), 83 (certain public service employees) or 84 (continuation of modified rate on changing employment) of the Consolidated Contribution and Insurability Regulations of 1996.[196]
6. A person who is regarded as not resident or not ordinarily resident in the State in accordance with the provisions of the Income Tax Acts and whose reckonable income for that year does not include income to which Chapter 3 of Part 4 or Part 43 of the Taxes Consolidation Act of 1997 applies.

---

191. As substituted by s. 19(1) SW&PA 2014 and amended by s. 17(b) SW&PA 2015. This amendment extended liability for social insurance contributions to spouses and civil partners of self-employed contributors who are not business partners or employees, where they perform the same or ancillary tasks in implementation of Directive 2010/41/EU on the application of equal treatment between men and women engaged in self-employment activity. For a case on this issue, *see Social Welfare Appeals Office Report 2019*, 114–117.
192. Article 94 of S.I. No. 312 of 1996 as substituted by S.I. No. 347 of 2014.
193. As amended by SWA 2006, s. 12.
194. Article 92 of S.I. No. 312 of 1996 as amended by S.I. No. 684 of 2010.
195. As amended by s. 26 and Sch. 3 SW&PA 2010.
196. As substituted by s. 6(9) SW&P(MP)A 2013.

§2. Basis for Calculation of Contributions

132. Self-employed contributors are liable for social insurance contributions on the basis of their 'reckonable income' or 'reckonable emoluments'. Section 2 of the Act defines 'reckonable emoluments' as 'emoluments (other than reckonable earnings and any other emoluments that may be prescribed) to which [the PAYE system] applies'.[197]

133. 'Reckonable income' is defined in section 2[198] as 'the aggregate income (excluding reckonable earnings, reckonable emoluments, and any other income that may be prescribed) from all sources for the contribution year as estimated in accordance with the Income Tax Acts', *but without regard to* (a) various tax exemptions,[199] or (b) in the case of a prescribed relative of a self-employed worker,[200] the provisions concerning married, divorced, and separated persons, 'after deducting from the income so much of any deduction allowed by virtue of the provisions of the definition of "capital allowance" in section 2(1)' of the Taxes Consolidation Act 1997.

134. When a self-employed contributor pays the contributions due with respect to any year, he or she is regarded as having paid a contribution with respect to each contribution week in that year.[201]

§3. Amount of Contribution

135. Self-employed contributors pay contributions of 4% of their reckonable income or emoluments or a minimum amount (currently EUR 500 per annum), whichever is greater.[202] Contributors who are not required by the Revenue Commissioners to make a tax return in any year (because of low income) only pay a fixed contribution (currently EUR 310 per annum).[203]

§4. Disregarding of Contributions

136. Unlike most employed contributions, contributions paid by self-employed contributors do not count for all benefits. However, the range of benefits to which

---

197. As amended by s. 8(b) SW&PA 2012 and s. 6(1) SW&P(MP)A 2013. This includes share-based remuneration realized, acquired or appropriated, as the case may be on or after 1 Jan. 2011, and the 'specified amount' within the meaning of s. 825C of the Taxes Consolidation Act of 1997. The later concerns the 'Special Assignee Relief Programme' which provides tax relief to employees who are assigned to work in Ireland from abroad.
198. As amended by s. 8 SW(MP)A 2008 and s. 2 SWA 2022.
199. Set out in ss 140, 195, 216C (substituted by SWLRPA 2006, s. 5), 216F, 231, and 232 of the Taxes Consolidation Act of 1997.
200. To whom para. 1 of Part 3 of Sch. 1 applies.
201. Section 21(1)(d). Conversely, when the contribution is not paid in full, *no* contributions are regarded as having been paid.
202. Section 21(1)(a) as amended by SWA 2010, s. 14 and SWA2012, s. 10.
203. Section 21(1)(b).

self-employed contributors are entitled has been expanded significantly in recent years. Section 21(1)(e) specifically provides that self-employed contributions are to be disregarded in determining whether the contribution conditions for any benefit other than State pensions (contributory), widow(er)'s (contributory) and surviving civil partner's (SCP's) pensions, guardian's payments (contributory), JB (self-employed), maternity benefit, adoptive benefit, paternity benefit, parent's benefit, treatment benefit or invalidity pension (IP) are satisfied.[204]

§5. Administration

137. As in the case of employees, the collection of self-employed contributions is largely integrated into the income tax system, and most functions are carried out by the Revenue Commissioners.

204. As amended by s. 26 and Sch. 3 SW&PA 2010, SWA2012, s. 10, s. 19 SW&P(MP)A 2013, ss 3, 5 & 9 SWA 2016, s. 6 and the Schedule to SWA 2019 and Parent's Leave and Benefit Act 2019, s. 26.

Chapter 4. Other Contributions

§1. Voluntary Contributors

138. The purpose of voluntary contributions was more relevant in the past when a wide range of employment (including self-employment) was not covered by social insurance. The intention was to allow a person with a record of compulsory insurance who fell outside the scope of social insurance (e.g., because of a change of job) to keep up his or her insurance record. Voluntary contributions are now of limited relevance, given the wide scope of compulsory insurance (and credited contributions) other than, perhaps, to persons leaving the workforce because of family responsibilities who will not be covered by insurance or to persons moving abroad to work (outside the EU/EEA) who wish to maintain the continuity of their Irish insurance record.[205]

139. Section 24 provides that when a person ceases to be an employed or self-employed contributor, other than by reaching pension age and has qualifying contributions with respect to not less than 520 contribution weeks, he or she shall, on making an application in the prescribed manner and within the prescribed period, be entitled to become an insured person paying contributions under the Act voluntarily.[206] Article 28 of S.I. No. 312 of 1996 provides that application must be made in writing to the Minister within sixty months of the end of the contribution year in which the person ceased to be an employed or self-employed contributor or in which a contribution was last credited to the person or such longer period as the Minister, having regard to the circumstances, may allow.[207] The occupational injuries insurance of any person is disregarded in determining his or her right to become, or to continue to be, a voluntary contributor, and the rate of voluntary contribution payable in any case shall not be affected by such insurance.[208] A voluntary contributor who becomes an employed or a self-employed contributor ceases to be a voluntary contributor.[209] Section 25(4)–(5) provides that a voluntary contributor is not entitled to illness benefit (IB), jobseekers benefit, maternity benefit, invalidity pension (IP), or treatment benefit (other than in prescribed circumstances).

§2. Optional Contributors

140. As we have seen, the High Court held in *D.P.P. v. McLoughlin*[210] that persons engaged in share fishing remunerated by a share of the profits from the catch were partners of, rather than employees of, the boat owner. A subsequent attempt by

205. In practice, such persons rarely avail themselves of voluntary insurance. Voluntary contributions could, however, be used by persons retiring early to continue their contribution record to pension age. There are currently about 3.000 contributors.
206. As amended by s. 3 SW&PA 2012.
207. As substituted by S.I. No. 38 of 2017.
208. Section 24(2).
209. Section 24(3)–(4) except insofar as is provided in s. 25(2).
210. [1986] IR 355.

the Minister/Department to deem the owner of the boat to be the employer was struck down by the High Court in *Griffiths v. Minister for Social Welfare*.[211] Subsequently, the Department attempted to approach the issue on a case-by-case basis, but the High Court has upheld the *McLoughlin* decision that fishers paid by share are partners.[212] The effect of this decision appears to be that any fisher remunerated wholly or mainly by share rather than by a set payment is to be considered *not* to be an employee.[213] While this may appear not to be in line with the economic realities of the situation, it would appear to be settled law in the absence of legislative reform.[214] Subsequent to the *Griffiths* decision, the Oireachtas introduced a new category of optional contributors whereby self-employed share fishers who were already paying Class S insurance could pay an additional contribution to gain entitlement to limited jobseeker's benefit, limited illness benefit, and treatment benefit.[215] This has not proved to be an attractive option, and a minimal number of people (currently zero) are insured in Class P.

§3. Credited Contributions

141. In conclusion, it should be noted that when persons who have built up a record of social insurance contributions are unable to continue to pay insurance because of the occurrence of a recognized contingency (such as unemployment or illness), they may be granted 'credited contributions', which will help to qualify them for future benefits. Generally credited contributions count only for the 'second' contributions requirement, that is, the requirement that a person has a certain number of contributions in a recent year or a yearly average of a certain number of contributions. Credited contributions are also granted to persons entering insurance for the first time to assist them in qualifying for short-term benefits should the need arise.[216]

142. Section 33 provides that regulations may provide for:

(a) making exceptions from the liability to pay contributions for any specified periods; and
(b) crediting contributions to insured persons for any specified periods, including, in particular, (i) periods for which there is an exception from the liability to pay contributions by virtue of paragraph (a); (ii) the period between the beginning

211. [1992] ILRM 44. For the suggestion that this decision is incorrect; *see* M. Cousins 'Social Welfare: Persons Engaged in Sharefishing – Employees or Self-Employed', DULJ 16 (1994): 207.
212. *Griffin v. Minister for Social, Community and Family Affairs*, High Court, unreported 2 Oct. 2001.
213. However, it should be noted that when a fisher has a contract that provides that he or she is paid a weekly wage (with an additional bonus payment), this may be considered to give rise to a contract of service.
214. *See contra* the old case of *Donnelly and Byrne v. Hanlon* [1893] 27 ILTR 73 but cf. *Scottish Insurance Commissioners v. McNaughton* [1914] SC 826.
215. Sections 28–30 as amended.
216. For an excellent overview of the policy issues involved, *see* D/SCFA, *Review of Credited Contributions*, 1999.

of the contribution year last preceding that in which they become insured persons and their entry into insurance; and (iii) periods in any contribution year in which they become or cease to be a homemaker within the meaning of section 108(2).

143. Article 56 of S.I. No. 312 of 1996 provides that an employment contribution (known as pre-entry credits) shall be credited to an insured person (other than a person insured for OIBs only) with respect to each complete contribution week from the beginning of the second-last contribution year preceding that in which his or her entry into insurance as an employed contributor occurred up to the date of such entry into insurance.

144. Articles 58, 59, 59A,[217] 60, 61,[218] 62,[219] 63A,[220] 63B,[221] 63C,[222] and 64 provide that an employment contribution shall be credited to an insured person:

(a) with respect to a day of duly notified incapacity for work or of proven unemployment in any contribution year;[223]
(b) with respect to any week in receipt of maternity benefits, health and safety benefits, adoptive benefits, invalidity pension, carer's allowance and benefits, PRETA, and disability allowance (DA);[224]
(c) with respect to any week in which an insured person is in receipt of carer's allowance, jobseeker's allowance (transition), or one-parent family payment when immediately prior to claiming the said allowance, the insured person was entitled to be credited with employment contributions by virtue of paragraph (a) or (b);[225]
(d) for any week during the whole or part of which he or she attends a course of training provided or approved of by FÁS, the National Tourism Development Authority, Teagasc, or Bord Íascaigh Mhara;[226]
(e) for any contribution week during the whole or part of which he or she is employed under a scheme known as Community Employment;
(f) with respect to any week during the whole or part of which he or she is participating in the Back-to-Education Allowance scheme or any other course of education or training approved by the Minister;

---

217. As inserted by S.I. No. 292 of 1997.
218. As amended by S.I. No. 509 of 2012.
219. As amended by S.I. No. 509 of 2012.
220. As inserted by S.I. No. 569 of 1998.
221. As inserted by S.I. No. 76 of 2001 and amended by S.I. No. 75 of 2003.
222. As inserted by S.I. No. 75 of 2003.
223. S.I. No. 391 of 2003 provides that a day of proven unemployment must be a day of unemployment within the meaning of what is now s. 62(5)(a), i.e., the person is capable of, available for, and genuinely seeking employment; *see* Part VII.
224. As amended by S.I. No. 338 of 2000.
225. As amended by S.I. No. 243 of 2013.
226. The reference to FÁS would appear to be redundant as the agency has been abolished, but s. 38(1)(c) of the Further Education and Training Act 2013 provides that statutory references to FÁS shall be construed as references to Solas (a Government agency responsible for Further Education and Training).

(g) with respect to each contribution week during which he or she avails himself or herself of parental leave or force majeure leave under the Parental Leave Act of 1998;
(h) with respect to each contribution week during which he or she avails himself or herself of additional statutory maternity or adoptive leave;
(i) with respect to each contribution week during which he or she avails himself or herself of statutory carer's leave, maternity leave, or adoptive leave;[227]
(j) for any week in the contribution year in which a person becomes or ceases to be a homemaker from the relevant date; and
(k) for any contribution week during which a volunteer development worker is employed as such in a developing country or engaged in preparatory training in the State prior to taking up employment in a developing country.[228]

145. Clearly, when an employed contribution is payable with respect to any week, no credited contribution is granted. In addition, when there are no employment contributions paid or credited with respect to an insured person for any two complete consecutive contribution years, then an employment contribution is *not* generally credited to that person unless, since the end of the second contribution year, twenty-six employment contributions have been paid with respect to such person.[229]

§4. Attributed Contributions

146. Recently a fourth category of contribution was created by s. 8 of the Social Welfare (COVID-19) (Amendment) Act 2020 in response to the COVID-19 pandemic – attributed contributions. Any person who, on or after 13 March 2020, is in receipt of PUP (whether paid before or after 5 August 2020) or is in receipt of Jobseeker's Benefit, Jobseeker's Benefit (Self-Employed) or Jobseeker's Allowance, but is otherwise entitled to PUP, will have paid social insurance contributions attributed to him/her at the same rate as previously paid by that person. This also applies to employees whose employer is, or was, in receipt of the Temporary Wage Subsidy or a subsidy payable under the COVID-19 employer refund scheme. Employees whose employers are in receipt of either of these subsidies do not pay this contribution and the employer has to pay a contribution of 0.5% on any reckonable earnings paid to the employee in excess of the temporary wage subsidy. So even though the employees covered by these arrangements do not pay a contribution in these circumstances, the contributions attributed to such employees are treated as paid contributions and not credited contributions.[230]

227. Thus, a person is granted a credit even when not entitled to a benefit payment while on leave.
228. 'Developing country' is defined as any country so listed by the Minister having regard to the designations of the UN, the World Bank, or the ILO and having consulted with the Minister for Foreign Affairs: s. 2.
229. Article 57.
230. These claimants are also deemed to have average weekly income or earnings in excess of EUR 300 in the contribution year 2021 for the purpose of claiming IB, JB or JB (Self-Employed) – S.I. No. 234 of 2023.

Chapter 5. Government Funding

147. Social insurance benefits are funded by contributions made by employers, employees, and the self-employed, with any deficit being made up by the State. All other social welfare payments are funded entirely by the State from general taxation.

§1. Full Payment Out of General Taxation

148. The full cost of all social assistance payments, child benefit, carer's support grants (CSGs), working family payment (WFP)) (and continued payment for qualified children) is met by the State from general taxation.[231]

§2. Residual Funding

149. Contributions paid by employers, employees, and the self-employed are paid into the Social Insurance Fund originally established under the SWA of 1952 (*see* now section 9 of the Act). The specific range of benefits funded from the Fund are set out in section 7 and include all social insurance benefits (listed in section 39) and a number of allowances and benefits payable to persons with an underlying entitlement to a social insurance payment. Insofar as contributions are insufficient to fund benefits due, the balance is funded by the Exchequer.

§3. Subsidies According to Fixed Criteria

150. There are no fixed criteria for State subsidies.

§4. Earmarked Taxes

151. There are currently no earmarked taxes that fund social welfare benefits and allowances.

231. Sections 139, 219–223, 224–226, 227–233, and 234–238, respectively.

Part III. Health Care

Introduction

152. This chapter looks at the legal provisions concerning healthcare. Under the Irish system, the healthcare system is almost entirely independent of the social security (or social welfare) system. Healthcare entitlement is set out in the Health Acts of 1947–2023.[232] It is the responsibility of the Department of Health and is administered by the HSE. For largely historical reasons, the DSP administers a limited number of insurance-based benefits (known as treatment benefits), which concern primarily dental, optical, and aural treatment.

153. The legislation in relation to healthcare is not, unlike social welfare legislation, always expressed in terms of legal rights to services, and there appears to remain some uncertainty about the legal basis underpinning the provision of healthcare.[233] As discussed in the coming sections, in many areas of health law, the legislation imposes a statutory duty to provide healthcare (e.g., section 52 of the HA, 1970). In others, it gives the health authorities the discretionary power to provide services but does not impose a statutory duty (e.g., section 52(1A) on long-term residential care services (LTRCS) or section 61 on home help services). Nonetheless, the statutory duty to provide a service does not necessarily imply a correlative right to services on the part of the public (nor, more specifically, a right to specific services within specific time periods). To date, issues that have been litigated in the UK courts – such as the scope of the statutory duty[234] or the extent to which the courts will intervene in health authority decisions as to the allocation of resources (including any possible impact of human rights law)[235] – have not been extensively litigated in Ireland.

---

232. Unfortunately, unlike the social welfare system, the legislation has not been consolidated by the Oireachtas and is somewhat of a maze. Helpfully, an administrative consolidation of the Health Act 1970 has been produced by the Law Reform Commission although it is not fully up to date at the time of writing. *See* http://revisedacts.lawreform.ie/eli/1970/act/1/front/revised/en/html. A similar consolidated version of the Health Act 1947 is also available at http://revisedacts.lawreform.ie/eli/1947/act/28/front/revised/en/html.
233. *See* the discussion in the excellent report by the Ombudsman, *Who Cares: An Investigation into the Right to Nursing Home Care in Ireland*, 2010.
234. *R v. Gloucestershire County Council, ex p Barry* [1997] AC 584; *R v. Sefton Metropolitan Borough Council, ex p Help the Aged* [1997] 4 All ER 532; *McGregor, application for judicial review* [2000] CSOH 317.
235. *R v. Cambridge Health Authority, ex p B* [1995] 1 WLR 898; *R v. North Derbyshire Health Authority, ex p Fisher* (1998) 10 Admin LR 27; *R v. North West Lancashire Health Authority, ex p A* [2000]

Chapter 1. Field of Application

§1. Territorial Field of Application

154. This section addresses two territorial issues. First, to which persons (territorially) does the Irish system apply? Second, in which territory can a person covered by the Irish healthcare system obtain treatment?

I. Who Is Entitled to Healthcare in Ireland?

155. The substantive provisions of the HA 1970 limit most eligibility for healthcare to persons who are 'ordinarily resident in the State'. Section 47A allows the Minister to issue guidelines to the HSE to assist it in deciding whether or not a person is ordinarily resident in the State for the purposes of sections 45 (full eligibility), 45A (over 70s and dependants), 46 (limited eligibility), 58 (GP services), 58A (GP over 70), 58B (GP under 6), 58D (GP for carers), 62A (termination of pregnancy) or 67E (contraception services).[236] The legal definition of 'ordinarily resident' is discussed elsewhere (Part XII, Chapter 3).

156. While the HA could, of course, define 'ordinary residence' in a particular manner, the guidelines are intended to assist in interpretation rather than to redefine the concept. The guidelines provide that a person will normally be regarded as an 'ordinarily resident' in Ireland if he or she has been living in Ireland for at least one year or if he or she satisfies the HSE that it is his or her intention to remain in Ireland for a minimum period of one year.[237] Examples of the evidence that may be sought in this context include proof of property purchase or rental, including evidence that the property in question is the applicant's principal residence; evidence of transfer of funds, bank accounts, pensions; documentation showing a right of residence; work permits or visas; statements from employers and others; and when necessary, the signing of an affidavit by the applicant. However, as set out in Part XII, the concept of 'ordinary residence' as interpreted by the courts does not necessarily require a minimum period of residence or intended residence of one year,[238] and it is arguable that if it is thought necessary to require this for access to healthcare services, an appropriate amendment to the HA would be necessary. The person's dependants must also satisfy the criterion of 'ordinary residence' to establish eligibility for health services; that is, the fact that a person has himself or herself established eligibility does not imply that all dependants are also eligible.

---

1 WLR 977; *R v. Swindon NHS Primary Care Trust ex p Rogers* [2006] EWCA Civ 392; *R (Condliff) v. North Staffordshire Primary Care Trust* [2011] EWCA Civ 910; [2011] EWCA Civ 910.

236. Section 47A of the 1970 Act as inserted by s. 5 of the HACEA 2013 and amended by HGPS 2014, s. 3; HGPS 2015, s. 3, HRTPA 2018, s. 26 and HMP(No. 2)A 2022, s. 3 and 5.

237. https://www.hse.ie/eng/services/find-a-service/eligibility.html.

238. *See Chubb European Group v. Health Insurance Authority* [2020] IECA 91 at [141].

157. However, section 45(7) provides that a person who is not ordinarily resident in the State but who, in relation to a particular service that is available to persons with full eligibility, is considered to be unable, without undue hardship, to provide that service, him/herself or his or her dependants shall be deemed to be persons with full eligibility in relation to that service.[239] Thus, a non-resident person may be granted full eligibility in a case of hardship.

158. The 'ordinary residence' rule is, of course, subject to the provisions of EU law. For the purposes of clarity, section 9 of the HAA 1991 specifically provides that the provisions relating to a person being ordinarily resident in the State are without prejudice to the due application of the provisions of Regulation 883/2004.

II. Healthcare Outside the State

159. Persons may be entitled to seek healthcare treatment abroad under EU Regulation 883/2004 on coordination of social security. In addition to persons temporarily abroad who are entitled to necessary treatment (persons covered by a European Health Insurance Card), Irish people can also seek permission to travel abroad to seek treatment under another EU healthcare system. In addition to the provisions of Regulation 883/2004, the EU has also adopted the Cross-Border Healthcare Directive 2011/24/EU, which is intended to clarify patients' rights to access treatment across EU borders and be reimbursed for that treatment. This is implemented in Irish law by the EU (Application of Patients' Rights in Cross-Border Healthcare) Regulations 2014.[240] In relation to reciprocal access to healthcare in the UK *see* above 28.

§2. Personal Field of Application

160. In terms of eligibility for healthcare, the HA of 1970 draws a distinction, which runs through the whole issue of access to public healthcare, between persons having 'full eligibility' for services and persons with 'limited eligibility'. Persons with 'full eligibility' are commonly described under the non-statutory name of 'medical-card holders'.[241] Subsequent policy changes introduced a new category of those with full eligibility for GP services only (known by the HSE as GP visit cards) (*see* below Chapter 2, §4).

161. Persons with full eligibility are defined in section 45(1) of the HA of 1970, which provides:

---

239. Substituted by HAA 1991, s. 2.
240. S.I. No. 203 of 2014 as extensively amended by S.I. No. 65 of 2015.
241. The HAA 1996 makes specific provision, however, in relation to the provision of certain health services to persons who contracted hepatitis C directly or indirectly from the use of Human Immunoglobulin-Anti-D or the receipt within the State of another blood product or a blood transfusion and to other prescribed classes of persons.

(1) A person in either of the following categories and who is ordinarily resident in the State shall have full eligibility for the services under this Part:
 (a) adult persons who, in the opinion of the HSE, are unable without undue hardship to arrange GP medical and surgical services for themselves and their dependants;
 (b) dependants of the persons referred to in paragraph (a).[242]

162. Section 45(2) provides that in deciding whether a person is unable without undue hardship to arrange GP medical and surgical services for themselves and their dependants, the Health Service Executive shall have regard to the person's overall financial situation (including the means of the spouse and civil partner, if any) in view of the person's reasonable expenditure in relation to himself or herself and his or her dependants if any.[243] Section 45(3) allows for the making of regulations to define persons with full eligibility, but it appears that no regulations have been made pursuant to that subsection and that the determination of who is entitled to 'full eligibility' is administered by a system of guidelines, with the HSE making individual decisions.

163. In addition to the general provision in section 45(1), there have been a number of categorical additions to the group of persons entitled to full eligibility (i.e., those over 70 years (subject to an income test) and children in respect of whom domiciliary care allowance (DCA) is payable).

164. Section 45A provides that a person who has attained the age of 70 years of age and is ordinarily resident in the State will have full eligibility for the services so long as the person's gross income does not exceed the relevant gross income limit.[244] Section 45A(2)–(3) provides for two different gross income limits depending on the civil status of the individual:

(i) if a person (I) is not married, (II) is not living together with another person as husband and wife, and (III) does not have a civil partner, his or her gross income limit is EUR 550 per week, not including the income from the portion of the person's savings or similar investments whose capital value does not exceed EUR 36,000, and
(ii) if persons (I) are married, (II) live together as husband and wife, or (III) are civil partners as respects each other, their combined gross income limit is EUR 1,050 per week, not including the income from the portion of their savings or similar investments whose capital value does not exceed EUR 72,000.[245]

242. As substituted by HAA 1991, 2 and amended by HAA 2005, s. 1.
243. Substituted by HAA 2005, s. 1.
244. Substituted by HA 2008, s. 3 and amended by HACEA 2013 and HACE(No. 2)A 2013. Prior to 1 Jan. 2009, person aged 70 and over qualified for full eligibility without any means test and there are various transitional provisions for such persons and their dependants in s. 45(5A) and 45A of the Act.
245. Section 2 of the Health (General Practitioner Service and Alteration of Criteria for Eligibility) Act 2020 (HGPSACEA) amends s. 45A and was commenced on 1 Nov. 2020. As amended, subs.

The manner in which gross income is to be calculated is set out in section 45A(5)–(6).

165. Section 45(5B) provides that a person who is a child within the meaning of section 186C of the Social Welfare Consolidation Act 2005 and in respect of whom a DCA is being paid shall have full eligibility.[246]

166. Finally, section 45(7) provides that a person who does not qualify under subsection (1) *or* who is not ordinarily resident in the State but who, in relation to a particular service that is available to persons with full eligibility, is considered by the HSE to be unable, without undue hardship, to provide that service or himself or herself or his or her dependants shall, in relation to that service, be deemed to be a person with full eligibility.[247]

167. Section 46 of the HA of 1970 provides that any person ordinarily resident in the State who is without full eligibility shall, subject to section 52(3), have limited eligibility for health services.[248]

168. Section 47 of the HA of 1970 provides for the establishment of an appeals system in relation to eligibility, but this has never been activated (although there are non-statutory review systems). A number of Acts, most recently section 2 of the Health (General Practitioner Service) Act (HGPSA) 2014, have provided for replacement of this section but have not been commenced at the time of writing. Part 9 of the HA of 2004 provides for the establishment of a broader complaints system regarding healthcare, which came into force on 1 January 2007. However, this is a 'complaints' rather than an appeals process, and the recommendations of a complaints officer are not legally binding on the service provider.[249] In addition, the Health Act 2007 (Care and Welfare of Residents in Designated Centres for Older People) (Amendment) Regulations 2022 (S.I. No 628 of 2022) provides for access to independent advocacy services and for complaint mechanisms for residents of such centres.

45A(8) now provides that 'civil partner' has the same meaning as in the Civil Partnership and Certain Rights and Obligations of Cohabitants Act 2010.

246. As inserted by HAA 2017, s. 2.

247. Substituted by HAA 1991, s. 2.

248. As substituted by HAA 1991, s. 3.

249. *See* the Health Act of 2004 (Complaints) Regulations, 2006 (S.I. No. 652 of 2006). In *Enguye v. HSE* [2011] IEHC 507, Gilligan J pointed out that the 'statutory remedy [in Part 9 of the Health Act, 2004] is the entitlement to make a statutory complaint to a complaints officer of the Health Service Executive and not an appeal mechanism' and, therefore, he did not consider that the opportunity to voice such a complaint as a matter of law, especially against the particular background circumstances of the case, was one that had to be undertaken prior to contending for judicial review.

Chapter 2. Benefits

§1. In-Patient Care

I. Definition of In-Patient Care and Acute In-Patient Services

169. Section 51 of the HA of 1970 defines 'in-patient services' as:

> institutional services provided for persons while maintained in a hospital, convalescent home or home for persons suffering from physical or mental disability or in accommodation ancillary thereto.[250]

'Institutional services', in turn, is defined in section 2 of the HA of 1947, as including:

(a) maintenance in an institution;
(b) diagnosis, advice, and treatment at an institution;
(c) appliances and medicines and other preparations;
(d) the use of special apparatus at an institution.[251]

'Acute in-patient services' are defined as in-patient services provided:

(a) in a hospital for the care and treatment of patients with acute ailments (including psychiatric ailments), and
(b) to persons requiring medically acute care and treatment (including care and treatment in respect of motherhood or termination of pregnancy).[252]

This distinction between in-patient services per se and acute in-patient services (which are a subset of in-patient services) related to the charging regime but charges for acute in-patient services were abolished as of April 2023.

II. Duty to Provide and Eligibility for In-Patient Services

170. Section 52(1) provides that the HSE *shall* make available in-patient services for persons with full eligibility and persons with limited eligibility. Section 52(1A) provides that the HSE *may* make available LTRCS. Section 67B further provides that the HSE *may* make available residential support services to persons with

250. Substituted by HAA 2013, s. 8 (though the wording of this part of the definition is the same as that original Act).
251. The legislation does not expressly make this link between the 1947 and 1970 Acts but in *K.(C.) v. Northern Area Health Board* [2003] IESC 34, the Supreme Court stated that 'it seems clear' that the legislature intended the words 'institutional services' in the 1970 Act to bear the same meaning as in the 1947 Act, while in *In re Article 26 of the Constitution and the Health (Amendment) (No. 2) Bill 2004* [2005] IESC 7 [2005] 1 IR 105, the Court simply quoted the definition from the 1947 Act without comment.
252. Substituted by HAA 2013, s. 8 and amended by HRTPA 2018, s. 26.

full eligibility and persons with limited eligibility. Given that both LTRCS and residential support services fall within the definition of in-patient services, it is arguable that the mandatory duty in section 52(1) applies to all such services and that sections 52(1A) and 67B are surplusages.

171. There is a fundamental distinction between persons with 'full eligibility' and those with 'limited eligibility' in terms of charges for services.[253] In the case of persons with full eligibility, these are not currently subject to any charges. The Health Services (In-Patient) Regulations of 1991 provide for the manner in which a person may avail his or her entitlement to in-patient services and the manner in which in-patient services may be made available to private patients.[254]

172. Section 52(3) provides that where a person with full eligibility or limited eligibility for in-patient services does not avail of or waives the right to avail of, some part of those services and instead avails of services not provided under section 52(1), then the person is deemed not to have full eligibility or limited eligibility, as the case may be, for those services. This then means that charges may be imposed for such services where, for example, a person who would be entitled to public services opts for private in-patient services in the same hospital.[255]

III. Charges for In-Patient Services

173. The legislation now distinguishes between:

- charges for in-patient services that do not involve acute care and treatment (section 53A);
- charges for long-term residential care (section 53B, which are to be in accordance with the Nursing Homes Support Scheme Act 2009 (NHSSA)); and
- charges for residential support services maintenance and accommodation contributions (section 67A–D).[256]

Thus, to summarize, sections 53A relates to hospital in-patient services (not involving acute care), while sections 53B and 67A-D relate to long-term residential care and residential support services. The provisions are, unfortunately, not a model of clear drafting.

174. Section 53A[257] of the HA of 1970 applies where in-patient services (not being LTRCS) are provided to a person in a hospital for the care and treatment of

253. The categories involved are discussed above.
254. S.I. No. 135 of 1991.
255. *See* s. 55 as substituted by HAA 2013, s. 13.
256. Previously s. 53C provided for charges for acute in-patient services but this has been repealed by the HAA 20023 as commenced by S.I. No. 165 of 2023 as of 17 Apr. 2023. The HAA 2023 also repealed the Health (Acute In-Patient) Charges Regulations 2021.
257. Charges for in-patient services were previously provided in s. 53 of the Act. This was repealed by the HAA 2013 from 2017.

patients with acute ailments (including any psychiatric ailments) and where a registered medical practitioner (designated by the HSE) has certified in writing that the person in receipt of such services does *not* require medically acute care and treatment in respect of any such ailment.[258] This section also applies to in-patient services being provided to a person who is a resident in a designated centre for older people (as defined in the HA 2007 (Care and Welfare of Residents in Designated Centres for Older People) Regulations 2009))[259] and who is not being provided with support under the NHSSA 2009.

175. Where section 53A applies, and notwithstanding section 67C concerning residential support services, charges may be made in respect of in-patient services as if those services were LTRCS provided by the HSE. These charges are to be determined by the average cost of LTRCS as determined by the HSE in its facilities, predominantly for the care of older people.

176. Section 53A is intended to allow a charge for a person in a hospital who is no longer receiving acute care or such a person in a public 'centre for older people' (aka public nursing home) where such a person is *not* receiving long-term residential care. The intention appears to be to allow the HSE to charge such persons so as to 'encourage' them to move to more appropriate services. Second, charges for LTRCS under the NHSSA are discussed below (paragraph 219). Finally, the maintenance and accommodation contributions (section 67A–D) apply to those requiring long-term in-patient services other than acute care and other than long-term residential care. It appears that this latter group applies to residential care provision in the disability, mental health and care of older people sectors. This is not, to put it mildly, a model of clear drafting.

177. Section 53B provides that charges shall be made for LTRCS in accordance with the NHSSA 2009. This is discussed below in paragraph 226.

178. Section 67A–D, as outlined above, applies to those requiring residential support services, i.e., long-term in-patient services other than acute care and other than long-term residential care.[260] 'Residential support services' is defined as any health or personal social service excluding: (a) acute in-patient services, (b) LTRCS, and (c) out-patient services provided under section 56, provided by or on behalf of the HSE to a person residing in accommodation that is a: (i) hospital, (ii) convalescent home, (iii) nursing home, or (iv) home or any other category of housing accommodation for persons with a physical, sensory, mental health or intellectual disability, or in accommodation ancillary thereto.[261]

258. Section 53A inserted by NSSA 2009, s. 34 and amended by HAA 2013, s. 11.
259. S.I. No. 236 of 2009.
260. As inserted by HAA 2013, and amended by HMPA 2014.
261. Section 67A as substituted by HMPA 2014, s. 42.

179. 'Accommodation' in relation to a person being provided with a health or personal social service that falls within the definition of 'residential support services', means: (a) accommodation provided to the relevant person by or on behalf of the HSE, or (b) if paragraph (a) does not apply and the ongoing costs of maintenance associated with the provision of that service to the person are met by or on behalf of the HSE, accommodation provided to the person pursuant to an arrangement that has been put in place for the purpose of facilitating the provision, in that accommodation, of that service.

180. 'Costs of maintenance' means the costs (other than excluded costs below) relating to the ongoing essential daily living requirements of the person and includes the costs of purchasing or paying for: (a) the person's food or other essential household provisions, (b) the person's electricity, gas, heating, refuse collection, water supply or other essential utilities, or (c) any combination of any such provisions and such utilities. 'Excluded costs' means: (a) the person's accommodation costs (if any), and (b) the costs (if any) associated with the provision of a health or personal social service to the person not already included.[262]

181. Section 67C provides that a person provided with residential support services by or on behalf of the HSE shall pay a financial contribution, in accordance with regulations made by the Minister under this section.[263] The relevant Regulations are the Health (Residential Support Services Maintenance and Accommodation Contributions) Regulations 2016.[264] The amount of the contribution is not to exceed 80% of the maximum daily rate of the State pension (non-contributory).[265]

182. Section 67C(7) provides that a contribution shall not be payable where the residential support services are provided to:

(a) a person under 18 years of age;
(b) a woman receiving services in respect of motherhood:
    (i) a woman receiving services for the purpose of termination of pregnancy under the HRTPA 2018;
(c) a person detained involuntarily under the Mental Health Acts 2001–2009;
(d) a person detained in a designated centre under the Criminal Law (Insanity) Act 2006;
(e) a person who has contracted Hepatitis C directly or indirectly from the use of Human Immunoglobulin Anti-D or the receipt within the State of another blood product or a blood transfusion;
(f) a person in respect of the treatment of infectious diseases prescribed under Part IV of the HA 1947;

262. *Ibid.* Why it is necessary to say that any costs not included are excluded is not immediately obvious.
263. Inserted by HAA 2013, s. 19 and amended by HMPA 2014, s. 43.
264. S.I. No. 467 of 2016 as amended by S.I. No. 106 of 2019 and S.I. No. 1 of 2022.
265. Section 67C(3)(a).

(g) a person who pays charges under section 53A (*see* above); or
(h) a person in receipt of State support under the NHSSA 2009.

183. Finally, section 67D allows the HSE to waive a contribution where: (i) it is necessary to do so in order to avoid undue financial hardship on the part of the person concerned or his or her dependants, (ii) it is necessary to do so, or that doing so would be of significant benefit, in advancing the medical, therapeutic, rehabilitative or health-related needs of the person concerned (including, where a care plan has been prepared for that person by or on behalf of the HSE, needs relating to meeting objectives specified in such a care plan), or (iii) it is reasonable to do so having regard to the extent to which the person concerned provides for his or her own maintenance or accommodation.[266]

184. Section 55(1) allows the Executive, subject to regulations, to make available in-patient services for persons who do not qualify under section 52 or who are deemed under section 52(3) not to have eligibility (i.e., where a person has opted not to avail of such services) and to charge for such services.[267]

§2. Out-Patient Care

I. Definition of Out-Patient Care

185. Section 56(1) of the HA of 1970 provides that:

> For the purpose of this section 'out-patient services' means institutional services other than in-patient services provided at, or by persons attached to, a hospital or home and institutional services provided at a laboratory, clinic, health centre, or other similar premises, but does not include:
>
> (a) the giving of any drug, medicine or other preparation, except where it is administered to the patient directly by a person providing the service or is for psychiatric treatment, or
> (b) dental, ophthalmic, or aural services.

186. The definition of 'out-patient services' was considered in *K.(C.) v. Northern Area Health Board*.[268] This case involved a dispute about the services being provided to a severely disabled man who required twenty-four-hour care at home. Finnegan P expressed the view that out-patient services and in-patient services were identical in nature and scope except that in-patient services were provided in an institution, and out-patient services were provided at home. On appeal, the State argued that this was incorrect and that out-patient services were not a 'home based

266. Inserted by HAA 2013, s. 19 and amended by HMPA 2014, s. 44.
267. As substituted by HAA 2013, s. 13. The charges are set out in the Fourth, Fifth and Sixth Schedule to the 1970 Act.
268. [2003] IESC 34.

equivalent of services to be provided in a hospital or other institution'.[269] The Supreme Court agreed. McGuiness J (*nemine dissentiente*) stated that:

> 57 In construing Section 56(1) as a whole, and in particular construing it in the context of Section 51, it is clear that the 'home' at which out-patient services are to be provided is an institutional home, such as a convalescent home or disabled persons' home as referred to in Section 51. If this interpretation is accepted, the meaning of Section 56 falls into place and the section describes what is normally considered as out-patient services – the situation where a person who is otherwise resident at his or her own home attends a hospital, health centre, clinic or other institution to obtain such medical services as x-rays, dressing of minor wounds, clinical tests and the like. The words of the section then assume their 'ordinary and natural sense' (*see* Craies on Statute Law (1971) (7th edition) on page 65).
>
> 58 This understanding of the word *'home'* in the subsection is also consistent with the meaning of *'institutional services'* as set out in Section 2 of the Health Act 1947, which makes it clear that such services (other than the provision of appliances, medicines and other preparations) are to be provided *'at an institution'*.

187. The judge went on to say that, in considering the submission on behalf of the applicant that services provided 'by persons attached to', a hospital or home must envisage the provision of these services at a person's own residence, the definition of 'institutional services' in section 2 of the 1947 Act is also relevant. Under section 56(1), out-patient services that are to be provided 'by persons attached to' a hospital or home are 'institutional services', which, under section 2 of the 1947 Act, are services to be provided 'at an institution'. McGuinness J took the view that the phrase 'by persons attached to' did not imply the provision of services at an individual's own home.

188. Therefore, the Supreme Court held that section 56 did not mean that the Health Board must provide for the person in his or her own home the equivalent care and maintenance service, both medical and practical, that he or she would receive as an in-patient in a hospital. The section provides for the establishment of an out-patient service, in the normal and ordinary sense of the term, at or attached to hospitals and other institutions.

II. Eligibility for Out-Patient Care

189. Section 56(2) provides that the HSE shall, subject to any regulations relating to the services under subsection (5), make out-patient services (as defined above) available to persons with full eligibility and persons of limited eligibility.[270]

269. At para. 47 of the judgment.
270. Subsections (2)–(5) substituted by HAA 1987, s. 1.

Section 56(3) states that the HSE shall make available out-patient services without charge for children with respect to diseases and disabilities of a permanent or long-term nature prescribed by the Minister with the consent of the Minister for Finance. The following diseases and disabilities are currently prescribed for the purposes of section 56(3): mental handicap, mental illness, phenylketonuria, cystic fibrosis, spina bifida, hydrocephalus, haemophilia, and cerebral palsy.[271]

190. Section 56(4) requires the HSE to make out-patient services available without charge for children with respect to defects noticed at a health examination provided under section 66.[272]

III. Charges for Out-Patient Services

191. Section 56(5) provides that regulations may: (i) provide for the imposition of charges for out-patient services including the giving of any drug, medicine, or other preparation in specified circumstances for persons who are not persons with full eligibility and are not children specified in subsection (3) or (4); and (ii) specify the amounts or the maximum amounts of such charges. Regulations under this subsection may also specify the circumstances in which a person's entitlement to out-patient services extends to services provided by a registered medical practitioner engaged in a consultant capacity in the provision of hospital services and may provide that, when a person's entitlement does not so extend, the HSE may charge for the provision of out-patient services such charges as may be approved of or directed by the Minister.[273]

192. The details of the charges are specified in the Health (Out-Patient Charges) Regulations of 2019.[274] These provide that a charge is to be made for out-patient services provided under section 56(2) of the Act at: (a) an emergency department, (b) an accident and emergency department, or (c) a casualty department.[275] The charge is EUR 100, payable by each person who avails of the services concerned, but it is made only in respect of the first occasion the service is provided in relation to each episode of care. A charge of EUR 75 is made for out-patient services at (a) a minor injury unit, (b) an urgent care centre, (c) a local injury unit, or (d) any other facility providing similar services (other than those covered by the high EUR 100 charge).[276]

193. Article 5 of the 2019 Regulations exempts:

(a) a person with full eligibility;

271. Health Services (Amendment) Regulations of 1987 (S.I. No. 114 of 1987).
272. As amended by s. 1 of the Health (Amendment) Act of 1987 and s. 7 of the Health (Amendment) Act of 1991.
273. Added by HAA 1991, s. 7.
274. S.I. No. 693 of 2019.
275. Article 3 of S.I. No. 693 of 2019.
276. Article 4 of S.I. No. 693 of 2019.

(b) a woman receiving services with respect to motherhood;
(c) a child up to the age of 6 weeks;
(d) a child suffering from diseases or disabilities prescribed under section 56(3);
(e) a child with respect to defects noticed at a health examination held under section 66;
(f) a person receiving services for the diagnosis or treatment of infectious diseases prescribed under Part IV of the HA of 1947;
(g) a person who is deemed, pursuant to section 45(7) of the Act, to be a person with full eligibility in relation to an out-patient service;
(h) a person who has a letter of referral from a registered medical practitioner;
(i) a person whose attendance results in admission as an in-patient
(j) a person who has contracted hepatitis C directly or indirectly from the use of Human Immunoglobulin-Anti-D or the receipt within the State of another blood product or a blood transfusion; or
(k) a relevant participant, within the meaning of section 2 of the Redress for Women Resident in Certain Institutions Act 2015.

§3. Nursing and Home Help Services

194. Section 60 of the HA of 1970 provides that:

> The Health Services Executive shall, in relation to persons with full eligibility and such other categories of persons and for such purposes as may be specified by the Minister, provide without charge a nursing service to give to those persons advice and assistance on matters relating to their health and to assist them if they are sick.

195. McGuiness J in *K.(C.) v. Northern Area Health Board* adopted a narrow interpretation of this provision.[277] She stated that in light of the ordinary and natural sense of the words 'advice and assistance on matters relating to their health and to assist them if they are sick', she did not consider that what was intended was the provision of a long-term virtually full-time (or even extensive part-time) nursing service for disabled persons in their own homes. Rather, she accepted the State's contention that what was in question was an advice and assistance service provided by the public health nurse.

196. Section 61(1) of the 1970 Act provides that:

> The Health Services Executive may make arrangements to assist in the maintenance at home of
>
> (a) a sick or infirm person or a dependant of such a person,

277. *K.(C.) v. Northern Area Health Board* [2003] IESC 34.

(b) a woman availing herself of a service under Section 62 (medical, surgical and midwifery services), or receiving similar care, or a dependant of such a woman,
(c) a person who, but for the provision of a service for him under this section, would require to be maintained otherwise than at home, either (as the Executive may determine in each case) without charge or at such charge as he considers appropriate.

197. In *K.(C.) v. Northern Area Health Board*,[278] Finnegan P held that there was no statutory right to services under this section, having regard to the use of the word 'may' rather than 'shall', and this finding was not appealed.[279] In that case on appeal, McGuinness J also relied on the wording of section 61 to support her interpretation of section 56 (discussed above). McGuinness J expressed the view that the words 'at home' in section 61 refer to the person's own residence as opposed to an institutional home. She suggested that section 61(1)(c) applies precisely to the circumstances of the person in that case.

§4. General Practitioner Services

198. Section 58 requires the HSE to make available without charge a GP medical and surgical service for:

(a) persons with full eligibility;
(b) adult persons with limited eligibility for whom, in the opinion of the Health Service Executive, and notwithstanding that they do not come within the category mentioned in section 45(1)(a), it would be unduly burdensome to arrange GP medical and surgical services for themselves and their dependants; and
(c) dependants who are ordinarily resident in the State of the persons referred to in paragraph (b).[280]

Section 58(4) provides that a person shall be deemed not to come within a category mentioned in paragraph (a) or (c) of subsection (1) for so long as that person has not attained the age of 6 years.[281]

199. Section 58(3) requires that insofar as it is considered practicable by the Health Service Executive, a choice of a medical practitioner should be offered under the GP medical and surgical service.[282]

278. As quoted in [2003] IESC 34.
279. However, speaking *obiter*, McGuinness J in the Supreme Court agreed with this interpretation: at para. 62 of her judgment.
280. Substituted by HAA 2005, s. 5.
281. Inserted by HGPSA 2014, s. 4.
282. Substituted by HAA 2005, s. 5. *See also* the Health Services Regulations of 1972, Art. 5.

200. As of 11 September 2023, a major expansion of the number of people entitled to free GP care to people earning up to the median income was announced. This appears to be on the basis of a revision in the income thresholds in internal guidelines rather than on the basis of any changes to the Acts or statutory instruments. A further extension is planned for November 2023.

201. In addition, to the general provisions in section 58, reforms have introduced eligibility for GP services for a number of specific groups. Section 58A provides for eligibility for GP services for persons (who are ordinarily resident in the State) aged 70 and over who have limited eligibility and whose gross income does not exceed the relevant gross income limit (currently EUR 700 per week for a single person and EUR 1,400 for a couple).[283]

202. Section 58B further provides GP services for children under 8 years of age who are ordinarily resident in the State.[284]

203. Finally, section 58D provides for GP services for persons in receipt of: (a) carer's benefit, (b) carer's allowance, or (c) domiciliary care allowance under the Social Welfare (Consolidation) Act of 2005.[285]

204. The Health Services (No. 3) Regulations of 1983 purport to limit the entitlement to GP services. These provide that services under section 58(1) shall not extend to persons between the ages of 16 and 25 who are dependants of persons who do not have full eligibility, except when it is considered that such a service should be made available to such a person so as to avoid undue hardship. Such a limitation of primary legislation by secondary regulations is almost certainly in breach of the Constitutional separation of powers.[286]

§5. Contraception Services

205. While contraceptive services might fall under other general categories of healthcare, section 67 of the HA now provides that the HSE shall make available without charge contraception services for women who are ordinarily resident in the State (a) who have attained the age of 17 years but not yet attained the age of 26 years, or (b) who are within such class or classes of ages as may be prescribed by

283. Inserted by HACEA 2013, s. 7. Details of how the income limit is calculated are set out in s. 58A.
284. Inserted by HGPSA 2014, s. 5. The Health (General Practitioner Service and Alteration of Criteria for Eligibility) Act 2020, s. 4 provided for the extension of this to children up to 8 and this was commenced from 11 Aug. 2023 by S.I. No. 401 of 2023.
285. Inserted by HGPSA 2018, s. 4.
286. *See Cooke v. Walsh* [1984] IR 710 in which a similar attempt to limit entitlement to health services by statutory instrument was *ultra vires* and void. The Regulations also purport to limit entitlement under ss 59(1) (drugs, medicines and appliances) and 67(1) (dental, ophthalmic and aural services).

the Minister.[287] S.I. No. 408 of 2023 prescribes women who have attained the age of 26 but have not yet attained the age of 31.[288]

206. 'Contraception services', means (a) applicable services or (b) relevant products or both, made available without charge under section 67E (a rather circular definition) while 'applicable services' means (a) such number of consultations with a scheme provider required by a woman in a year for the purposes of obtaining a prescription for accessing relevant products, and (b) the fitting (including such further follow-up consultation as is necessary) and removal by a scheme provider of a long-acting reversible contraceptive device.[289]

§6. Maternity Care

207. Although maternity care in hospitals would appear to have come within the general definition of 'in-patient services',[290] discussed above, section 62 of the HA of 1970 now makes specific provision for maternity care 'provided otherwise than as' in-patient care. Section 62(1) provides that:

> The Executive shall make available medical, surgical and midwifery services for attendance to the health of women in respect of motherhood.[291]

The legislation provides that medical, surgical and midwifery services under section 62(1) are to be provided 'otherwise than as' in-patient services and that no charge can be made for such services.[292]

208. Section 62 further provides that:

> (2) A woman entitled to receive medical services under this section may choose to receive them from any registered medical practitioner who has entered into an agreement with the Executive for the provision of those services and who is willing to accept her as a patient.

287. As inserted by HMP(No. 2)A 2022 which was commenced on 30 Aug. 2022 insofar as it relates to the insertion of s. 67E(7)–(11) and on 14 Sep. 2022 as to the remaining provisions of Part 3 (contraceptive services). *See* S.I. Nos 425 and 452 of 2022. *See also* Health Act 1970 (Section 67E) (Payments in respect of Contraception Services) Regulations 2022 (S.I. No. 451 of 2022) which provide for the services to be provided and fees to be paid to medical practitioners and pharmacists in respect of the free contraception scheme for women aged 17–25.

288. Health Act 1970 (Section 67E) (Prescription of Further Age to Whom Contraceptive Services Will Be Made Available Without Charge) Regulations 2023, S.I. No. 408 of 2023.

289. Section 67E(11) which also defines 'scheme provider' and 'relevant products'. The latter means 'contraceptive drugs, medicines and products (including long-acting reversible contraceptive devices and emergency contraceptives) for the time being (a) standing approved by the Heath Service Executive, or (b) on the Reimbursement List within the meaning of section 2(1) of the [Health (Pricing and Supply of Medical Goods) Act 2013]'.

290. The definition of acute in-patient services now specifically included 'care and treatment in respect of motherhood', as inserted by HAA 2013.

291. As amended by HAA 2013, s. 18.

292. As inserted by HAA 2013, s. 18.

(3) When a woman avails herself of services under this section for a confinement taking place otherwise than in a hospital or maternity home, the Executive shall provide without charge obstetrical requisites to such extent as may be specified by regulations made by the Minister.

209. The current version of section 62 is a significant change to the original version as interpreted by the courts.[293] Until 2013, Section 62 simply provided that the HSE should make available 'medical, surgical and midwifery services' for attendance to the health of women with respect to motherhood. This wording dated back – in more or less identical terms – to the HA of 1953, when, of course, many births would have taken place at home. However, in *O'Brien v. South Western Area Health Board*, the Supreme Court held that section 62(1) should be interpreted as requiring a health board to make available appropriate medical, surgical, and midwifery services, but that that obligation 'would be fully complied with by the provision of medical, surgical and midwifery services *within the confines* of a hospital' (emphasis added).[294] Accordingly, it rejected the applicant's claim that section 62 created a legally enforceable right to the provision or funding of home midwifery services.[295] At most, Geoghegan J (*nemine dissentiente*) suggested that section 62(3) indicated that 'the Oireachtas clearly had in mind the possibility at least that the midwifery services provided by a health board might include home midwifery services'.

210. In *Teehan v. Health Service Executive*, the applicant (who had previously had a caesarean birth) requested that midwifery services be made available to her for a home birth.[296] The HSE refused on the basis that under the agreement between the HSE and self-employed midwives, clinical indemnity is not available to midwives attending a home birth if, *inter alia*, the mother has previously had a caesarean section. The applicant sought a declaration that the HSE had unlawfully fettered its discretion and applied a blanket policy without assessment of her individual suitability. O'Malley J in the High Court recalled that the Supreme Court ruling in *O'Brien* had established that there is no statutory obligation on the HSE to provide for a home birth service although it had the discretion to do so if it considers it appropriate so to do. The HSE is entitled to adopt such policy guidelines as it sees fit, provided they are not 'wholly unreasonable'. O'Malley J did not consider that the HSE approach, in this case, was unreasonable and refused the reliefs sought.

293. The amendment was introduced during the passage of the Bill in the Dáil and was described by the Minister responsible as being 'to clarify the current situation that maternity services for women are provided by or on behalf of the HSE, both in a hospital context and in a community or home setting.' *See* https://www.oireachtas.ie/en/debates/debate/seanad/2013-07-18/13/.

294. [2003] IESC 56.

295. *See also Maguire v. South Eastern Health Board* [2001] IEHC 11 and *Tarrade v. Northeastern Area Health Board* [2002] IEHC 32 in which the High Court had, somewhat surprisingly, rejected the applicants' claims as moot (the children having been born by the time the case came to hearing) and consequently also refused to consider whether the applicants had the right claimed that might entitle them to damages.

296. [2013] IEHC 383.

211. In *Spruyt v. Southern Health Board,* the applicant sought an order directing the Board to provide the services of a midwife for the birth of her child. The Board had made arrangements with a registered medical practitioner rather than a midwife. Giving the *ex tempore* decision of the court, Finlay C.J. said:

> There is no dispute that the Section applies whether a person with such eligibility is anxious to have their child born in a hospital or maternity home or at home, and that there is no difference in the extent of the obligation, though there may be differences in the method of providing it between those two situations. The Health Authority has under subsection (3) an obligation where a confinement is to take place otherwise than in a hospital or maternity home to provide without charge obstetrical requisites, and that obligation has been carried out in this case.
>
> The issue which arises, in this case, is whether the midwifery service mentioned in the subsection can be provided by a registered medical practitioner or whether it must be provided by a midwife registered under the Nurses Act. I am satisfied that the conclusion reached by the learned High Court Judge that midwifery services can be provided by a registered medical practitioner is the correct conclusion and the proper interpretation of the section.[297]

212. The Chief Justice also addressed the issue of the scope of service, which could be provided under section 62. He said:

> The only other point which arises in the case is that I am satisfied that the statutory obligation which is contained in section 62(1) can only be provided by a Health Board if it enters into arrangements with a registered medical practitioner or a registered midwife to provide the attendance to the health in respect of motherhood of any particular woman having a child at home. It could not under any circumstances be discharged merely by an offer to indemnify such a person with eligibility against the cost of their own choice and arrangement with a private practitioner, either consisting of a midwife or a registered medical practitioner … [The Board's] offer to indemnify the applicants against the cost of taking the services of a registered midwife who is prepared to act in relation to this birth, but not to provide personal insurance for any midwife prepared to enter into a contract with the applicants is not a purported discharge of their obligation under the section, but rather an ex gratia arrangement.

The 2013 amendments mean that 'medical, surgical and midwifery services for attendance to the health of women in respect of motherhood' (or 'care and treatment in respect of motherhood' as now worded in s. 51) are now provided as part of general in-patient services (section 52) rather than under section 62 while section 62 now refers only to the provision of such services 'provided otherwise than as in-patient services'. The drafting is again not a model of clarity and the introduction

297. Supreme Court, unreported, 14 Oct. 1988 at p. 2.

of such a significant legal change without adequate explanation or debate is hardly desirable (although it is not clear that this has led to much change in practice).

213. In *Tierney v. North Eastern Health Board*, the High Court considered a challenge to a decision to cease to provide maternity services at a particular local hospital.[298] The Court considered that the provision of maternity services arose in the context of the general obligations pursuant to the HA of 1970. Ó Caoimh J pointed to the fact that under section 62 of the Act of 1970, there were certain obligations to make available medical, surgical, and midwife services with respect to motherhood. However, he went on to say that:

> While the obligations in question are clear in this regard, it is to be noted that nowhere in the section is there any indication as to where the provision in question is to take place … I believe that this obligation must be construed on a rational basis enabling a Health Board to choose where the provision in question will take place as long as the decision that is taken in this regard is not such as to preclude the provision of the service for women residing in any part of its catchment area.

Accordingly, he upheld the arrangements arrived at by the board in that case. The Supreme Court upheld this decision.[299] Denham J ruled that:

> The Act of 1970 gives a general duty to the respondent to provide services, such as maternity services. This obligation is stated in sections of the Act of 1970, including s. 62. However, the statute does not mandate where the services should be provided. The respondent may meet its obligation by providing the services anywhere in its region. The terms of s. 38(3) and s. 38(4) refer to the provision and maintenance, and to the discontinuance of the provision and maintenance, of premises, including a hospital, and not to services.
>
> There is an express scheme provided for the discontinuance of hospital premises. Section 38(3) refers to 'any premises' referred to in s. 38(1), and section 38(4) expressly provides that a health board shall not exercise its powers under s. 38(3) in relation to the discontinuance of a hospital, sanatorium or home, save with the consent of the Minister. In essence, these subsections refer to premises – and not to the provision of services.
>
> The decisions as to the provision of services, whether to open, modify or close a department of a hospital, are made under the implied powers which the

298. [2004] IEHC 306.
299. *Tierney v. North Eastern Health Board* [2010] IESC 43. This decision must be read in the light of the changes to ss. 51 and 62 introduced by HAA 2013 but it is not clear that these changes would affect the outcome of the case given that the HSE is still obliged to 'make available' maternity services.

respondent has to provide the services mandated by the Act of 1970. Consequently, I am satisfied that the respondent has the power to close a department in a hospital and that it did not act *ultra vires* in making the decision in issue.[300]

§7. Termination of Pregnancy

214. Following the approval of the Thirty Sixth Amendment to the Irish Constitution, the broader provision of termination of pregnancy services is allowed under Irish law. This is regulated by the HRTPA 2018. Section 62A of the 1970 Act provides that the Executive shall make available without charge medical, surgical and midwifery services for the purpose of termination of pregnancy in accordance with sections 9, 10, 11 or 12 of the 2018 Act for women who are ordinarily resident in the State.[301]

§8. Healthcare for Children

215. While children are obviously covered by the general provisions on in-patient, out-patient, and GP services outlined above and the specific GP services for children under 6, the HA also make specific provision in relation to children's health. Section 63 provides that the Executive shall make available without charge medical, surgical, and nursing services for children up to the age of 6 weeks whose mothers are entitled to avail themselves of services under section 62 (medical and midwifery care for mothers). This is known as the Maternity and Infant Care Scheme.[302] In addition, section 66 provides for a free health examination and treatment service for children under the age of 6 years at clinics, health centres, or other prescribed places; and a free health examination and treatment service for pupils attending any primary school or who are taught at home.[303] However, subsection (5) provides that section 66 shall not be construed as authorizing the Executive to provide any general domiciliary service or any services as mentioned in sections 52, 56 or 67.

§9. Dental Treatment

216. Section 67(1) requires the Executive to make dental, ophthalmic, and aural treatment and dental, optical, and aural appliances available for persons with full

300. *Ibid.*, at 16.
301. Inserted by the Health (Regulation of Termination of Pregnancy) Act 2018, s. 26.
302. No amendment was made to s. 63 on the significant amendment to s. 62 by HAA 2013 which altered the scope of persons covered by that section. However, it is not clear that this led to any change in the scope of the Maternity and Infant Care Scheme in practice.
303. As amended by the Irish Medicines Board (Miscellaneous Provisions) Act 2006, s. 27.

eligibility,[304] while subsection (2) requires the Executive to make dental, ophthalmic, and aural treatment and dental, optical, and aural appliances available with respect to defects noticed at an examination under the service for children mentioned in section 66. Charges cannot be made under this section.

217. Section 1 of the Health (Amendment) Act (HAA) of 1994 specifically provides that the HSE shall make available without charge, for children who have attended any primary school or who are taught at home under a specified age, specified dental health services.[305]

§10. Pharmaceuticals and Appliances

218. Section 59 of the Act concerns drugs, medicines and medical and surgical appliances.[306] It provides a number of mechanisms whereby persons can be assisted with access to these items. First, it provides for the provision of certain drugs to persons with full eligibility. Section 59(1) provides that the HSE shall make arrangements for the supply without charge to persons with full eligibility of drugs, medicines and medical and surgical appliances on the Reimbursement List within the meaning of section 2(1) of the Health (Pricing and Supply of Medical Goods) Act (HPSMGA) 2013.[307]

219. Formerly, such medication was free for such persons with full eligibility, but the Health (Amendment) (No. 2) Act (HA(No. 2)A) 2010 introduced a small charge (known as the prescription charge) for such medication. This inserted a new subsection (1A) which provides that, notwithstanding section 59(1), a person with full eligibility is to be charged an amount of EUR 0.50, or such other amount as may be determined by regulations, per item supplied to that person on prescription (currently EUR 1.50 is prescribed).[308] The maximum amount payable in respect of items supplied in a month to an adult person and his or her dependants is EUR 10 (or such other amount as may be determined by regulations, currently EUR 15).[309] (But *see* below in relation to persons aged 70 or over).

304. As amended by the Irish Medicines Board (Miscellaneous Provisions) Act 2006, s. 28.
305. As amended by the Irish Medicines Board (Miscellaneous Provisions) Act 2006, s. 29. The Health (Dental Services for Children) (Amendment) Regulations, 2009 (S.I. No. 248 of 2000) prescribe the age of 15 and the following services: (a) a dental health screening service; (b) a preventive dental treatment service; (c) a primary care dental treatment service with respect to defects noted during a screening examination carried out under (a). These regulation purport to amend S.I. No. 248 of 2000 but appear simply to repeat the wording of that Regulation.
306. As substituted by the HMPA of 2001. 'Drugs' are defined in s. 59(12) as drugs that are prescribed by a registered medical practitioner or a registered dentist and includes medicines, and medical and surgical appliances, that are so prescribed.
307. As amended by HPSMGA 2013, s. 30. References to listed drugs, etc., below are to this Reimbursement List. Despite the fact that, as discussed below, charges are now made for such drugs, etc., the phrase 'without charge' has been retained in s. 59(1).
308. SI. No. 464 of 2022.
309. Section 59(1B) substituted by HAA 2017, s. 3. The amount of EUR 15 is prescribed by S.I. SI. No. 464 of 2022.

220. However, the following persons remain excluded from such charges:

(a) children who are in the care of the Health Service Executive under the Child Care Acts 1991–2007;
(b) persons to whom are supplied specified controlled drugs;[310] and
(c) persons who are of a class specified by the Minister in regulations made under this section.[311]

Section 59(4)[312] allows, *inter alia*, the Minister to prescribe other 'classes of persons' who are not to be charged the prescription charge. This power has been exercised to prescribe asylum seekers living in direct provision and refugees living in emergency reception and orientation centres under the Irish Refugee Protection Programme.[313]

221. Section 59A provides a separate charging regime for persons who have attained the age of 70 years and their dependants.[314] This provides that the amount of charge under section 59(1A) per item is EUR 2.00 or such other amount as may be determined by regulations (currently EUR 1.00), and the maximum amount payable per month is EUR 20 or such other amount as may be determined by regulations (currently EUR 10).[315]

222. Second, section 59 provides for subsidization of the cost of drugs, medicines and medical and surgical appliances for persons with limited eligibility (or those with full eligibility who choose to buy medicines). This is known as the Drug Payment Scheme. Section 59(2) provides that if a person with limited eligibility, or a person with full eligibility who does not avail himself or herself of arrangements under subsection (1), incurs expenditure on a listed drug, medicines and medical and surgical appliances obtained on prescription for the treatment of the person or his or her dependants, the HSE shall make arrangements to meet the balance of the cost, or a prescribed proportion thereof of the person's being supplied with such drugs, medicines and medical and surgical appliances. The Health Services Regulations of 1972 (as amended) provide that when the cost of supplying a person or his or her dependants for the relevant period (i.e., the period beginning on the first day of any month and ending on the last day of that month) with prescribed drugs,

310. Within the meaning of the Misuse of Drugs (Supervision of Prescription and Supply of Methadone) Regulations 1998 or such other regulations as may be made by the Minister under s. 5 of the Misuse of Drugs Act 1977 for the purpose of preventing the misuse of controlled drugs, in respect of those specified controlled drugs.
311. Section 59(1C) as inserted by HA(No. 2)A 2010, s. 1.
312. As substituted by HA (No. 2)A 2010, s. 1.
313. Prescribed by S.I. No. 382 of 2015 and S.I. No. 635 of 2016 respectively. The payment to those in direct provision, known officially as the 'daily expenses allowance', is now made under the European Communities (Reception Conditions) Regulations 2018 [S.I. No. 230 of 2018].
314. As inserted by HAA 2017, s. 4.
315. S.I. No. 465 of 2022.

medicines, and medical and surgical appliances exceeds EUR 80, the amount met by the HSE is the amount by which the cost exceeds EUR 80.[316]

223. Third, section 59(3) of the Act provides for the provision, without charge, of listed drugs, medicines or medical and surgical appliances to persons with certain diseases or disabilities of a permanent or long-term nature.[317] This is known as the Long-Term Illness Scheme. The following diseases and disabilities are hereby prescribed for the purposes of section 59(3) of the Act: mental handicap, mental illness, phenylketonuria, cystic fibrosis, spina bifida, hydrocephalus, haemophilia, cerebral palsy, diabetes mellitus, diabetes insipidus, epilepsy, Parkinsonism, acute leukaemia, muscular dystrophies, and multiple sclerosis.[318] Arrangements for the supply of drugs and medicines to persons suffering from mental illness in pursuance of section 59(3) of the Act are confined to persons under the age of 16 years.[319]

§11. Nursing Home Care

I. Introduction

224. The area of nursing home care has been a legally controversial one in Irish law. The fundamental legal issue has been whether nursing home care formed part of general 'in-patient services' discussed above or whether it constituted a separate service. The categorization of nursing home care was considered in *In Re Maud McInerney, a Ward of Court.*[320] The case involved the issue as to whether the Health Board was entitled to change for the nursing home services provided to the person concerned. The Board argued that the service provided was 'institutional assistance', within the meaning of section 54 of the HA of 1953, a term that meant 'shelter and maintenance' and for which the Board was legally entitled to make charges. The Supreme Court held in *McInerney* that the person concerned was in receipt of more than mere shelter and maintenance and that there was an element of medical care involved. Accordingly, the Court held that the care provided involves 'in-patient services' wherever the patient is in receipt of any medical care over and above pure maintenance. Obviously, in very many cases, persons in nursing home care were in receipt of such care and accordingly, this fell within the category of in-patient services. The implications of this were two-fold: first, persons had a statutory entitlement to such services in accordance with their eligibility categorization (as discussed above). Second, charges could only be charged against persons with full eligibility in accordance with the relevant provisions of the HA.

316. As substituted by S.I. No. 577 of 2017 and amended by S.I. No. 77 of 2022.
317. As amended by HPSMGA 2013, s. 30.
318. Health Services (Amendment) Regulations of 1971, Art. 8 (S.I. No. 277 of 1971) as implicitly amended by S.I. No. 64 of 1975.
319. Health Services (Amendment) Regulations 1971, Art. 9 (S.I. No. 277 of 1971). Given the wording of s. 59(3), it is not clear that confining the provision of such drugs to persons under a certain age is *intra vires*.
320. [1976–1977] ILRM 229.

225. The fact that nursing home services are normally 'in-patient' services appears to have been conceded by the State in the *Health Bill Reference*[321] case. However, the practice in relation to access to nursing home care was entirely different, and a separate scheme of entitlement operated as though nursing home care was *not* an in-patient service.[322]

226. The NHSSA, 2009 has now inserted a new subsection in section 52, which provides that:

> (1A) The Health Service Executive may make available long-term residential care services within the meaning of the Nursing Homes Support Scheme Act 2009.

Section 51 (in-patient services) includes a definition of 'LTRCS' as meaning 'long-term residential care services within the meaning of the Nursing Homes Support Scheme Act 2009'.[323] Section 53B now specifies that charges can be imposed for LTRCS in accordance with the NHSSA 2009. Section 33 of the NHSSA 2009 sets out specific provisions in relation to charges for care services within the meaning of the definition of 'LTRCS' (in section 3(1)(a)(i) of NHSSA).[324] Section 52(1) of the HA 1970 has not, however, been amended, and it is arguable that nursing home care is now both an in-patient service and 'LTRCS' as defined in the NHSSA (*see* below paragraph 231). This would imply that the HSE has a mandatory duty to provide such services under section 52(1) and that section 52(1A) is otiose, although section 53B means that charges can be imposed in line with the NHSSA. However, the Department of Health appears to take the view that rights and duties in relation to nursing home care arise solely under the NHSSA.

227. The Health (Nursing Homes) Act 1990 came into force on 1 September 1993 and provided a regulatory framework for the provision of and access to nursing home care.[325] The Act (as amended by the Health (Nursing Homes) (Amendment) Act of 2007) and Regulations made thereunder were intended to clarify the legal and practical position in relation to these issues, to introduce the registration system for nursing homes, and to provide a system for assessing entitlement to public nursing home care and/or subventions towards the cost of care in private nursing homes.

228. A 'nursing home' is defined as 'an institution for the care and maintenance of more than two dependent persons' (i.e., persons who require assistance with the activities of daily living by reason of physical or mental infirmity).[326] Various institutions are excluded from this definition, such as 'mental institutions', 'maternity

321. [2005] IESC 7; [2005] 1 IR 105.
322. *See* earlier editions of this book.
323. Substituted by HAA 2013, s. 8. This implies that LTRCS is a sub-category of in-patient services.
324. *See* below, para. 231.
325. M. Cousins, 'The Health (Nursing Homes) Act 1990', Gazette of the Law Society of Ireland (1994), 15–18.
326. Sections 1 and 2 of the Health (Nursing Homes) Act of 1990.

homes', and institutions where the majority of patients are priests or members of religious orders. All nursing homes must be registered with the Executive, who must keep a list of registered nursing homes. The Act sets out the grounds upon which registration may be refused or removed.

II. Nursing Home Support Scheme Act, 2009

229. The Nursing Homes Support Scheme (better known as the 'Fair Deal' although the title does not appear in the legislation) came into effect on 27 October 2009.[327] The Scheme introduced a much-needed reform of the system of support for nursing home care and provided some much-needed clarity in this area. However, unlike the social welfare legislation, which provides for payment of benefits as of right and is thus, demand-led, the NHSSA 2009 does not explicitly provide for a right to 'State support' and attempts to ensure that the operation of the Scheme will be contained within the financial resources provided. Section 5 of the NHSSA provides that:

> (2) The Scheme is established for the purpose of giving financial support under this Act in respect of care services in accordance with this Act out of the resources allocated to the Scheme in each year in accordance with *subsection (4)* and shall consist of the provision of financial support in respect of care services for the purposes of and in accordance with the provisions of this Act and any guidelines issued under *section 35.*
>
> …
>
> (4) In the financial year 2009 and in each subsequent financial year the Executive shall, out of such monies as are available to it for that financial year from monies provided by the Oireachtas, allocate such amount as the Minister determines, with the consent of the Minister for Finance, for the provision of financial support under this Scheme in that financial year.

Thus, the intention appears to be to limit the amount of expenditure under the scheme in any year to the amount of financial resources available to the HSE and regardless of the actual level of demand for the Scheme in that year.

230. Section 2 of the Health (Amendment) (No. 3) Act 1996 (now repealed by the HAA 2004) provided:

> (1) A health board, in performing the functions conferred on it by or under this Act or any other enactment, shall have regard to (*a*) the resources,

327. An administrative consolidation of the Act is available at http://revisedacts.lawreform.ie/eli/2009/act/15/front/revised/en/html.

> wherever originating, that are available to the board for the purpose of such performance and the need to secure the most beneficial, effective and efficient use of such resources, ...[328]

In *O'Brien v. South Western Area Health Board*,[329] Ó Caoimh J. held that:

> if a clear statutory obligation exists, economic considerations cannot override the requirement of the section and I am satisfied that s. 2 ... cannot be construed as overriding any clear statutory obligation to provide a specific service.

On appeal, the Supreme Court did not find it necessary to consider the issue as it dismissed the appeal on other grounds. Nonetheless, Ó Caoimh J's interpretation would appear to be correct in principle. However, section 5(2) of the NHSSA 2009 provides a much more specific limitation in relation to services provided under that Act, and, in this case, it is submitted that the clear wording of section 5 does limit the statutory duty to provide support under the NHSS.[330]

Long-term residential care services

231. The concept of LTRCS is defined in the NHSSA (section 3(1)) as including (a) (i) maintenance, health or personal care services, or any combination thereof, provided by or on behalf of the Executive to a person (I) whilst the person resides in and is maintained in a facility (A) that is publicly designated in writing by the Executive as a facility predominantly for the care of older people, ... and (B) in which nursing care is provided on the basis that at no time should there be less than one registered nurse present in the facility who is available to provide nursing care for the persons maintained in the facility, and (II) subject to subsection (2), for (A) a period of not less than thirty consecutive days, or (B) periods in the aggregate amounting to not less than thirty days within a period of twelve consecutive months, or (ii) maintenance, health or personal care services, or any combination thereof, provided to a person whilst the person resides in and is maintained in an approved nursing home[331] (I) in which nursing care is provided on the basis that at no time should there be less than one registered nurse present in the approved nursing home who is available to provide nursing care for the persons maintained in the approved nursing home, and (II) subject to subsection (2), for (A) a period of not less than thirty consecutive days, or (B) periods in the aggregate amounting to not less than thirty days within a period of twelve consecutive months. Section 3(2) provides that where the Executive is satisfied that a person who is or is to be provided with care

---

328. *See* now s. 7(5) of the HA 2004 which provides that in performing its functions, the HSE shall have regard to '(d) the resources, wherever originating, that are available to it for the purpose of performing its functions, and (e) the need to secure the most beneficial, effective and efficient use of those resources'.
329. Unreported, High Court, 5 Sep. 2002.
330. *See Kavanagh v. Legal Aid Board* [2001] IEHC 149; *O'Donoghue v. Legal Aid Board* [2004] IEHC 413.
331. This concept is also defined in the NHSSA, s. 3.

services is unlikely to ever cease to require care services during the person's lifetime, then the durational requirements of the definition of LTRCS shall not apply in the case of that person. However, paragraph (b) of the definition provides that LTRCS does not include: (i) medically acute care and treatment in an acute hospital, (ii) respite care, (iii) rehabilitative care for (I) a period of less than twelve consecutive months, or (II) periods in the aggregate amounting to less than twelve months within a period of twenty-four consecutive months, or (iv) out-patient services made available pursuant to section 56 of the HA 1970.

232. Thus the definition of LTRCS comprises:

(a) (i) 'maintenance, health or personal care services' (ii) provided by or on behalf of the HSE (iii) to a person residing in and being maintained in an HSE designated facility for the care of older people (iv) in which nursing care is provided (v) for a certain minimum period (unless the person is unlikely to ever cease to require care services during the person's lifetime) or
(b) (i) 'maintenance, health or personal care services' (ii) provided to a person residing in and being maintained in an approved nursing home (iii) in which nursing care is provided (iv) for a certain minimum period (again subject to the above proviso).

The first category of services covers nursing care provided by or on behalf of the HSE directly in an HSE designated facility for the care of older people, while the second covers care in private (approved) nursing homes. Based on the discussion above, it would seem clear that LTRCS generally falls within the category of in-patient services as defined in section 52 of the HA of 1972.

233. Section 5(5) provides that the Scheme is to be operated subject to the principles that applicants who are determined by the HSE to need care services are to be informed of all relevant facilities and approved nursing homes and subject to the availability of a long-term residential care bed, the applicant may select the relevant facility or approved nursing home in which to receive care services.

Care needs assessment

234. A person who wishes to apply for State support must first, in principle, apply for a care assessment (in practice, there is one combined application form that covers all aspects of the application).[332] A care needs assessment of a person comprises an evaluation of:

(a) the person's ability to carry out the activities of daily living, including:
  (i) the cognitive ability;
  (ii) the extent of orientation;
  (iii) the degree of mobility;

332. Section 7(1) of the NHSSA 2009 (all references in this section are to the NHSSA unless otherwise stated).

(iv) the ability to dress unaided;
(v) the ability to feed unaided;
(vi) the ability to communicate;
(vii) the ability to bathe unaided; and
(viii) the degree of continence of the person;

(b) the family and community support that is available to the person;
(c) the medical, health and personal social services being provided to or available to the person both at the time of the carrying out of the assessment and generally;
(d) any other matter that affects the person's ability to care for himself or herself; and
(e) the likelihood of a material alteration in the circumstances referred to in paragraphs (a)–(d) during the lifetime of the person.[333]

235. When the HSE receives a care needs assessment report, it must, after considering the report as soon as practicable after its receipt, make a determination as to whether or not the person needs care services.[334] A person who has been determined to need care services may apply for state support under section 9, and a financial assessment (means test) is carried out. The details of the financial assessment are set in Chapter 6 of Part XI.

236. On receipt of the financial assessment, the HSE is required to 'determine an application for State support in accordance with the method of calculation of State support set out in section 14'.[335] Section 14 provides that the amount of State support payable under the Scheme shall be expressed as a weekly amount and shall be determined on the basis of the assessed weekly means and by applying the equation:

$$S = T - M$$

where S is the weekly amount of State support, T is the total weekly cost of the care services provided to the person concerned, and M is the assessed weekly means of the person.

237. Section 12 provides that State support is to be provided: (a) by the transfer by the Executive of the appropriate amount of State support to the relevant facility, or (b) by the payment by the Executive of the appropriate amount of State support to the proprietor of the approved nursing home in which the person resides and is being maintained.

238. The NHSSA also provides for what is known as 'ancillary State support' whereby the persons concerned can charge some of the cost of care (over and above

333. Section 7(6).
334. Section 7(8). A refusal may be reviewed after six months or earlier if there is a material change in circumstances: s. 8.
335. Section 11(1).

that covered by State support) against his or her assets.[336] This support is to be repaid to the HSE on the death of the person receiving care services, the transfer of any part of the interest in a charged asset of any person who has requested the payment of ancillary support, the adjudication as a bankruptcy of the person in respect of whom the payment of ancillary support was made (or of a partner who also applied for such support). However, repayment can be deferred in certain cases where the asset is the principal residence of the surviving partner.

239. In order to apply for and receive State support, a person must be ordinarily resident in the State.[337]

240. The HSE may review – either at its own initiative or at the request of the persons – the care assessment, financial assessment or ancillary support payable.[338] In addition, a person may submit an appeal where he or she is aggrieved by a decision in rclation to:

(i) Care needs assessment (section 7(8)).
(ii) Financial assessment (section 11(1)).
(iii) Ordinary residence (section 7(1)).
(iv) Failure to provide information (sections 10(7) and 11(1)).
(v) Ancillary State support (section 16).
(vi) A revised decision (section 30(4)).
(vii) The hardship provision concerning transferred assets (section 31(2) and (5)).

The appellant must give the HSE a notice in the specified form, stating the reasons for the appeal, not later than forty working days after notice of the decision was given to him or her.[339]

241. The NHSSA specifically provides that the appeals officers shall be independent in the performance of their functions.[340] The appeals officer is not confined to the grounds on which the decision of the HSE was based but may decide the matter, which is the subject of the appeal, as if it were being decided for the first time. The procedure for appeals is to be laid out in guidelines by the HSE under section 35. The appeals officer's decision is to be in writing and may include a decision to refer the matter concerned back to the HSE for reconsideration in accordance with such directions as the officer thinks appropriate. A copy of the decision is to be sent to the appellant and the HSE together with the officer's reasons for the relevant decision. A person (including the HSE) aggrieved by the decision may appeal to the High Court on a point of law.

336. Sections 15–20.
337. Sections 6 and 7.
338. Section 30.
339. Section 32.
340. Section 32(3)(a).

242. In conclusion, the question arises as to whether the NHSSA provides the sole source of rights and duties in relation to nursing home care or whether a duty to provide nursing home care still exists under section 52(1) of the HA of 1970. As we have seen above, nursing home care has been recognized by the Supreme Court as falling within the scope of section 52(1). This provision has never been amended. A separate subsection concerning LTRCS – described by the then Minister as a 'technical provision' – was inserted in section 52 (a section titled 'Provision of in-patient services') by the NHSSA. There is nothing necessarily inconsistent with a statutory provision providing a duty to provide in-patient services in general and a separate provision allowing the provision of a sub-category on in-patient services.[341] Given that the Oireachtas could have amended section 52(1) to exclude LTRCS, its 'decision' not to do so should imply a decision not to exclude nursing home care from the concept of in-patient services.[342] Thus, it is arguable that a person may still seek to be provided with nursing home care under section 52, and the HSE is under a statutory duty to provide such services.

§12. Psychiatric Treatment

243. Entitlement to psychiatric treatment is provided separately from entitlement to general healthcare. The relevant legislation is contained in the Mental Health Acts of 1947–2018. The Mental Health Act of 2001 (as amended) largely replaces previous legislation dating back to 1947 and provides for involuntary admission to hospitals of psychiatric patients, the establishment of a Mental Health Commission, and related issues. As this is a specialist area of medical care, it will not be addressed in this book.[343]

§13. Treatment Benefit

244. Unlike the other services discussed in this chapter, the treatment benefit scheme is administered by the DSP. The statutory provisions as to treatment benefits are extremely brief. Section 138(1) of the Social Welfare (Consolidation) Act of 2005 simply provides that a person shall, subject to the satisfaction of the prescribed conditions, be entitled to such treatment benefit as may be specified by regulations. Subsection (2) (as amended by SWP(No.2)A 2009 and s. 12 SWA 2021) provides that such regulations may specify the payment of the whole or any part of the cost of any of the following:

---

341. *See also* the discussion in the Ombudsman's report: *Who Cares: An Investigation into the Right to Nursing Home Care in Ireland*, 2010, p. 99.

342. The principle of *generalia specialibus non derogant* (general things do not derogate from special things) would not seem to apply here where the specific provision comes after the general provision and does not explicitly amend a well-established rule.

343. Readers are referred to A.M. O'Neill, *Irish Mental Health Law* (Dublin, First Law, 2005) and to the annotation of the Mental Health Act of 2001 by Mary Keys in *Irish Current Law Statutes*.

(a) dental treatment;
(b) optical treatment and appliances;
(c) hearing aids and specialized contact lenses, subject to a maximum grant of EUR 500 per hearing aid;[344] and
(d) non-surgical hair replacement for persons suffering from hair loss (other than physiological hair loss) resulting from a disease or treatment for a disease, subject to a maximum grant of EUR 500.[345]

The details of the actual treatment benefit scheme have always been set out in Regulations.[346]

245. Unlike the other healthcare schemes, entitlement to treatment benefits is based on social insurance contributions. The current contribution requirements are somewhat convoluted and increase with the age of the claimant.[347] In brief, these provide that a person:

(a) who is under the age of 21 years must have thirty-nine paid contributions between the date of his or her entry into insurance and the relevant date; or
(b) who is of or over the age of 21 years and under the age of 29 years must have (i) thirty-nine paid contributions between the date of his or her entry into insurance and the relevant date; and (ii) (I) paid or credited contributions in respect of not less than 39 contribution weeks in the relevant contribution year, or (II) paid contributions in respect of not less than 26 contribution weeks in both the relevant contribution year and the contribution year immediately before the relevant contribution year; or
(c) who is of or over the age of 29 years must have (i) 260 paid contributions between the date of his or her entry into insurance and the relevant date, and (I) paid or credited contributions in respect of not less than 39 contribution weeks in the relevant contribution year, or (II) paid contributions in respect of not less than 26 contribution weeks in both the relevant contribution year and the contribution year immediately before the relevant contribution year.[348]

246. Article 96, as amended by Article 4 of S.I. No. 259 of 2022, provides that a dependent spouse, civil partner or cohabitant is entitled to treatment benefits when the contribution conditions (specified above) are satisfied by his or her spouse, civil partner or cohabitant. Article 97 goes on to provide that upon the death of an insured person whose dependent spouse, civil partner or cohabitant at the date of the death,

---

344. *See* S.I. No. 77 of 2021. A claimant is entitled to a grant for contact lenses once every two years or such other frequency as the Minister may, from time to time, determine – S.I. No. 360 of 2022.
345. As amended by SWA 2021, s. 12 and *see* S.I. No. 259 of 2022. The scheme also covers treatment provided to a claimant in other member states of the EU and in the UK – Art. 105(2) of S.I. No. 142 of 2007 as amended by S.I. No. 716 of 2020.
346. SW(CCP&C)R, Ch. 12 as amended by S.I. No. 578 of 2009, S.I. No. 720 of 2011, S.I. No. 381 of 2017, S.I. No. 77 of 2021, S.I. No. 259 of 2022 and S.I. No. 360 of 2022.
347. SW(CCP&C)R, Art. 94 as substituted by S.I. No. 381 of 2017 and amended by S.I. No. 259 of 2022.
348. SW(CCP&C)R, Art. 94, as amended by S.I. No. 381 of 2017 and S.I. No. 259 of 2022.

was or would have been entitled to treatment benefits under Article 96, the dependent spouse, civil partner or cohabitant continues to be entitled to treatment benefits for as long as that person remains a widow or widower, surviving civil partner or surviving cohabitant as the case may be.[349] Finally, Article 98 provides that when an insured person, at any time between the age of 60 and attaining pensionable age, is or would be entitled to treatment benefits, he or she continues throughout his or her life to be so entitled.[350]

247. Section 138(5) provides that the Minister may by order appoint a day on which the scheme shall expire.

349. SW(CCP&C)R, Art. 97 as amended by Art. 4 of S.I. No. 259 of 2022.
350. As substituted by S.I. No. 381 of 2017.

Part IV. Family Allowances

248. This part looks at the current family support payments under the social welfare system, including CB, increases with respect to qualified adults and children, guardian's payments, maternity benefits, parent's and paternity benefits and lone parents' payments.

249. The Irish Constitution imposes some limits on the support available to different types of families. Article 41.1.1 of the Constitution provides that:

> The State recognises the Family as the natural primary and fundamental unit group of Society, and as a moral institution possessing inalienable and imprescriptible rights, antecedent and superior to all positive law.

Article 41.3.1 goes on to state that:

> The State pledges itself to guard with special care the institution of marriage, on which the family is founded, and to protect it against attack.

In *Hyland v. Minister for Social Welfare*, the Supreme Court held that a provision of the SW Acts, which treated an unmarried couple more favourably than a married couple, was a breach of the positive obligations cast upon the State by Article 41.3.1.[351] However, in *MacMathúna v. Attorney General*, the Supreme Court rejected a challenge to the constitutionality of providing various tax and welfare supports to lone parents on the basis that there were abundant grounds for distinguishing between the needs and requirements of single parents and those of married persons living and rearing a family together and that once such a disparity had been justified, the courts could not seek to assess the extent of the disparity.[352]

250. The introduction of a system of civil partnership in Ireland in the Civil Partnership and Certain Rights and Obligations of Cohabitants Act 2010 (CPCROCA 2010) has led to an important reform of the social welfare code.[353] The code has

351. [1989] IR 624. *See also H v. Eastern Health Board* [1988] IR 747.
352. [1995] 1 IR 484 at 495.
353. For the purposes of the Act, 'civil partnership' means: (a) a civil partnership registration referred to in s. 3(a) of CPCROCA 2010, or (b) a legal relationship referred to in s. 3(b) of CPCROCA 2010: s. 2 as inserted by SWPA 2010, s. 15. In 2015, the Irish Constitution was amended to provide for same-sex marriage – *see* Art. 41.4.

been modified to treat civil partners[354] in the same general manner as married couples and so, for example, SCPs[355] are now entitled to the same contributory pension entitlements as widows and widowers. No constitutional issue would seem to arise in this regard, given that civil partners are not treated *more favourably* than a married couple. The social welfare code now also recognizes the status of 'cohabitant' (i.e., persons 'living together as a couple in an intimate and committed relationship'). However, such couples do not have the same rights as married couples and civil partners. The reform has led generally to the same treatment of unmarried opposite-sex and same-sex couples. In some areas, this has positive financial effects for same-sex couples in that the definition of a qualified adult has now been extended to same-sex couples. On the other hand, however, the cohabitation rules (both as a bar to certain payments and as a factor in the means test) have also been extended to such couples. These rules are discussed in more detail as they arise.

251. A significant proportion of Irish employers already pay *occupational* maternity and parental benefits. However, *statutory* obligations to compensate for these risks has been confined to the social welfare legislation. The Parental Leave Act 1998 introduced a right to parental leave (*see* paragraph 294), but this was unpaid, and there is *no* parental benefit. However, maternity leave has now been extended to twenty-six weeks with benefit (and the possibility of a further sixteen weeks unpaid). The Paternity Leave and Benefit Act 2016 introduced a *paternity* leave and benefit for fathers of two weeks. Finally, the Parent's Leave and Benefit Act 2019 has now provided for two weeks' *parent's* leave and benefit.

---

354. For the purposes of the Act, 'civil partner' means a civil partner within the meaning of CPCROCA 2010: s. 2 as inserted by SWPA 2010, s. 15.
355. 'Surviving civil partner' means one civil partner of a couple who were both parties to the same civil partnership and whose civil partner is deceased and includes one civil partner of a couple who were both parties to the same civil partnership, who would otherwise be a surviving civil partner but for the fact that his or her civil partnership has been dissolved being a dissolution that is recognized as valid in the State: s. 2 as inserted by SWPA 2010, s. 15.

Chapter 1. Child Benefit

§1. Beneficiaries and Conditions

252. CB is a universal payment (i.e., it is not means-tested and not subject to payment of social insurance contributions).[356] CB is payable with respect to a child if:

(a) he or she is under the age of 16 or if between 16 and 18, he or she is receiving full-time education, or is by reason of physical or mental infirmity incapable of self-support and likely to remain so for a prolonged period;
(b) he or she is ordinarily resident in the State;[357] and
(c) he or she is not detained in a children's detention school and is not undergoing imprisonment or detention in legal custody.[358]

253. A child who resides with his or her parent (or other qualified person) and that person's spouse, civil partner or cohabitant outside the State when that person or the person's spouse, civil partner or cohabitant is a member of the Defence Forces or the civil service and is outside the State in the service of the government, the State, or an international organization; or is a volunteer development worker; or is an insured person employed outside the state with respect to whom employment contributions are payable in accordance with section 31, is deemed to be a qualified child under section 219(2). In addition, the territorial rules will often be overridden by EU Regulations 883/2004 on the coordination of social security.[359]

254. Full-Time Education: A child is regarded as receiving full-time education while attending on a full-time basis a course of full-time instruction by day at an institution of education.[360] However, the following courses are excluded from the definition of a course of full-time instruction:

---

356. Sections 219–223 and the SW(CCP&C)R, Arts 159–161 as amended. In *X v. Ireland,* 23851/20 and 24360/20, 22 Jun. 2023, the European Court of Human Rights held that CB was paid as of right and must be taken as generating a proprietary interest for the purposes of Art. 1 of Protocol No. 1 of the Convention. However, it held that that CB did not fall within the scope of Art. 8 of the Convention.
357. On ordinary residence, *see* Part XII, Ch. 3. In Case 2019/03, the Appeals Officer noted that the term 'ordinarily resident' is not defined in the legislation and that, therefore, decision makers can apply discretion having regard to the circumstances of the case, including the length of absence. In the instant case, the children had been absent from the State for a period of six months when the decision to disallow child benefit was made and the Appeals Officer concluded that the children were not ordinarily resident in the State at that time – Social Welfare Appeals Office Annual Report 2019, p. 44.
358. Section 219(1) as substituted by SWMPA 2008, s. 20. This reduced the maximum age for CB from 19 to 18. Limited transitional provisions were introduced in the SWMPA 2008.
359. For example, where a person is employed in Ireland but his or her children reside in another Member State of the EU.
360. In Case 2017/03, a child was regarded as receiving full-time education, even though not attending his school because of bullying, in circumstances in which he was still registered as a pupil there and where there was a significant amount of cooperation and interaction with the school – *Social Welfare Appeals Office Annual Report* 2017, 49.

(a) courses provided or approved by Solas (other than Youthreach) and with respect to which an allowance is payable;
(b) courses that form part of an employment or work experience scheme;
(c) courses that arise from employment;
(d) courses that comprise, in an academic year, a period of work experience with respect to which remuneration is paid, when such period exceeds the time spent receiving instruction or tuition at an institution of education; or
(e) courses provided or approved by Teagasc, when, in an academic year, such training or instruction comprises a period of work experience that exceeds the time spent receiving instruction or tuition at an institution of education.

255. A child is regarded as continuing to receive full-time education:

(a) for periods during an academic year when that child is not attending an institution of education arising from the temporary interruption to the provision of a course of education by an institution of education; and
(b) for the period immediately following the completion by that child of part of a cycle of education, when such part finishes between 1 May and 30 June in an academic year, up to and including the next following 30 September, except in relation to a child who completes the final part of a cycle of education and terminates his or her attendance at a course of full-time instruction at an institution of education.

256. Normal Residence: CB is payable to the person with whom a qualified child normally resides.[361] CB is normally payable to the mother on the basis that the child is deemed by Regulation to be 'normally resident' with her. This a clearly discriminatory procedure, which is, however, allowed by EU law because of the exclusion of family benefits from the scope of Directive 79/7.[362] A person (other than a person to whom section 219(2) applies) is not qualified for CB unless he or she is habitually resident in the State.[363]

257. The detailed rules in relation to 'normal residence' are set out in Article 159 of the Social Welfare (Consolidated Claims, Payments and Control) Regulations of 2007 (SW(CCP&C)R). Rule 1 provides that a qualified child, who is resident with more than one of the following persons: his mother, stepmother, father, or stepfather, is regarded as normally residing with the person first so mentioned and with no other person. However, when the persons are resident in separate households, the child is regarded as normally residing with the person with whom he or she resides

361. Section 220.
362. *See also Barber v. Secretary of State for Work and Pensions* [2002] EWHC Admin. 1915 in which the English High Court rejected a challenge to similar UK provisions under the ECHR, albeit on somewhat unconvincing grounds.
363. Section 220(3). As to habitual residence, *see* Part XII, Ch. 3.

for the majority of the time.[364] Thus, if the parents are living in separate households, and the child spends the majority of the time with the father, CB will be payable to the father rather than to the mother.

258. A qualified child who is resident with one only of the persons mentioned in Rule 1 is regarded as normally residing with that person and with no other person, provided that person is the father, and he is cohabiting with a woman as husband and wife, this Rule shall not apply with respect to the child when the father so elects, and, on such an election, the child shall be regarded as normally residing with the woman with whom the father is cohabiting (Rule 3). Subject to Rule 8, a qualified child, who is resident elsewhere than with a parent or a step-parent and whose mother is alive, is, when his mother is entitled to his or her custody whether solely or jointly with any other person, regarded as normally residing with his or her mother and with no other person (Rule 4). Subject to Rule 8, a qualified child, who is resident elsewhere than with a parent or a step-parent and whose father is alive, is, where his or her father is entitled to his or her custody whether solely or jointly with any person other than his mother, regarded as normally residing with his or her father and with no other person (Rule 5). Rule 6 provides that a qualified child to whom none of the foregoing Rules applies is regarded as normally residing with the woman who has care and charge of him or her in the household of which he or she is normally a member and with no other person provided that where there is no such woman in that household, he or she shall be regarded as normally residing with the head of that household and with no other person. (Rules 4 and 5 are subject to Rules 7 and 8 below). Rule 7 provides that when the normal residence of a qualified child is to be determined under Rule 3 or 4 and the person with whom the child would thus be regarded as normally residing has abandoned or deserted him or her or has failed to contribute to his or her support, the relevant Rule shall cease to apply with respect of that child, and the person with whom the child shall be regarded as normally residing shall be determined in accordance with Rule 6. Rule 7 states that when the normal residence of a qualified child is to be determined under Rule 4 or 5, and the person with whom he or she would thus be regarded as normally residing has abandoned or deserted him or her or has failed to contribute to his or her support, the relevant Rule shall cease to apply with respect to that child, and the person with whom the child shall be regarded as normally residing shall be determined in accordance with Rule 6. Finally, Rule 8 states that when normal residence would be decided under Rule 4 or 5 above and when a qualified child has been placed in foster care, or with a relative by the Health Service Executive under section 36 of the Child Care Act of 1991, and has been in such care for a continuous period of six months, he or she shall be regarded as normally residing with the woman who has

364. As amended by S.I. No. 265 of 2000. *See* an appeals officer's decision on such an issue: *Social Welfare Appeals Office Report 2003*, 16–17. In *O v. Minister for Social Protection*, High Court, 2 Oct. 2020, Faherty J held that the denial of CB to the child's father, with whom the child was not resident, in circumstances in which the child's mother could not claim CB because she did not satisfy the habitual residence test, did not involve unlawful discrimination contrary to Art. 40.1 of the Constitution or Art. 14 ECHR. Neither was Art. 159 SW(CCP&C)R *ultra vires* because of this outcome and the fact that the father could not claim CB was not due to any unconstitutional omission in the 2005 Act.

care and charge of him or her in the household of which he or she is normally a member and with no other person, provided that when there is no such woman in that household, he or she shall be regarded as normally residing with the head of that household and with no other person.[365]

259. In summary, CB is normally payable to the mother (or stepmother), and it is the adult, not the child, who is entitled to the payment – *see Michael (a minor) v. Minister for Social Protection.*[366] However, when the child is living full-time with the father (or stepfather) only, then CB will be payable to the father. When the parents reside in separate households, CB is payable to the parent with whom the child resides the majority of the time. If the child resides 50% of the time with each parent, the mother is paid. When the parents are dead, the child has been abandoned, or the child is in foster care, CB is payable to the woman who has care and charge of the child in the household in which the child lives (or the head of the household when there is no such woman in the household). Finally, when a child is placed in an institution on a voluntary basis, CB is payable to the person who would normally get the benefit, provided that person is making adequate contributions towards the cost of the child's maintenance in the institution. When the child is placed in an institution as a result of a court order, CB is only payable if the child returns home on a regular basis.

§2. AMOUNT OF THE BENEFIT

260. CB of EUR 140 per month is payable in respect of each child, though increased payments are payable with respect to multiple births.[367] CB is not taxable.

§3. DISQUALIFICATIONS

261. Section 249(15) specifically provides that CB shall be paid only in the State.[368] However, this is frequently overridden by EU law on coordination of family benefits. In addition, where a qualified person is absent from the State, an application on his/her behalf for CB may be accepted from such person as the Minister thinks fit[369] The habitual residence condition (HRC) also applies to CB. In *Michael (a minor) v. Minister for Social Protection,*[370] the Supreme Court held that the denial of CB to asylum seekers, because they are not regarded as habitually resident in the State, was not unconstitutional as the State was entitled to impose restrictions on inward migration. In the same case, the European Court of Human Rights rejected the argument that the right-to-reside requirement was discriminatory under

365. Rule 8 inserted by S.I. No. 859 of 2007.
366. [2019] IESC 82.
367. Section 221 as amended.
368. Section 249.
369. Section 223.
370. [2019] IESC 82.

article 14 of the European Convention on Human Rights and held that the applicants in a relevantly similar position, in terms of legal status, to the chosen comparators, i.e., parents with a legal right to reside in Ireland.[371]

262. However, CB is a 'family benefit' under EU law and is subject to EU rules on coordination of benefits. Therefore, the HRC cannot be applied against a person covered by Regulation 883/2004 with regard to coordination of family benefits to disqualify him or her from benefits.

371. *X v. Ireland,* 23851/20 and 24360/20, 22 Jun. 2023.

Chapter 2. Increase for a Qualified Child

§1. Beneficiaries and Conditions

263. Entitlement to an increase with respect to a 'qualified child' is set out in the Act in the sections dealing with the main payment.[372] A 'qualified child' is defined as a person who is ordinarily resident in the State, is not detained in a children detention centre, and, in the case of long-term payments, is under the age of 18 or is over the age of 18 and under the age of 22 and is receiving full-time education, or, in the case of short-term payments, is under the age of 18 or who is over 18 for the three months immediately following the completion or leaving by the person of second-level education or the completion of the Leaving Certificate.[373]

264. When a person is in receipt of a social welfare payment, he or she will, in general,[374] be entitled to an increase with respect to a qualified child (IQC) who 'normally resides' with the person. The concept of normal residence is defined in Article 13 of the Social Welfare (Consolidated Claims, Payments and Control) Regulations of 2007. Article 13(2) provides that the person with whom a qualified child shall be regarded as normally residing is to be determined in accordance with the rules of priority set out in the following sub-articles:

(1) A qualified child shall, subject to sub-articles (4)–(11), be regarded as normally residing with his or her parents.[375]
(2) A qualified child who is resident with one parent only shall be regarded as normally residing with that parent and with no other person provided when that parent is a member of a household that the parent so elects.
(3) Notwithstanding that a qualified child does not reside with one of his or her parents, the qualified child may be regarded as normally residing with the parent who has custody of the child and who is contributing substantially to the child's maintenance.[376]
(4) Notwithstanding the provisions of sub-Article (4), a qualified child resident with one parent who is living apart from the other parent and who is not claiming or in receipt of benefit or assistance shall be regarded as residing with the other parent if that other parent is contributing substantially to the child's maintenance.
(5) If one parent dies, a qualified child shall be regarded as normally residing with the other parent, provided that that parent is maintaining the child.

---

372. For example, entitlement with jobseeker's benefit is set out in s. 66.
373. Section 2(3) as amended by SWMPA 2008, s. 9. During the latter three-month period, a person is disqualified for JA so the intention is to ensure that a person does not lose entitlement to an IQA while he or she is statutorily disqualified for JA.
374. Increases are not payable with working family payment (WFP), death benefit by way of parent's pension under the OIB scheme, guardian's payment, and WNCP (in the latter case because widow(er)s with dependent children will be entitled to OFP).
375. 'Parent' means a parent or step-parent.
376. Departmental guidelines take this to mean contributing at least the equivalent of the IQC (including, when appropriate, contributions in kind).

(6) When the normal residence of a qualified child is to be determined under sub-Article (6) or (7), and the person with whom the child would thus be regarded as normally residing has abandoned or deserted the child or failed to contribute substantially to the child's maintenance, sub-Article (6) or (7) shall cease to apply with respect to that child, and the person with whom the child shall be regarded as normally residing shall be determined in accordance with sub-Article (9).

(7) A qualified child whose normal residence does not fall under the foregoing sub-articles shall be regarded as normally residing with the head of the household of which the child is normally a member and with no other person.

(8) A qualified child who is a refugee within the State from another country shall be regarded as normally residing with the head of the household of which the child is for the time being a member and with no other person.

(9) When a qualified child is resident in an institution, the child shall be regarded as normally residing only with the person (if any) who contributes towards the cost of the child's maintenance in the institution, and with whom the child would, under this Article, be regarded as normally residing, if the child were not resident in an institution.

265. The 'normal residence' rules in relation to OFP are slightly different and are set out in Article 128. This Article provides that, for the purposes of OFP and subject to sub-Article (2), a qualified child is to be regarded as normally residing with a qualified parent when: (a) the child is resident with that parent, and (b) that parent has the main care and charge of the child.

266. Article 128(2) provides that a qualified child who is resident in an institution is regarded as normally residing with the qualified parent when that parent contributes towards the cost of the child's maintenance in the institution and with whom the child would, under sub-article (1), be regarded as normally residing if the child were not resident in an institution.

267. Finally, Article 128(3) provides that a qualified child may, in such circumstances as an officer of the Minister considers appropriate, be regarded as normally residing with the qualified parent who is resident in an institution. 'Institution' means: (a) a hospital, convalescent home, or home for persons suffering from a physical or mental disability or accommodation ancillary thereto; (b) any other similar establishment providing residence, maintenance, or care for the persons therein; or (c) any prison, place of detention, or other establishments to which Articles 218 and 219 of the Social Welfare (Consolidated Claims, Payment and Control) Regulations of 2007 apply.

§2. Amount of the Benefit

268. Increases with respect to a qualified child are now payable at two rates, one for children under the age of 12 (currently EUR 38 per week) and a higher rate for children over the age of 12 (currently EUR 45 per week). The increase, unlike CB, is payable to the person in receipt of the payment. In the case of a couple (i.e., a married couple who are living together or a man and woman cohabiting as husband and wife), a half-rate increase is payable when the spouse or partner is not a qualified adult of the claimant. Increases may be taxable, depending on the taxable status of the underlying payment.[377]

269. Increases with respect to a qualified child are not payable when (i) a weekly benefit or assistance (other than SWA),[378] (ii) an increase with respect to a qualified adult (IQA), or (iii) a further IQC is payable to or in respect of the same child in the same period.[379] The legislation now specifically allows the payment of an IQC and the guardian's payment (contributory) and (non-contributory) and OIB death benefit by way of pension at the same time.[380]

---

377. In *Ó Síocháin v. Neenan* [1999] I IR 533, the Supreme Court held that an IQC payable as part of the widow's (contributory) pension was the income of the widow for income tax purposes and, as widow's (contributory) pension is taxable, therefore, liable to tax.
378. Once off payments such as OIB funeral grant and widowed and SCP grant and the monthly DCA are excluded.
379. Section 247(2) as amended.
380. Section 247(2A)–(2B) inserted by SW(No.2)A 2019, s. 13.

Chapter 3. Guardian's Payment

§1. Beneficiaries and Conditions

270. There are two payments for orphaned or abandoned children:[381] contributory guardian's payment (formerly, orphan's contributory allowance) and non-contributory guardian's payment (formerly, orphan's non-contributory pension).[382]

271. The term 'orphan' is defined as meaning a qualified child:

(a) both of whose parents are dead; or
(b) one of whose parents is dead or unknown or has abandoned and failed to provide for the child and whose other parent:
 (i) is unknown; or
 (ii) has abandoned and failed to provide for the child

where that child is not residing with a parent, adoptive parent or step-parent.[383]

272. Thus, the definition of 'orphan' goes far beyond the strict meaning of the term and includes children, both of whose parents are alive when the parents have abandoned and failed to provide for the child. Formerly, the definition referred (in (b)(ii)) to one parent having abandoned *or* refused or failed to provide for the child. Under this definition, an appeals officer was able to find that a mother who was in prison, while she arguably had not 'abandoned' her children, had failed to provide for them, and they thus satisfied the statutory definition of 'orphan'.[384] However, this definition was altered in 2005 so that it now requires one parent to have abandoned *and* failed to provide, which would appear to involve a more onerous test.

381. Sections 130–133, 168, 169 and 171 of the 2005 Act as amended.
382. Renamed by SWLRPA 2006, s. 4.
383. Section 2. On the meaning of 'abandoned', *see* the appeals officers' decisions in *Social Welfare Appeals Office Report 2001*, 23–24; and *Social Welfare Appeals Office Report 2005*, 20–21 (although these tend to turn on the facts of the case rather than legal principles). In Case 2012/11, an Appeals Officer noted that there was nothing in the Social Welfare Acts indicating a minimum time that must pass before abandonment may be deemed to have occurred – *Social Welfare Appeals Office Annual Report*, 29. In Case 2015/04, an Appeals Officer ruled that abandonment included the failure of a parent to provide for the emotional and physical necessities in life so that even though the father in the instant case had paid occasional maintenance in respect of his children, they had still been abandoned by him for the purpose of the contributory guardian's payment – *Social Welfare Appeals Office Annual Report 2015*, 55. *See also* Case 2016/06 – *Social Welfare Appeals Office Annual Report 2016*, 55. In Case 2017/07, an Appeals Officer ruled that occasional contact and intermittent financial support cannot counteract what amounts to abandonment and failure to provide – *Social Welfare Appeals Office Annual Report 2017*, 53. The *Social Welfare Appeals Office Report 2013* states that Appeals Officers refer to the Supreme Court decision in *Northern Area Health Board v. An Bord Uchtála* [2002] IESC 75 in deciding whether a child has been 'abandoned'. *See also* Cases 2015/04, 2016/06 and 2017/07, cited above and Case 2018/318/70, *Social Welfare Appeals Office Annual Report 2018*, 146. However, this Supreme Court case concerns a different statutory context (the Adoption Acts), and it is not necessarily clear that it is appropriate to adopt the approach taken by the Court in this context to the interpretation of the term 'orphan'.
384. *Social Welfare Appeals Office Report 2003*, 19.

273. The contribution condition for contributory guardian's payment is that one of the following persons has qualifying contributions for not less than twenty-six contribution weeks:

(a) a parent of the orphan; or
(b) a step-parent of the orphan.[385]

274. Section 133 provides that contributory guardian's payment is to be paid to the guardian of the orphan to whom the allowance is payable. However, section 133(2) provides that contributory guardian's payment may, if the Minister thinks fit, be paid instead to some other person for the benefit of the orphan.

275. There are analogous provisions in relation to the means-tested non-contributory guardian's payment.[386] Section 168 provides that, subject to a means test, non-contributory guardian's payment shall be payable with respect to an orphan (as defined above). Unlike the contributory payment, the habitual residence rule applies to the non-contributory payment.[387]

§2. Amount of the Benefit

276. The rate of the benefit is set out in Part 1 of Schedule 2 of the Act. Guardian's payment is not payable for any period when a foster care allowance is made under Part VI of the Child Care Act of 1991 and regulations made thereunder.[388]

385. Section 131.
386. Sections 168–171.
387. Section 168(5) as amended by s. 11 SWPA 2014.
388. Sections 130(2) and 168(4) as amended by SWPA 2007, s. 17.

Chapter 4. Maternity Benefit

§1. Beneficiaries and Conditions

277. Section 47 provides that a woman is entitled to a maternity benefit when:[389]

(i) it is certified by a doctor (or otherwise to the satisfaction of the Minister) that it is expected that she will be confined in a specified week or that she has been confined;
(ii) in the case of an employed contributor, it is certified by her employer that she is entitled to leave under section 8 of the Maternity Protection Act of 1994;[390]
(iii) in the case of a self-employed person, she must have been in insurable self-employment; and
(iv) she satisfies the contribution conditions.[391]

278. 'Confinement' means labour resulting in the issue of a living child, labour after twenty-four weeks of pregnancy resulting in the issue of a child, whether alive or dead or labour resulting in the issue of a child who, at birth, weighs not less than 500 grams, whether alive or dead.[392] Maternity benefit is not payable to a commissioning woman in a surrogacy situation. In *Z v. A Government Department*, Case C-363/12, 18 March 2014, the Court of Justice ruled that EU law did not require the State to provide maternity or adoptive benefits to a commissioning mother whose genetic child was born through surrogacy. In *G v. Department of Social Protection* [2015] IEHC 419, O'Malley J held that a commissioning mother in a surrogacy situation could not rely on the Equal Status Acts to argue that the social welfare code discriminated unlawfully against her by not providing her with maternity benefit when such benefit is provided to birth and adoptive mothers.

279. In the event of the death of the mother following the week of her confinement and before the expiry of the payment to her of the maternity benefit to which she was entitled, the father has certain leave entitlements. When it is certified by his employer that a man who satisfies the contribution conditions is entitled to leave

389. Sections 47–51 and the SW(CCP&C)R, Arts 29–35, as amended.
390. Section 37.
391. The contribution requirements do not apply to a woman who was in receipt of health and safety benefit at any time during pregnancy: s. 47(2). Departmental guidelines state that a person who is pregnant but who does not satisfy these contribution conditions and who is not in receipt of wages from her employer may be considered to satisfy the conditions of being available for and genuinely seeking employment during pregnancy including her confinement in hospital or at home unless there are other factors that could call into question her general availability for work. Accordingly, such persons may qualify for jobseeker's benefit or allowance.
392. Section 51(1)(a) as amended by s. 5 SW(No.2)A 2019. For the UK case law on this issue, *see* Nicholas Wikeley, Anthony Ogus & Eric Barendt, *The Law of Social Security*, 5th ed. (London: Butterworths, 2002), 561.

under the Maternity Protection Act, then he shall be entitled to benefit similar to that if he were a woman who was entitled to maternity leave.[393]

280. An employed person must have: (a) at least thirty-nine contributions paid in the twelve months before the first day of maternity leave, or having been in insurable self-employment, she satisfies the contribution conditions for self-employed women, or (b) at least thirty-nine contributions paid since first starting work and either at least thirty-nine contributions paid or credited in either the second-last complete contribution year before the beginning of the benefit year in which she claims maternity benefit or in a subsequent complete contribution year before the first day on which she claims such benefit or at least twenty-six contributions paid in each of the second- and third-last contribution years.[394] A self-employed claimant must have fifty-two qualifying contributions paid in the second- or third-last complete contribution year or in a subsequent complete contribution year before the first day on which she claims such benefit or, where she was previously an employed contributor, at least thirty-nine employment contributions in the twelve months immediately before the first day for which maternity benefit is claimed.

§2. Amount of the Benefit

281. The weekly rate of maternity benefit is the amount of IB which the claimant would receive if she was entitled to that benefit or EUR 262, whichever is greater.[395] Payment of the benefit is for a maximum of twenty-six weeks, beginning not later than two weeks before the end of the expected week of confinement and ending not earlier than four weeks thereafter.[396] In the case of premature births, the period of entitlement is extended for a period equivalent to the duration between the actual date of birth of the baby and two weeks before the expected date of confinement – section 15 of the SWA 2017. There is an optional additional sixteen weeks leave under the Maternity Protection Act, but benefit is not payable during this period.

§3. Disqualifications

282. A woman is disqualified for a maternity benefit during any period for which the benefit is payable in which she engages in any occupation other than domestic duties in her own household or when she fails, without good cause, to attend or submit to medical examinations.[397] The standard detention in legal custody and absence

393. Section 47(4) as amended by SWA 2005, s. 7.
394. Section 48. Volunteer development workers only need at least thirty-nine qualifying contributions since entry into insurance and before the first day of maternity leave – Art. 31 of S.I. No. 142 of 2007.
395. Section 49(1) as amended by SWA 2022, s. 5.
396. Section 47(5) as amended by SWA 2006, s. 7 with effect from 1 Mar. 2007.
397. Section 40.

from the state disqualifications[398] also apply to a maternity benefit, although the latter is subject to so many exceptions as to be almost meaningless in practice.[399] A maternity benefit is payable in the following circumstances to claimants who are absent from the state: (i) during such period as the Minister may allow, having regard to the circumstances of the case, if the absence is temporary and for the specific purpose of receiving treatment for incapacity that commenced before the person left the State; (ii) while she is a person who is 'posted' under Article 98 of the Social Welfare (Consolidated Contributions and Insurability) Regulations of 1996 (SW(CCI)R of 1996);[400] and (iii) while on holidays for a period or periods not exceeding six weeks in total during the period of entitlement to the benefit.[401]

283. A woman is disqualified for a maternity benefit during any period for which the benefit is payable in which she engages in any occupation other than domestic duties in her own household or when she fails, without good cause, to attend or submit to medical examinations. She will also be disqualified while imprisoned or detained in legal custody except where she is detained for the treatment of mental illness or infectious disease (though the disqualification does apply to a woman who is found not guilty by reason of insanity pursuant to the Criminal Law (Insanity) Act 2006) – Article 218(1)(a) of SI No. 142 of 2007. The disqualification of convicted prisoners for maternity benefit would appear to be unconstitutional in light of *PC v. Minister for Social Protection* [2017] IESC 63.

A claimant will also be disqualified if s/he participates in a Community Employment scheme that commences after 16 January 2012[402] or in a Solas scheme or national internship scheme.[403] In addition, persons who are employed abroad and continue to be insured under the SW Acts may be paid a maternity benefit. Finally, a maternity benefit may be paid to a claimant in the other EU Member States in accordance with Council Regulation 883/2004.

398. Though the disqualification of convicted prisoners would appear to be unconstitutional in light of *PC v. Minister for Social Protection* [2017] IESC 63.
399. Section 249.
400. SW(CCP&C)R, Art. 217(c).
401. S.I. No. 12 of 2017.
402. Section 247B.
403. Section 247A.

Chapter 5. Adoptive Benefit and Health and Safety Benefit

284. Adoptive benefit is analogous to a maternity benefit and is paid for a continuous period of twenty-four weeks from the placement of the child to an adoptive parent.[404] Section 58(1) of the 2005 Act, as amended by section 10 of the Family Leave and Miscellaneous Provisions Act 2021 (FLMPA), provides that an adopting parent is a qualifying adopter or a surviving parent. A qualifying adopter is, in relation to an employed contributor, (a) the member of an adopting couple (of whom neither is the mother or father of the child) who is an employee and who is chosen by the couple to be the qualifying adopter or (b) in any other case, an employee, who is not a surviving parent in relation to the child, who is adopting a child. In relation to self-employed contributors, a qualifying adopter is (a) the member of an adopting couple (of whom neither is the mother or father of the child) who is chosen by the couple to be the qualifying contributor and in whose care the child has been placed or (b) in any other case, a person who is not a surviving parent who is adopting a child. A couple for these purposes is defined as 'a married couple, a couple who are civil partners of each other or a cohabiting couple',[405] while a surviving parent is a spouse, civil partner or cohabitant of a qualifying adopter where the qualifying adopter has died.[406]

285. A person is disqualified for receipt of adoptive benefit while s/he is imprisoned or detained in legal custody though the disqualification of convicted prisoners would appear to be unconstitutional in light of *PC v. Minister for Social Protection* [2017] IESC 63.

286. Health and Safety Benefit is a weekly payment to women who are granted health and safety leave under the Maternity Protection Act of 1994.[407] Health and safety leave is granted to an employee by her employer when the employer cannot remove a risk to the employee's health or safety during her pregnancy or while she is breastfeeding or cannot assign her alternative safe employment. Under the Maternity Protection Act of 1994, such an employee is entitled to health and safety pay from her employer for the first twenty-one days of leave followed by a health and safety benefit (if the qualification conditions are satisfied).

404. Sections 58–61 as amended.

405. Section 2 of the Adoptive Leave Act 1995 as amended by s. 5(a) of the FLMPA 2021.

406. Section 2 of the Adoptive Leave Act 1995 as amended by s. 5(a) of the FLMPA 2021 (in relation to employed contributors) and s. 58(1) of the 2005 Act as amended by s. 10(a) of the FLMPA 2021 (in relation to self-employed contributors).

407. Sections 52–56 as amended by SWMPA 2008, s. 16. Adopted in implementation of EU Directive (92/85/EC) on the introduction of measures to encourage improvements in the safety and health at work of pregnant workers and workers who have recently given birth or are breastfeeding.

Chapter 6. Paternity Benefit

§1. Beneficiaries and Conditions

287. Paternity benefit is payable to a relevant parent, other than the mother of the child, in respect of a period during which that parent provides care in relation to a child.[408] In the case of an employee, the employer must certify that the relevant parent is entitled to paternity leave under the Paternity Leave and Benefit Act 2016[409] (though paternity benefit is also payable to persons employed abroad as volunteer development workers who have at least thirty-nine paid contributions since their entry into insurance).[410] Where the relevant parent is self-employed and the child in question is being adopted, a certificate of placement must be issued in relation to the child. Alternatively, a declaration of eligibility and suitability must be issued in relation to the child and particulars in writing provided of the day of placement or expected day or placement.[411] In the case of a person in insurable self-employment, the relevant parent in a couple who is adopting is the member of the couple concerned who is chosen by the couple to be the relevant parent for this purpose.[412] A couple for this purpose is a married couple, a couple who are civil partners of each other or a cohabiting couple. Where the relevant parent is self-employed and is the father of the child or spouse, civil partner or cohabitant of the mother of the child or a parent of the child under section 5 of the Children and Family Relationships Act 2015 where the child is a donor-conceived child, it must be certified by a registered medical practitioner, or otherwise to the Minister's satisfaction, that it is expected that the child's mother will be confined in a week specified in the certificate or that the mother has been confined.[413] The contribution conditions for paternity benefit are the same as for maternity benefit except that the first option for satisfying contribution conditions for maternity benefit, viz., having at least 30 paid contributions in the twelve months before the first day of leave or having been in insurable self-employment, the claimant satisfies the contribution conditions for self-employed claimants, does not apply.[414]

§2. Amount and Duration of Benefit

288. Paternity Benefit is equivalent to the amount of IB that the claimant would receive if s/he was entitled to that benefit or EUR 262 per week,[415] whichever is the greater and in the case of an employee, is payable for the period of paternity leave

408. Section 61A–E, inserted by s. 31 of the Parental Leave and Benefit Act 2016, as amended, and S.I. No. 442 of 2016.
409. Section 61B(1)(a) inserted by s. 31 of the Parental Leave and Benefit Act 2016.
410. *See* Art. 5 of S.I. No. 442 of 2016.
411. Section 61B(1)(b)(i).
412. Section 61A(1) as amended by s. 12 of the FLMPA 2021.
413. Section 61B(1)(b)(ii).
414. Section 61C.
415. Section 61D as amended by SWA 2022, s. 7.

to which the parent is entitled under the 2016 Act or, in the case of a surviving parent, the amount of transferred paternity leave to which s/he is entitled under the 2016 Act.[416] Paternity benefit in all other cases is payable for a maximum of two consecutive weeks, commencing any time within six months of the birth or adoption of the child.[417] Where a self-employed person becomes entitled to maternity benefit or adoptive benefit, payment of paternity benefit is postponed to the day immediately after the last day for which maternity or adoptive benefit is claimed.[418] Where a self-employed person is entitled to paternity benefit where it is certified that the mother of the child will be confined in a specified week, payment may be postponed in the event that the date of confinement occurs after the expected week of confinement.[419] Payment may also be postponed for a maximum period of six months when the child in relation to whom the relevant parent is entitled to paternity benefit is hospitalized.[420]

§3. Disqualifications

289. Regulations may provide for disqualifying a person from receiving paternity benefit where, during the period for which benefit is payable, the parent engages in any form of insurable employment, insurable (occupational injuries) employment, insurable self-employment, any employment referred to in paragraphs 1, 2, 3 or 6 of Part 2 of Schedule 1 to the 2005 Act or any self-employment referred to in paragraph 1 or 5 of Part 3 of Schedule 1 to the 2005 Act.[421] A claimant will also be disqualified while he is absent from the State other than on holidays for a period or periods not exceeding two weeks in total during the period of entitlement to the benefit. A claimant is also disqualified if s/he is imprisoned or detained in legal custody except where s/he is detained for the treatment of mental illness or infectious disease (though it does apply to a person who is found not guilty by reason of insanity pursuant to the Criminal Law (Insanity) Act 2006) – Article 218(1)(a) of SI No. 142 of 2007. The disqualification of convicted prisoners for paternity benefit would appear to be unconstitutional in light of *PC v. Minister for Social Protection* [2017] IESC 63. In addition, a claimant will be disqualified if s/he participates in a Community Employment scheme that commences after 16 January 2012[422] or in a Solas scheme or national internship scheme.[423]

---

416. Section 61B(7)(a).
417. Section 61B(7)(b)–(c).
418. Section 61B(8).
419. Section 61B(9) and Art. 5 of S.I. No. 442 of 2016.
420. Section 61B(10) and Art. 5 of S.I. No. 442 of 2016.
421. Section 61E and Art. 5 of S.I. No. 442 of 2016.
422. Section 247B.
423. Section 247A.

Chapter 7. Parent's Benefit

§1. Beneficiaries and Conditions

290. Parent's Benefit is payable to each parent of a child under the age of two or of a child who has been placed with them for adoption within the previous 104 weeks where (a) the relevant parent is (i) an employed contributor and it is certified by the relevant employer that s/he is entitled to parent's leave under the Parent's Leave and Benefit Act 2019 or (ii) is in insurable self-employment, (b) in either case, the relevant parent satisfies the prescribed contribution conditions and (c) the parent uses the leave to provide care and assistance to the child.[424] Where the relevant parent dies, the outstanding benefit is transferred to the surviving parent.[425] Where the surviving parent is an employee, this arises where the relevant parent died on or before the expiration of the period of entitlement concerned and where the surviving parent's employer certifies that the employee is entitled to transferred parent's leave under section 16(1) of the 2019 Act. Where the surviving parent is not an employee, this arises where the relevant parent died before the expiry of the 104th week following the date of birth or placement of the child. The surviving parent is entitled to the benefit to which the deceased parent was entitled, less any benefit already paid to that parent. The contribution conditions are the same as for maternity benefit.[426]

§2. Amount and Duration

291. The weekly rate of Parent's Benefit is an amount equal to the greater of the amount of IB which the claimant would receive if entitled to that benefit or EUR 262.[427] Parent's Benefit may be claimed concurrently with the Back to Work Family Dividend. A parent is only entitled to one Parent's Benefit in respect of any one child, and where the birth of the child is part of multiple births of two or more children or where a person adopts two or more children at the same time, only one Parent's Benefit is payable to the relevant parent in respect of the children concerned.[428] However, where a child had been adopted, the fact that another party obtained Parent's Benefit in respect of the child prior to its adoption shall not prevent a relevant parent claiming Parent's Benefit in respect of the child after its adoption.[429] This benefit is payable for a continuous period of seven weeks or for seven separate periods of leave, each consisting of not less than one week.[430]

424. Section 61F–J, inserted by s. 29 of the Parent's Leave and Benefit Act 2019, as amended, and S.I. No. 554 of 2019.
425. Section 61G(11).
426. Section 61H.
427. Section 61I as amended by SWA 2022, s. 9.
428. Section 61G(5).
429. Section 61G(6).
430. Section 61G(10) as amended by s. 15 of the FLMPA 2021 and s .8 of SWA 2021, commenced by S.I. No. 334 of 2022.

292. Where the child is hospitalized, payment of the benefit may be postponed for up to six months but not longer than seven days immediately after the day of discharge of the child. In the case of a parent who is self-employed, payment may be postponed for up to twelve weeks where seasonal variations in the volume of work in his or her business, profession or vocation means that s/he cannot claim the benefit within the period of 104 weeks from the date of birth or placement of the child.[431] Where the relevant parent is an employee, payment may be postponed by a period of up to twelve weeks where parent's leave has been postponed pursuant to section 13 of the Act because the taking of leave would have a substantial adverse effect on the operation of the employer's business, profession or vocation.[432] Where parent's leave has been postponed because the parent could not take leave within two years of the date of the child's birth or placement due to the requirement to give six weeks' notice of the intention to take leave, benefit may also be postponed for up to six weeks.[433] The death of the child does not affect entitlement to Parent's Benefit.[434] Parent's Benefit is payable in respect of all children born or placed for adoption after 1 November 2019.

§3. Disqualifications

293. The grounds for disqualification in respect of Parent's Benefit are the same as for Paternity Benefit.[435]

431. Section 61G(15) as amended by s. 15 of the FLMPA 2021.
432. Section 61G(16)(b) and Art. 5 of S.I. No. 554 of 2019.
433. Section 61G(16)(a) as amended by s. 15 of the FLMPA 2021 and Art. 5 of S.I. No. 554 of 2019.
434. Section 61G(14).
435. Section 61J and Arts 5 and 6 of S.I. No. 554 of 2019.

Chapter 8. Parental Leave

294. The Parental Leave Acts 1998–2019 make provision for *unpaid* leave for fathers and mothers to look after young children. Parental leave may be taken either as a continuous block of twenty-six weeks or, with the agreement of the employer, broken up over a period of time. The Acts also provide for limited paid leave (force majeure leave), which must not exceed three days in any twelve consecutive months, or five days in any thirty-six consecutive months, to enable employees to deal with family emergencies resulting from injury or illness of a family member. Parents who take parental leave may be entitled to receive a credited contribution for each week taken. This will ensure that their existing coverage for social welfare benefits is fully maintained.

Chapter 9. Payments to Qualified Adults

§1. Beneficiaries and Conditions

295. In the case of most weekly social welfare payments, an increase is payable when the claimant has a qualified adult. This entitlement is provided for in the chapter of the Acts dealing with individual payment.[436] State pension (non-contributory) and blind pension (BP) have different rules, which are outlined in Part VIII. A somewhat different approach also applies in relation to SWA (*see* Part X). An IQA is not payable with CA or benefit, nor with a maternity benefit. IQAs are not payable with the lone parents' and widow(er)s' payments.

296. Section 2(2), as amended, defines a 'qualified adult', subject to sections 134 (bereavement grants), 187 (SWA), and 297 (tapered IQAs), as meaning, in relation to any person:

(a) a spouse, civil partner or cohabitant of that person[437] who is wholly or mainly maintained by that person but does not include:
  (i) a spouse, civil partner or cohabitant of that person in employment (other than subsidiary employment or employment of inconsiderable extent as specified in paragraph 4 or 5 of Part 2 of Schedule 1);
  (ii) a spouse, civil partner or cohabitant of that person who is self-employed;
  (iii) a spouse, civil partner or cohabitant of that person who is entitled to, or is in receipt of, any benefit, pension, assistance, or allowance (other than half-rate CA payable under section 186A or SWA) under Part 2 or 3 of the Act;
  (iv) a spouse, civil partner or cohabitant of that person who, by virtue of the provisions of section 68(1) or 147(2) (relating to trade disputes), is or would be disqualified for receiving JB, JB (self-employed) or jobseeker's allowance in his or her own right with the exception of a spouse who qualifies as a qualified adult by virtue of regulations made under paragraph (c);
  (v) a spouse, civil partner or cohabitant of that person who is entitled to or is in receipt of an allowance, the rate of which is related to the rates of JB, JB (self-employed) or jobseeker's allowance with respect to an approved course of training;
  (vi) a spouse, civil partner or cohabitant of that person who is entitled to or in receipt of an allowance with respect to participation in the Vocational Training Opportunities Scheme (VTOS);
  (vii) a spouse, civil partner or cohabitant of that person who is entitled to or in receipt of an allowance with respect to participation in the Back-to Education Allowance, Back-to-Work Allowance, Back-to-Work Enterprise Allowance, Part-Time Job Incentive or the national internship scheme;

436. For example, entitlement to an IQA in the case of illness benefit is set out in s. 43.
437. References to civil partner, etc., are inserted by SWPA 2010, s. 15.

(viii) a spouse, civil partner or cohabitant of that person, where that person is in receipt of jobseeker's allowance, and the spouse, civil partner or cohabitant is a participant under a Community Employment scheme.[438]

(b) a person over the age of 16 years being wholly or mainly maintained by that person and having the care of one or more than one qualified child who normally resides with that person when that person is (i) a single person, (ii) a widow, (iii) a widower; (iv) a married person who is not living with and is neither wholly or mainly maintaining, nor being wholly or mainly maintained by, such married person's spouse; or (v) an SCP, or (vi) a civil partner who is not living with and is neither wholly or mainly maintaining, nor being wholly or mainly maintained by, his or her civil partner;[439]

(c) any person whom the Minister may by Regulations specify to be a qualified adult for the purposes of the Act.

297. For the purposes of determining entitlement to an IQA,[440] 'spouse' means each person of a married couple who are living together, and (b) 'civil partner' means each civil partner of a couple who are both parties to a civil partnership who are living together. Also, for these purposes, references to a spouse or civil partner in the definition of 'qualified adult' contained in section 2(2) and regulations made under that provision shall be read as including a party to a marriage or civil partnership (as appropriate) that has been dissolved, being a dissolution that is recognized as valid in the State.[441]

298. Section 2(2)(a) would have meant that any person who was in employment (other than subsidiary employment or employment of inconsiderable extent) or self-employment or in receipt of most social welfare payments was not classified as a qualified adult, even if he or she was 'wholly or mainly maintained' by the claimant. However, in the exercise of the power provided under section 2(2)(c), Regulations provide that a spouse who is wholly or mainly maintained by a person is, subject to sections 187 and 297, a qualified adult in relation to that person, when the spouse is: (i) in employment or self-employment; or (ii) entitled to or in receipt of disablement benefit, death benefit, half-rate CA (under section 186A), guardian's payment (contributory) and (non-contributory), and to no other benefit or assistance (other than SWA).[442]

299. A person (being one of a couple) is generally considered to be wholly or mainly maintaining his or her spouse, civil partner or cohabitant when the weekly

---

438. As inserted by s. 3 SWA 2022.
439. As amended by SWPA 2010, s. 15. Arguably it might have been preferable to have reviewed the definition of qualified adult rather than simply adding civil partners to a rather complex structure.
440. The specific sections where this applies are listed in s. 3(10) as substituted by SWPA 2010, s. 16.
441. Section 3(11) as substituted by SWPA 2010, s. 16.
442. SW(CCP&C)R, Art. 6 as substituted by S.I. No. 604 of 2011 and amended by S.I. No 616 of 2022. Though, however, sensible as it might be, one might question whether it is *intra vires* the Minister to include persons who are specifically excluded by the primary legislation.

income of that spouse, civil partner or cohabitant does not exceed EUR 100.[443] However, a person in receipt of jobseeker's allowance, DA or FA who is one of a couple is regarded as wholly or mainly maintaining his or her spouse, civil partner or cohabitant, though in the case of a claimant of JA, not where the spouse, civil partner or cohabitant commenced participating in a Community Employment scheme on or after 1 January 2023.[444] A person who is one of a married couple who are not living together is considered to be wholly or mainly maintaining his or her spouse when that spouse is not cohabiting with another person as husband and wife, and that spouse's weekly income does not exceed EUR 100, and the person is contributing towards the maintenance of his or her spouse by a weekly amount that is equal to or in excess of the amount of the IQA payable with jobseeker's allowance. Thus, this provision brings within the definition of 'qualified adult', a person who is in employment or self-employment but whose income does not exceed EUR 100 per week and who is wholly or mainly maintained by the claimant (as defined above). It also includes persons who are in receipt of the limited number of social welfare payments with specific purposes outlined in Article 6(b).

300. A person who is: (i) a single person, (ii) a widow, (iii) a widower, (iv) a married person who is not living with and is neither wholly or mainly maintaining, nor being wholly or mainly maintained by, such married person's spouse, (v) an SCP or (vi) a civil partner who is not living with and is neither wholly or mainly maintaining, nor being wholly or mainly maintained by, his or her civil partner, is considered to be wholly or mainly maintaining another person when that other person, being over the age of 16 years of age and having the care of one or more than one qualified child of the first-mentioned person, resides with the first-mentioned person and his or her weekly income does not exceed EUR 100.[445] This provision provides a definition of 'wholly or mainly maintaining' for the purposes of section 2(2)(b).

301. Weekly income is calculated:

(a) insofar as it comprises earnings from employment as an employee, by reference to the weekly average of the gross amount of all such earnings received in the previous two months when earnings are received monthly or in the previous six weeks when earnings are received weekly or fortnightly;
(b) insofar as it comprises income from any form of self-employment, by reference to the weekly amount of such income calculated by dividing the income in the last complete income tax year by fifty-two;
(c) insofar as it consists of income from property (other than property referred to in paragraph (d)) that is invested or otherwise put to profitable use or is capable of

---

443. SW(CCP&C)R, Art. 7 as substituted by S.I. No. 604 of 2011. As a result of the introduction of the 'half-rate' carer's allowance, S.I. No. 700 of 2007 introduced specific rules as regards JA, DA, and farm assistance. *See* now Art. 3 of S.I. No. 604 of 2011.
444. *See* S.I. No. 128 of 2023.
445. SW(CCP&C)R, Art. 7. As a result of the introduction of the 'half-rate' carer's allowance, S.I. No. 700 of 2007 introduced specific rules as regards JA, DA, and farm assistance in SW(CCP&C)R, Art. 7(2A).

being but is not invested or put to profitable use, by reference to a week of the yearly value of the property, calculated as follows:

(i) the first EUR 20,000 of the capital value of the property shall be excluded;

(ii) the weekly value of so much of the capital value of the property as exceeds EUR 20,000 but does not exceed EUR 30,000 shall be assessed at EUR 1 per each EUR 1,000; and

(iii) the weekly value of so much of the capital value of the property as exceeds EUR 30,000 but does not exceed EUR 40,000 shall be assessed at EUR 2 per each EUR 1,000; and

(iv) the weekly value of so much of the capital value of the property as exceeds EUR 40,000 shall be assessed at EUR 4 per each EUR 1,000; and

(d) insofar as it consists of income from any other source (including rent or any other periodical payment receivable for the possession and use of property in all lands, tenements and hereditaments), by reference to the normal weekly amount of such income;[446]

(e) in relation to claims for State pension, income or property of which a person deprives himself or herself in order to qualify for an IQA or a higher rate of IQA than that which should otherwise be paid shall be taken into account in assessing weekly income.[447]

302. In calculating this weekly income, any sums received by way of disablement benefit, death benefit, 'half-rate' CA, CB, guardian's payment (contributory) and (non-contributory), DCA or any sum received by way of payment from the HSE in respect of a child boarded out are disregarded.[448] Compensation awards made by the Hepatitis C Compensation Tribunal and the HIV Compensation Tribunal, together with judicial awards to compensate people who contracted either such illness from the use of certain blood products, are similarly disregarded, as are awards made by the Residential Institutions Redress Board, awards paid to people with disabilities caused by Thalidomide, awards paid under the Health (Repayment Scheme) Act 2006, payments made by the Residential Institutions Statutory Fund Board, payments made to women who worked in the Magdalen Laundries and payments made by the Stardust Victims' Compensation Tribunal or made pursuant to recommendations proposed by the Scoping Inquiry into the CervicalCheck Screening Programme, payments made under a package of support measures for women diagnosed with cervical cancer since 2008, payments made under the Lourdes Hospital Redress Scheme, the Lourdes Hospital Payment Scheme and the Surgical Symphysiotomy Scheme, bursaries from the Department of Education and Skills 1916 Bursary Fund, University Higher Educational Scholarships for adult learners to a maximum value of EUR 7,000, payments made by Sports Ireland under the International Carding Scheme, payments made by the N. Ireland Victims and Survivors'

446. SW(CCP&C)R, Art. 8.

447. SW(CCP&C)R, Art. 8(1A) as inserted by Art. 3 of S.I. No. 616 of 2011. This does not apply to an assignment of a farm of land of which the assignor is the owner and/or occupier only to a child or children of the assignor – Art. 8(1B). Where the income or value of the property assessed under sub-Art. 1A has reduced since the date of calculation, the calculation may be revised downwards – Art. 8(1C).

448. SW(CCP&C)R, Art. 8(2) as amended by Art. 3 of S.I. No. 447 of 2012.

Service in accordance with the Victims and Survivors (N. Ireland) Order 2006 and Special Transport Grants made as part of the School Transport Scheme for Children with Special Educational Needs.[449] A deciding officer or appeals officer who considers that the periods mentioned in Article 8 would not be appropriate in any case to determine the amount of weekly income may have regard to such other periods that appear to be appropriate for that purpose – Article 8(4).

303. The definition of 'qualified adult' covers three different groups of person: (i) spouses (including cohabitees) who are wholly or mainly dependent on the claimant (subject to the list of exclusions set out above, including those in employment, self-employment, or in receipt of social welfare and certain other allowances); (ii) persons over sixteen who are caring for the claimant's child(ren); and (iii) spouses specified by regulations to be qualified adults, that is, persons wholly or mainly maintained by the claimant who are in employment or self-employment but are earning less than EUR 100 per week.

304. In the case of section 2(2)(b), a lower age limit of 16 is provided. However, no specific age limit is set in relation to subsections (a) and (c). Departmental guidelines suggest that, while social welfare legislation does not specify the age at which a person has to be to be considered a qualified adult, it is reasonable for deciding officers to refuse to award an IQA for a person under age 18 on the basis that he or she is not an adult (except when he or she is legally married or in section 2(2)(b) cases). This is on the basis, *inter alia*, of the fact that legal definitions of an 'adult' include 'a person who attains full age' and of the age of majority as 'age 18 years or, if married before that age, age on marriage'. It might, however, be preferable to underpin this approach in legislation, given the fact that, in some cases, persons under the age of 18 are considered to be 'adults' for the purposes of an IQA.

305. When a claimant or beneficiary of IB, JB, injury benefit, incapacity supplement, IP, State pension (contributory), jobseeker's allowance, FA, or DA would be entitled to an increase with respect to his or her spouse but for the fact that the spouse's weekly income exceeds the prescribed limit and the spouse's weekly income is less than a maximum amount (currently EUR 250 per week), a tapered rate of increase is payable, depending on the precise level of income. This is to ensure that persons whose income is somewhat over the basic EUR 100 per week limit do not lose the entire IQA.[450]

§2. Amount of the Benefit

306. The rate of the IQA varies from scheme to scheme and is currently set at about 66%–70% of the main rate. However, in the case of qualified adults over the pension age, the IQA is somewhat higher, and the objective has been set to increase this to the full State pension (non-contributory) rate over time.

449. SW(CCP&C)R, Art. 8(3) as amended.
450. Section 297 and SW(CCP&C)R, Arts 9–11.

§3. DISQUALIFICATIONS

307. An IQA is not normally payable to a person who is absent from the State/ resides outside the State or is undergoing detention in legal custody, but this rule is subject to certain exceptions.[451]

451. Section 249. *See* paras 756 and 782.

Chapter 10. OFP and Lone Parents' Payments

308. One-parent family payment (OFP) is a means-tested payment that is made to men or women who are caring for a child or children without the support of a partner.[452] Social Welfare Miscellaneous Provisions Act (SWMPA) 2010 introduced an important reform of the OFP scheme whereby it is payable only where the claimant has at least one child aged up to 7 (or up to 16 in certain limited circumstances).[453] (As long as a claimant has at least one child under the relevant age, s/he may claim for older children up to the age of 18 or 22, where the dependant is in full-time education).

§1. Beneficiaries and Conditions

309. To qualify for OFP, a person must be a 'qualified parent'. A 'qualified parent', subject to regulations under section 177, is defined as:

(a) a widow;
(b) a widower;
(c) a separated spouse;
(d) an unmarried person;
(e) a person whose spouse or civil partner has been committed in custody to prison or place of detention for not less than six months;
(f) an SCP;
(g) a civil partner who is not living with the other civil partner of the civil partnership, or
(h) a person who is not a party to a civil partnership;

who is the parent, step-parent, adoptive parent, or legal guardian of at least one relevant child who normally resides with that person.[454] He or she must not have

452. The main provisions are set out in ss 172–178 of the Act and the SW(CCP&C)R, Arts 124–130.
453. A person who does not qualify for OFP because his/her youngest child has reached a prescribed age threshold may claim Jobseeker's Allowance where the youngest child is not yet 14 and the claimant is not a cohabitant – s. 148A as inserted by s. 10 of the Social Welfare and Pensions (Miscellaneous Provisions) Act 2013, and as amended by s. 5 of the Social Welfare (Miscellaneous Provisions) Act 2015. *See* further, para. 508. A person qualifying for Jobseeker's Allowance also qualifies for credited contributions – *see* S.I. No. 243 of 2013. Where a claimant of OFP is in employment or self-employment on the date his or her youngest child reaches the prescribed age threshold, s/he may apply for Back-to-Work Family Dividend, as to which, *see* paras 538 et seq. This payment may also be claimed by, *inter alia*, a person who ceases to claim or be entitled to OFP by reason of the claimant being in employment or self-employment or commencing employment or self-employment within four weeks of the date of ceasing to claim or be entitled to OFP.
454. Section 172(1) as substituted by s. 13 of the SWMPA 2008 and amended by SWPA 2010, s. 20 and SWPA 2011, s. 9. For the definitions of 'civil partner', etc., *see* para. 250. Anyone who, as a result of the war in Ukraine, has come to Ireland from Ukraine with their children but without their spouse

attained pensionable age.[455] A widow(er) who has remarried or entered into a civil partnership is *not* regarded as a widow(er) of his or her former spouse for these purposes.[456] Likewise, an SCP who enters into a new civil partnership or marries is not regarded as an SCP of his or her former civil partner.[457] Conversely, an otherwise qualified parent does not cease to be so because of the fact that (i) the person's marriage has been dissolved, being a dissolution that is recognized as valid in the State, or (ii) the person's civil partnership has been dissolved, being a dissolution that is recognized as valid in the State.[458]

310. Separated Spouse or Civil Partner: A person is to be regarded as being a separated spouse or civil partner if he or she and his or her spouse or civil partner have lived apart from one another for a continuous period of at least three months immediately preceding the date of his or her claim for OFP and continue to so live apart.[459]

311. The term 'lived apart' is one that is featured in family law in both this jurisdiction (in section 5 of the Family Law (Divorce) Act of 1996) and in the UK and has received extensive judicial consideration. There would appear to be no reason why this would not also be relevant in the area of social welfare law. In *McA v. McA*,[460] the High Court discussed the meaning of the term and followed the approach adopted in the English case of *Santos v. Santos*.[461] McCracken J held that the phrase 'lived apart' must be construed as meaning something more than mere physical separation. He stated:

> Marriage is not primarily concerned with where the spouses live or whether they live under the same roof, and indeed there can be a number of circumstances in which the matrimonial relationship continues even though the parties are not living under the same roof as, for example, where one party is in a hospital or an institution of some kind or is obliged to spend a great deal of time away from home in the course of his or her employment. Such separations do not necessarily constitute the persons as living apart from one another. Clearly, there must be something more than mere physical separation, and the mental or intellectual attitude of the parties is also of considerable relevance. I do not think one can look solely either at where the parties physically reside

or partner and who has temporary protection under Council Directive 2001/15/EC is entitled to OPFP as a separated or unmarried person as long as the Directive remains in force – S.I. No. 355 of 2023.

455. Section 173 as substituted by SWLRPA 2006, s. 22 and amended by SWPA 2011, s. 9.
456. Section 172(2)(b) as substituted by SWPA 2010, s. 20.
457. Section 172(2)(ba) as inserted by SWPA 2010, s. 20.
458. Section 172(3)(c) as substituted by SWPA 2010, s. 20.
459. Article 125 and Art. 125A as inserted by Art. 2 of S.I. No. 355 of 2023.
460. [2001] 1 IR 457. This case has been followed by an appeals officer: *see Social Welfare Appeals Office Annual Report 2001*, 23.
461. [1972] 2 All ER 246.

or at their mental or intellectual attitude towards the marriage. Both of these elements must be considered and in conjunction with each other.[462]

312. Accordingly, he had 'no doubt that, just as parties who are physically separated may in fact maintain their full matrimonial relationship, equally parties who live under the same roof may be living apart from one another'. An appeals officer held that when an emotional bond subsisted between the spouses, a person could not be considered separated solely because her husband, who had been deported from Ireland by the Minister for Justice, was separated from her by 'geography and circumstance'.[463]

313. Unmarried Person: A person is to be regarded as being an unmarried person if, not being a married person or a party to a civil partnership, he or she is the parent of a qualified child. The term 'parent' is deemed to include the adoptive parent, in the case of a child who has been adopted under the Adoption Acts of 1952 to 1991 (or under such other form of adoption as the Minister considers appropriate in the circumstances).[464]

314. Prisoner's Spouse or civil partner: A person is to be regarded as being a prisoner's spouse or civil partner if he or she is the spouse or civil partner of a person who: (a) is in prison or place of detention, and (b) has for a period of not less than six months immediately preceding the date of claim been in custody by order of a court or a responsible authority, or is committed in custody by a court or a responsible authority for a period of not less than six months.[465] OFP continues to be paid for four weeks after the release of the spouse or civil partner from the prison or place of detention.[466]

315. Relevant child: A 'relevant child' means a person:

(a) who is ordinarily resident in the State;
(b) is not detained in a children detention school, and
(c) has (i) not attained the age of 16 years where the claimant of OFP is qualified for a BP or a CA or the child is a child in respect of whom DCA is in payment;[467] or (ii) has not attained the age of 12 years in respect of any claim for OFP made between 3 May 2012 and 3 July 2013, 10 years in respect of any such

462. [2001] 1 IR 457. *See also* the approach of the Australian courts in *Staunton-Smith v. Secretary, Department of Social Security* (1991) 14 AAR 325.
463. *Social Welfare Appeals Office Report 2003*, 29.
464. Article 126 as substituted by Art. 5(a) of S.I. No. 447 of 2012. The requirement as to parenthood is now in the primary legislation (para. 309 above).
465. Article 127 as substituted by Art. 12(c) of S.I. No. 604 of 2011.
466. Section 176 as substituted by s. 5(3) of SW&P Act 2012.
467. Section 172(1) as inserted by SWPA 2011, s. 9 and as amended by s. 11 SWA 2016.

claim made between 4 July 2013 and 2 July 2014 and 7 years in respect of any such claim made on or after 3 July 2014.[468]

The effect of this provision is that, OFP will only be payable in respect of a person with a child under 7 (unless DCA is payable in respect of that child or the claimant of OFP is also entitled to BP or a CA). The Upper Tribunal rejected a human rights challenge to similar provisions in the UK on the basis that, although the reduction in the age of entitlement could have a disproportionate impact on mainly female claimants, the policy was objectively justified, i.e., it pursued a legitimate aim and there was a reasonable relationship of proportionality between the means employed, and the aims sought to be realized.[469]

316. Section 173A provides that in the case of a surviving spouse, SCP or a surviving cohabitant (who had been living together at the date of the death of the spouse/partner/cohabitant) where the child is over the age at which OFP ceases to be payable in respect of him/her, OFP is payable for up to two years or until the child reaches the age of 18. Section 173B provides that in a similar situation where the child is within two years of the age at which OFP ceases to be payable in respect of him/her, OFP remains payable for up to two years.[470] These provisions introduce discrimination between; (i) certain spouses, civil partners and cohabitants; and (ii) all other claimants of OFP (of whom a majority would appear to be unmarried and separated lone parents). Although the ECtHR has allowed different treatment of married couples in the context of a widow's pension scheme,[471] it is rather more difficult to identify any rationale for this difference in treatment in the context of the means-tested OFP scheme. It would appear that the rationale for this approach relates to the view held by many members of the general public and many members of the Oireachtas that widows should receive favourable treatment. It may be that members of the judiciary would be inclined to follow these views, but one would be reliant on a degree of judicial deference to the policy options chosen by the Oireachtas/Minister in this area as it is not clear that there is a policy rationale.

317. Normal Residence of a Qualified Child: A qualified child is regarded as normally residing with a qualified parent or other person to whom OFP is payable when: (a) the child is resident with that parent or other person, and (b) that parent or other person has the main care and charge of the child.[472] A qualified child who is resident in an institution is regarded as normally residing with the qualified parent or other person when that parent or other person contributes towards the cost of the child's maintenance in the institution and is the person with whom the child

468. Section 172(1) as amended by s. 14(a) SWA 2012.
469. *VL v. Secretary of State for Work and Pensions* [2011] UKUT 227.
470. As inserted by SWMPA 2010, s. 25 and amended by SWPA 2010, s. 20.
471. *Mata Estevez v. Spain*, App. 56501/00, 10 May 2001.
472. Article 128 as substituted by Art. 5(b) of S.I. No. 447/2012.

would be regarded as normally residing if the child were not resident in an institution. A qualified child may, in such circumstances as an officer of the Minister considers appropriate, be regarded as normally residing with the qualified parent or other person who is resident in an institution.

318. 'Institution' means:

(a) a hospital, convalescent home, or home for persons suffering from physical or mental disability or accommodation ancillary thereto;
(b) any other similar establishment providing residence, maintenance, or care for the persons therein; or
(c) any prison, place of detention, or other establishment to which Articles 218 and 219 of the Social Welfare (Consolidated Claims, Payment and Control) Regulations of 2007 apply.

319. *Efforts to Obtain Maintenance:* Separated claimants and unmarried parents are no longer required to make efforts to obtain maintenance from a liable relative – S.I. No. 355 of 2023.

§2. Means Test

320. OFP is a means-tested payment, and the means test is set out in Part 5 of Schedule 3 of the Act. This is broadly similar to the means test applying to the State pension (non-contributory) (*see* Part XI). However, in the case of OFP, to encourage the employment of lone parents, claimants of OFP are allowed to earn gross weekly earnings (including wages and profit from any form of self-employment) of up to EUR 165 per week together with half the weekly earnings in excess of that amount before their OFP is affected. When a person's weekly earnings exceed the lower amount, an amount of EUR 165 and half the weekly earnings in excess of that amount are disregarded (subject to the upper threshold, at which entitlement ceases). Persons entitled to OFP before 5 January 2012 who exceed this limit can retain a portion of OFP for a transitional period of up to six months.[473]

321. Both personal and child maintenance payable by the other spouse or parent are assessed as means. However, housing costs of up to EUR 95.23 a week can be offset against maintenance payments, with half the balance of maintenance being assessed as means of establishing entitlement to OFP[474] (though where working family payment (WFP) and OFP are payable to or in respect of a person in respect of the same period, only one maintenance disregard applies).[475] 'Housing costs' means 'rent or repayment of a loan entered into solely for the purpose of defraying

473. Section 173(4) as substituted by SWMPA, 2010 s. 25(3) and s. 173(5C) as inserted by s. 7 of the SWA, 2011.
474. Rule 1(2)(b)(ii) of Part 5 of Sch. 3.
475. Article 174(m) of S.I. No. 142 of 2007 as substituted by Art. 4(b) of S.I. No. 634 of 2019.

money employed in the purchase, repair, or essential improvement of the residence in which the qualified parent is residing'.[476]

322. When a recipient of OFP is receiving maintenance payments by way of a court order (i.e., a maintenance order or an order of the court made in a separation agreement),[477] he or she is liable to transfer to the Minister payments made to that person insofar as they exceed the lesser of EUR 4,952 p.a. in respect of housing costs or the annual housing costs actually incurred by that person.[478] In practice, this may be applied when the maintenance payments have not been assessed in deciding his or her rate of payment. Failure to comply with a request to transfer maintenance payments may result in a reduction of the OFP by the amount that the person is liable to transfer.[479]

§3. Amount of the Benefit

323. OFP is payable at a flat rate, with increases for qualified children as appropriate.[480] Certain 'secondary benefits' are payable with OFP.

§4. Disqualifications

324. A person is not entitled to OFP if he or she is absent from the State or if he or she is undergoing detention in legal custody (subject to certain exceptions),[481] and the habitual residence rule also applies.[482] Section 249(10) provides that a person is disqualified for OFP where he or she is undergoing imprisonment (except where regulations otherwise provide) though this provision is legally questionable in light of the Supreme Court decision in *C v. Minister for Social Protection.* In general, the marriage or remarriage of a parent terminates entitlement to OFP, as does entering into a civil partnership.[483] A person is also disqualified for OFP if and so long as he or she and another person are 'living as a couple in an intimate and committed relationship' (*see* below, paragraph 330).[484] Finally, a claimant will be disqualified if s/he participates in a Community Employment scheme that commences after 16 January 2012[485] or in a Solas scheme or national internship scheme.[486]

476. *Ibid.*
477. Section 344(1).
478. Section 358 and Art. 130 of S.I. No. 142 of 2007 as amended by Art. 5(c) of S.I. No. 447 of 2012.
479. Section 358(3).
480. Section 174 as amended by SWLRPA 2006, s. 22.
481. Section 249.
482. Section 173(6).
483. Section 173(2) as substituted by SWPA 2010, s. 20.
484. Section 175 as substituted by SWPA 2010, s. 20.
485. Section 247B.
486. Section 247A.

§5. LEGAL ISSUES

325. Discrimination Between Men and Women: As outlined above, both lone parents and widow(er)s payments are now made on a gender-neutral basis. However, there remains 'historical' discrimination between the genders in that a number of single-gender schemes still exist – in particular, the deserted wife's benefit – although these are no longer open to new claims. The EU Directive on equal treatment does not apply, as the deserted wife's benefit does not fall within the material scope of the Directive.[487] In a number of cases, discrimination against men was challenged before the Irish courts on constitutional grounds. In *Lowth v. Minister for Social Welfare,* a deserted husband argued that the failure to provide a deserted husband's payment was in breach of Articles 40.1, 40.3 and 41 of the Constitution.[488] However, the Supreme Court ruled against the plaintiff on the basis that Article 40.1 did not require that all citizens be treated identically without recognition of differences in relevant circumstances. Persons could be classified and treated differently once this classification was for a legitimate legislative purpose. In the particular circumstances, the Court was satisfied that there were ample grounds for the Oireachtas to conclude that deserted wives were in general likely to have greater needs than deserted husbands so as to justify the legislation.

326. The Cohabitation Disqualification: The cohabitation disqualification applies to the various payments that can be loosely described as lone parents' or survivors' payments.[489] When a person is cohabiting, he or she is thereby disqualified from receiving any of these payments. Cohabitation, in this context, is thus an absolute bar to payment and not merely a factor that is taken into account in deciding the level of payment to be made. Cohabitation is also a factor for other means-tested payments such as jobseeker's allowance, but in these cases, it is a factor that affects the level of payment (if any) and *not* an absolute bar. The Oireachtas (i.e., in reality, the DSP) has taken advantage of the introduction of civil partnership legislation (which introduced a new concept of 'cohabitant') to make a significant (and perhaps not well-recognized) change in the law in this area. Although the concept of cohabitation remains, it has been extended to same-sex couples *and* substantially redefined. As it is important to emphasize the difference in approach (and as the old approach will remain relevant for pre-2011 periods), we outline first the former approach and then look at the current position.

327. Prior to 1 January 2011, the concept of cohabitation was defined in the SW Acts as involving 'living with another person as man and wife'. There had been no

487. Article 3 of Directive 79/7/EEC, and *see Lowth v. Minister for Social Welfare* [1998] 4 IR 321 at 329–330. It seems likely that were this to be challenged under the European Convention on Human Rights, the Irish courts would find the difference in treatment justified following *Runkee and White v. United Kingdom*, Apps. 42949/98 and 53134/99, 10 May 2007.

488. [1998] 4 IR 321. *See also Dennehy v. Minister for Social Welfare*, High Court, unreported 26 Jul. 1984. For a criticism of the *Lowth* judgment, *see* G. Hogan, 'The Supreme Court and the Equality Clause', Bar Review 4 (1998): 116.

489. Section 175 (OFP), s. 124(3) (widow(er)'s (contributory) pension), s. 166 (widow's (non-contributory) pension).

attempt to provide a more detailed statutory definition, and when the issue came before the High Court, Gannon J stated that he considered 'it unwise for the Court to supply a definition when the legislature has refrained from doing so'.[490]

328. The High Court upheld the Departmental view that it was not necessary that there be any financial support of the claimant by the 'cohabitee' to determine that cohabitation existed in a case in which the Court rejected the argument that the cohabitation rule should be interpreted in a purposive manner so as only to apply when actual financial support was being provided.[491] In that case, Gannon J approved the comments of the English courts in *Thomas v. Thomas*,[492] in which it was stated that:

> Cohabitation' means living together as husband and wife and … consists in the husband acting as a husband towards the wife and the wife acting as a wife towards the husband.

329. Gannon J refused to follow a number of Canadian cases in which it had been held that the concept of 'living together as husband and wife' should be construed in light of the purposes of the legislation so as to refer to the financial relationship of the couple and not to their sexual or social relationship.[493]

330. From 1 January 2011, the Act states that a person is disqualified for certain payments 'if and so long as he or she is a cohabitant'.[494] 'Cohabitant' means a cohabitant within the meaning of section 172(1) of the Civil Partnership and Certain Rights and Obligations of Cohabitants Act 2010 (CPCROCA 2010).[495] Section 172(1), in turn, provides that:

> a cohabitant is one of 2 adults (whether of the same or the opposite sex) who live together as a couple in an intimate and committed relationship and who are not related to each other within the prohibited degrees of relationship or married to each other or civil partners of each other.[496]

490. *Foley v. Moulton* [1989] ILRM 169.
491. *Foley v. Moulton* [1989] ILRM. 169. *See* G. Whyte, 'Social Welfare Law: The Cohabitation Rule', DULJ 11 (1989): 187.
492. [1948] KB 294.
493. *Re Proc and Minister for Community and Social Services* (1975) 53 DLR (3d) 512; *Re Stoikiewicz* and *Filas* (1979) 92 DLR (3d) 128. A similar approach has been adopted by the New Zealand courts – *Ruka v. Department of Social Welfare* [1997] I NZLR 154 – but rejected in Australia: *Lambe v. Director-General of Social Services* (1983–1984), 52 ALR 128.
494. *See*, for example, s. 124 which relates to widow's, etc. (contributory) pension and s. 175 as regards one-parent family payment (as substituted by SWPA 2011, s. 9(6)).
495. Section 2 as amended by SWPA 2010, s. 15.
496. Section 172(4) of the CPCROCA 2010 provides that two adults are within a prohibited degree of relationship if (a) they would be prohibited from marrying each other in the State, or (b) they are within the prohibited degrees of relationship set out in the Third Schedule to the CPCROCA 2010 (which includes close family relationships).

Section 172(2) provides that in determining whether two adults are cohabitants, all the circumstances of the relationship should be taken into account and, in particular:

(a) the duration of the relationship;
(b) the basis on which the couple live together;
(c) the degree of financial dependence of either adult on the other and any agreements in respect of their finances;
(d) the degree and nature of any financial arrangements between the adults, including any joint purchase of an estate or interest in land or joint acquisition of personal property;
(e) whether there are one or more dependent children;
(f) whether one of the adults cares for and supports the children of the other; and
(g) the degree to which the adults present themselves to others as a couple.[497]

Finally, section 172(3), for the avoidance of doubt, provides that a relationship does not cease to be an intimate relationship for the purpose of this section merely because it is no longer sexual in nature.[498]

331. In summary, the 2010 law marks an important change in the cohabitation rule. The rule has now been extended to same-sex couples, but the test is no longer whether a couple is living together 'as man and wife' but rather 'living together as a couple in an intimate and committed relationship'.

332. The 2010 Act has now been considered in a number of court rulings. In *D.C. v. D.R.*, Baker J pointed out that the legislation required that a cohabiting relationship be more than one of mere friendship and that it must involve or have involved sexual intimacy.[499] She held that 'the various indices of the relationship and the public presentation of that relationship must be taken as a whole and in the context of the social mores and perhaps even of the age of the participants in the relationship'.[500] She further held that:

> the test requires the court to determine whether a reasonable person who knew the couple would have regarded them as living together in a committed and intimate relationship, and that the individual and many factors in how they are perceived must be taken into account.[501]

---

497. Section 2 of the Act refers only to the first subsection of s. 172 of CPCROCA 2010. However, as the further subsections of that section are relevant to whether or not a person is a cohabitant within the meaning of s. 172(1), it is submitted that subs. 172(2) and (3) must also be considered by the social welfare adjudication authorities.
498. The provision indicates that the term 'intimate' refers to sexuality (not necessarily a common-sense interpretation) and suggests that a relationship which has been sexual has been intimate while also suggesting that a relationship which has never been sexual would not fall within the scope of s. 172(1). However, this remains to be seen.
499. [2015] IEHC 309.
500. At para. 106 of her judgment.
501. At para. 107.

333. In *M.W. v. D.C.*, the Court of Appeal ruled that:

> The legal concept of living together as a couple for the purposes of s. 172 does not require two persons to live physically at all times in the same shared premises. Hence, notwithstanding that a couple may not be physically living day by day in the same residence … , s. 172 envisages that a court may decide on all the relevant facts that they, nonetheless continued to live together as a couple during that period.[502]

334. The current Departmental Guidelines on Cohabitation set out a number of criteria for assessing cohabitation:

- the duration of the relationship;
- the basis on which the couple live together;
- the degree of financial dependence of either adult on the other and any agreements in respect of their finances;
- the degree and nature of any financial arrangements between the adults including any joint purchase of an estate or interest in land or joint acquisition of personal property;
- whether there are one or more dependent children;
- whether one of the adults cares for and supports the children of the other;
- the degree to which the adults present themselves to others as a couple.[503]

335. The basic principle behind the social welfare provisions is that the primary responsibility is on the spouse or parent to provide maintenance. Support from the spouse or parent can involve an obligation to seek maintenance and/or the liability to maintain provisions.

336. The Liability to Maintain:[504] The SW Acts of 1989 and 1990 introduced the provisions concerning the liability of family members to maintain persons and to repay payments to the Department. Section 2(7) provides that – subject to Part 12 – 'liable relative' means:

(a) a man who is liable to maintain all or any of the following:
  (i) his (I) spouse; (II) his former spouse where the marriage has been dissolved, being a dissolution that is recognized as valid in the State; (III) his civil partner; (IV) his former civil partner where the civil partnership has been dissolved, being a dissolution that is recognized as valid in the State; while all or any of the persons specified in clauses (I)–(IV) are, or is, in receipt of an allowance or a benefit, and (ii) any qualified child of his in respect of whom an increase in allowance or a benefit is payable to the other parent of that qualified child, or

502. [2017] IECA 255 at para. 29. *See also G.R. v. Regan* [2020] IEHC 89.
503. Operational Guidelines on Cohabitation at https://www.gov.ie/en/publication/d258d8-cohabitation/. These factors are discussed in more detail in the Guidelines
504. Sections 2(7), 344–359 and the SW(CCP&C)R, Arts 250–255.

(b) a woman who is liable to maintain all or any of the following:
   (i) her (I) spouse; (II) her former spouse where the marriage has been dissolved, being a dissolution that is recognized as valid in the State; (III) her civil partner; (IV) her former civil partner where the civil partnership has been dissolved, being a dissolution that is recognized as valid in the State; while all or any of the persons specified in clauses (I)–(IV) are, or is, in receipt of an allowance or benefit, and (ii) any qualified child of hers in respect of whom an increase in allowance is payable to the other parent of that qualified child.[505]

337. For the purposes of sections 173 [OFP] and 189 [SWA] and without prejudice to any obligations imposed by law or otherwise, section 345[506] provides that (a) a man is liable to maintain (i) his spouse[507] or civil partner, and (ii) any child of his, being a child who is under the age of 18 years or (save for the purposes of section 189) who is of or over that age and under the age of 22[508] years and is receiving full-time education or instruction by the day at any university, college, school or other educational establishments, and (b) a woman is liable to maintain (i) her spouse or civil partner, and (ii) any child of hers, being a child who is under the age of 18 years or (save for the purposes of section 189) who is of or over that age and under the age of 22[509] years and is receiving full-time education or instruction by day at any university, college, school or other educational establishment. The provisions apply to OFP and SWA, but we will focus here on OFP.

338. The Department can require any liable relative to repay some or all of the amount of a payment made to a claimant. The maximum amount to be deducted cannot exceed the total social welfare payment being paid to the claimant. If the liable relative does not contribute, the Department can apply to the District Court for an order directing the person to make the repayments.[510]

339. The detailed provisions in relation to the determination of the contribution are set out in Regulations prescribed under section 346(2). When a claim for OFP is being investigated, the claimant is asked for the identity of the liable relative who is not normally interviewed at the claim stage but is informed of his or her potential liability by letter. After a claim is awarded and if it is deemed that the liable relative may be in a position to contribute, then he or she is contacted by the Department at that stage and may be interviewed. The liable relative and his or her employer are

---

505. As substituted by SWPA 2015, s. 11(a). Note that while the CPCROCA 2010 imposes maintenance obligations on certain cohabitants, the Oireachtas did not chose to extend the liable relative provisions to cohabitants.
506. As amended by SWPA 2010, s. 24.
507. Section 344(1) as amended by SWPA 2015, s. 11(b) provides, *inter alia*: '"spouse" in relation to a person who has been married more than once refers only to the last spouse of that person and for this purpose that last spouse shall be read as including the person to whom, but for the fact that the marriage has been dissolved, being a dissolution recognised as valid in the State, that person would be married'.
508. Substituted by SWLR&PA 2006.
509. *Ibid.*
510. Section 356.

obliged to provide information to the Department in relation to the amount of a contribution. Failure to provide requested information constitutes an offence.[511]

340. The amount that the liable relative is liable to contribute for the purposes of section 346 is calculated as: (a) the weekly value of any property belonging to the liable relative (not being property personally used or enjoyed by him or her) that is invested or otherwise put to profitable use by the liable relative or which, though capability of investment or profitable use, is not invested or put to profitable use by the liable relative, and the weekly value of the property is calculated as follows: (i) the first EUR 20,000 of the capital value of the property shall be excluded; (ii) the weekly value of so much of the capital value of the property as exceeds EUR 20,000 but does not exceed EUR 30,000 shall be assessed at EUR 1 per each EUR 1,000; (iii) the weekly value of so much of the capital value of the property as exceeds EUR 30,000 but does not exceed EUR 40,000 shall be assessed at EUR 2 per each EUR 1,000; (iv) the weekly value of so much of the capital value of the property as exceeds EUR 40,000 shall be assessed at EUR 4 per each EUR 1,000, but no account shall be taken under any other provision of this Article of any appropriation of the property for the purpose of current expenditure; and the weekly value of (b) gross income, other than income from property assessed under paragraph (a), actually received or likely to be received in the contribution year in which the liability is calculated (or any other contribution year that appears to the deciding officer or appeals officer to be appropriate), less the amount of (i) any allowable contribution referred to in Regulations 41 and 42 of the Income Tax Employments (Consolidation) Regulations of 2001; (ii) any income tax payable under the provisions of the Income Tax Acts as defined in section 1 of the Taxes Consolidation Act of 1997; (iii) any contributions payable under section 13(2)(b) and Regulations made under section 14 or section 21; (iv) any contributions payable under section 5 of the Health Contributions Act of 1979; (v) any maintenance payments being paid by the liable relative with respect to his or her spouse and his or her child or children, when such maintenance payments have been taken into account in deciding the amount of allowance payable to the said spouse or parent of his or her children; (vi) an amount, not exceeding EUR 4,952 per annum, of any rent or repayment of a loan entered into solely for the purpose of defraying money employed in the purchase, repair, or essential improvement of the residence in which the liable relative is residing but when the liable relative has remarried or is cohabiting as husband and wife with another person who is in employment or self-employment, the amount allowed shall be one-half of the rent or repayment, not exceeding EUR 2,476 per annum.[512]

341. The amount calculated above is further reduced by; (a) a weekly amount equal to the personal rate of OFP plus EUR 19.05, and (b) an amount of the IQC payable with OFP (currently EUR 26) with respect to each qualified child of the liable relative normally residing with him or her and for whom he or she has the main care and charge.

---

511. *Ibid.*
512. SW (CCP&C) R, Art. 251.

342. The weekly amount to be paid by the liable relative is either: (a) the amount calculated in accordance with Article 251 above; (b) the amount of weekly allowance in payment to the person, or parent of the person as the case may be, whom the liable relative is liable to maintain; or (c) in the case of the qualified child of an unmarried person, an amount not exceeding the maximum amount set out in section 23(2)(a) of the Family Law Maintenance of Spouses and Children Act of 1976 (as amended by the Courts Act of 1991) with respect to each qualified child.[513]

343. The Minister is empowered to take action in the District Courts to seek enforced payment of contributions due by way of instalment orders or attachment of earnings orders.[514] The latter order is directed to the person who has the liable relative in his or her employment to make specified deductions from his or her earnings and to pay the amounts deducted to the District Court clerk for transmission to the Department. Such actions would normally only be considered when the liable relative has failed to comply with the determination on contributions due, although it appears that no such action has in fact gone to court to date. The Minister may apply to the District Court for an order directing the arrest and imprisonment of the person for non-compliance with an order.

344. Maintenance payments made under a court order offset in whole or in part contributions due by a liable relative.[515]

345. There are several difficulties with regard to the practical operation of this legislation. First, the Supreme Court held, in relation to the enforcement of earlier liable relative provisions, that the question as to the claimant's initial entitlement to the payment (and any consequent liability to maintain it) may be reopened in the District Court.[516] The Act was amended in 1998 to remove the power of the District Court to 'fix the amount of the contribution to be made', but this does not address the issue as to whether a contribution is due at all or not. Second, it is unclear whether the liable relative will be allowed to rely on defences, such as the fact that circumstances of the case (including the conduct of the claimant) would make it repugnant to justice to order the liable relative to contribute. In the area of family law, such a defence would mean that the relative would not be liable for maintenance, but it is not clear whether the same rules will apply in the social welfare area. In the UK case of *National Assistance Board v. Wilkinson*,[517] the Divisional Court, considering similar UK legislation, held that a husband was not liable to contribute

513. Article 252.
514. Sections 346–356.
515. Section 357.
516. *Board of Public Assistance for the South Cork Public Assistance District v. O'Regan* [1949] IR 415. In that case, the Supreme Court considered a case stated in relation to an application to the District Court to enforce an application to recover payments made to the respondent's wife. A majority of the Court held that the wife was not eligible to receive public assistance and that, therefore, the public assistance authority was not entitled to recover from the husband. However, O'Byrne J did say that he would not deal with a case where the granting of assistance depended upon a disputed question of fact (as opposed to law).
517. [1952] 2 All ER 255.

if his wife had been guilty of adultery or desertion. However, the Court of Appeal in *National Assistance Board v. Parkes*[518] held that the correct basis for this decision was the phrase in the UK legislation that required the Court to 'have regard to all the circumstances'.[519] The Irish legislation contains no such phrase, and the old Irish case of *McEvoy v. Guardians of the Kilkenny Union*,[520] which interprets the Irish Poor Law provisions from which our current legislation is derived, is the authority for the proposition that liability to maintain is absolute and that the behaviour of the spouse is irrelevant.

346. Finally, there is an issue as to whether an agreement between the parties to transfer property might affect the liability to maintain. One spouse may agree to transfer property to the other on the basis that no maintenance or only a low maintenance payment is to be made. It is well established that one party cannot contract out of his or her right to maintenance.[521] Nonetheless, should a subsequent application for maintenance be made, the courts may take into account all the relevant facts, including any property transfer.[522] The UK authorities are unanimous that an agreement between the parties will not relieve a spouse from liability to maintain, although, under the UK legislation, it could be taken into account in deciding the appropriate contribution to be required.[523] In the absence of any case law to date, it is difficult to predict how the liable relatives' provisions may be interpreted. However, it is clear that the legal rules concerning the recovery of contributions from the liable relative through the courts are not properly integrated with the operation of the family law provisions applied by the courts.

347. Maintenance and Social Welfare Payments: The SWA of 1989 amended the Family Law (Maintenance of Spouses and Children) Act of 1976 to provide that lone parents' payments payable to the applicant should not be taken into account in assessing the amount of maintenance to be awarded. The purpose was to ensure that lone parents' families would be adequately maintained by the absent spouse or father and that the amount of maintenance would not be subsidized by payment of social welfare, there is some evidence that maintenance orders were being set at reduced levels because the applicants had social welfare entitlements. However, as a Review of OFP notes (p. 106), it is not clear that this provision was applied to any extent by the family courts in practice.[524]

518. [1955] 2 All ER 1.
519. *See* James Casey 'The Supplementary Benefits Act: Lawyer's Law Aspects', NILQ 19 (1968): 1.
520. (1896) 30 ILTR 156.
521. *H.D. v. P.D.* Supreme Court, unreported, 8 May 1978 and s. 27 of the Family Law (Maintenance of Spouses and Children) Act of 1976.
522. *O.C. v. T.C.* High Court, unreported, 9 Dec. 1981.
523. *National Assistance Board v. Prisk* [1954] 1 All ER 400; *National Assistance Board v. Parkes* [1955] 2 All ER 1; *Hulley v. Thomson* [1981] 1 All ER 1128.
524. Note also that s. 51(2) provides that in relation to an application under the 1976 Act to the payment of expenses incidental to the birth of child, the court shall not take into account the fact that the mother is entitled to a maternity benefit.

Part V. Incapacity to Work, Disability and Care

348. This part looks at the main payments with respect to sickness and disability, as well as care. There are three main sickness and disability benefits: illness (formerly, disability) benefit, invalidity pension, and disability allowance – in addition to the occupational injuries scheme, which is discussed in the next part. There is also a 'partial capacity benefit' (PCB) which is intended to provide an opportunity for people with disabilities, who are assessed to have an employment capacity that is restricted when compared to the norm, to avail of employment opportunities while continuing to receive an income support payment. The main features of these schemes are outlined below. In addition, there is a means-tested BP, which originated as an old-age pension payable to persons under pension age who were unable to work because of blindness.[525] There are two main care payments: CA and benefit. There is also a DCA payable to children who require constant care or supervision.[526] Arising from the COVID-19 pandemic, an IB (COVID-19) payment was introduced on an emergency basis in 2020 but terminated as of 30 September 2022.

525. Section 161.
526. This replaces the scheme of the same name operated by the HSE under s. 61 of the Health Act of 1970. The mobility allowance and motorised transport grant operated by HSE were closed to new claims in 2013 and a promised replacement scheme has yet to appear.

Chapter 1. Illness Benefit

349. IB is a payment for people who are incapable of work because of sickness or disability.[527] From 2009, changes in legislation provided that a person's entitlement to IB is limited to two years. Prior to 2023, there was no statutory sick pay in Ireland. However, the Sick Leave Act 2022 provides for sick leave and pay and came into effect from 1 January 2023.

§1. Beneficiaries and Conditions

350. IB is payable to any person under pension age (*see* paragraph 545 for any day of incapacity for work that forms part of a period of interruption of employment when that person satisfies the contribution conditions (*see* below).[528] Following the SW(No.2)A 2019, the reason for the period of interruption of employment must be as a direct result of the person concerned being incapable of work and for no other reason (*see* paragraph 792).[529]

351. *Day of Incapacity for Work:* A day of incapacity for work is a day on which a person is 'incapable of work'.[530] However, IB is not payable for the first three days of any period of incapacity for work.[531] Sunday is not included as a day of incapacity for work, and any day on which a person is paid holiday pay by his or her employer is also not generally treated as a day of incapacity.[532] Any day when a person fails to prove that he or she is incapable of work or on which he or she does any work other than that rehabilitative work specified in Article 24(3) and (4) will not be treated as a day of incapacity for work.[533] Any three days of incapacity within a period of six consecutive days will be treated as a period of incapacity for work, and any two such periods not separated by more than three days shall be treated as one period of incapacity.[534] This means that if a person goes back to work and becomes incapable of work again within three days, he or she will be entitled to a benefit without the waiting period, but if he or she has two periods of incapacity that are separated by more than three days, the person is not entitled to a benefit for the first three waiting days of the second period.

527. Sections 40–46 and the SW(CCP&C)R, Arts 20–28. Renamed by SWLRPA 2006, s. 4.
528. Section 40(1).
529. Section 40(1)(ab) as inserted by SW(No.2)A 2019.
530. Section 40(3)(a).
531. Section 40(2) as amended by s. 5 of SWA 2020.
532. Section 40(3).
533. SW(CCP&C)R, Art. 21.
534. Section 40(3)(d). Section 40(3)(e) provides an exception to this in the case of a person who has been in receipt of illness benefit for not less than 1,560 days (five years), whereby any two periods of incapacity not separated by more than thirteen weeks are treated as one. This is to allow a 'trial period' for a long-term disabled person to go back to work without losing entitlement to illness benefit should he or she subsequently prove incapable of work.

352. Period of Interruption of Employment: Any three days of interruption of employment (i.e., a day that is a day of incapacity for work or a day of unemployment),[535] whether consecutive or not, within a period of six consecutive days will be treated as 'a period of interruption of employment', and any two such periods not separated by more than thirteen weeks will be treated as one period of interruption of employment.[536] Thus, a person who, having been incapable, returns to work for more than thirteen weeks will have to establish a new period of interruption of employment and will not be entitled to a benefit for the waiting period. Any day with respect to which a woman is entitled to and in receipt of a maternity benefit will be treated as a day of incapacity for work for the purposes of reckoning periods of interruption of employment only.[537] Thus, a woman who has been receiving a maternity benefit and who then claims IB because of incapacity for work can have the days on which she received the maternity benefit counted as part of the period of interruption of unemployment. However, a woman who was in receipt of a maternity benefit on any of the three days prior to her claim for IB is not entitled to IB for the waiting period.[538] This means that women transferring from a maternity benefit to IB will normally have established a period of interruption of unemployment and will be entitled to IB after the waiting period.

353. Incapable of Work: 'Incapable of work' means incapable by reason of some specific disease of bodily or mental disablement or deemed, in accordance with regulations, to be so incapable.[539] There is no more detailed statutory definition of 'incapacity', nor does there appear to be any Irish case law on the issue.[540] The departmental guidelines on Medical Certification state that in the case of temporary incapacity:

> If the claimant is unable to follow his usual occupation but could be fit for a less demanding form of work, he may be regarded as incapable of work if it is likely that he will soon be able to return to his former occupation.[541]

354. However, in the longer-term:

> The certifier should consider if the physical and mental condition of the claimant is such that he is capable of performing alternative work, which he could

535. Section 40(3)(b).
536. Section 40(3)(c).
537. SW(CCP&C)R, Art. 25.
538. Section 40(6). Unlike most other benefits, a maternity benefit itself does not have waiting days.
539. Section 2(1). *See* Robert Clark, *Annotated Guide to Social Welfare Law* (London: Sweet & Maxwell, 1995), 66–68. Thus, incapacity due to pregnancy *per se* does not fall within the statutory definition, although a pregnancy related illness could give rise to incapacity in this sense.
540. For the UK case law, *see* Anthony Ogus & Eric Barendt, *The Law of Social Security*, 3rd ed., (London: Butterworths, 1982 and 1988). 150–156.
541. The guidelines quoted here no longer appear on the DSP website but there is nothing to suggest that the approach has changed.

reasonably be expected to undertake after taking into account his training, education, experience and age.

355. In some circumstances, one can be deemed to be incapable of work even though a person is not so incapable.[542] This can happen when a person is under medical care for a disease or disablement[543] and when it is certified by a doctor that because of the disease or disablement, he or she should not work and he or she does not work, or a person is a probable source of infection with a disease specified as an infectious disease under the HA of 1947, and he or she abstains from work on the written order or advice of a doctor.[544]

356. Night Workers: When a person is employed to work continuously from one day until the next (e.g., on a night shift), that person will be regarded as being employed: (a) only on the first day, when the first day is Monday to Friday and when the employment on the first day is longer than on the second day, or when the first day is Saturday; or (b) in any other case, on the second day.[545] When a person is regarded as being employed on only one of two days and a person is incapable of work on the other day, he or she will be deemed to be incapable of work for the other day.

§2. Contribution Conditions

357. The contribution conditions for IB require that a person must have:[546]

- 104 weeks reckonable paid contributions since he or she first entered insurable employment; and
- 39 paid or credited contributions in the second-last contribution year before the year in which the claim is made (13 of which must be paid contributions);[547] or
- 26 weeks paid at the appropriate class in each of the second-last and third-last contribution years.

542. SW(CCP&C)R, Art. 20.
543. In R.(S) 4/93, a Social Security Commissioner ruled that a pregnant woman advised not to work due to a health risk could be deemed incapable with respect to a period when she was under medical care to establish whether she had contracted a disease but not otherwise, as pregnancy is not, of itself, a disease or disablement. Such a person might now qualify for a health and safety benefit, *see* para. 286.
544. *See* the Infectious Diseases Regulations 1981 (SI 390 of 1981) as amended on numerous occasions most recently by SI 258 of 2022 and SI 245 of 2023.
545. SW(CCP&C)R, Art. 22.
546. Section 41 (as amended by SWMPA 2008, s. 15) and SW(CCP&C)R, Art. 27. Persons who are in receipt of various social welfare payments are exempt from the thirteen paid contributions requirement: s. 41(11) and SW(CCP&C)R. Art. 28.
547. If there are not thirteen paid contribution in the relevant year, the following years may be used instead: the two contribution years before the relevant year, the last complete contribution year, or the current contribution year.

§3. Amount of the Benefit

358. IB is payable at a flat rate with increases for qualified adults and qualified children as appropriate.[548] The personal rate of the benefit depends on the previous weekly earnings. In theory, this is a contribution condition and is included in section 41, but in practice, it affects the rate of the benefit rather than the qualification therefor. A person must have reckonable weekly earnings in excess of a prescribed amount in the relevant contribution year.[549] The prescribed amount is currently EUR 300 per week.[550] This is calculated by taking the reckonable weekly earnings in the relevant year and dividing by the number of paid contributions in that period. In the case of a person whose reckonable weekly earnings are less than EUR 32 per week, he or she shall be deemed to have reckonable earnings of EUR 32 per week. When the reckonable weekly earnings are less than EUR 300 but are EUR 32 or more, the person will be entitled to a reduced rate of the benefit.[551] 'Household benefits' are not generally payable with IB.

§4. Duration of the Benefit

359. Any person who satisfies the above contribution conditions may receive IB for up to one year.[552] To requalify for the benefit, a person must have thirteen paid contributions begun or ended since the last day for which he or she was entitled to the benefit (and satisfy the relevant contribution conditions). Up until 2008, a person who had 260 or more paid contributions could receive IB indefinitely up to the age of 66. However, the SWMPA 2008 introduced a major change in relation to new claims from 5 January 2009; such persons now will only be entitled to IB for a maximum of two years (624 days) without requalifying.[553]

§5. Disqualifications

360. A person will be disqualified for IB for a period of up to nine weeks if he or she (a) becomes incapable of work through his or her own misconduct; or (b) fails without good cause to comply with such requirements as may be specified by the regulations, including but not necessarily limited to: (i) attending or submitting

548. Sections 42 & 43.
549. Section 41(1)(c). This requirement does not apply to a volunteer development worker who returns to Ireland.
550. SW(CCP&C)R, Art. 26 as amended by S.I. No. 604 of 2008. Claimants of Pandemic Unemployment Payment (PUP) or of Jobseeker's payments who had an underlying entitlement to PUP are deemed to have had weekly average earnings or income in excess of EUR 300 in 2021 for this purpose – S.I. No. 234 of 2023.
551. SW(CCP&C)R, Art. 27 and Sch. 6-6A as amended by S.I. No. 604 of 2008.
552. Section 44 as amended by SWLRPA 2006, s. 4 and SWPA 2010, s. 3.
553. Section 44(1A) as inserted by SWMPA 2008, s. 15 and amended by SWPA 2010, s. 3. Section 44(1C) and (1D) set out 'savers' for specific groups.

to any medical or other examination or treatment; or (ii) complying with instructions relating to his or her incapacity issued by a registered medical practitioner, refraining from behaviour likely to hinder his or her recovery, or being available to meet with an officer of the Minister or medical assessor regarding his or her claim for IB.[554]

361. A person in receipt of or entitled to IB is not allowed to engage in work.[555] However, Section 46(1B) allows an exemption from disqualification for receipt of IB while engaging in such class or classes of employment or training and subject to such circumstances and conditions as may be prescribed.[556] The Regulations provide that a person shall not be disqualified for receipt of IB where that person, having become incapable of following his or her normal occupation and with the prior written permission of an officer of the Minister, undertakes a course of training for a specified period of time with a view to taking up some other occupation.[557]

362. In addition, a person may engage in the following limited work *without* prior written permission or specified period of time: (a) light work for which no remuneration is, or would normally be, payable; (b) work undertaken primarily as a part of his or her treatment while he or she is a patient in, or of, a hospital, sanatorium, or other similar institution and his or her weekly earnings with respect to that work do not exceed EUR 50; and (c) work under a scheme that is, in the opinion of the Minister, charitable in character and purpose and his or her weekly earnings for that work do not exceed EUR 50.[558]

363. A person will also be disqualified if he or she is absent from the State (subject to certain exceptions) or is undergoing detention in legal custody (again, subject to certain exceptions).[559] This is also subject to the provision of EU law and, in particular, Regulation 883/2004. Finally, a claimant will be disqualified if s/he participates in a Community Employment scheme that commences after 16 January 2012[560] or in a Solas scheme or national internship scheme.[561]

554. Section 46 as substituted by SWPA 2007 and SW(CCP&C)R, Art. 24.
555. Section 46(1A) as amended by s. 12(2)(b) SW&PA 2010.
556. Section 46(1B) inserted by s. 12(2)(b) SW&PA 2010 and SW(CCP&C)R, Art. 24.
557. Article 24 as inserted by S.I. No. 43 of 2012.
558. *Ibid.*
559. Section 249. *See* Part XII, Chs 3 and 4.
560. Section 247B.
561. Section 247A.

Chapter 2. Invalidity Pension

364. IP is a payment for people who are incapable of work in the long term because of sickness or disability.[562]

§1. Beneficiaries and Conditions

365. To be entitled to IP, a person must be:

(a) permanently incapable of work, and
(b) satisfy the contribution conditions.[563]

Following the SW(No.2)A 2019, the reason for the incapacity must be as a direct result of the person concerned being incapable of work and for no other reason (*see* paragraph 792.[564]

366. The definition of 'incapacity for work' has already been discussed in relation to IB (*see* paragraphs 355–363). A person will be regarded as being permanently incapable of work if, immediately before the date of claim of IP:

(a) he or has been continuously incapable of work for a period of one year, and it is shown to the satisfaction of a deciding officer or an appeals officer that the person is likely to continue to be incapable of work for at least a further year; or
(b) the person is incapable of work, and evidence is adduced to establish to the satisfaction of a deciding officer or an appeals officer that the incapacity for work is of such a nature that the likelihood is that the person will be incapable of work for life.

However, he or she will not be so regarded when it is subsequently shown to the satisfaction of a deciding officer or an appeals officer that he or she is no longer likely to continue to be incapable of work for at least a further year or for life, as the case may be.[565]

367. In practice, most claimants of IP will have been in receipt of IB for considerably more than one year before qualifying for a pension. A person who considers that he or she qualifies for IP can submit a claim to the Department at any time. In addition, when a medical referee examining someone for IB considers that he or she is likely to qualify for IP, the medical referee will recommend to the Department that the person be transferred to IP. The Department will then inform

562. The provisions in relation to invalidity pension are set out in ss 118–122 and SW(CCP&C)R, Arts 76–78.
563. Section 118.
564. Section 118(1)(a) as inserted by SW(No.2)A 2019.
565. SW(CCP&C)R, Art. 77.

the person of this option (assuming that he or she satisfies the contribution conditions). It is, of course, open to a person to submit a claim for IP in any other case.

§2. Contribution Conditions

368. To qualify for IP, a person must have:

(a) at least 260 paid contributions since his or her entry into insurance, and
(b) at least 48 paid or credited contributions in the last or second-last complete contribution year before the 'relevant date'.[566]

'Relevant date' means any date subsequent to the commencement of a period of incapacity for work when evidence is adduced to establish to the satisfaction of a deciding officer or an appeals officer that the incapacity for work is of such a nature that the likelihood is that the person will be incapable of work for life.[567]

§3. Amount of the Benefit

369. IP is payable at a flat rate with increases for qualified adults and qualified children as appropriate.[568] 'Household benefits' are generally payable with an IP. Any person who satisfies the above contribution conditions may receive IP indefinitely up to pension age (provided that he or she continues to satisfy the eligibility conditions). Section 113A now provides that a person in receipt of an IP immediately before reaching pension age will automatically qualify for a State pension.[569]

§4. Disqualifications

370. The Act provides for disqualification for IP when the person fails without good cause to comply with such requirements as may be specified by the regulations, including but not necessarily limited to: (a) attending or submitting to any medical or other examination or treatment, (b) complying with instructions relating to his or her incapacity issued by a registered medical practitioner, (c) refraining from behaviour likely to hinder his or her recovery, and (d) being available to meet with an officer of the Minister or medical assessor regarding his or her claim for IP.[570]

566. Section 119 as amended by s. 4(c) SWA 2016. Self-employed contributions count towards entitlement to IP.
567. Section 119(2) and Art. 53.
568. Sections 121 & 122.
569. As inserted by SWLRPA 2006, s. 11 and amended by SW(MP)A 2015.
570. Section 118(3) substituted by SWPA 2007, s. 16, and SW(CCP&C)R. Art. 78.

371. A person in receipt of or entitled to IP is not allowed to engage in work except that he or she may, with the prior written permission of an officer of the Minister, for a specified period of time, undertake the following types of work or training: (a) having become permanently incapable of following his or her usual occupation, a course of training with a view to taking up some other occupation, or (b) light work for which no remuneration is or would ordinarily be payable.[571]

372. A person is also disqualified if he or she is undergoing detention in legal custody (subject to certain exceptions and to EU law)[572] or if s/he participates in a Community Employment scheme that commences after 16 January 2012[573] or in a Solas scheme or national internship scheme.[574]

571. SW(CCP&C)R, Art. 78(3) as inserted by S.I. No. 43 of 2012.
572. Section 249, and *see* Part XII, Chs 3 and 4.
573. Section 247B.
574. Section 247A.

Chapter 3. Partial Capacity Benefit

373. PCB is intended to provide an opportunity for people with disabilities who are assessed to have an employment capacity that is restricted when compared to the norm to avail of employment opportunities while continuing to receive an income support payment.[575] This benefit is intended to replace previous 'exemption' arrangements where people on IB or IP could get permission to work part-time for rehabilitative or therapeutic purposes and keep their social welfare payment.

§1. Beneficiaries and Conditions

374. A person is entitled to PCB where he or she: (i) has a profound restriction on his or her capacity for work in relation to the capacity for work of a person of the same age who has no such restriction; (ii) is in receipt of IB for at least twenty-six weeks or IP; and (iii) is under pension age.[576] However, section 46A(3)–(5) provides that a person who does not have a profound restriction may still be entitled to PCB at a reduced rate, although the Act specifically provides that a person who has only a mild restriction on his or her capacity for work is *not* entitled to PCB.[577] The reduced rates that emerge in secondary legislation are payable where the person has a severe or moderate (as opposed to profound) restriction.

375. Article 28A of the SW(CCPC)R provides that a claimant is to be regarded as having a profound restriction on his or her capacity for work where he or she has a residual capacity for work which is not more than a quarter of the norm in relation to the capacity for work of a person of the same age who has no such restriction.

376. Although the terms are not used in the primary legislation, the Regulations define 'severe' and 'moderate' as involving a residual capacity for work which is not more than half or four-fifths of the norm, respectively.[578]

377. Partial capacity benefit cannot be claimed in respect of a period more than thirteen weeks before the claimant commenced employment where the claim is made before commencement of employment or in respect of any period more than three weeks after commencement of employment where the claim is made after employment has commenced – s. 11, SWA 2022.

---

575. Sections 46A-D as inserted by SW&PA 2010 and SW(CCP&C)R, Art. 28A–28G as inserted by S.I. No. 43 of 2012 and amended by S.I. No. 340 of 2013.
576. Section 46A.
577. This is defined in legislation as a capacity for work which is not materially different to the capacity for work of a person of the same age who has no such restriction.
578. Article 28C.

§2. Contribution Conditions

378. Because PCB depends on the previous receipt of IB or IP, there are no separate contribution requirements.

§3. Amount of the Benefit

379. Section 46D provides that rate of PCB in the case of a person with a profound restriction is the weekly rate of IB or IP that was being paid to that person on the day immediately before the day for which PCB is awarded, including any increase in that benefit or pension, where payable. Persons with a 'severe' and 'moderate' restriction are entitled to 75% or 50% of this rate, respectively.[579]

380. PCB is payable for a maximum period of 156 weeks.[580]

§4. Disqualifications

381. A person will also be disqualified if he or she is absent from the State (subject to certain exceptions) or is undergoing detention in legal custody[581] or if s/he participates in a Community Employment scheme that commences after 16 January 2012[582] or in a Solas scheme or national internship scheme.[583]

382. Article 28G provides that a person shall be disqualified from receiving PCB for up to nine weeks if he or she fails without good cause to: (a) attend for, or submit to, any medical or other examination, (b) comply with any medical advice and instructions provided by a registered medical practitioner relating to his or her incapacity, (c) see an officer of the Minister or medical assessor and to answer any reasonable enquiries by any such officer relating to his or her claim for PCB.

579. Schedule 7A.
580. Section 46C but this may be less as outlined in Art. 28F.
581. Section 249. *See* Part XII, Chs 3 and 4.
582. Section 247B.
583. Section 247A.

Chapter 4. Disability Allowance

383. DA is a means-tested payment for people who are substantially restricted in undertaking employment in the long term because of sickness or disability.[584,585]

§1. Beneficiaries and Conditions

384. To be entitled to DA, a person must:

(1) be between the ages of 16 and pension age (*see* paragraph 545;
(2) by reason of a specified disability, be substantially restricted in undertaking employment of a kind, which if the person were not suffering from that disability, would be suited to his or her age, experience, and qualifications; and
(3) satisfy the means test.[586]

DA is subject to the HRC (*see* Part XII, Chapter 3). Following the SW(No.2)A 2019, the reason for the restriction must be as a direct result of the person concerned being incapable of work and for no other reason (*see* paragraph 792.[587]

385. A person is regarded as being substantially restricted in undertaking suitable employment by reason of a specified disability when he or she suffers from an injury, disease, congenital deformity, or physical or mental illness that has continued or, in the opinion of a deciding officer or an appeals officer, may reasonably expect to continue for a period of at least one year. However, he or she shall not be so regarded when it is subsequently shown to the satisfaction of a deciding officer or an appeals officer that he or she is no longer likely to continue to be substantially restricted for a period of at least one year.[588]

§2. Means Test

386. The means test,[589] which is broadly similar to that applying to jobseeker's allowance, includes means from:

---

584. Sections 209–212 and SW(CCP&C)R, Arts 137–140. In *Petecel v. Minister for Social Protection* [2020] IESC 41, the Supreme Court ruled that disability allowance has been correctly classified as a special non-contributory allowance under EU Regulation 883/2004 and that it was not a social security benefit for the purposes of that Regulation.
585. This payment replaces the disabled person's maintenance allowance administered by the regional health boards under the auspices of the Department of Health. Responsibility for this payment transferred from the Department of Health to the Department of Social Welfare on 2 Oct. 1996.
586. Section 210.
587. Section 210(1)(ba) as inserted by SW(No.2)A 2019.
588. Article 137.
589. Part 2 of Sch. 3.

- most property owned by the person and/or by his or her spouse (but excluding property personally used or enjoyed by the person);
- all income that the person and/or spouse may reasonably expect to receive in the coming year (with certain exceptions);
- the value of any advantage accruing to the person or spouse from the use of property (other than a domestic dwelling or farm building, owned and occupied, furniture, and personal effects) that is personally used or enjoyed by the person or spouse, and the value of any advantage from the leasing of a farm of land; and
- any property that the person or spouse have deprived themselves of either directly or indirectly so as to qualify for assistance.

The detailed provisions of the means tests are set out in Part XI, Chapter 2.

§3. AMOUNT OF THE BENEFIT

387. A DA is payable at a flat rate with increases for qualified adults and qualified children as appropriate.[590] 'Secondary benefits' are generally payable with a DA. Any person who satisfies the above eligibility conditions may receive a DA up to pension age.

§4. DISQUALIFICATIONS

388. The Act allows for disqualification for DA when the person fails without good cause to comply with such requirements as may be specified by the regulations, including but not necessarily limited to: (a) attending or submitting to any medical or other examination or treatment, (b) complying with instructions relating to his or her incapacity issued by a registered medical practitioner, (c) refraining from behaviour likely to hinder his or her recovery, and (d) being available to meet with an officer of the Minister or medical assessor regarding his or her claim for DA. The Act states that a person is not disqualified for receipt of DA while engaging in such class or classes of employment or training and subject to such circumstances and conditions as may be prescribed.[591] In addition, section 210(9) provides that a person shall not be disqualified for receipt of a DA while engaging in a prescribed course of education, training or development.[592] Although the Regulations do not specifically prescribe such employment, they do allow earnings from 'employment or self-employment of a rehabilitative nature', which, by implication, would appear to allow such work.[593]

590. Section 211 as amended by SWPA 2007, s. 9, SW(MP)A 2010, s. 12, SWPCRA 2018, s. 17 and SWA 2021, s. 13.
591. Section 212 substituted by SWPA 2007, s. 26.
592. As inserted by SW(No.2)A 2019.
593. SW(CCP&C)R, Art. 147 as substituted by S.I. No. 783 of 2021 and amended by S.I. No. 614 of 2022.

389. Previously, a person was not entitled to receive DA for any period during which he or she was resident in an institution (with certain exceptions). However, this disqualification was abolished with effect from 3 January 2007.[594]

390. A person is also not entitled to DA if he or she is temporarily resident outside the State or undergoing detention in legal custody (subject to certain exceptions).[595] Section 249(6) provides that a person is disqualified for DA where he or she is undergoing imprisonment (except where regulations otherwise provide) though this provision is legally questionable in light of the Supreme Court decision in *C v. Minister for Social Protection* (*see* paragraphs 782–784). A claimant will also be disqualified if s/he participates in a Community Employment scheme that commences after 16 January 2012[596] or in a Solas scheme or national internship scheme.[597]

594. SWA 2006, s. 11.
595. Section 249 as amended by SWPA 2008, s. 10 (*see* below Part XII, Chs 3 and 4).
596. Section 247B.
597. Section 247A.

Chapter 5. Blind Pension

391. BP is a means-tested payment payable to blind persons.[598,599]

§1. Beneficiaries and Conditions

392. To qualify for BP, a person must have attained the age of 18 years but not have reached pensionable age, must be 'blind', satisfy the means test, and be habitually resident in the State. Section 161A(b) provides that, to qualify for a BP, a person must be 'so blind that he or she either cannot perform any work for which eyesight is essential or cannot continue his or her ordinary occupation'.

§2. Means Test

393. The means test for BP is broadly the same as that for the State pension (non-contributory) (*see* Part XI).

§3. Amount of the Benefit

394. BP is payable at a flat rate with increases for qualified children as appropriate.[600] It is payable over pension age. The normal 'qualified adult' rules do not apply to a BP. Increases are payable when the claimant is living with or is wholly or mainly maintaining his or her spouse, civil partner or cohabitant who has not attained pension age and is not in receipt of a payment set out in section 161C(2).[601] Additional payments are made when the person is living alone. 'Household benefits' are generally payable with a BP.

598. Sections 161–161E as substituted by SWLRPA 2006, s. 20.
599. The blind pension originated as an old-age pension payable at a younger age to blind persons. *See* the discussion in *Harvey v. Minister for Social Welfare* (1989) IR 213 in which the Supreme Court rejected an argument that the blind pension was *not* an old-age (non-contributory) pension and upheld J Blayney's decision that it was merely the old-age pension payable at an earlier age to a person who suffers from blindness. However, the current statutory provisions have evolved since that decision and it may well be that, should the question arise, a different answer would be arrived at today. There is also a blind welfare allowance (BWA) currently administered by the HSE on behalf of the Department of Health which is payable as a supplement with other social welfare schemes, SWPA 2008, ss 12–14 provided for this payment to be taken over by DSP but these provisions have not yet been commenced (presumably as the purpose of the BWA is entirely unclear). As long ago as 1986, the Commission on Social Welfare recommended that BWA should be phased out.
600. Section 161B as substituted by SWLRPA 2006, s. 20.
601. Section 161C as substituted by SWLRPA 2006, s. 20 and amended by s. 26 and Sch. 3 SW&PA 2010. Spouse and civil partner includes a party to a marriage/civil partnership that has been validly dissolved, s. 161 as substituted by SWLRPA 2006, s. 20 and amended by s. 19(5)(b) SW&PA 2010.

§4. DISQUALIFICATIONS

395. A person is generally disqualified for payment of a BP when he or she is receiving a contributory pension.[602] A person may also be disqualified while undergoing detention in legal custody.[603] Section 249(9) provides that a person is disqualified for BP where he or she is undergoing imprisonment though this provision is legally questionable in light of the Supreme Court decision in *C v. Minister for Social Protection* (*see* paragraphs 782–784. A BP is not normally payable when the person is temporarily resident outside the State, and the HRC applies.[604] A claimant will also be disqualified if s/he participates in a Community Employment scheme that commences after 16 January 2012[605] or in a Solas scheme or national internship scheme.[606]

602. Section 161E(1) subject to sub-ss (2) and (3) (as substituted by SWLRPA 2006, s. 20).
603. Section 249, *see* Part XII, Chs 3 and 4.
604. Section 249(7) subject to s. 249(8), and s. 161A(d). *See* Part XII, Chs 3 and 4.
605. Section 247B.
606. Section 247A.

Chapter 6. Carer's Allowance

§1. Beneficiaries and Conditions

396. CA is a means-tested payment to persons providing full-time care and attention to a 'relevant person' who requires care.[607] To be entitled to CA, a person must be a carer; that is, a person must be residing with and providing full-time care and attention to a relevant person.[608] In limited circumstances, a person not residing with the care recipient but providing full-time care and attention can qualify for the allowance.[609] In addition, the carer must: (i) not be engaged in employment or self-employment (subject to some exceptions), (ii) be at least 18 years old, and (iii) not be residing in an institution.[610] 'Institution' means: (a) a hospital, convalescent home, or home for persons suffering from a physical or mental disability or accommodation ancillary thereto and any other similar establishment providing residence, maintenance, or care for the persons therein; or (b) a private dwelling where a person is boarded under an arrangement with the HSE.[611] The carer must also satisfy the HRC.

397. The following additional conditions apply to a non-resident carer: there must be a direct system of communication (such as a telephone or alarm system) between the carer's residence and that of the caree, and the caree must not already be receiving full-time care and attention within his or her own residence from another person.[612]

398. 'Relevant person' means a person (other than a person in receipt of a constant attendance allowance under the occupational injuries scheme) who has such a disability that he or she requires full-time care and attention and who has attained the age of 16 or who is under 16 and is a person in respect of whom a payment of DCA is being made.[613]

399. A relevant person is not to be regarded as requiring full-time care and attention unless:

(1) he or she has such a disability that he or she requires from another person:
   (a) continual supervision and frequent assistance throughout the day in connection with normal bodily functions; or

607. Sections 179–186 and SW(CCP&C)R, Arts 131–136.
608. Section 179(1)(a).
609. Section 179(1)(b) and art. 133.
610. Article 132 (as amended by art. 2 of S.I. No. 76 of 2021) but *see* art. 136(1) (as substituted by SI 76 of 2021) as to the circumstances in which a person may be regarded as providing full-time care and attention *and* engage in employment or self-employment (*see* below). Quaere whether the age condition is *intra vires* given the definition of 'carer' in s. 179 (which imposes no age condition).
611. Section 164 and Art. 133.
612. Article 133.
613. Section 179(1) as substituted in part by s. 9 SW(No.2)A 2019.

(b) continual supervision to avoid danger to him or herself; and

(2) he or she is likely to require full-time care and attention for at least twelve consecutive months.[614]

400. The phrases 'requires … continual supervision and frequent assistance throughout the day in connection with normal bodily functions' and 'continual supervision to avoid danger to him or herself' are based on UK law in relation to attendance allowance and, subsequently, disability living allowance. There has been extensive judicial consideration of the meaning of these phrases by the UK courts.[615] However, the precise language used is not the same as the Irish wording; the legislative context is not the same, nor is the UK interpretation self-evidently correct. It could not be said that the Irish courts would (or indeed should) necessarily follow the UK interpretation.

401. A carer may continue to be regarded as providing full-time care and attention to a care recipient when he or she would qualify for payment of an allowance but for the fact that either he or she or the relevant person is undergoing medical or other treatment of a temporary nature in an institution for a period or periods of no longer than thirteen weeks; where he or she would qualify for payment of an allowance but for the fact that the relevant person has been permanently admitted to an institution, and the maximum period for payment of the allowance does not exceed twelve weeks; or where he or she is attending a nonresidential course of rehabilitation training provided by an organization (recognized by the Minister for Health for the purposes of the provision of such training); or a non-residential day care place approved by the Minister.[616] A carer may also be regarded as providing full-time care and attention to a relevant person under 16 in respect of whom DCA is being paid, where he or she would qualify for payment of CA but for the fact that the relevant person is undergoing medical or other treatment of a temporary nature in an institution for a period not longer than twenty-six weeks.[617]

---

614. Section 179(4) as amended by SW(MP)A 2015. A person may be required to attend or submit to such medical or other examination as may be required and may be disqualified for failing to do so without good cause: s. 185.

615. *R v. National Insurance Commissioner ex parte Secretary of State for Social services* [1981] 1 WLR 1017; *In re Woodling* [1984] 1 WLR 384; *R v. Secretary of State for Social Services ex parte Connolly* [1986] 1 All ER 998; *Mallinson v. Secretary of State for Social Security* [1994] 1 WLR 630; *Cockburn v. Chief Adjudication Officer* and *Secretary of State for Social Services v. Fairey* [1997] 3 All ER 844; *Stewart v. AG for Scotland* reported in R(DLA) 2/00. *See Wikeley, Ogus and Barendt*, 694–703.

616. SW(CCP&C)R, Art. 136 as substituted by S.I. No. 76 of 2021 and amended by S.I. No. 201 of 2022. A person in receipt of CA may continue to be regarded as providing full time care and attention to a child in respect of whom DCA is payable where the child is undergoing medical or other treatment in a hospital or other institution for a period of up to twenty-six weeks in a twelve-month period – S.I. No. 201 of 2022 – or where a child born on or after 1 Jan. 2023 and otherwise eligible for Domiciliary Care Allowance remains in hospital immediately after birth for the purpose of receiving medical or other treatment – S.I. No. 324 of 2023.

617. SW(CCP&C)R, Art. 136(1A) as inserted by S.I. No. 201 of 2022.

402. A carer is allowed to engage in employment or self-employment or to undertake training or education for not more than 18.5 hours per week (provided that adequate provision is made for the care of the relevant person).[618]

403. Finally, Article 136(1)(e) now provides that a carer may be regarded as providing full-time care and attention to a relevant person where the number of hours providing such care is not less than thirty-five hours in a period of seven consecutive days, and care is provided on any five days, whether consecutive or not, within a period of seven consecutive days.[619] This is intended 'to set a minimum hours condition for which a carer can be regarded as providing full-time care and attention' (per the Explanatory Note to the Regulations). It is not clear whether this broadly follows existing practice or whether it is intended to reflect a change in how 'full-time care and attention' is assessed. However, the provision states that such a person *may* (rather than *shall*) be regarded as providing full-time care and attention so its implications remain to be seen in practice. It also remains necessary for the relevant person to *require* full-time care and attention even if these hours of care are provided in practice.[620]

§2. Means Test

404. The means test for the CA is generally similar to that in relation to the State pension (*see* Part XI).[621] However, when the income of a carer and his or her spouse is being assessed under the means test, the first EUR 665 of weekly income is disregarded, that is, not taken into account. When the carer's spouse receives a pension that is a social welfare pension paid by another state, an amount of that pension equal to the maximum rate of a State pension (contributory) is not taken as means. The first EUR 350.50 of weekly income enjoyed by a single carer is not assessed under the means test.[622]

§3. Amount of the Benefit

405. CA is payable at a flat rate with increases for qualified children as appropriate (however, no increases for qualified adults apply).[623] 'Secondary benefits' are generally payable with a CA. The rate of the allowance is currently significantly

618. SW(CCP&C)R, Art. 136 as amended by S.I. No. 76 of 2021.
619. As substituted by S.I. No. 76 of 2021.
620. *See*, for example, the *Social Welfare Appeals Office Annual Report 2021*: Case Study 37: Carer's Allowance Care Required (which predated the adoption of this provision) where the evidence was that the carer provided care 'from early in the morning until late in the evening' but the Appeals Officer concluded that the evidence did not indicate the need for assistance with normal bodily functions throughout the day or that the care recipient required continual supervision in order to avoid danger to herself and, therefore, it had not been established that she required full-time care and attention within the meaning of the legislation.
621. Part 5 of Sch. 3.
622. Article 144 as amended by S.I. No. 783 of 2020.
623. Section 181.

higher than the standard social assistance rate. When a person is caring for more than one person, a higher rate of allowance is payablc (and a lesser increase is payable when the person cared for is over pension age). Increases with respect to qualified children are payable, but no IQA is payable with CA.

406. The SWPA of 2007 introduced a new 'half-rate' CA.[624] This is payable to persons over the age of 18, not resident in an institution and in receipt of other social welfare payments under Part 2 or Part 3 of the 2005 Act (other than jobseeker's benefit, jobseeker's benefit (self-employed), jobseeker's allowance, back to work family dividend, supplementary welfare allowance), or in respect of whom an increase for a qualified adult is paid to another party, who satisfy the rules as to providing care. This half-rate allowance is not payable where the carer gets credited contributions in respect of any period of proven unemployment. It may, however, be paid where the carer is engaged in employment, self-employment or any course of education or training where it is shown to the satisfaction of a deciding or appeals office that adequate provision has been made for the care of person requiring carer and the aggregate duration of the employment, self-employment, education or training does not exceed 18.5 hours a week.[625]

§4. Disqualifications

407. The normal temporary residence outside the State and detention in legal custody disqualifications do not apply to CA, although a person who is absent for any length of time or in legal custody may not satisfy the other qualification conditions (*see* above). The HRC applies to CA.[626] A claimant will also be disqualified if s/he participates in a Community Employment scheme that commences after 16 January 2012[627] or in a Solas scheme or national internship scheme.[628]

624. Section 186A as inserted by SWPA 2007, 24 and SW(CCP&C)R, art. 136A and 136B as inserted by S.I. No. 76 of 2021.
625. Art. 136B of S.I. No. 142 of 2007 as inserted by S.I. No. 76 of 2021.
626. Section 180(2).
627. Section 247B.
628. Section 247A.

Chapter 7. Carer's Benefit

§1. Beneficiaries and Conditions

408. A carer's benefit is a payment made to insured people who leave the workforce to provide full-time care and attention to persons who require full-time care and attention.[629] While entitlement to a carer's leave and benefit is intended to operate in a complementary manner, entitlement to leave – which is set out in the Carer's Leave Act of 2001 – is separate from entitlement to a benefit, that is, unlike a maternity benefit, entitlement to a carer's benefit is not dependent on entitlement to a carer's leave. To be entitled to a carer's benefit, a person must be a carer; that is, a person must be at least 16 years old and be residing with and providing full-time care and attention to a relevant person.[630] A carer will be regarded as providing full-time care and attention where the number of hours providing such care is not less than thirty-five hours in a period of seven consecutive days, and care is provided on any five days, whether consecutive or not, within a period of seven consecutive days.[631] A carer will also be regarded as providing full-time care and attention where (a) s/he or the relevant person is undergoing medical or other treatment of a temporary nature in an institution for a period no longer than thirteen weeks, or (b) the person being cared for is attending a non-residential course of rehabilitation training provided by an organisation (being an organisation recognised by the Minister for Health and Children for the purposes of the provision of such training), or a non-residential place of day care approved by the Minister for Health. Where a child is admitted to an institution on a full-time basis for the purpose of receiving medical or other treatment of a temporary nature or where a child born on or after 1 January 2023 and otherwise eligible for DCA remains in hospital immediately after birth for the purpose of receiving medical or other treatment, CB remains payable for not more than twenty-six weeks in a twelve-month period – S.I. No. 324 of 2023.

409. In addition, the carer must:

(i) have been engaged in remunerative 'full-time' employment as an employed contributor for not less than eight weeks (whether consecutive or not) within the relevant period;[632]

---

629. Sections 99–107 and SW(CCP&C)R, Arts 52–58 as amended by S.I. No. 623 of 2021.

630. Section 99(1). In practice, a person will only qualify from the age of 19 years as they will only have the relevant contribution record at that age. The definition of 'relevant person' is identical to that set out above in relation to the carer's allowance.

631. Art. 56(c) of S.I. No. 142 of 2007 as inserted by Art. 4 of S.I. No. 623 of 2021.

632. Generously defined as employment for an aggregate of not less than sixteen hours per week or not less than thirty-two hours in a fortnight within the eight week period prior to the claim. Section 300(5). 'Relevant period' means the twenty-six weeks immediately before the first day for which the benefit is claimed. A person taking adoptive leave, health and safety leave, maternity leave, parental leave, parent's leave or paternity leave may claim Carer's Benefit if s/he was engaged in remunerative full-time employment for eight weeks in the period of twenty-six weeks prior to the period of twenty-six weeks immediately before the first day in respect of which a claim to Carer's Benefit is made or in a period which consists of two or more periods that, taken together, amount to a period of twenty-six weeks in the fifty-two weeks prior to the period of twenty-six weeks

(ii) not engage in employment, self-employment, education, or training of more than 18.5 hours per week and not earn more than EUR 332.50 per week as an employee;[633] and

(iii) satisfy the contribution conditions.

A person will not be regarded as requiring full-time care and attention unless the person has such a disability that he or she requires from another person (a) continual supervision and frequent assistance throughout the day in connection with normal bodily functions, or (b) continual supervision in order to avoid danger to himself or herself.[634]

410. As in the case of CA in limited circumstances, persons not residing with the care recipient but providing full-time care may qualify for a benefit.[635]

§2. Contribution Conditions

411. The contribution conditions are that the person must have at least 156 paid contributions and must have thirty-nine paid contributions in the second-last contribution year before the benefit year in which the claim is made, or in the twelve months immediately prior to the first day for which the benefit is claimed, or twenty-six weeks in the second- and third-last contribution years before the beginning of the benefit year (the latter condition is to allow job sharers to benefit).[636]

§3. Amount of the Benefit

412. A carer's benefit is payable at a flat rate with increases for qualified children as appropriate (however, no increases for qualified adults apply).[637] 'Household benefits' are not payable with the benefit, as it is considered to be a short-term payment. When a person is caring for more than one person, a higher rate of allowance is payable. A benefit is payable for up to 104 weeks, whether consecutive or not.[638]

§4. Disqualifications

413. A person is not entitled to a carer's benefit if he or she is absent from the State or if he or she is undergoing detention in legal custody (subject to certain

immediately before the first day in respect of which a claim to Carer's Benefit is made – SW(CCP&C)R, Art. 57A, as inserted by Art. 4(c) of S.I. No. 623 of 2021.

633. SW(CCP&C)R, Art. 57 as amended by Art. 4(b) of S.I. No. 75 of 2008 and Art. 4(b) of S.I. No. 623 of 2021.
634. Section 99(2) as amended by SW(MP)A 2015.
635. *See* above para. 397 and SW(CCP&C)R, Art. 54.
636. Section 101.
637. Section 102.
638. Section 103 as amended by SWLRPA 2006, s. 7.

exceptions).[639] A person who, having been in receipt of a benefit for a period of less than six weeks, ceases to be entitled to such benefit, is disqualified for receipt of the benefit with respect to the same person for six weeks from the last day on which he or she was entitled to the benefit.[640] A claimant will also be disqualified if s/he participates in a Community Employment scheme that commences after 16 January 2012[641] or in a Solas scheme or national internship scheme.[642]

639. Section 249.
640. Section 106.
641. Section 247B.
642. Section 247A.

Chapter 8. Carer's Support Grant

414. A CSG (formerly known as respite care grant) is an annual payment to a carer (whether in receipt of another social welfare payment or not).[643]

§1. Beneficiaries and Conditions

415. 'Carer' is defined as a person ordinarily resident in the State who has attained the age of 16 and:

(a) is in receipt of or entitled to a carer's benefit, CA or DCA;
(b) (repealed);
(c) is providing full-time care and attention to a person who is in receipt of an increase of disablement pension under section 78 with respect to the need for constant attendance;
(d) resides with and has provided, is providing, or is likely to provide full-time care and attention for such periods and on such date as may be prescribed to a relevant person; or
(e) subject to prescribed conditions and circumstances, does not reside with but has provided, is providing, or is likely to provide full-time care and attention for such periods and on such date as may be prescribed to a relevant person.[644]

416. The definition of 'relevant person' means a person who is ordinarily resident in the State and is so incapacitated that he or she requires full-time care and attention.[645] CSG is also payable where a child is admitted to an institution on a full-time basis for the purpose of receiving medical or other treatment of a temporary nature or where a child born on or after 1 January 2023 and otherwise eligible for DCA remains in hospital immediately after birth for the purpose of receiving medical or other treatment.[646]

417. CSG is not subject to any contribution conditions or means test.

§2. Amount of the Benefit

418. A CSG is payable at an annual rate, currently EUR 1,850,[647] and is payable on the first Thursday in June of each year.[648]

---

643. Sections 224–226 and SW(CCP&C)R, Arts 162–171. Renamed by SWPA 2015.
644. SW(CCP&C)R, Art. 165 provides that for the purposes of paras (d) and (e), on the date on which the grant is payable, the carer shall have provided full-time care and attention, be likely to provide full-time care and attention, or a combination of both, to the relevant person for a continuous period of not less than 183 days, such period to include the date on which the grant is payable. Art. 168 sets out the conditions for non-resident carers.
645. Section 224(1).
646. S.I. No. 324 of 2023.
647. Section 225 as amended by SWA, 2020, s. 11.
648. SW(CCP&C)R, Art. 163.

§3. DISQUALIFICATIONS

419. Section 225(2), as amended,[649] provides that a grant is not payable to a carer when:

(a) he or she engages in employment, self-employment or any course of education or training (but *see* below);[650]
(b) he or she is entitled to or in receipt of JB or JA;
(c) he or she is in receipt of credited contributions with respect to proven unemployment;
(d) the relevant person is resident in an institution.

420. For these purposes, 'institution' means a hospital, convalescent home or home for people suffering from a physical or mental disability or ancillary accommodation, a nursing home for the care and maintenance of dependent elderly people, or any other similar establishment providing residence, maintenance, or care.[651]

421. The ban on employment is subject to the exception that a person *is* allowed to engage in employment, self-employment or any training or course of education provided that the aggregate duration of such activities does not exceed 18.5 hours per week *and* that adequate provision has been made for the care of the relevant person.[652]

422. As set out above, the carer must be ordinarily resident in the State. Article 166 of the Regulations provides that the carer must not be resident in an institution.[653] However, Article 167 sets out circumstances in which a carer may continue to be regarded as providing full-time care and attention, including when:

(a) the carer is undergoing medical or other treatment of a temporary nature in an institution for a period or periods amounting to not more than thirteen weeks;
(b) the relevant person is (i) undergoing medical or other treatment of a temporary nature in an institution, or (ii) temporarily being cared for by, or temporarily residing with, another person, for a period or periods amounting to not more than thirteen weeks;
(c) the relevant person is attending (i) a non-residential course of rehabilitation training provided by an organization (being an organization recognized by the Minister for Health for the purposes of the provision of such training), or (ii) a non-residential place of day care approved by the Minister for Health and Children; or

649. Section 225(2)(d) was deleted by s. 169(c) of the SWPA 2008.
650. As amended by SW&PA 2007; s. 225(3) and SW(CCP&C)R, Art. 169 as amended.
651. Section 224(1).
652. SW(CCP&C), Art. 169 as substituted by S.I. No. 623 of 2021.
653. SW(CCP&C), Art. 166.

(d) the carer is undertaking such training or course of education outside the home as the Minister may determine from time to time subject to the limits with respect to duration imposed by article 169, i.e., up to 18.5 hours per week; and
(e) the number of hours providing such care is not less than thirty-five hours in a period of seven consecutive days, and care is provided on any five days, whether consecutive or not, within a period of seven consecutive days.[654]

423. Finally, a carer is disqualified for receiving the grant if and for so long as the caree fails without good cause to attend or submit to the medical examination.[655]

654. Section 225(4) and SW(CCP&C), Art. 167 as amended by S.I. No. 623 of 2021.
655. Section 226 and SW(CCP&C), Art. 171.

Chapter 9. Domiciliary Care Allowance

424. DCA is a monthly payment to assist with the costs of caring for a severely disabled child who needs full-time care and attention substantially beyond what is normally required by a child of the same age.[656] Previously DCA was operated on the basis of guidelines by the HSE.[657] However, SWPA 2008 provided a detailed statutory basis for the scheme, and from 1 April 2009, it has been administered by the DSP.

§1. Beneficiaries and Conditions

425. DCA is payable to a 'qualified person' in respect of a qualified child'. In order to be a qualified child for the purposes of DCA, a child must:

(a) be under the age of 16; and
(b) have a severe disability requiring continual or continuous care and attention substantially in excess of the care and attention normally required by a child of the same age (the level of disability caused by that disability must be such that the child is likely to require full-time care and attention for at least twelve consecutive months).[658]

The Departmental guidelines state that it uses 'a set of consistent and objective guidelines in determining the medical (sic.) eligibility of children for the scheme' which were revised, most recently in 2013.[659] Claims are assessed by designated Departmental medical assessors who have received training in disability evaluation.

426. To be a qualified person:

(a) the child must normally reside with that person;[660]
(b) the person must provide for the care of the child, and
(c) at the date of the making of the application for DCA, the person must be habitually resident in the State (or must be a member of the Defence Forces or a civil servant in the service, outside the State, of the Government, the State or an international organization; or a volunteer development worker; or an insured person

656. Section 186B–H as inserted by SWPA 2008, s. 15 as amended and SW(CCP&C)R, Art. 140A–140F (as inserted by S.I. No. 162 of 2009).
657. SWPA 2008, s. 17 sets out transitional arrangements in relation to the DCA payments made by HSE.
658. Section 186C as substituted by SWMPA 2010, s. 26. The *Social Welfare Appeal Office Report 2010* and the *Social Welfare Appeal Office Report 2013* set out a number of decisions as to how appeals officer are interpreting the care requirement (though the issues are of a factual rather than legal nature).
659. *Operational Guidelines: Domiciliary Care Allowance*, 2020. For the medical guidelines *see* https://assets.gov.ie/37034/fdb0f1b14efd46d894d807c136128fdc.pdf.
660. Normal residence is determined in accordance with Art. 13 of SW(CCP&C)R, *see* S.I. No. 162 of 2009.

employed outside the State in respect of whom Irish employment contributions are payable and with whom the child resides).[661]

427. There is no contribution requirement or means test. The child must be ordinarily resident in the State or satisfy the requirements of section 219(2) (i.e., where the parent or guardian is a member of the Defence Forces or a civil servant, etc., residing outside the State (as above), and must not be detained in a children detention school.[662]

§2. Amount of the Benefit

428. The current rate of DCA is EUR 330 per month.[663] A half-rate payment may be payable in respect of children who reside on a part-time basis with the carer (*see* below).

§3. Disqualifications

429. A child is not entitled to DCA, where he or she is detained in a children's detention school.[664] Generally, DCA is not payable for any period during which a child is resident in an institution.[665] 'Institution' means a hospital, convalescent home or home for children suffering from a physical or mental disability or ancillary accommodation and any other similar establishment providing residence, maintenance or care where the cost of the child's maintenance in that institution is being met in whole or in part by or on behalf of the Executive or the Department of Education and Science.[666] However, a reduced allowance may be payable where the child in an institution is temporarily resident with the qualified person for a period of not less than two days in any one week.[667] DCA will continue to be payable in respect of a qualified child who has been admitted to an institution on a full-time basis for the purpose of receiving medical or other treatment of a temporary nature for not more than twenty-six weeks in a twelve-month period.[668] Similarly, where a child born on or after 1 January 2023 remains in hospital immediately after birth for the purpose of receiving medical or other treatment, this allowance is payable for not more than twenty-six weeks in a twelve-month period.[669] A claimant will also be disqualified for receipt of DCA if s/he participates in a Community Employment

661. Section 186D. The provisions in relation to persons working abroad are adopted from s. 219(2).
662. Section 186C(c) as substituted by SWMPA 2010, s. 26.
663. As amended by s. 16 of SWA 2022.
664. Section 186C(d) as substituted by SWMPA 2010, s. 26.
665. Section 186E. In *Donnelly v. Minister for Social Protection* [2022] IESC 31 the Supreme Court held that this disqualification was not contrary to the guarantees of equality in Art. 40.1 of the Constitution or Art. 14 of the European Convention on Human Rights.
666. Section 186B.
667. Section 186E(2).
668. Section 186E(3) and S.I. No. 162 of 2009 as amended by S.I. No. 200 of 2022.
669. *See* S.I. No. 129 of 2023.

scheme that commences after 16 January 2012[670] or in a Solas scheme or national internship scheme.[671] Finally, the (a) legal detention in custody and (b) 'temporary residence outside the State' rules apply in respect of DCA – in the case of residence outside the State after the first three weeks of any such absence in a calendar year.[672]

670. Section 247B.
671. Section 247A.
672. Section 249(17) (as inserted by SWPA 2008, s. 16) and S.I. No. 162 of 2009.

Part VI. Industrial Accidents and Occupational Diseases

Chapter 1. The Occupational Injuries Scheme

§1. Field of Application

I. Personal Field of Application

430. This part looks at the Occupational Injuries Code.[673] The scope of the Occupational Injuries Code is determined by two factors: first, the claimant must be working in insurable (occupational injuries) employment (*see* paragraphs 99–106 of Part II) and, second, the illness must be the result of an occupational accident or prescribed disease or injury (*see* paragraphs 433–443 in this part). In general terms, the vast majority of employees, irrespective of age, are covered for occupational injuries. However, self-employed persons are *not* covered for occupational injuries.

431. When a claim for an OIB is made (or a declaration is sought that an accident or disease is an occupational accident or disease), the Minister may direct that the relevant employment shall be treated as having been insurable (occupational injuries) employment, notwithstanding that, by reason of a breach of a statutory provision passed for the protection of employed persons, the contract of employment was void or the employee not lawfully employed.[674]

II. Territorial Field of Application

432. Except when Ministerial Regulations otherwise provide, OIBs are not payable with respect to an accident happening while the insured person is outside of the State.[675] This exclusion is subject to the EU Regulations on Social Security for Migrant Workers (Regulation 883/2004) and bilateral agreements (where relevant). The EU Regulations provide that when a person is working for an employer in another EU country, he or she is generally covered by the social security laws of

673. Sections 69–98 and the Social Welfare (Consolidated Occupational Injuries) Regulations, 2007 (S.I. No. 102 of 2007) (hereafter, SW(COI)R).
674. Section 73(1). *See* the general discussion as to the position of such employments at para. 70.
675. Section 73(3). *See also* SW(COI)R, Art. 30 as to occupational diseases.

that country. However, if a person is posted by an Irish employer to work in another EU country and remains subject to Irish social welfare law, coverage for OIBs continues under Irish legislation. In addition, the EU Regulation provides for the assimilation of facts occurring in different Member States so that where legal effects are attributed to the occurrence of certain facts or events, the competent Member State must take account of like facts or events occurring in any Member State as though they had taken place in its own territory.[676]

§2. Concept of 'Occupational Accident'

433. The Occupational Injuries Code applies with respect to a personal injury[677] caused by an accident arising out of and in the course of employment (occupational accidents) and with respect to prescribed diseases and prescribed personal injury not so caused but that is a result of the nature of the employment (occupational diseases). The accident or disease must have occurred or developed on or after 1 May 1967.

I. Accident

434. The meaning of the term 'accident' is not self-evident, and considerable case law has been built up around the import of this word.[678] 'Accident' was defined in *Fenton v. Thorley* as 'an unlooked-for mishap or an untoward event which is not expected or designed'.[679] An 'accident' has been held to include deliberate acts by a third party, and the fact that the event was foreseeable has been held not to prevent it from being considered to be an accident.[680] The main use of the term has been to distinguish an event (which can be an accident) from a process (which cannot).[681] Thus, an injury sustained as a result of an ongoing series of incidents, none of which could be regarded as an accident, will not be regarded as having been

676. Article 5 of Regulation 883/2004.

677. In UK law, 'personal injury' has been understood as referring to 'hurt to body or mind': *Jones v. Secretary of State for Social Services* [1972] AC 944 at 1019. It is clear from the case law that a disease can fall within the concept of injury (although it often may not be possible to identify an 'accident' by which it was caused).

678. Nicholas Wikeley, Anthony Ogus & Eric Barendt, *The Law of Social Security*, 5th ed. (London: Butterworths, 2002), 722–726; Robert Clark, *Annotated Guide to Social Welfare Law* (London: Sweet & Maxwell, 1995), 127–130. There are very few Irish cases interpreting the Occupational Injuries Code. In contrast, there are numerous workmen's compensation cases on issues such as the term 'accident' – many of which are referred to by Clark – but one would have to question how relevant many of them are today given the significant changes in work practices.

679. [1903] AC 413.

680. *Trim Joint District School v. Kelly* [1914] AC 667. However, there must still be an accident. Thus, a suspension of an employee for suspected misconduct, while it might come as a surprise cannot be an accident: *Chief Adjudication Officer v. Oakley* [1997] EWCA Civ. 1170.

681. *Chief Adjudication Officer v. Faulds* [2000] 2 UKHL 26. *See also Kelly v. Cement Ltd* [1940] IR 86 and the discussion in the Northern Ireland case of *R. (Curry) v. National Insurance Commissioners* [1974] NI 102.

caused by an occupational accident. (Such an injury might, however, constitute a prescribed disease, depending on the circumstances.)

435. The House of Lords in *Faulds* established that 'accident' and 'injury' must be treated as conceptually distinct so that 'injury caused by accident' is not the same as 'accidental injury'.[682] Thus there must be a separate causative event or incident which can be described as 'an accident'. So in *Scullion,* a person who suffered a heart attack while at work – without any separate event or incident causing that attack – was held not to have suffered from an 'accident'.[683] However, in the old worker's compensation case of *Larkin v. CIE,* the Irish Supreme Court ruled that a railway shunter who died as a result of cardiac disease shortly after moving a heavy points lever had suffered from personal injury by accident.[684] In contrast, the English Court of Appeal in *Scullion* stated that to succeed, Mr Scullion would have to show that his heart attack was brought on by, for example, lifting a heavy bundle of papers or a (work-related) incidence of stress.[685] Clearly, a worker involved in physical labour is more likely to succeed in such a case, and the distinctions drawn by the courts are not always entirely satisfactory.[686]

436. The House of Lords in *Faulds* also reviewed the law in relation to the distinction between an accident and a process.[687] A fireman claimed an industrial injuries benefit (the UK equivalent of injury benefit) on the basis that he had attended many fatal accidents, which had resulted in his suffering from post-traumatic stress disorder. The House of Lords held that it was necessary to identify an accident that had caused injury to the claimant; the fact that a person had suffered stress or developed a physical or psychological illness as a result of a stressful occupation would not, in itself, qualify him or her for an award of benefit. Even so, it was possible to find that persons in stressful occupations had suffered an accident or a series of accidents (although the distinction between an accident and a process might be difficult to discern).[688] The word 'accident' as required to be given its normal meaning and regard should be held to such factors as expectation and foreseeability, whether an accident was exceptional, and the nature of the claimant's occupation.

---

682. *Chief Adjudication Officer v. Faulds* [2000] UKHL 26.
683. *Secretary of State for Work and Pensions v. Scullion* [2010] EWCA Civ 310. *See also* the old Irish cases of *O'Hara v. Hayes* (1910) 44 ILTR 71 (heart attack not, in itself, an accident) and *Dennis v. Midland Railway* [1920] 2 IR 154 (catching pneumonia while exposed to bad weather did not, in itself, amount to injury by accident).
684. [1962–1963] Ir. Jur. Rep. 73.
685. *Secretary of State for Work and Pensions v. Scullion* [2010] EWCA Civ 310 at 22 and 54.
686. *Clover, Clayton & Co. Ltd. v. Hughes* [1910] AC 242. *See also Fyfe Coal Co. Ltd. v. Young* [1940] AC 479.
687. *Chief Adjudication Officer v. Faulds* [2000] UKHL 26.
688. *See Mullen v. Secretary of State for Work and Pensions* [2002] SC 251, where the Court of Sessions found that, on the facts of that case, repeated back injuries were accidents rather than a process. *See also* an appeals officer's decision that stress arising from bullying and harassment at work involved the cumulative effect of a series of incidents arising out of and in the course of employment: *Social Welfare Appeals Office Report 2002*, 19–20.

II. Link to the Contract of Employment

437. An occupational accident is one that arises 'out of and in the course of employment'.[689] This phrase – which has given rise to even more debate than the meaning of the word 'accident' – is generally accepted to mean that (a) the accident must have been caused or linked to some risk relating to the claimant's employment, and (b) it must have occurred during the course of employment.[690] The meaning of this phrase has been modified by section 72, which sets out certain rules for determining when an accident may be regarded as having arisen out of and in the course of employment. There is a presumption that an accident that occurred *in the course of* employment arose *out of* that employment.[691] This presumption is rebuttable, however, so that in appropriate cases, an employer may be able to show that, even though the claimant suffered an injury while at work, the accident was not attributable to the employment.

438. In addition, when an accident: (a) arises in the course of employment; (b) is caused by another person's misconduct, misbehaviour, or negligence or by steps taken in consequence of any such misconduct, negligence, or misbehaviour or by the behaviour or presence of an animal or is caused by or consists in the insured person being struck by any object or by lightning; and (c) the insured person did not directly or indirectly cause or contribute to the happening of the accident by his or her conduct outside the employment or by any act not incidental to the employment, such accident *shall be* treated as having arisen out of the insured person's employment.[692]

439. Disobeying instructions does not necessarily debar an employee from claiming OIBs. The fact that, at the time of the accident, the employee was acting in contravention of any statutory or other regulations pertaining to the employment or of any orders given by the employer or was acting without instructions from the employer shall not affect a claim for benefit provided that (a) the accident would have been deemed to be an occupational accident had the act not been done in contravention of regulations or without instructions from the employer, as the case may be, and (b) the act was done for the purposes of and in connection with the employer's trade or business.[693]

440. The position of apprentices injured while on training is governed by section 72(6), which creates a rebuttable presumption that accidents occurring to an

689. Nicholas Wikeley, Anthony Ogus & Eric Barendt, *The Law of Social Security*, 5th ed. (London: Butterworths, 2002), 727–743; Robert Clark, *Annotated Guide to Social Welfare Law* (London: Sweet & Maxwell, 1995), 130–135.
690. *Chief Adjudication Officer v. Rhodes* [1999] 2 All ER 859.
691. Section 72(1).
692. Section 72(2).
693. Section 72(3).

apprentice while attending a technical school or other place of training or instruction are occupational accidents if attendance was with the employer's consent or under his or her direction or if attendance was required by the contract of apprenticeship.

441. Accidents happening to an insured person at the place of employment and while that person is taking steps, in an actual or supposed emergency, to rescue persons or property are also deemed to have arisen out of and in the course of employment.[694]

III. Accidents on the Way to Work

442. Accidents occurring while commuting to and from work (to or from the normal place of residence) are deemed to be occupational accidents provided that they occur in the course of an unbroken journey to or from work to carry out or having carried out the duties of employment.[695]

§3. Concept of 'Occupational Disease'

443. Section 87(1) provides that the Occupational Injuries Code shall also apply to prescribed diseases and prescribed personal injuries that are not caused by accident but that are a result of the nature of the employment. Subsection 2 obliges the Minister to prescribe a disease or injury for the purpose of this section in relation to insured persons when he or she is satisfied that (a) it ought to be treated as a risk of their occupations and not as a risk common to all persons, and (b) it is such that, in the absence of special circumstances, the attribution of particular cases to the nature of the employment can be established or presumed with reasonable certainty. The relevant Regulations list over sixty medical conditions that are prescribed as occupational diseases or injuries with respect to specified occupational activities.[696] In

694. Section 72(5).
695. Section 72(4) and SW(COI)R, Art. 16. This alters the original position whereby an accident on the way to or from work was not, without more, an accident arising out of and in the course of employment. *See* an appeals officer's decision on the meaning of 'unbroken' in *Social Welfare Appeals Office Report 1997*, 20 in which it was held that a motorcyclist's short break in a café to avoid heavy rain did not bring him outside the statutory provisions. However, injuries sustained in a fall while leaving a church were not accepted for OIB purposes on the basis that the journey was considered to be broken, and a parent who injured his back while putting a child into a car seat was disallowed on the basis that the journey had not yet commenced: *Social Welfare Appeals Office Report 2006*, 12.
696. SW(COI)R, Sch. 4. The EU has drawn up a number of recommendations on occupational diseases: Recommendation to the Member States concerning the adoption of a European schedule of occupational diseases and Commission Recommendation 66/462 on the conditions for granting compensation to persons suffering from occupational diseases; Recommendation concerning the adoption of a European schedule of occupational diseases, 90/326/EEC; and most recently Commission Recommendation 2003/670/EC concerning the European schedule of occupational diseases. These are not legally binding, but the Court of Justice of the European Union has held that

relation to the vast majority of these conditions, the Regulations provide for a rebuttable presumption that the condition is a result of the nature of the employment.[697] However, it is also possible to provide individual proof of an employment link in certain circumstances. When an insured person has developed a disease, other than occupational deafness, that is prescribed in relation to that person, that disease may be regarded as being a result of the nature of that person's employment, even when such employment is not prescribed, if relevant medical and other proof can be provided.[698] The Regulations also provide for the determination of the time at which a person is to be treated as having developed a prescribed disease or injury and regulate the circumstances in which any such disease or injury is to be treated as having recrudesced or as having been contracted or received afresh.[699]

§4. Medical Care

444. The cost of medical care that, in the opinion of the Minister, is reasonably and necessarily incurred by the insured person as a result of an occupational injury or disease and that is not otherwise provided for under the HA, the Mental Health Acts, or the Treatment Benefit Scheme (section 138) is payable out of the Social Insurance Fund.[700] For the purpose of this scheme, medical care comprises GP and specialist care; nursing care at home (except when a constant attendance allowance is payable) and institutional nursing care; pharmaceutical and other medical or surgical supplies; dental and optical treatments and appliances; care provided by professionals allied to the medical profession, such as physiotherapists and chiropodists; and travel expenses to and from the place where medical care is provided.[701] As the decision on a claim for a medical care allowance is entrusted to the Minister, as opposed to a deciding officer, it would appear that there is no statutory right of appeal against such a decision to an appeals officer.

445. The amount payable is the cost of the medical care that is (in the opinion of the Minister) reasonably appropriate and necessarily incurred.[702] When a person receives medical care as an in-patient in a hospital or similar institution, the amount payable shall not exceed the maximum amount chargeable under section 53 of the HA of 1970 or under the Mental Treatment Act of 1945.[703] When a person is eligible for services under the HA, the Mental Health Acts, or the Treatment Benefit

---

national courts are required to take them into account in interpreting national provisions, Case 322/88, *Grimaldi v. Fonds des maladies professionnelles* [1989] ECR 4407.

697. Article 24.
698. Article 22. However, this would not appear to allow individual proof where the disease itself is not prescribed as in an appeals officer decision (Occupational Injury Benefit Case 2) in which a person who had acquired asthma at work from handling penicillin was not covered, as although, occupational asthma arising from exposure to certain agents is prescribed, exposure to penicillin is not among them.
699. Articles 25–27.
700. Section 86(1).
701. Section 86(9).
702. Section 86(4).
703. Section 86(3).

Scheme but does not avail him or herself of such services, the amount payable is limited to what would have been payable had the person availed him or herself of these services. The appropriate cost for the care provided is determined by the Minister. The Minister may decide to pay the allowance to such persons as he or she thinks fit and, in particular, when the cost of medical care is due to the HSE.

446. In practice, expenditures under this heading are very low, and persons injured in occupational accidents or suffering from occupational diseases receive medical care under the general healthcare provisions (*see* Part III).

§5. Injury Benefit (Incapacity to Work)

447. Injury benefit is payable to persons who are incapable of work as a result of an occupational accident or disease.

I. Conditions of Eligibility

448. If a person is incapable of work as a result of an occupational accident or disease, he or she is entitled to injury benefit from the fourth day of such period of incapacity.[704] A person capable of work may be deemed to be incapable of work when s/he is under medical care in respect of an occupational disease or disablement, and it is certified by a registered medical practitioner that by reason of such disease or disablement, the person should abstain from work and s/he does not work, or s/he is a probable source of infection with a disease specified in regulations under the HA 1947 to be an infectious disease, and the person abstains from work in pursuance of written order or written advice of a registered medical practitioner. A day or days may be deemed to be a day or days of incapacity for work and form part of a period of interruption of employment if it or they fall immediately after the end date of a period of incapacity for work – S.I. No. 242 of 2019. A day of paid holiday leave is not treated as a day of incapacity.[705] Injury benefit can only be claimed for a maximum of 156 days (six months), beginning from the date of the accident. A person under the age of 16 is not entitled to injury benefit except insofar as may be provided by Regulations.[706] Injury benefit is not payable with respect to pneumoconiosis, byssinosis, occupational asthma, or occupational deafness.[707] In such cases, the person may only claim disablement benefit. Notwithstanding section 87(5), which allows the Minister to vary the benefits payable in the case of occupational diseases, it is not clear whether the exclusion of specific diseases could be justified in law.[708]

704. Section 74(1) and (2), as amended by s. 8 SWA 2020.
705. Section 53(2).
706. Section 74(7). SW(COI)R, Art. 7 and Sch. 1 provide for the payment of an injury benefit to such persons when they are in full-time employment.
707. SW(COI)R, Art. 36. *See* s. 87(5).
708. *See*, by analogy, the approach of the Canadian Supreme Court, which held that the exclusion of chronic pain from the workers' compensation scheme was in breach of the Canadian Charter of

II. Amount of Benefit

449. The personal rate of injury benefit is currently equivalent to the standard personal rate of IB (though a lower rate of benefit is payable to claimants under the age of 16 engaged in part-time work[709]). Section 76 provides for increases in the benefit with respect to qualified adults and/or children. When a person suffers two or more successive occupational accidents, section 79 provides that Regulations may allow for adjusting the amount of the injury benefit or disablement benefit payable.

III. Disqualifications

450. A person is disqualified for receiving injury benefit for a period not exceeding nine weeks if he or she fails without good cause (a) to attend, or to submit to, medical examination, or (b) to submit to appropriate medical treatment for the injury or loss of a faculty (provided that he or she shall not be disqualified for receiving injury benefit or disablement benefit for refusal to undergo a non-minor surgical operation).[710]

451. In addition, a person is disqualified for receiving injury benefit or an increase of disablement benefit by way of incapacity supplement for such period not exceeding nine weeks as may be determined under the Act if he or she fails without good cause (a) to comply with a doctor's instructions relating to his or her incapacity, (b) to refrain from behaviour that is likely to hinder his or her recovery, or (c) to see an officer of the Minister or a medical assessor and to answer any reasonable enquiries by any such officer relating to his or her claim. Injury benefit remains payable while a person is absent from the State and/or undergoing detention in legal custody, subject to certain restrictions.[711] A claimant will also be disqualified if s/he participates in a Community Employment scheme that commences after 16 January 2012[712] or in a Solas scheme or national internship scheme.[713]

§6. Disablement Benefit (Loss of a Faculty)

452. Disablement benefit is payable with respect to a person who has suffered a 'loss of faculty' as a result of an occupational accident or disease.

Rights as it did not correspond to the actual needs and circumstances of person suffering from chronic pain: *Martin v. Workers' Compensation Board of Nova Scotia*, 2003 SCC 54.

709. *See* currently S.I. No. 618 of 2022.
710. SW(COI)R, Art. 75.
711. SW(COI)R, Arts 71–72.
712. Section 247B.
713. Section 247A.

I. Conditions of Entitlement

453. A person who suffers from an occupational injury or disease is entitled to disablement benefit when he or she suffers as a result of the accident from a loss of a physical or mental faculty assessed at not less than 15%.[714] It is *not* necessary to prove incapacity to work to be entitled to disablement benefit. Assessment of loss of a faculty is made by a deciding officer in accordance with the general principles set out in section 75(4). Thus, the disabilities to be taken into account are all disabilities (whether or not involving a loss of earning power or additional expense) to which a person may be expected to be subject during the period taken into account as compared with a person of the same age and gender whose physical and mental condition is normal. Such disabilities are treated as having been incurred as a result of the relevant loss of a faculty except when they were the result of a congenital defect or an injury or disease received or contracted before the relevant accident or disease, or received or contracted after, and not directly attributable to, such accident or disease. The assessment is made without reference to the particular circumstances of the claimant other than age, gender, and physical and mental condition and is made by reference to disabilities that are prescribed by Regulation as amounting to 100% disablement.

454. Section 75(5) provides that Regulations may direct that a prescribed loss of a faculty shall be treated as resulting in a prescribed degree of disablement.[715] Section 75(6) provides for the making of a provisional assessment of disablement when there is a possibility of change in the condition of the claimant.

455. Disablement benefit is not payable for the first three days after the accident occurred or the disease was contracted. Moreover, if a person is incapable of work as a result of the accident or disease, he or she cannot claim disablement benefit while remaining so incapable during the period of 156 days (six months), beginning with the day of the relevant accident or commencement of illness.[716]

---

714. Section 75(1) as amended by s. 3 SWA 2011. Where an assessment of disablement refers to the period before 1 Jan. 2012, a claimant qualifies for disablement benefit if s/he has a loss of faculty of at least 1% – s. 75(1A) inserted by s. 3(b) SWA 2011. On disablement benefit generally, *see* Nicholas Wikeley, Anthony Ogus & Eric Barendt, *The Law of Social Security*, 5th ed. (London: Butterworths, 2002), 751–759; Robert Clark, *Annotated Guide to Social Welfare Law* (London: Sweet & Maxwell, 1995), 142–144.

715. SW(COI)R, Art. 8 and Sch. 2 set out the prescribed degrees of disablement for fifty-five different types of injury (seven of which are assessed at 100% disablement), while Art. 21 and Sch. 5 specify the rules to be followed in assessing degrees of disablement in respect of occupational deafness. Art. 8(3) does provide, however, that where, as a result of the injury the claimant may be expected to be subject to greater disabilities than would normally be incurred as a result of such an injury or the part of the body by which the injury was sustained would not, apart from that injury, have been normal at the date of the assessment, the prescribed degree of disablement may be adjusted to such figure as is reasonable in the circumstances of the case.

716. Section 75(3).

II. Amount of Benefit

456. When disablement is assessed at less than 20%, a benefit is payable as a gratuity fixed in accordance with a prescribed scale.[717] When such disablement is assessed at not less than 15%,[718] and when the period of assessment is for life or a period exceeding seven years, a person may opt, before the gratuity is paid, for the substitution of a weekly pension for the gratuity.[719] Again, the rate of the pension is fixed in accordance with a prescribed scale. When disablement is assessed as amounting to 20% or more, disablement benefit is payable as a weekly pension, which varies in accordance with the degree of disablement from a prescribed minimum when the claimant has suffered 20% disablement to a prescribed maximum when the claimant has suffered 100% disablement.[720]

457. An incapacity supplement is payable as an increase to disablement benefit when a person is, as a result of the relevant loss of a faculty, incapable of work and likely to remain permanently so incapable.[721] A person may be treated as being so incapable, notwithstanding that the loss of a faculty is not such as to prevent the person from being capable of work when it is likely to restrict him or her to earn not more than a prescribed amount.[722] A person in receipt of such a supplement also qualifies for further increases with respect to qualified adults and children.[723]

458. When disablement pension is payable with respect to an assessment of 50% or more, and when, as a result of the relevant loss of a faculty, a person requires constant attendance, the disablement pension is supplemented by a constant attendance allowance, except when the person is receiving medical treatment as an in-patient in a hospital or similar institution.[724]

459. When a person suffers two or more successive accidents covered by the Code, regulations may provide for adjusting (a) injury benefit or disablement benefit, or the conditions for the receipt of either such benefit, in any case where the person has received or is entitled to a disablement gratuity; and (b) any increase in respect of adult and/or child dependants, incapacity supplement or constant attendance allowance.[725]

717. Section 75(8). This scale is updated annually by regulation.
718. One per cent where the period to be taken into account in assessing disablement began before 1 May 1990 – s. 75(11)(a) – and 10% where the period of assessment began on or after 1 May 1990 but before 1 Jan. 2012 – s. 75(11)(b) as inserted by s. 3(f) SWA 2011.
719. Section 75(10) as amended by s. 3(e) SWA 2011.
720. Part 3 of Sch. 2, as amended annually.
721. Section 77 as substituted by SWA 2010, s. 6 and amended by SWMPA 2010, s. 8. Renamed by SWLRPA 2006, s. 4.
722. Section 77(2(a)).
723. Section 77A(1) as substituted by SWMPA 2010, s. 8.
724. Section 78.
725. Section 79.

III. Disqualification

460. A person is disqualified for receiving disablement benefit for such period not exceeding nine weeks if he or she fails without good cause: to attend or to submit him/herself to a medical examination or to submit him/herself to such medical treatment as is considered appropriate in his/her case by the registered medical practitioner in charge of the case or by a medical referee (other than for refusing to undergo a surgical operation not being of a minor character).[726] A claimant will also be disqualified if s/he participates in a Community Employment scheme that commences after 16 January 2012[727] or in a Solas scheme or national internship scheme.[728]

461. A person is disqualified for receiving incapacity supplement for a period not exceeding nine weeks on the same basis as applies to injury benefit (above, paragraphs 450–451.

462. Disablement pension remains payable while a person is absent from the State and/or undergoing detention in legal custody, subject to certain restrictions.[729]

§7. Death Benefit

463. Death benefit is payable when an insured dies (i) *as a result of* an accident arising out of and in the course of employment, or (ii) when, immediately before the death, he or she was entitled to disablement pension with respect to a disablement assessed at 50% or more.[730]

464. The benefit is payable as follows:

(i) The widow(er) or SCP of the deceased is entitled to a death benefit.[731] A widow(er) is disqualified for benefit if he or she remarries, enters into a civil partnership or if and so long as he or she is a cohabitant.[732] However, he or she will not lose entitlement to a death benefit merely because he or she is divorced from the former spouse. Increases in the rate of a death benefit are payable (a) when the claimant has qualified children, and (b) when he or she has reached pensionable age and is living alone.

726. Section 91 as amended and SW(COI)R, Art. 75.
727. Section 247B.
728. Section 247A.
729. SW(COI)R, Arts 71–72.
730. Section 80–84.
731. Section 81(1) as amended by SWPA 2010, s. 17. Death benefit for parents (s. 82) was discontinued by the SWPA 2011.
732. Section 81(3) & (4) as amended by SWPA 2010, s. 17.

(ii) Orphans – A death benefit is payable to an orphan who is a child or step-child of the deceased or who was wholly or mainly maintained by the deceased at the date of his or her death.[733]

(iii) Funeral expenses – Finally, a lump sum payment (currently EUR 850) is payable for funeral expenses.[734]

§8. Miscellaneous

465. Notice of Accidents: By virtue of section 88, Regulations may provide for requiring an insured person to give notice of an accident, with respect to which injury benefit or medical care allowance may be claimed, to his or her employer within a prescribed time. (When the insured person dies as a result of the accident within this prescribed time, the obligation to notify may pass to another prescribed person). Section 89 provides that regulations may require employers to report such accidents to a prescribed person within a prescribed time, to furnish to such person any information required for the determination of claims for injury benefit, and to take such other steps as may be prescribed to facilitate the giving of notices of accidents for which injury benefit may be claimed, the making of claims for such benefit, and the determination of such claims.[735]

466. Rehabilitation: By virtue of section 94, the Minister may make such contributions towards the cost of rehabilitation services for persons entitled to disablement benefit as he or she may, with the consent of the Minister for Public Expenditure and Reform, determine.

467. Medical Research: Section 95 empowers the Minister to promote research into the causes, incidence, and methods of prevention of occupational accidents and diseases and to finance such research from the Social Insurance Fund.

733. Section 83.
734. Section 84(1).
735. The relevant regulations for both of these sections are S(COI)R, Arts 49–50.

Part VII. Unemployment and Low-Income Families

468. This part looks at support for low income and unemployed persons under the social welfare system. There are three main unemployment payments: a contributory JB for employees, a contributory jobseeker's benefit for self-employed people and a means-tested jobseeker's allowance.[736] In addition, farm assist is a means-tested payment payable to low-income farmers. Working family payment (formerly FIS) is payable to families in low-income employment,[737] while Back-to-Work Family Dividend (BTWFD) applies to parents who return to work having claimed certain welfare payments.

736. A pre-retirement allowance was abolished for new claims with effect from 4 Jul. 2007.
737. In addition, there are administrative Back-to-Work and Back-to-Education schemes for persons on social welfare payments who wish to take up work or education.

Chapter 1. Provision of Work

§1. Labour Mediation

469. Labour mediation does not form part of the Irish social security system and is the responsibility of the Workplace Relations Commission established under the Workplace Relations Act 2015.

§2. Vocational Training

470. Vocational training is also not considered as part of the Irish social security system and is the responsibility of Solas which was established under the Further Education and Training Act 2013.

§3. Direct work provision

471. Currently, direct work provision is limited to 'social employment' schemes such as Community Employment or the Rural Social Scheme which are targeted a specific disadvantaged groups such as long-term unemployed persons. Although several of these schemes are administered by the Department of Social Protection they are not generally considered as part of the social security system and are not provided on a statutory basis.

Chapter 2. Jobseeker's Benefit

§1. Beneficiaries and Conditions

472. A person is entitled to JB for any 'day of unemployment' that forms part of a 'period of interruption of employment' provided that he or she is under pensionable age on the day for which the benefit is claimed, proves unemployment in the prescribed manner,[738,739] satisfies the contribution conditions, and has sustained a substantial loss of employment in any period of seven consecutive days (except in the case of a person engaged in casual employment or a person employed as a retained firefighter).[740] These requirements are discussed below.

473. Period of Interruption of Employment: The rule in relation to entitlement to JB is that the benefit is payable with respect to any 'day of unemployment' that is part of a 'period of interruption of employment'. A 'period of interruption of employment' is defined as any four 'days of interruption of employment' (i.e., a day of unemployment or of incapacity for work), whether consecutive or not, within a period of seven consecutive days.[741] Any two such periods not separated by a period of more than twenty-six weeks are to be treated as one period of interruption of unemployment.[742] Periods spent on various work experience and training schemes, not exceeding a one-year duration, do not break a period of interruption of employment (or up to two years in the case of the VTOS).[743] The result of these rules is that entitlement to JB is established on a daily basis. However, to establish initial entitlement, a person must be out of work as a result of unemployment or incapacity for any four days in a period of seven consecutive days. A benefit is not payable for the first three days in any period of interruption of employment except as provided for by regulations made with the consent of the Minister for Public Expenditure and Reform.[744]

474. Day of Unemployment: A day is not treated as a day of unemployment[745] unless the person is capable of work, he or she is available for work (or is deemed

738. The details of the benefit (unimaginatively renamed in SWLRPA 2006, s. 4) are set out in ss 62–68 of the Act and in the SW(CCP&C)R, Arts 44–52.

739. Traditionally this was done by signing on at a labour exchange – SW(CCP&C)R, Art. 52 – but s. 62(1A), inserted by SW&PA 2010, s. 4(c) now provides that a person may prove unemployment by making a declaration for that purpose by means of an electronic communication. *See* now SW(CCP&C)R, Art. 52 (as inserted by Art. 4 of S.I. No. 250 of 2012).

740. Section 62(1) as amended by SW&P(MP)A 2013, s. 9. *See* generally *Clarke's* extensive discussion of the relevant sections.

741. Section 62(5)(c) as amended by SWA 2012, s. 16(1)(b)(i)(I)–(II).

742. *Ibid.*

743. Section 62(8) as substituted by SWMPA 2008, s. 17 and as amended by SW&PA 2010, s. 29(2), and SW&P(MP)A 2013, ss 3(2) and 19.

744. Section 62(4) as substituted by H(PPEMPI)A 2020, s. 7. The power to waive the three day waiting rule was exercised during the COVID-19 pandemic – *see* S.I. Nos 95, 164, 223 and 310 of 2020 and S.I. Nos 34 and 161 of 2021.

745. On the concept of 'unemployment', *see Louth v. Minister for Social Welfare* [1993] 1 IR 339; *Director-General of Social Services v. Thomson* (1981) 38 ALR 624; *McAuliffe v. Secretary, Department of Social Security* (1990) 23 ALD 284, upheld at (1992) 28 ALD 609. An appeals

to be or exempted from being so available), and is genuinely seeking but is unable to obtain employment suitable for him or her having regard to age, physique, education, normal occupation, place of residence, and family circumstances.[746] A day is not treated as a day of unemployment if the person does any paid or remunerative work[747] on that day unless that work could have been done by the person in addition to his or her usual employment and outside the ordinary working hours of that employment[748] and the remuneration or profit from the occupation does not exceed EUR 7,500 annually, or EUR 144 weekly or at least 117 contributions have been paid by the person in either of the last three years or the last three complete contributions years or the work constitutes employment as a retained firefighter or the work is subject to an agreement at the Workplace Relations Commission or the Labour Court under which the person is retained in their occupation by their employer without undertaking any gainful employment for that employer and the total weekly remuneration does not exceed EUR 144 and is paid for a period not exceeding thirteen weeks.[749]

475. In the case of any person engaged in share fishing, s/he must show, in respect of any day for which benefit is claimed, that it is not a day on which s/he is engaged in share fishing, and it is a day in respect of which s/he made reasonable efforts to obtain such work, but there was no work available for him/her on or in connection with, the fishing vessel of which s/he is a crew member because of adverse weather conditions or because the vessel is undergoing repairs or maintenance (other than such repairs or maintenance that s/he would normally be required to do).[750]

476. In the case of persons engaged on temporary employment contracts whereby they are obliged to be available for *up to* thirty-nine hours of work per week, appeals officers held that, while the existence of an employment contract was indicative of employment, it was not, of itself, sufficient grounds for holding that the individuals concerned were 'not unemployed' on days when they did not actually work. It was necessary to examine the reality of the extent of employment, and in cases in which there was very limited employment and the claimants showed that

---

officer has held that, on the facts of the specific case and having regard to the specific terms and conditions involved, a person on a career break was not unemployed: *Social Welfare Appeals Office Report 2010*, 25–26.

746. Section 62(5)(a) as substituted by SW&P(MA)A 2013, s. 12.

747. For a discussion of the concept of 'remunerative work' (albeit in a somewhat different statutory context) *see Saunderson v. Secretary of State for Work and Pensions* [2012] ScotCS CSIH 102.

748. In Case 2015/13, which concerned a claim for Jobseeker's Benefit by a claimant who worked on a casual basis in a factory and who was also engaged in small scale farming, an appeals officer indicated that, in the absence of any refusal of an offer of work by reason of his farming obligations, the claimant could be said to have always carried out his farming outside the hours of employment and alongside that employment – *Social Welfare Appeals Office Annual Report 2015*, 73.

749. SW(CCP&C)R, Art. 44 as amended by Art. 4 of S.I. No. 254 of 2013 and Art. 2 of S.I. No. 651 of 2018 and Art. 2 of S.I. No. 362 of 2023.

750. Section 63.

they were available for alternative work, the statutory condition of being 'unemployed' might be regarded as being fulfilled. Conversely, when the level of employment was considerable and/or the claimants were not interested in alternative work, they could not be considered to be unemployed.[751]

477. Available for Employment: A person must be 'available for employment' (or be deemed to be or exempted from being available).[752] A person is regarded as being available for employment if he or she can show to the satisfaction of the Minister that he or she is willing and able, at once, to take up an offer of suitable full-time employment.[753] It is accepted that, in practice, a person may require a day or two to make necessary arrangements. The relevant Regulations provide that a person will not be regarded as being available for employment if he or she imposes unreasonable restrictions on (a) the nature of the employment, (b) the hours of work, (c) the rate of remuneration, (d) the duration of the employment, (e) the location of the employment, or (f) other conditions of employment that he or she is prepared to accept.[754] In determining what constitutes suitable full-time employment, regard must be accorded to (a) the skills, qualifications, and experience of the person concerned; (b) the period for which the person has been unemployed; and (c) the availability of employment vacancies within travelling distance from his or her residence. The requirement that the person be available to take up 'full-time' work may have a disproportionate impact on women, as more women than men wish to avail themselves of part-time work – often because of family responsibilities. If this requirement were to be challenged under EU law, it would be required to be objectively justified, that is, to be shown that it was a necessary part of the overall unemployment payment system, which aims to compensate people who are unable to find full-time work and not to act as a subsidy to those who only wish to work part-time.[755]

---

751. *Social Welfare Appeals Office Report 2003*, 12.
752. Section 62(5)(a)(ii) as amended by SW&P(MP)A 2013, s. 12.
753. Article 15 of the SW(CCP&C)R, and DSP, *Jobseekers Benefit Guidelines*. *See* the approach of the Canadian courts in *Faucher v. CEIC* (1997) 215 NR 314 in which the court ruled that persons otherwise considered to be available for work should not be considered not available because they had sought to establish their own business. An appeals officer summarily held that a person attending a part-time driving course to enhance her employment opportunities did not preclude her being available for employment – noting that many persons in full-time employment complete such training: *Social Welfare Appeals Office Report 2003*, 19–20.
754. *Ibid.* Employment as a retained fire fighter is not regarded as an unreasonable restriction on availability for employment in certain circumstances – *see* Art. 4 of S.I. No. 254 of 2013. In *Solovastru v. Minister for Social and Family Affairs* [2011] IEHC 532, the applicant – a Romanian national – required a work permit to be able to take up work as an employee. The Department argued that where a person is available only to take up a particular form of employment – e.g., self-employment – he is not as a consequence in a position to satisfy the availability condition. In principle, this approach seems correct and has long been adopted in the UK (*see*, for example, R (U) 1/82(T)). Unfortunately, Dunne J. did not discuss at all the meaning of 'available for employment' although she appears to have assumed (at p. 17) that the Department's view was correct.
755. *See* R.(JSA) 4/02 in which a Social Security Commissioner upheld similar UK legislation albeit that (unlike the Irish law) the UK rules excluded those with caring responsibilities from the requirement.

478. Departmental guidelines provide that a person who moves to a location where his or her prospects of getting suitable employment have been significantly reduced will not be considered to be available for work. In deciding whether a move to a location imposes unreasonable restrictions on availability for work, regard should be accorded to the reasons for the move. For example, the guidelines state that people who relocate to be near family or relatives or under a resettlement programme would be regarded as indigenous residents.[756]

479. In the short-term, a person could be regarded as available when he or she is seeking to be re-employed in his or her usual employment. However, over a longer period, a person would be required to be available for any suitable employment having regard to his or her skills, qualifications and experience, and health status. A person who is not legally able to work (e.g., a non-EU national without a work permit) could not be considered available for employment.

480. Genuinely Seeking Work: A person must be genuinely seeking work that is suitable for him or her, having regard to his or her age, physique, education, normal occupation, place of residence, and family circumstances.[757] The relevant regulations provide that a person is regarded as genuinely seeking employment if he or she can show that he or she has, in the relevant period, taken reasonable steps that offer him or her the best prospects of obtaining employment.[758] These steps include:

(a) Applications for employment made to persons:
   (i) who have advertised the availability of employment; or
   (ii) who appear to be in a position to offer employment.
(b) Seeking information on the availability of employment from:
   (i) employers;
   (ii) advertisements;
   (iii) persons who have placed advertisements that indicate that employment is available; or
   (iv) employment agencies.
(c) Availing themselves of reasonable opportunities for training that is suitable in their circumstances.
(d) Acting on advice given by an officer of the Minister or other placement service concerning the availability of employment.
(e) Taking steps towards establishing themselves in self-employment.

481. The taking of one step on a single occasion is not considered to be sufficient to prove that a person is genuinely seeking work unless taking that step is all that is reasonable for the person concerned to do. In deciding whether a person has taken the steps that are reasonable in his or her case, regard must be given to his or

756. This approach is broadly supported in Canadian jurisprudence: *Canada (AG) v. Dodsworth* [1984] 2 FC 193; *Canada (AG) v. Whiffen* (1994) 165 NR 145.
757. Section 42(4).
758. SW(CCP&C)R, Art. 16 as amended by Art. 6 of S.I. No. 447 of 2012 and DSP *Jobseekers Benefit Guidelines*.

her circumstances, including, in particular, (a) his or her skills, qualifications, and experience; (b) the steps that he or she has taken previously to seek employment; (c) the availability and location of vacancies for employment; (d) the duration of his or her period of unemployment; and (e) his or her family circumstances.

482. Substantial Loss of Employment: A person is regarded as having sustained a 'substantial loss of employment' in any period of seven consecutive days when he or she has lost one day of insurable employment; provided that his or her reckonable earnings or income are reduced as a consequence of the loss of employment.[759] In establishing if there has been a substantial loss, deciding officers will seek to establish the normal level of employment over a preceding period (normally thirteen weeks) and compare it with the current level. However, a longer period can be used if the thirteen-week period is not representative of the normal level.[760]

483. Casual Employment: As set out above, persons in casual employment are not subject to the 'substantial loss' requirement. A person is considered to be engaged in 'casual employment' when:

(a) he or she is normally employed for periods of less than a week;
(b) the number of days and the days of the week on which he or she is employed in each period varies with the level of activity in the employer's business; and
(c) on the termination of each period of employment, he or she has no assurance of being re-employed with the same employer.[761]

484. In determining whether a person is engaged in casual employment, account is taken of employment in the six months immediately preceding the first day of the claim for the benefit; however, when a deciding officer or appeals officer considers that this period is not appropriate to determine whether a person is engaged in casual employment, such other period as appears to be appropriate may be considered.[762]

485. Night Workers: When a person is employed to work continuously from one day until the next (e.g., on a night shift), that person will be regarded as being employed (a) only on the first day, when the first day falls on Monday through Friday and when the employment on the first day is longer than on the second day, or when the first day is Saturday; or (b) in any other case, on the second day.[763] When a person is regarded as being employed on only one of two days and s/he is not employed or is deemed to be available for employment throughout part of the other day, s/he will be deemed to be available for employment throughout the other day.

759. SW(CCP&C)R, Art. 49 as amended by Art. 5 of S.I. No. 254 of 2013.
760. In one case where the applicant was on maternity leave for six months, an Appeals Officer indicated that the Department should have regard to the fifty-two-week period prior to her Jobseeker's Benefit claim – *Annual Report of the Social Welfare Appeals Office 2019*, 82.
761. SW(CCP&C)R, Art. 51.
762. *See Social Welfare Appeals Report 2004*, 9–10 for cases where appeals officers held that dockers with no assurance of being re-employed were 'casual' rather than part-time employees and so not subject to the 'sub-loss' rule.
763. SW(CCP&C)R, Art. 22.

486. Persons over 65 – By virtue of S.I. No. 36 of 2021, claimants who have reached the age of 65 do not have to comply with the requirements in relation to availability for work, genuinely seeking work, signing-on and activation for the labour market.

§2. Contribution Conditions

487. The contribution conditions require a person to have (1) at least 104 employment or optional contributions or at least 156 self-employment contributions paid in the period between entry into insurance and the day for which the benefit is claimed; (2) at least thirty-nine contributions paid or credited (of which at least thirteen must be paid)[764] in the second-last complete contribution year before the beginning of the benefit year in which the benefit is claimed; and (3) reckonable weekly earnings[765] in excess of a fixed amount (currently, EUR 300)[766] in the relevant contribution year.[767] Reduced rates of benefits are payable when the average reckonable weekly earnings are less than that amount. As an alternative to the second contribution requirement, a person must have at least twenty-six reckonable contributions paid in each of the second- and third-last complete contribution years before the beginning of the benefit year in which the claim is made.[768] This is to facilitate atypical workers (such as job sharers) in qualifying for the benefit.

§3. Amount of the Benefit

488. The amount of JB payable will depend on a number of factors. Chief of these is whether the claimant has a qualified adult or child.[769] Reduced rates of JB are payable where a claimant refuses, without good cause: (a) to attend a meeting designed to improve her knowledge of employment, work experience, education,

764. Article 48A of SW(CCP&C)R (as inserted by S.I. No. 24 of 2009) provides that a person who fails to satisfy this condition will qualify if he or she has thirteen paid contributions in either of the two contribution years preceding the governing contribution year or in a subsequent contribution year.
765. Or income in the case of a person qualifying for jobseeker's benefit by virtue of having paid optional contributions – s. 64(1)(c)(ii).
766. By virtue of s. 64(6)(c) and (f), a person has reckonable weekly earnings or income in respect of a period of interruption of employment commencing on or after 5 Jan. 2009 if s/he has weekly earnings or income that do not exceed EUR 149.99, or are between EUR 149.99 and EUR 219.99 or between EUR 219.99 and EUR 299.99.
767. Section 64(1), as amended by SWMPA 2008, s. 18 and SWA 2019, s. 3, and SW(CCP&C)R, Art. 47 (as amended by S.I. No. 604 of 2008) and Art. 48. This condition does not apply to a claim for jobseeker's benefit made by a person within the three benefit years of that person's return to the State having been a volunteer development worker overseas – s. 64(8). Claimants of Pandemic Unemployment Payment (PUP) or of Jobseeker's payments who had an underlying entitlement to PUP are deemed to have had weekly average earnings or income in excess of EUR 300 in 2021 for this purpose – S.I. No. 234 of 2023.
768. Section 64(1)(b)(ii).
769. Section 66 as amended by SWA 2021, s. 11. By virtue of S.I. No. 96 of 2020 as amended by S.I. No. 376 of 2020, the amount of qualified adult allowance payable with JB was temporarily increased in response to the COVID-19 pandemic.

training or development courses available to her; or (b) to have her education, training or development needs assessed; or (c) to participate in prescribed schemes of employment or work experience or courses of education, training or development.[770] Reduced rates of benefit are also payable to claimants whose reckonable weekly earnings are less than the prescribed amount.[771]

489. Section 16 of the SWPA 2012 fixes the amount of JB payable to the claimant by reference to the number of days per week that the claimant is unemployed. The maximum rate of benefit is payable where the claimant is unemployed for six days in the week, 80% of the maximum rate where the claimant is unemployed for five days, 60% where s/he is unemployed for four days, 40% where s/he is unemployed for three days and 20% where s/he is unemployed for two days. No benefit is payable when a claimant is unemployed for only one day in a week.[772]

490. JB is payable at a flat rate with increases for qualified adults and qualified children as appropriate.[773] Non-statutory 'secondary benefits' are not generally payable with JB. The benefit is payable for up to 156 days (i.e., twenty-six weeks) in the case of a person who is under age 18 and for up to 234 days (nine months) in the case of a person over age 18 who has at least 260 paid contributions.[774] Once this benefit period has been exhausted, a person must work thirteen weeks of insurable employment before requalifying for the benefit. Workers on short-time (i.e., systematically working fewer days in a working week than is normal in the employment concerned) are restricted in their entitlement to JB so that the total number of days in respect of which benefit is claimed and the number of days worked shall not exceed five, and in such cases, the daily rate of benefit is one-fifth the weekly rate.[775]

§4. DISQUALIFICATIONS

491. A range of disqualifications for JB is set out in legislation. A person is disqualified if he or she is absent from the State (subject to exceptions under EU law).[776] However, a person is not disqualified for the first two weeks of a period of holidays, while representing Ireland in an amateur capacity at an international sporting event, or during such period as the Minister may allow, having regard to the circumstances of the case, if the absence is temporary and a result of force majeure.[777] A person is also disqualified if he or she is undergoing detention in legal custody.[778]

770. Section 62A and B (inserted by SW&P(MP)A 2013, s. 12).
771. Section 65A inserted by SWA 2010, s. 7(5) and as amended by s. 9 of SWA 2021.
772. Section 62(10A) inserted by SW&PA 2012, s. 16(b).
773. Sections 65 & 66.
774. Section 67 as amended by SWMPA 2008, s. 18 and SWA 2012, s. 12.
775. Section 62(11) as amended by SWA 2012, s. 16(1)(f).
776. Section 249.
777. SW(CCP&C)R, Art. 219.
778. Section 249. The disqualification of convicted prisoners for receipt of State Pension (Contributory) was declared unconstitutional in *PC v. Minister for Social Protection* [2018] IESC 57 and it would

Persons on a Solas, Community Employment scheme, national internship scheme and the Rural Social Scheme are also disqualified for the benefit.[779]

492. Section 68A provides that a person is not entitled to JB while attending a course of study, other than in prescribed circumstances and subject to prescribed conditions.[780] A person is deemed to be attending a course of study (a) for three months immediately following the completion or the leaving by that person of second-level education or the completion by him or her of the leaving certificate examination whichever is later, (b) for the duration of an academic year, or (c) for the period immediately following the completion of one academic year, other than the final academic year, up to the beginning of the following year.[781] The exemptions provide that a person is not disqualified for JB where the person is undertaking a Junior Certificate or Leaving Certificate course as part of the Department of Education and Skills' Youthreach programme or is a mature student[782] or is participating in an activity within the meaning of Article 120(4) of SW(CCP&C)R, i.e., persons aged between age 18 and 21 years who are deemed to be available for work while attending certain approved courses of education.[783]

493. A person may be disqualified for the benefit for up to nine weeks if he or she has:

(1) lost his or her employment through his or her own misconduct or has voluntarily left employment without just cause;[784]
(2) has refused an offer of suitable employment;[785]
(3) has failed or neglected to avail him or herself of any reasonable opportunity of obtaining suitable employment, or

---

seem to follow that the disqualification of convicted prisoners in respect of other insurance payments is similarly unconstitutional. However, a convicted prisoner is not generally available for work and therefore cannot qualify for JB.

779. Section 68(4)–(5) and s. 247A(a) as amended by SW&P(MP)A 2013, s. 19.

780. As inserted by SWMPA 2010, s. 7. The definitions of 'course of study', etc., are as set out in s. 148 in relation to jobseeker's allowance (*see* para. 516 below).

781. Section 68A(3).

782. Within the meaning of s. 1 of the Local Authorities (Higher Education Grants) Act 1968 as amended by s. 2 of the Local Authorities (Higher Education Grants) Act 1992.

783. Article 47A as inserted by S.I. No. 327 of 2016.

784. On misconduct, *see Canada (AG) v. Tucker* [1986] FC 329; *Canada (AG) v. Brisette* [1994] 1 FC 684; *Smith v. Canada (AG)* [1998] FC 529; *Foley v. Department of Family and Community Services* [2002] AATA 626; *Canada (AG) v. Grantstorm* 2003 FCA 485; *Mishibinijima* v. *Canada (AG)* 2007 FCA 36. The Canadian case law has been reviewed by the Social Security Tribunal of Canada: *N. P. v. Canada Employment Insurance Commission*, 2014 SSTGDEI 11. On voluntary leaving, *see Crewe v. Social Security Commissioner* [1982] 2 All ER 745; *Tanguay v. CEIC* (1985) 68 NR 154; and the Social Security Commissioner's decision at [2005] UKSSCSC CJSA_2507_2005.

785. Employment is not be deemed to be suitable if it is in a situation vacant as a result of a trade dispute; employment in the district where the person was last employed at a rate of pay lower or on conditions less favourable that s/he would be used to or employment in another district at a rate of pay lower or conditions less favourable that those generally observed, s. 47(6). A person may be disqualified on this ground *and* found to be not available for work: *Canada (AG) v. Michael*, 23 Mar. 1994.

(4) being a person under the age of 55, s/he is dismissed by reason of redundancy and has obtained a redundancy payment in excess of a prescribed amount, currently EUR 50,000.[786]

494. In the US, the Supreme Court has ruled that the religious clauses of the US Constitution prohibit the application of disqualifications for unemployment benefits in the case of an action arising from a religious belief, such as, for example, when a person refuses to accept employment where he or she would have to work on Sunday, contrary to his or her beliefs.[787] The case law under the ECHR, in contrast, indicates that a requirement to work on a particular day, contrary to one's religious beliefs, is not a breach of Article 9 of the Convention (which concerns freedom of religion).[788] The issue has not yet been considered by the Irish courts.

495. A person may also be disqualified for the benefit for up to nine weeks if s/he persists in refusing, for more than three weeks and without good cause, (i) to attend a meeting designed to improve her knowledge of employment, work experience, education, training or development courses available to her, or (ii) to have her education, training or development needs assessed, or (iii) to participate in prescribed schemes of employment or work experience or courses of education, training or development.[789]

496. A person who has lost employment by reason of a stoppage of work that was a result of a trade dispute at the factory, workshop, farm, or other premises or place at which he or she was employed is disqualified for the benefit so long as the stoppage of work continues, except in a case when he or she has, during the stoppage of work, become bona fide employed elsewhere in the occupation that he or she usually practises or has become regularly engaged in some other occupation.[790] This disqualification does not apply to a person who is not participating in or

786. Section 68(6)(a)–(e) and SW(CCP&C)R, Art. 50. *See generally* Robert Clark, *Annotated Guide to Social Welfare Law* (London: Sweet & Maxwell, 1995) & Anthony Ogus & Eric Barendt, *The Law of Social Security*, 3rd ed. (London: Butterworths, 1982 and 1988), 97–110.

787. *Sherbert v. Verner* (1963) 374 US 398; *Thomas v. Indiana Employment Security Division* (1981) 450 US 707; *Hobbie v. Unemployment Appeals Committee of* Florida (1987) 480 US 136; *Frazee v. Illinois Department of Employment Security* (1989) 489 US 829.

788. *See Konttinen v. Finland*, App. 24949/94, 3 Dec. 1996; *Stedman v. UK*, App. 29107/95, 9 Apr. 1997; and *Kosteski v. Macedonia*, App. 55170/00, 13 Apr. 2006. Although the Court's subsequent jurisprudence has given more weight to the rights of those with religious beliefs, it has yet to consider this issue directly: *Eweida v. United Kingdom* (2013) 57 EHRR 213.

789. Section 62A(5) and 62B(3) inserted by SW&P(MP)A 2013, s. 12 and S.I. Nos 259 of 2013 and 440 of 2014.

790. Section 68(1)–(3). On the 'trade dispute' disqualification, *see* Robert Clark, *Annotated Guide to Social Welfare Law* (London: Sweet & Maxwell, 1995), 105–111 and Anthony Kerr & Gerry Whyte, *Irish Trade Union Law* (Butterworths, Abingdon, 1985). In *Zwarich v. Canada (AG)* [1987] 3 FC 253 and *Meredith v. CEIC* 1989 FCJ 1117, the Canadian Federal Court of Appeal held that a similar provision was not in breach of the provisions of the Canadian Charter of Rights guaranteeing freedom of association. Similarly, in *Ohio Bureau of Employment Svcs. v. Hodory*, 431 U.S. 471 (1977), the US Supreme Court held that the denial of unemployment benefits to a person whose unemployment was due to a labour dispute was not unconstitutional. *See also Lyng v. Automobile Workers*, 485 U.S. 360 (1988).

directly interested in the trade dispute that caused the stoppage of work. The purpose of this disqualification is to attempt to ensure 'neutrality' in relation to trade disputes, that is, that the State is not seen to subvert strikers. However, the perceived harshness of this approach led to the establishment in 1982 of a Social Welfare Tribunal to consider further cases of this kind. When a person has been found by a deciding officer and an appeals officer to be subject to the trade dispute disqualification, the person may apply to the Tribunal for an adjudication that he or she is entitled to the benefit (notwithstanding the disqualification). The Tribunal has regard, *inter alia*, to the reasonableness or otherwise of employers and employees in relation to the trade dispute.[71]

791. Sections 331–333. *See Robert Clark's* extensive treatment of this in *Annotated Guide to Social Welfare Law* (London: Sweet & Maxwell, 1995) at 301–310.

Chapter 3. Jobseekers Benefit (Self-Employed)

497. A new insurance-based scheme for people who lose their self-employment was introduced in 2019.[792]

§1. Beneficiaries and Conditions

498. In order to claim JB (Self-Employed), a claimant must:

(a) be under pensionable age in the week for which the benefit is claimed;
(b) satisfy the contribution conditions set out in section 68D;
(c) not be engaged in self-employment, subject to section 68K(3);
(d) be capable of work;
(e) be genuinely seeking, but unable to obtain, suitable employment having regard to age, physique, education, normal occupation, place of residence and family circumstances, and
(f) must prove unemployment in the prescribed manner.[793]

499. Section 68C(2) authorizes the Minister to make regulations specifying the circumstances in which a person may be regarded as being available for and genuinely seeking employment, while subsection 3 provides that a person may prove unemployment by means of electronic communication in a prescribed manner – *see* further S.I. No. 551 of 2019. Subsection 4 provides that a person shall not be entitled to this benefit where s/he had four days of insurable employment (other than as a retained firefighter) in any payment week.

Genuinely seeking employment – The requirement that a claimant be genuinely seeking employment is the same for JB (Self-Employed) as it is for JB.[794]

Proving unemployment – A claimant may prove unemployment by making a declaration that s/he has not engaged in self-employment since the date of his/her claim to benefit and that s/he has lost self-employment involuntarily and not as a result of a planned temporary or seasonal closure of the business. The Minister may require the claimant to sign a written declaration to this effect at a Departmental office or to make the declaration in such other manner as the Minister considers appropriate, including by way of electronic communication.[795]

Week of unemployment – The relevant regulations purport to define 'week of unemployment' for the purpose of this scheme,[796] even though this concept does not feature in the statutory conditions of eligibility and the Minister is not given any

792. Section 68B–K of the 2005 Act as inserted by s. 5 of the Social Welfare Act 2019; S.I. No. 551 of 2019 as amended by S.I. No. 540 of 2022.
793. Section 68C(1).
794. *See* SW(CCP&C)R, Art. 16, as amended by Art. 7 of S.I. No. 551 of 2019.
795. SW(CCP&C)R, Art. 52G, inserted by Art. 4 of S.I. No. 551 of 2019.
796. SW(CCP&C)R, Art. 52A, inserted by Art. 4 of S.I. No. 551 of 2019. S.I. No. 540 of 2022 provides that any week, where a person is a self-employed contributor solely in respect of income or emoluments arising from an approved retirement fund (or ARF) and that person (i) has sustained the loss of self-employment in their usual occupation, and (ii) the loss occurred not earlier than the first day

explicit power to define it for the purpose of this scheme.[797] Notwithstanding that, the definition in the regulations imports two additional requirements that a claimant be available for employment and not follow any occupation except in certain prescribed circumstances, which requirements are almost identical to those listed in the corresponding part of the definition of 'day of unemployment' for the purposes of JB.[798] While the Minister is empowered by section 68C(2) to make regulations specifying the circumstances in which, *inter alia*, a person is or is not to be regarded as being available for employment, given that these two requirements are not explicitly listed in the conditions of eligibility set out in the Act, it is at least arguable that they are *ultra vires*.

Night workers – When a person is employed to work continuously from a time on any day until a time on the following day, that person will be regarded as being employed (a) only on the first day, where the employment on the first day is longer than that on the second day and in that case the first day is not treated as a day of unemployment, and (b) only on the second day in any other circumstances and in that case the second day is not treated as a day of unemployment.[799] When a person is regarded as being employed on only one of two days and s/he is not employed or is deemed to be available for employment throughout part of the other day, s/he will be deemed to be available for employment throughout the other day.

Persons over 65 – By virtue of S.I. No. 36 of 2021, claimants who have reached the age of 65 do not have to comply with the requirements in relation to availability for work, genuinely seeking work, signing-on and activation for the labour market.

§2. Contribution Conditions

500. A claimant must have: (a) either 104 paid employment or optional contributions or 156 paid self-employment contributions in the period between entry into insurance and the week for which benefit is claimed; (b) at least 52 paid self-employment contributions in the second-last complete contribution year before the beginning of the benefit year in which the claim is made; and (c) reckonable weekly income in excess of EUR 300 in the governing contribution year[800] or average reckonable weekly income as specified in paragraphs (a)–(c) of subsection 4 in that

---

of the second last complete calendar year before the year in which his or her application for jobseeker's benefit (self-employed) is made, shall be regarded as a week of unemployment. The intention is to ensure that a self-employed contributor in receipt of income solely from an ARF is not debarred from JB to which they would otherwise be entitled.

797. The phrase 'week of unemployment' does feature in s. 68H dealing with duration of payment of Jobseeker's Benefit (Self-Employed).

798. *See* above, paras 474–476.

799. SW(CCP&C)R, Art. 52B inserted by Art. 4 of S.I. No. 551 of 2019.

800. That is, the second-last complete contribution year before the beginning of the benefit year which includes the day for which benefit is claimed – *see* s. 2(1). Claimants of Pandemic Unemployment Payment (PUP) or of Jobseeker's payments who had an underlying entitlement to PUP are deemed to have had weekly average earnings or income in excess of EUR 300 in in 2020 or 2021 for this purpose – S.I. No. 234 of 2023.

year.[801] Those paragraphs specify the following levels of weekly income respectively – less than EUR 149.99; between EUR 150 and EUR 219.99; or between EUR 220 and EUR 299.99. The requirement to have a certain reckonable weekly income in the governing contribution year does not apply to a volunteer development worker to Ireland from a developing country in the year of return or in the following two years.[802]

§3. Amount and Duration of Benefit

501. The rate of JB (Self-Employed) is currently the same as that of JB.[803] The weekly rate is reduced by 20% for each day of insurable employment that the claimant has in the payment week[804] and is also reduced by EUR 44 for each week that a claimant fails, without good reason, to attend a meeting for the purpose of providing the claimant with information intended to improve his or her knowledge of the employment, work experience, education, training and development opportunities available to him or her or fails without good reason to participate in, agree to participate in or avail himself or herself of an opportunity to participate in any prescribed scheme or programme of employment or work experience or course of education, training or development considered appropriate having regard to the education, training and development needs of the claimant and his or her personal circumstances.[805] There are three reduced weekly rates of benefit for claimants who have reckonable weekly earnings of less than EUR 300 in the governing contribution year,[806] and these rates may be further reduced where a claimant fails, without good reason, to attend a meeting for the purpose of providing the claimant with information intended to improve his or her knowledge of the employment, work experience, education, training and development opportunities available to him or her or fails without good reason to participate in, agree to participate in or avail himself or herself of an opportunity to participate in any prescribed scheme or programme of employment or work experience or course of education, training or development considered appropriate having regard to the education, training and development needs of the claimant and his or her personal circumstances.[807] Increases are paid where the claimant has a qualified adult and/or qualified children.[808] Where the spouse, civil partner or cohabitant of the claimant is not a qualified adult, only half of the normal increase in respect of a qualified child residing with the claimant will be paid, and where that spouse, civil partner or cohabitant has weekly income in excess of a prescribed amount, no such increase will be paid.[809]

801. Section 68D(1).
802. Section 68D(3).
803. Section 68E(1).
804. Section 68E(3).
805. Section 68E(2).
806. Section 68F(1) as amended.
807. Section 68F(2) as amended.
808. Section 68G as amended.
809. Section 68G(4)–(5).

502. Where a claimant has fewer than 260 self-employment contributions in the period between entry into insurance and the week for which JB (Self-Employed) is claimed, the benefit is payable for a maximum of twenty-six weeks.[810] This increases to thirty-nine weeks, where the claimant has more than 260 self-employment contributions during the same period.[811] In both cases, any week where a person is entitled to payment shall be treated as a week of unemployment, and any two such weeks not separated by more than twenty-six weeks shall be treated as the same claim.[812] However, where a claimant's entitlement to JB (Self-Employed) expires after his/her 65th birthday, s/he may continue to claim this benefit for any week of unemployment where s/he has paid fifty-two self-employment contributions in the governing contribution year and has qualifying contributions in respect of not less than 156 self-employment contribution weeks between entry into insurance and the week for which JB (Self-Employed) is claimed.[813] Any days of unemployment in respect of which the claimant receives 20% of the weekly rate of JB (Self-Employed) because s/he has a day or days of insurable employment in the same week are taken into account for the purpose of calculating the maximum duration of payment.[814] A claimant may requalify for benefit when s/he has fifty-two paid self-employment contributions since the last week, for which s/he was entitled to benefit and a minimum of twelve months have elapsed since that week.[815] The payment of JB or Jobseeker's Allowance in any week in respect of which a claimant is entitled to JB (Self-Employed) is treated as if the latter benefit was paid – section 68H(4) – while the payment of Short-Term Enterprise Allowance Scheme in respect of any week of unemployment that includes a day in respect of which a claimant is entitled to JB (Self-Employed) is treated as if the latter benefit was paid in respect of that day – section 68H(5)(b).

§4. Disqualifications

503. Where a person is in receipt of a reduced rate of JB (Self-Employed) because s/he refuses or fails, without good cause, to attend a meeting arranged by the Department for the purpose of providing him or her with information intended to improve his or her knowledge of the employment, work experience, education, training and development opportunities available to him or her or to attend for or submit to an assessment of that person's education, training or development needs or to participate in or agree to participate in or avail of an opportunity of participating in a prescribed scheme or programme of employment or work experience or

810. Section 68H(1)(a).
811. Section 68H(1)(b).
812. Section 68H(3).
813. Section 68H(6).
814. Section 68H(5)(c).
815. Section 68H(2).

course of education, training or development, s/he will be disqualified for a period not exceeding nine weeks where s/he persists in refusing to comply with any of these requirements.[816]

504. A person is disqualified for receiving JB (Self-Employed) while employed under the Community Employment or Rural Social Schemes,[817] while attending a course of study on the same terms as applicable in relation to JB[818] or while participating in a Solas or national internship scheme.[819] A person is also disqualified for receipt of JB (Self-Employed) for a period not exceeding nine weeks where s/he has received or is entitled to receive any money in excess of a prescribed amount in respect of the sale or disposal of his or her self-employment business.[820] A person is also disqualified for receiving JB (Self-Employed) while absent from the State[821] or while undergoing detention in legal custody, except where regulations provide otherwise.[822]

816. Section 68I(5). After any such period of disqualification, a claimant will be subject to further reduced rates of benefit and further periods of disqualification where s/he refuses, without good cause, to comply with these requirements – s. 68I(6). By virtue of s. 68H(5)(a), any period of disqualification imposed in this context is treated as though it were a period in respect of which Jobseeker's Benefit (Self-Employed) was paid for the purpose of determining duration of entitlement.
817. Section 68K(1).
818. Subsection 68K(2), (4) and (5) and SW(CCPC)R 2007, Art. 52D, as inserted by Art. 4 of the Social Welfare (Consolidated Claims, Payments and Control) (Amendment) (No. 11) (Jobseeker's Benefit (Self-Employed)) Regulations 2019. SW(CCPC)R 2007, Art. 52E, as inserted by Art. 4 of the Social Welfare (Consolidated Claims, Payments and Control) (Amendment) (No. 11) (Jobseeker's Benefit (Self-Employed)) Regulations 2019, currently fixes this sum at EUR 50,000.
819. Section 247A(a) as amended by SW&P(MP)A 2013, s. 19.
820. Section 68K(3).
821. However, a person is not disqualified for the first two weeks in any calendar year that s/he is absent from the State provided s/he does not engage in any gainful employment during the absence or, in the case of a claimant aged over 65, for any temporary absence from the State provided s/he does not engage in gainful employment during the absence, or, while representing Ireland in an amateur capacity at an international sporting event, or during such period as the Minister may allow, having regard to the circumstances of the case, if the absence is temporary and a result of force majeure – Art. 217(d) as amended by Art. 12 of S.I. No. 551 of 2019 and Art. 2 of S.I. No. 495 of 2022.
822. Section 249(1). *See* further, Part XII, Chs 3 and 4.

Chapter 4. Jobseeker's Allowance

§1. Beneficiaries and Conditions

505. A person is entitled to jobseeker's allowance[823] for any 'day of unemployment' that forms part of a 'period of interruption of employment' provided that he or she is over age 18 and under pensionable age, that is on the day for which the allowance is claimed, proves unemployment in the prescribed manner, qualifies under the means test'[824] and proves that he is habitually resident in the State.[825] When a person is entitled to an allowance and benefit, he or she may opt for either payment – whichever is most beneficial.[826] This allows, for example, Community Employment workers reverting to an unemployment payment to claim a long-term allowance (and the associated secondary benefits), which might be more advantageous than claiming the benefit. However, a person cannot claim both payments on the same day.[827]

506. An attempt to impose a further requirement on homeless applicants was declared *ultra vires* in *Kozinceva v. Minister for Social Protection*.[828] Here the Court of Appeal, *per* Haughton J, held that requiring a homeless person to provide evidence that she was currently residing in a particular catchment area for the purpose of claiming Jobseeker's Allowance was *ultra vires* the Minister as this was not provided for by legislation and had the effect of unlawfully denying the applicant access to the administrative process for determining her claim for this allowance.

507. As in the case of JB, to qualify for an allowance, a person must be available for employment (or be deemed to be[829] or exempted from being so available) and be genuinely seeking employment.[830] In addition, a person must now participate or agree to participate, if requested to do so by an officer of the Minister in a course of education, training or development which is considered appropriate by the officer having regard to the training and education needs of the person and his or her personal circumstances.[831] The rules in relation to 'day of unemployment',

823. The details of the payment are set out in ss 140–148 of the Act and in the SW(CCP&C)R, Arts 116–121. Renamed in SWLRPA 2006, s. 4.
824. Section 141 as amended by SWPA 2010, s. 5. The latter provision is described as clarifying the calculation of entitlement to jobseeker's allowance where weekly means comprise earnings from insurable employment. In determining a week of unemployment, the practice is to include a day only once in any computation where that day is part of a week of unemployment in respect of which jobseeker's allowance is paid. This amendment ensures the Act is not ambiguous as regards applying this practice.
825. *See* further paras 763 et seq.
826. However, jobseeker's allowance and jobseeker's benefit are both not payable in respect of the same day: s. 147(6).
827. Section 147(6).
828. [2020] IECA 7.
829. *See* SW(CCP&C)R, Art. 120.
830. Section 141(4) as substituted by SWPA 2009, s. 5. The concepts have been discussed above in relation to jobseeker's benefit.
831. Section 141(4)(d) as substituted by SWPA 2009, s. 5.

availability for work, genuinely seeking work, disqualifications, and so on are, in general, very similar if not identical to those that apply in relation to JB and will not be discussed again here in detail.[832]

508. A person who does not qualify for OFP because his/her youngest child has reached a prescribed age threshold qualifies for jobseeker's allowance where the youngest child is not yet 14 and the claimant is not a cohabitant.[833] This applies even if the claimant was not previously in receipt of OFP. This payment is referred to as Jobseeker's Transitional Payment,[834] and claimants of this payment are exempt from the requirement to be available for and genuinely seeking full-time employment.

509. As in the case of JB, a person is not entitled to an allowance for the first three days of unemployment except as provided for by regulations made with the consent of the Minister for Public Expenditure and Reform.[835] In addition, an allowance is not payable for less than a day. A person is not regarded as unemployed with respect to any day on which he or she is working under a contract of employment (written or otherwise) or is in receipt of wages.

510. Any period of continuous employment under the community employment scheme, Rural Social Scheme or various other training and employment schemes is disregarded in treating any two continuous periods of employment not separated by more than fifty-two weeks as one continuous period of employment.[836]

§2. Means Test

511. The means test includes means from the following:

- most property owned by the person and/or by his or her spouse (but excluding property personally used or enjoyed by the person);
- all income that the person and/or spouse may reasonably expect to receive in the coming year (with certain exceptions);

---

832. In *Douglas v. Minister for Social Protection* [2012] IEHC 27 (an *ex tempore* judgment) the High Court ruled that a decision by an appeals officer that a law student, who was seeking work which was not inconsistent with perhaps eleven hours of lectures per week, was not available for work did not constitute an error of law (at para. 9).
833. Section 148A, inserted by s. 10 of the Social Welfare and Pensions (Miscellaneous Provisions) Act 2013, as amended by s. 5 of the Social Welfare (Miscellaneous Provisions) Act 2015.
834. Though that phrase is not used in the 2005 Act where the marginal note to s. 148A refers to jobseeker's allowance.
835. Section 141(2)(a) as substituted by H(PPEMPI)A 2020, s. 8. This power was exercised during the COVID-19 pandemic – *see* S.I. Nos 94, 163, 222 and 309 of 2020 and S.I. Nos 33 and 162 of 2021.
836. Section 141(5) as amended.

- the value of any advantage accruing to the person or spouse from the use of property (other than a domestic dwelling or farm building, owned and occupied, furniture, and personal effects) that is personally used or enjoyed by the person or spouse and the value of any advantage from the leasing of a farm of land;
- any property that the person or spouse has deprived him or herself of either directly or indirectly so as to qualify for an allowance; and
- the value of any 'benefit and privilege' enjoyed by the person or spouse, including the estimated value to the household of all income earned by the spouse from employment or self-employment.

512. The detailed provisions of the means tests are set out in Part XI.

§3. Amount of the Benefit

513. Jobseeker's allowance is payable at a flat rate with increases for qualified adults and qualified children as appropriate.[837] When each member of a couple is entitled to an allowance, the amount payable is limited to that which would be payable were the couple treated as a claimant and qualified adult (i.e., about 1.7 times the individual rate).[838] While higher rates of payment have in the past been payable to persons who were 'long-term' unemployed, the standard rates are currently the same for all allowance claimants. Limited 'secondary benefits' (e.g., a Christmas bonus) are payable with long-term jobseeker's allowance (i.e., a person who has been unemployed for fifteen months or more). The allowance is payable indefinitely to pension age.

514. A reduced rate of allowance is payable to claimants under 25 years who are not entitled to an increase in respect of a qualified child.[839] However, there are a number of exceptions to this rule. The reduction does not apply to a person who, immediately before the week of unemployment for which jobseeker's allowance was claimed, was in receipt of one-parent family payment, widow(er)'s or SCP's (non-contributory) pension or CA (*see* section 142(1)(*a*)(ii)) or who is entitled to an increase in respect of a qualified child.[840] Nor does it apply to a claimant in receipt of DA immediately before such a claim; or a person who at any time during twelve months before he or she reached the age of 18 years was in the care of the HSE under an order of the High Court, or a court order under Part III, IV, IVA, or VI of

837. Sections 142 and 146.
838. Section 144. In this context, 'couple' means a married couple who are living together, both civil partners of the same civil partnership who are living together, both cohabitants: s. 144 as substituted by SWPA 2010, s. 19. This cap on the payment of Jobseeker's Allowance to each member of a couple does not apply to claimants under the age of 25 receiving a reduced rate of allowance pursuant to s. 142A – *see* s. 142A(3).
839. Section 142A inserted by SW&PA 2009, s. 6(c) and amended by SW&PA 2013, s. 9(1)(a). On the compatibility of such a lower rate with the ECHR *see R v. Secretary of State for Work and Pensions ex parte Reynolds* [2005] UKHL 37 in which the House of Lords upheld similar rules in the UK. *See also Gosselin v. Quebec* 2002 SCC 84 for a related issue under the Canadian Charter of Rights (again the challenge was rejected by the Canadian Supreme Court).
840. Section 142A(1)(c).

the Child Care Act 1991, or under a voluntary care arrangement under section 4 of the Child Care Act 1991, or under an accommodation arrangement under section 5 of the Child Care Act 1991; or a claimant in receipt of housing supports in his or her own right.[841]

§4. Disqualifications

515. A person is disqualified for an allowance while he or she is an inmate of an institution maintained wholly or partly out of public money or by a local authority, or when he or she is employed in a community employment or rural social scheme[842] or while participating in a Solas or national internship scheme.[843] The general disqualifications that apply to a benefit in relation to trade disputes, leaving or losing employment, refusing work or training, etc., also apply to an allowance, as do disqualifications for detention in legal custody and residence, temporary or permanent, outside the State.[844] Section 249(6) provides that a person is disqualified for JA where he or she is undergoing imprisonment though this provision is legally questionable in light of the Supreme Court decision in *C v. Minister for Social Protection* (*see* paragraphs 782–784).

516. A person is not entitled to receive an allowance while attending a course of study, other than in limited prescribed circumstances.[845] 'Course of study' means a full-time day course of study, instruction, or training that may take place over more than one academic year at any institution of education.[846] A person is regarded as attending a course of study for three months immediately following the completion of second-level education or the completion of the Leaving Certificate (whichever is later), for the duration of the academic year (including term vacations), or for the

841. Section 142A(4) as amended by SW(No.2)A 2019, s. 6(1)(c).
842. Section 147(1).
843. Section 247A(b) as amended by SW&P(MP)A 2013, s. 19.
844. Sections 147(2)–(5) and 249(6). *See* Part XII, Chs 3 and 4. Note that in *Munteanu v. Minister for Social Protection* [2017] IEHC 161, O'Malley J ruled that JSA was a special non-contributory cash benefit within the meaning of Arts 3 and 70 of EU Regulation 883/2004 on the coordination of social security. She also held that, for the purposes of EU Directive 2004/38 EC (the Residence Directive), JSA was to be characterised as 'social assistance' rather than a financial benefit intended to assist a person entering the labour market. This view was followed by the Court of Appeal in that case at [2019] IECA 236 and in *Razneas v. Chief Appeals Officer* [2022] IECA 227.
845. There are a number of decisions in other jurisdictions in relation to similar but not identical provisions. *See*, in particular, *Secretary, Department of Social Security v. Jordan* [1998] 604 FCA; *Chief Adjudication Officer v. Weber* [1997] EWCA Civ. 1998; *Flemming v. Secretary of State for Work and Pensions* [2002] EWCA Civ. 641.
846. Section 148 as amended by SWMPA 2010, s. 24. 'Institute of education' means a school, university, or college of a university, an institution of higher education designated under the Higher Education Authority Act 1971, any institution to which the Qualifications (Education and Training) Act of 1999 applies, any institution established under the Regional Technical Colleges Act of 1992, any institution incorporated under the Dublin Institute of Technology Act of 1992, any other institution to which the Local Authorities (Higher Education Grants) Acts, 1968–1992, apply, and any other institution as may be prescribed. An appeals officer held that a full-time course in a language school was not such a 'course of study' as the school was not within the definition of 'institution': *Social Welfare Appeals Office Report 2003*, 21–22.

period immediately following the completion of one academic year (other than the final academic year). The exemptions provide that a person is not disqualified for jobseeker's allowance where the person is undertaking a Junior Certificate or Leaving Certificate course as part of the Department of Education and Skills' Youthreach programme or is a mature student[847] or is participating in an activity within the meaning of Article 120(4) of SW(CCP&C)R, i.e., persons aged between age 18 and 21 years who are deemed to be available for work while attending certain approved courses of education.[848] The main purpose of this disqualification, introduced in 1993, is to ensure that students do not qualify for an allowance during the term holidays – particularly the summer holidays.[849]

517. Unlike the benefit, the jobseeker's allowance is subject to the HRC.[850]

847. Within the meaning of s. 1 of the Local Authorities (Higher Education Grants) Act 1968 as amended by s. 2 of the Local Authorities (Higher Education Grants) Act 1992.
848. SW(CCP&C)R, Art. 121 as substituted by S.I. No. 327 of 2016.
849. Prior to the provision, a full-time student would not, in general, have been entitled to allowance as he or she would not have been available for employment. *See Douglas v. Minister for Social Protection* [2012] IEHC 27 and *Landry v. Canada (AG)* (1992) 152 NR 164; but *see also* the more flexible approach taken by the Australian Federal Court in *Director-General of Social Services v. Thomson* (1981) 38 ALR 624.
850. Section 141(9). *See* Part XII, Ch. 3.

Chapter 5. Farm Assist

518. FA is a means-tested scheme for low-income farmers.[851,852] Unlike the previous smallholder's assistance, which was unemployment assistance payable to farmers, who were not included on the Live Register, FA provides a disregard for earned income and thus provides a greater incentive for small farmers to generate income from farming.

§1. Beneficiaries and Conditions

519. To qualify for FA, a person must be a farmer, aged between 18 and pensionable age, and satisfy a means test.[853]

520. A 'farmer' is defined as a person engaged in farming, while 'farming' is defined as farming farmland in the State, including commonage, which is owned and used for the purposes of husbandry, or leased and used for the purposes of husbandry, or does not form part of a larger holding and is used for the purposes of husbandry, by the claimant.[854] 'Husbandry' means the working of the land with the object of extracting the traditional produce of the land.[855] This includes the cultivation of crops or trees (forestry) and the keeping of livestock and poultry.

521. Departmental guidelines state that tenure in the land should be verified by reference to relevant source documentation, for example, the Land Registry Office, a lease agreement, etc. Ownership may include joint-ownership. When the land is neither owned nor leased, FA may be payable only when the land used does not form part of a larger holding. This includes cases in which the claimant is farming a holding with respect to which he or she has an intestacy share that has not been officially registered. It also includes situations in which two or more siblings with an intestacy share in a farm jointly manage the same holding. When two or more persons farm what may originally have been a single unit but is now claimed to be made up of separate units, the guidelines state that deciding officers must satisfy themselves that what was the original farm is now managed as two separate entities/businesses, for example, that the claimant has his or her own herd number.

522. It is not sufficient for a person simply to own a farm. As outlined above, the legislation prescribes that the claimant him or herself must be engaged in farming. Therefore, a person who owns a farm but leases, lets, or rents out the entire holding does not satisfy this condition and cannot, therefore, qualify for FA. If, however, the claimant is personally engaged in farming part of the holding and also leases, lets, or rents a portion of the farm to another person, he or she may qualify for a payment.

851. Sections 213–218.
852. Self-employed fishermen or fisherwomen on low income may qualify for Jobseeker's Allowance, known in this context as Fish Assist.
853. Section 214.
854. Section 213(1).
855. *Ibid.*

523. There is no minimum acreage requirement. However, the guidelines also state that deciding officers must satisfy themselves that the land would reasonably be considered to be a farm that is used by the claimant for the purposes of husbandry. For example, when a claimant resides in a dwelling on a large site, for example, one or two acres, and he or she has a large vegetable garden, it may be reasonable to conclude that, while the claimant may be engaged in husbandry, the land does not constitute a farm and the person is not engaged in farming. Conversely, the claimant may be engaged in intensive farming on a small acreage, as, for example, with pig or mushroom farming, which would satisfy the condition.

§2. Means Test

524. The means test for FA is set out in Part 5 of Schedule 3 (*see* Part XI). In contrast to most other tests, the test for FA provides a specific incentive for the claimant to increase his or her earnings, as only 70% of additional earnings (less disregard for children) are taken into account as means.

§3. Amount of the Benefit

525. FA is payable at a flat rate with increases for qualified adults[856] and qualified children as appropriate.[857] When each member of a couple is entitled to FA or one is entitled to various welfare payments and the other to FA, the amount payable is limited to that which would be payable were the couple treated as a claimant and qualified adult (i.e., about 1.7 times the individual rate).[858] FA is payable indefinitely to pension age.

§4. Disqualifications

526. A person is disqualified for FA while he or she is employed under community employment or the rural social scheme or participating in Back to Work, Part-Time Job Incentive,[859] Solas or national internship schemes.[860] In addition, a farmer is not entitled to FA while attending a course of study (other than in prescribed circumstances).[861]

---

856. Provided that they are not resident outside the State or in prison or otherwise detained in legal custody – SWPA 2014, s. 8.
857. Section 215, as amended by s. 17 SWP&CRA 2018, and 216.
858. Section 217 as amended by SWPA 2010, s. 19 and SWA 2019, s. 6.
859. Section 218(1).
860. Section 247A(b) as amended by SW&P(MP)A 2013, s. 19.
861. Section 218(2)–(4). This disqualification is the same as that applicable to jobseeker's allowance, *see* above para. 516.

527. The general disqualifications in relation to detention in legal custody also apply to FA.[862] Section 249(6) provides that a person is disqualified for FA where he or she is undergoing imprisonment though this provision is legally questionable in light of the Supreme Court decisions in *C v. Minister for Social Protection* (*see* paragraphs 782–784). In addition, the disqualification for residence outside the State that is applicable to jobseeker's allowance under section 249(6) also applies to FA.

862. Section 249(6).

Chapter 6. Working Family Payment

528. A WFP is intended to provide income support for employees on low earnings with children and thereby preserve the incentive to remain in employment in circumstances in which the employee might only be marginally better off than if he or she were claiming other social welfare payments.[863]

§1. Beneficiaries and Conditions

529. To qualify for a WFP, a person must be a member of a 'family', must be engaged in *remunerative full-time employment as an employee* (self-employment is *not* eligible), and must satisfy a means test. A 'family' is defined in section 227 as (a) a person who is engaged in remunerative full-time employment as an employee, (b) when such person is living with or wholly or mainly maintaining his or her spouse,[864] civil partner or cohabitant, that spouse, civil partner or cohabitant, and (c) a child or children.[865] Section 9 of the SWPA 2014 provides that where a person is living apart from his or her spouse or civil partner and children, s/he may still claim WFP if s/he is maintaining the spouse or civil partner and contributing substantially towards the maintenance of the children and provided that the spouse or civil partner is not claiming any social welfare payments (other than certain prescribed exceptions). However, this provision has not yet been brought into force. A 'child' means a qualified child as defined in section 2(3), who normally resides with that family, and 'spouse' includes a party to a marriage that has been validly dissolved. When a WFP is payable with respect to a particular family for any period, no person who was included in that family at the beginning of such period is to be regarded as a member of any other family during that period.[866]

530. Regulations provide that a person is to be regarded as being engaged in remunerative full-time employment as an employee when he or she is engaged in remunerative employment[867] (other than community employment, national internships scheme or under the rural social scheme), which is expected to continue for a period of a minimum of three months and the number of hours worked per fortnight is not less than thirty-eight or when the aggregate number of hours worked by him or her and his or her spouse is not less than thirty-eight hours per fortnight.[868]

863. Sections 227–233 and the SW(CCP&C)R, Arts 172–177. Prior to 1 Jan. 2018, this payment was known as Family Income Supplement – s. 8 of the Social Welfare Act 2017.

864. 'Spouse' includes a person who is divorced where the divorce is recognized in Irish law.

865. As amended by SWPA 2010, s. 2010.

866. Section 230A, as inserted by SWPA 2014, s. 10(b).

867. In R 1/93(FC) a Northern Ireland Social Security Commissioner held that a student nurse in receipt of a bursary was not in *remunerative* employment.

868. SW(CCP&C)R, Art. 175. In *R v. Ebbw Vale and Methyr Tydfil SBAT, ex parte, Lewis* [1982] 1 WLR 420, the English Court of Appeal held that a person who was absent from work through illness was not engaged in remunerative work in this period for the purposes of the UK family income supplement scheme. In Case 2016/20, an appeals officer ruled that a student nurse working thirty-nine hours per week in a nine month paid job placement that was part of her course of studies qualified for WFP – *See Social Welfare Appeals Office Annual Report 2016*, 78.

531. In *Healy v. Minister for Social Welfare*,[869] the plaintiff claimed that the disqualification of persons employed in community employment by regulation was *ultra vires* by the Minister. However, Carroll J held that the general definition of 'remunerative full-time employment' by Regulation was a valid exercise of the Ministerial power to promulgate delegated legislation in that it filled in the details and gave effect to principles and policies contained in the Statute itself. She did not find it necessary, on the facts of that case, to decide whether the specific exclusion of community employment was *ultra vires* the Minister.

§2. Weekly Income

532. 'Weekly family income' is defined as the amount of *net* income received in a week by a family (i.e., less tax, pay-related social insurance (PRSI), and universal social charge), less any income of a child of that family.[870] To be assessable, the income must be received by the family. Thus in Case 2019/318/67, the Chief Appeals Officer ruled that no account should have been taken of the profits of a company of which the claimant's spouse was a director where the profits are used to finance the company's debts.[871] Regulations provide that weekly family income is to be calculated or estimated:

(a) insofar as it comprises earnings from employment as an employee, by reference to the weekly average of the amount of such earnings received in the two months immediately prior to the date on which the claim for a WFP has been made when such earnings are received at monthly intervals, or in the four weeks immediately prior to such date when such earnings are received at weekly or fortnightly intervals;[872]
(b) insofar as it comprises income from any form of self-employment, by reference to the weekly amount of such income calculated or estimated by dividing the income in the twelve months preceding the date of the claim by fifty-two;
(c) insofar as it consists of income from any other source, by reference to the normal weekly amount of such income.[873]

533. When, in any case, a deciding officer or appeals officer considers that the periods mentioned above would not be appropriate to determine the amount of

869. [1998] IEHC 145; [1999] 1 ILRM 72.
870. Section 227 as amended by SWLRPA 2006, s. 31 and SWPA 2011, s. 11. In Case 2019/34, an appeals officer ruled that account had to be taken of maintenance payable under a court order even where the appellant had confirmed that the maintenance was not being paid regularly – *Social Welfare Appeals Office Annual Report 2019*, 76.
871. *Social Welfare Appeals Office Annual Report 2019*, 121.
872. In Case 2017/36, an appeals officer ruled that unpaid leave could not be taken into account in calculating average weekly family income for the purpose of WFP – *Social Welfare Appeals Office Annual Report 2017*, 79.
873. Article 173(1). In Case 2019/34, an appeals officer ruled that maintenance due under a court order has to be taken into account even where the order is not being honoured – Social Welfare Annual Report 2019, p. 76.

weekly family income, he or she may give regard to such other period that appears to him or her to be appropriate for that purpose.[874]

534. In calculating or estimating weekly family income, the following items are disregarded:[875]

(a) any sums received by way of death benefit by virtue of orphan's pension, guardian's payment (contributory) or (non-contributory), CA or benefit, SWA, CB, early childcare supplement, or FIS;
(b) any sums received by way of allowance for domiciliary care of disabled children under the HA of 1970;
(c) any sums received by way of a rent allowance under Regulations made under section 23 of the Housing (Private Rented Dwellings) Act of 1982;
(d) any sums from the investment or profitable use of property (not being property personally used or enjoyed by the person concerned), other than when it consists of income from rent or any other periodical payment receivable for the possession and use of property in all lands, tenements, and hereditaments;[876]
(e) payments by the Health Service Executive (HSE) with respect to a child who is boarded out;
(f) in the case of a qualified applicant under a scheme administered by the Minister for the Gaeltacht and known as Scéim na bhFoghlaimeoirí Gaeilge, any income received under that scheme with respect to a person who is temporarily resident with the qualified applicant, together with any other income received with respect to such temporary resident;
(g) any money received from a charitable organization being a body whose activities are carried on otherwise than for profit (but excluding any public or local authority) and one of whose functions is to assist persons in need by making grants of money to them;
(h) any income arising from employment of a casual nature by the HSE as a home help;
(i) any payments made in accordance with the Magdalen Commission Report for the benefit of women who worked in the Magdalen Laundries;
(j) ex gratia payments made under the Lourdes Hospital Redress Scheme, the Lourdes Hospital Payment Scheme and the Surgical Symphysiotomy ex gratia Scheme;
(k) *ex gratia* payments made by the Stardust Victims' Compensation Tribunal;
(l) payments received under the Department of Education and Skills 1916 Bursary Fund;
(m) payments made by the Minister of Health to women diagnosed with cervical cancer since 2008;

874. Article 173(2).
875. Article 174 as amended.
876. Substituted by S.I. No. 148 of 2007.

(n) any payment made by Sport Ireland under the International Carding Scheme or by the N. Ireland Victim and Survivor Service in accordance with the Victims and Survivors (Northern Ireland) Order 2006;
(o) up to EUR 95.23 of maintenance payments and one-half of any maintenance payment in excess of that figure that are used to meet the weekly housing actually incurred by a claimant of WFP;[877] and
(p) a Special Transport Grant payable by the Minister for Education and Skills in respect of a child with special educational needs;
(q) any payment made under the Tusla Bursary Scheme for Children in Care and Aftercare;
(r) any payment made under the Probation Service's KickStart Scholarship scheme;
(s) any payment made under the Compensation Scheme for young people who suffered harm while in the care of Kerry Child and Adolescent Mental Health Service; and (t) any payment made under the Troubles Permanent Disablement Payment Scheme (Northern Ireland).

§3. Amount of the Benefit

535. The rate of WFP is calculated as a percentage of the difference between the 'weekly family income' and a set scale, which varies in accordance with the size of the family. This scale is normally adjusted on an annual basis in line with general increases in social welfare rates. Section 229 provides that the weekly rate of WFP is to be 60% of the amount by which the weekly family income is less than the amount appropriate in the particular case under section 228, as substituted by s. 10 of the Social Welfare Act 2022. Once a person qualifies for WFP, it is payable at a minimum rate (currently, EUR 20 per week).

536. WFP is payable for a period of fifty-two weeks, beginning on the date on which it is receivable, and, except where Regulations otherwise provide,[878] the weekly rate of WFP payable is not affected by any change of circumstances during that period.[879] However, in practice, WFP rates are increased in line with the general increases in social welfare rates, although this is not specifically provided for

877. However, where a claimant of WFP is also entitled to OPFP, maintenance payments are disregarded in the assessment of means for only one of those payments – S.I. No. 634 of 2019.
878. SW(CCP&C)R, Art. 176 as substituted by Art. 4 of S.I. No. 235 of 2013 provides for increases in WFP where there is an increase in the number of children in the family or where a claimant of WFP was also in receipt of OPFP and the latter payment ceased by virtue of the claimant's youngest child attaining the age at which OPFP ceases to be payable. Section 229(3), as inserted by SWPA 2014, s. 10(a) empowers the Minister to provide for a change in the rate of WFP payable where there is a change in the entitlement of members of the family concerned to any benefit or assistance under the 2005 Act or a change in the composition of the family. However, this provision has not yet been brought into force.
879. Section 230. Section 230(2) as substituted by SWPA 2014, s. 10(b) provides that where the claimant ceases to be engaged in remunerative full-time employment, WFP is discontinued immediately

by the legislation. WFP is payable to the member of the family (other than a child) who is engaged in remunerative full-time employment as an employee or, when there are two members of the family so engaged, to the member whose weekly income as calculated for the purposes of WFP forms the greater part of the weekly family income.[880]

§4. DISQUALIFICATIONS

537. By virtue of section 230(2),[881] a claimant who ceases to be engaged in remunerative full-time employment loses his/her entitlement to WFP immediately.[882]

---

and where such a claimant subsequently requalifies for WFP before the end of that fifty-two week period, payment recommences at the rate payable at the start of the period. However, this provision has not yet been brought into force.

880. Section 231.

881. As substituted by SWPA 2014, s. 10(b).

882. At the date of writing, however, this provision had not yet been commenced.

Chapter 7. Back-to-Work Family Dividend

538. In 2015, a new scheme, BTWFD, was introduced to encourage parents claiming jobseeker's payments or OFP or participating in certain specified schemes, approved training courses or employment or work experience schemes or courses of education or development to return to work.[883] There is no means test for this scheme.

§1. Beneficiaries and Conditions

539. In order to be eligible for BTWFD, a claimant must:

(a) be under pensionable age;
(b) on or after 5 January 2015, (i) have ceased to claim or be entitled to JB, JB (Self-Employed) or Jobseeker's Allowance (other than Jobseeker's Transitional Allowance) or an allowance payable in respect of specified schemes[884] (including an allowance payable to a person who claimed OPFP or Jobseeker's Transitional Allowance immediately before participating in a specified scheme) by reason of the claimant or his/her spouse, civil partner or cohabitant being in employment or self-employment[885] or commencing employment or self-employment within four weeks of the date of ceasing to claim or be entitled to the relevant payment *or* (ii) have ceased to claim or be entitled to OPFP by reason of the claimant being in employment or self-employment or commencing employment or self-employment within four weeks of the date of ceasing to claim or be entitled to OPFP or by reason of the claimant's youngest child reaching the age at which entitlement to OPFP ceases and the claimant being in employment or self-employment on that date;
(c) immediately before the date on which the person ceased to claim or be entitled to any of the payments in paragraph b, have been in receipt of an increase in respect of at least one qualified child who normally resides with the claimant;
(d) in the case of payments other than OPFP or Jobseeker's Transitional Allowance, immediately before the date on which s/he ceased to claim or be entitled to the payment concerned, in any continuous period of unemployment have been in receipt of such payment for not less than 312 days of unemployment, of which not less than 156 days occurred in the twelve-month period commencing immediately before that date;[886] and

883. Section 238A–F, inserted by s. 8 of the Social Welfare (Miscellaneous Provisions) Act 2015; S.I. No. 180 of 2015.
884. These are Community Employment schemes, Tús schemes, Rural Social Schemes, Gateway, the national internship scheme, approved courses of training and a number of schemes listed in S.I. No. 180 of 2015.
885. Employment or self-employment outside the State does not count for this purpose – *see Social Welfare Appeals Office Annual Report 2015*, at 84–85.
886. Section 238B(1), inserted by SW(MP)A 2015, s. 8. For this purpose, account is taken of periods spent in receipt of COVID-19 Pandemic Unemployment Payment – SWA 2021, s. 15.

(e) be habitually resident in the State.[887]

540. By virtue of section 238B(3), a person is not entitled to this payment where that person or, where appropriate, his/her spouse, civil partner or cohabitant is in receipt of any welfare other than guardian's payment (non-contributory), widowed or SCP grant, DCA, weekly or monthly discretionary payments of SWA pursuant to section 198 or payments of SWA in kind, in respect of exceptional needs, in urgent cases or for burial expenses pursuant to sections 200, 201, 202 and 206 respectively. That subsection further provides that a person is not entitled to this payment if s/he or, where appropriate, his/her spouse, civil partner or cohabitant is in receipt of a 'continued payment' for qualified children (i.e., where s/he continues to receive payment of a qualified child increase for a period of up to thirteen weeks after returning to the labour force has been in receipt of social welfare or having participated in a Community Employment scheme).[888] A person is also not entitled to BTWFD if s/he or, where appropriate, his/her spouse, civil partner or cohabitant participates in any prescribed schemes of employment, training, education, work experience or development, including Community Employment, Tús, Gateway, Rural Social Scheme or the national internship scheme. A person who is temporarily incapacitated from work will be able to receive the dividend in conjunction with IB or injury benefit for up to six weeks.[889]

§2. Amount of the Benefit

541. Section 238D provides for the rates of payment. For the first year of entitlement, the dividend is payable weekly at a rate (currently) of EUR 36.00 per child under the age of 12 and EUR 40.00 per child aged 12 and over, subject to an overall ceiling of the rate payable in respect of four such qualified children.[890] The weekly rate payable for the second year is half that payable in the first year, subject to an overall ceiling of half the rate payable in respect of four such qualified children. Any child participating in education, training, supported employment or work placement scheme in his or her own right or claiming social welfare in his/her own right or treated as a qualified child or qualified adult for the purpose of any other person claiming social welfare will not be taken into account for the purpose of calculating the dividend.[891]

542. The dividend is payable for a maximum period of 104 weeks.[892] The dividend may be payable in respect of separate periods, subject to the aggregate of those periods not exceeding 104 weeks and there being no more than three such separate periods. If a person returns to claim a social welfare payment during the two-year

887. Section 238B(5).
888. Note that this payment ceased to be payable on the enactment of SW(MP)A 2015 – *see* s. 234(1A) inserted by SW(MP)A 2015, s. 7.
889. Section 238B(4).
890. Section 238D(1).
891. Section 238D(2).
892. Section 238C.

period, the dividend will cease to be paid. However, payment of the dividend may recommence for the unexpired portion of the two-year period if the person or his/her spouse, civil partner or cohabitant returns to the labour force.

§3. Disqualification

543. A person will be disqualified for receipt of BTWFD if s/he or, where appropriate, his/her spouse, civil partner or cohabitant, ceases to be employed or self-employed.[893]

893. Section 238B(3)(c).

Part VIII. Pensions

544. This part looks at the main social security payments available for older people and survivors. There are currently two main 'old-age' pensions: the State contributory pension (formerly, the old-age contributory pension) and the State non-contributory pension (formerly, the old-age non-contributory pension).[894] The State transition pension (formerly the retirement pension) has been abolished for new claims with effect from 1 January 2014.[895] This part also looks at the widows' and widowers' pensions, which now also include surviving civil partners (SCPs). There are two widow(er)s' and SCPs' pensions – contributory and non-contributory – and a one-time widowed parent and SCP grant (discussed in Part IX).

894. Renamed by SWLRPA, 2006, s. 4.
895. By SWPA 2011. This pension is not payable to a person who attains the age of 65 years on or after 1 Jan. 2014.

Chapter 1. State Pension (Contributory)

§1. Beneficiaries and Conditions

545. To qualify for a contributory pension, a person must have attained pensionable age and satisfy the contribution requirements.[896,] Pension age is currently 66.[897]

§2. Contribution Conditions

546. The general contribution requirements are that a person must:

(a) have entered insurable employment before attaining the age of 56;[898]
(b) have a certain number of paid contributions since the entry into insurance; and
(c) have a minimum 'yearly average' of paid or credited contributions.[899]

547. 'Entry into insurance' means, subject to section 108(8)(a), the date on which a person first becomes an insured person by virtue of section 12(1) (as an employed contributor), except when he or she becomes an insured person for occupational injuries purposes only, or (b) the date on which he or she first becomes an insured person by virtue of section 20 (as a self-employed contributor).[900] Section 108(8) provides that when a person became a self-employed contributor on 6 April 1988 (when insurance for self-employment was introduced) and at any time prior to that date was an employed contributor, the date on which the person first entered into insurance or 6 April 1988, whichever is the more favourable to him or her, is regarded as the date of entry into insurance.

548. The minimum number of paid contributions required is now 520 (ten years) since 2012.[901]

---

896. Sections 108–113 and the SW(CCP&C)R, Arts 59–67 as amended. In *P.C v. Ireland*, 26922/19, 1 Sep. 2022, the European Court of Human Rights held that SPC represented a proprietary interest within the meaning of the Court's case law on Art. 14 of the Convention.
897. The SWPA 2011 provided for an increase in pension age ultimately to 68 by 2028. However, this was repealed by SWA 2020, s. 17.
898. Self-employed contributors who entered insurance for the first time on or after 6 Apr. 1988 before the age of 62 and who were not previously employed contributors qualify for a half-rate of State Pension (Contributory) provided they paid at least 260 contributions – s. 109(3)(e). In *Meagher v. Minister for Social Protection* [2015] IESC 4, the Supreme Court held that s. 21(1)(d), which deemed self-employed contributors to have paid contributions for each week in a contribution year where the appropriate amount of self-employment contribution had been paid, could not be interpreted to enable someone to continue to acquire contributions after reaching pensionable age so as to qualify for the half-rate State Pension (Contributory).
899. Section 109. There is a range of variations on these requirements set out in the legislation in transitional cases to take account of the reduction in pensionable age from 70 to 66 during the 1970s, s. 84(3)–84(6).
900. Section 108(5).
901. Section 109(1)(b) as substituted by s. 364 and Sch. 6 SWCA 2005. *See* s. 109(1)(b)(i)–(ii) in relation to persons also relying on voluntary contributions.

549. Section 113A provides for automatic entitlement to a pension for a person who is in receipt of IP immediately before retirement age.[902]

550. The issue that perhaps gives rise to most disputes in relation to the contributory pension is the operation of the 'yearly average' rule. 'Yearly average' is defined as:

> the average per contribution year of contribution weeks in respect of which [the] claimant has qualifying [i.e., paid] contributions, voluntary contributions or credited contributions in the period commencing either –
>
> (a) on 5 January 1953 in case the claimant is a man, or on 6 July 1953, in case the claimant is a woman, or
> (b) at the beginning of the contribution year in which the claimant's entry into insurance occurred (if after the dates set out in (a)).[903]

The average is rounded up or down to the nearest whole number.[904] (*See* paragraph 555 et seq. below in relation to a possible alternative qualification route for persons who do not satisfy the yearly average).

551. A person is required to have a yearly average of contributions (paid or credited) from the time of entering insurable employment (or from 1953, whichever is later) up to the last complete contribution year before reaching the pension age of 48 to qualify for a full pension. Alternatively, a person can satisfy an 'alternative yearly average' from 1979 (when the pay-related social insurance (PRSI) system was introduced).[905] A yearly average of twenty is sufficient to qualify for a slightly reduced pension, and a yearly average of as low as ten will qualify for a pro rata pension.[906] The rationale behind the rule is to ensure that a person has a reasonable record of contributions to the social insurance fund over his or her working life. However, the manner in which the rule operates can mean that a person who has paid a certain number of contributions may fail to qualify for a pension or may qualify for a lower pension than a person with a lower number of contributions. For example, a person who enters insurable employment late in life (but before age 56) and works reasonably continuously up to pension age will qualify for a full pension (because the denominator of years worked is small). In contrast, a person who entered insurable employment at a young age, took a significant number of years off, perhaps because of family responsibilities, and returned to insurable employment may have a lower average (as the denominator is much larger).

902. As inserted by SWLRPA 2006, s. 11.
903. Section 108(2). The reason for the different dates for men and women is that, for administrative reasons, men and women had different contribution years at that time.
904. As inserted by SWA 2012, s. 3.
905. Section 108(2).
906. Section 109(8).

552. This issue was considered in the case of *Kingham v. Minister for Social Welfare*,[907] in which a technical argument in relation to the construction of the relevant legislation was rejected by Lynch J, who, however, indicated that he had considerable sympathy with the case being advanced. A broader argument might be made that the operation of the 'yearly average' rule is so unreasonable as to be unconstitutional.[908] However, while the rule can, in some cases, lead to seemingly anomalous results, it does have a clear rationale and does not directly discriminate against any particular class of person. It would seem unlikely that a court would strike down this rule on a broad constitutional argument.

553. A further issue in relation to the yearly average arises in relation to persons (mainly women) with home duties. Many women have worked at an early age, taken time out of the paid labour force after marriage or childbirth, and returned to paid work later in life. Such women would tend to be adversely affected by the yearly average. To address this issue, a 'homemakers' disregard' was introduced in 1994. This means that complete contribution years spent as a homemaker, commencing on or after 6 April 1994, in which the person does not have any credited or voluntary contributions, can be disregarded for the purposes of calculating the yearly average contributions for the old-age contributory pension up to a maximum of twenty years.[909] A 'homemaker' is defined as a person who:

(a) is resident in the State,[910] or is a person entitled to CB under section 219(2) and is under pension age;
(b) is not engaged in remunerative employment, other than employment of inconsiderable extent; and
(c) either:
  (i) resides with and cares for a child under 12 years of age on a full-time basis; or
  (ii) provides full-time care and attention to a person who is so incapacitated as to require full-time care and attention within the meaning of section 179(4); and
(d) other than in the case of such class or classes of person as may be prescribed, makes application to be regarded as a homemaker in the prescribed manner and within the prescribed time.[911]

907. Unreported, High Court, 25 Nov. 1985.
908. *Morgan v. Park Developments* [1983] ILRM 156. In *Harvell v. Chater* 87 F. 3d. 371 the US Circuit Court of Appeals upheld a somewhat similar requirement under the US Constitution on the basis that it was rationally based and free from invidious discrimination. It has been proposed that the system should be changed to one of 'total contributions'.
909. Section 108(3).
910. Quaere whether the residence condition is compatible with EU law in certain cases. *See SF v. Secretary of State for Work and Pensions* [2013] UKUT 175 in which the UK Upper Tribunal ruled that, in a case falling within the scope of Regulation 1408/71 (now Regulation 883/2004), the UK authorities must take into account, for the purpose of calculating a person's pension entitlements and having regard to an analogous approach in UK law (known as 'home responsibilities protection'), the periods during which the person was in receipt of other EU child payments (while resident in another EU country) as if they were periods of receipt of UK child benefit.
911. Section 108 as amended by s. 11 (a) SW&PA 2008.

554. The effect of this is that up to twenty years in which a person does not have social insurance contributions (and during which that person was a homemaker) can be taken away from the denominator in calculating the yearly average, thereby improving the average and the person's chances of qualifying for a pension (or a higher pension).

555. Arising, in part, from the criticisms of the 'yearly average' approach, it is proposed to introduce an alternative 'total contribution' approach whereby pension will be based on the total contributions paid by a contributor rather than their yearly average.[912] As part of a move towards this approach, an alternative 'aggregated contribution' approach has been introduced. Section 109(6A) provides that in the case of a claimant who reached pension age on or after 1 September 2012 and who, on or after 30 March 2018, would be entitled to the maximum State pension (contributory) but for the fact that he or she does not satisfy the 'yearly average', that persons shall have a right to State pension (contributory) at a rate calculated under the 'the aggregated contributions method'.[913]

556. Section 109(6B) provides that the rate is calculated by multiplying the rate of State pension (contributory) by the percentage obtained when the aggregate number of (i) contributions reckonable for State pension (contributory) (including a maximum of 520 credited contributions), and (ii) home caring periods (up to a maximum of 1,040), is divided by 2,080 (i.e., 40 years' contributions) and multiplied by 100. The total reckonable contributions cannot exceed 2,080, i.e., the percentage cannot exceed 100.

557. The homemaker's disregard (above) does not work in the case of the 'aggregated contribution' method, and therefore, the concept of a 'home caring period' was introduced. 'Home caring period' means any contribution week during which a person:

(a) was aged 16 or over but under pension age and was resident in the State, or was a person entitled to CB under section 219(2);
(b) was not engaged in remunerative employment, other than employment of inconsiderable extent,[914] or does not have a paid or credited or voluntary contribution reckonable for State pension (contributory) purposes;
(c) was not in receipt of a weekly payment under this Act, other than a carer's benefit or allowance or DCA, and
(d) can demonstrate that, due to the nature and extent of his or her home carer responsibilities, he or she was unable to engage in insurable employment or self-employment.

912. *See* Government of Ireland, *A Roadmap for Pensions Reform 2018 2023,* 2018. Most recently it has been proposed that this will be introduced from January 2024. *See* https://www.gov.ie/en/press-release/6b939-minister-humphreys-announces-landmark-reform-of-state-pension-system-in-ireland/
913. Section (6A), (6B) and (6C) inserted by s. 9(b) SWP&CRA 2018.
914. Under para. 5 of Part 2 of Sch. 1.

'Home carer' is to be construed accordingly.[915] The Minister may by regulations make provision for the conditions required to be satisfied in order to qualify for home caring periods, including the class or classes of person who may be regarded as a home carer, the class or classes of persons in respect of whom a home carer may provide care and the evidence that may be offered by a person to demonstrate the nature, extent and duration of home caring. S.I. No. 40 of 2019 provides, *inter alia*, that a person shall be regarded as a home carer for any week that person, being over the age of 16, resides with and exercises full parental responsibility for a child under the age of 12 or for any week the person is in receipt of carer's benefit, carer's allowance or domiciliary care allowance or for any week the person provides continuous supervision and regular assistance throughout the day to a person aged 12 or over with the activities of daily living including those linked to personal care, food provision and nursing care, where the person receiving the care does not receive full time assistance within his/her residence from a person other than the applicant. A home carer may be regarded as providing continuous supervision and regular assistance to a person where either the home carer, or the person to whom continuous supervision and regular assistance is provided, is undergoing medical or other treatment of a temporary nature in an institution for a period not longer than thirteen weeks or the person to whom continuous supervision and regular assistance is being provided attends a non-residential course of rehabilitation training provided by an approved organisation or an approved non-residential place of day care or, where it is shown to the satisfaction of the Minister that adequate provision is being made for the care of the person to whom continuous supervision and regular assistance is provided, the home carer engages in employment, self-employment or undertakes an approved course of training or education for, in each case, not more than fifteen hours a week.

558. Because of the fact that the pensionable age is the same for both men and women, Ireland has been spared the litigation on this issue under EU equality law that has occurred in some other EU countries. There are, however, a number of issues that could potentially be challenged under EU equality law, in particular, Directive 79/7/EEC on equal treatment in social security.[916]

559. It might be argued that the operation of the yearly average rule (*see* above) indirectly discriminates against women, and, as we have seen, the homemakers' disregard, which goes some way to address this, only applies from 1994. This issue was argued before an appeals officer of the SWAO.[917] The appellant had worked from 1945 to 1954 and had then given up work upon her marriage. She returned to work in 1974 when her youngest child finished school. In 1991, having reached the age of 65, she applied for the retirement pension and was refused on the basis that her yearly average of twenty-one was below the statutory requirement of twenty-four. She argued that the operation of the rule was indirectly discriminatory in that

915. Section 108(2) as inserted by s. 9(a)(i) SWP&CRA 2018.
916. *See* generally S. Prechal & N. Burrows, *Gender Discrimination Law of the EC* (Aldershot: Dartmouth, 1990).
917. M. Cousins, 'Indirect Discrimination in Social Welfare', ILT 11 (1993): 147–151.

it was more likely to affect women than men and suggested that she should only be required to satisfy the averaging requirement over the period of her working life but excluding those years when she was not available to take up work because of family responsibilities.[918] The appeals officer, however, rejected the appeal. He held that the averaging requirement was justified by the need to protect the Social Insurance Fund and that the averaging requirement affected a number of different categories of pensions (not just persons with home duties) and, accordingly, that the averaging condition was not in breach of EU law.

560. A second issue is the treatment of part-time workers under Irish social welfare law. Prior to 1991, most part-time workers (working less than eighteen hours per week) were excluded from social insurance, but since 1991, the vast majority of part-time workers have been included in the social insurance scheme. However, as a result of the contribution conditions for pensions, current claimants may not qualify for a pension on the basis that they were excluded from insurance in the period before 1991. Prima facie, this might appear to be contrary to EU law, as the majority of part-time workers are women. At one time, it appeared that the EU Court of Justice was of the view that unfavourable treatment of part-time workers was likely to be in breach of Directive 79/7/EEC.[919] However, in a number of cases, appeals officers upheld the Irish position.[920] The subsequent jurisprudence of the EU Court has held that a provision that impacts disproportionately on part-time workers is not necessarily in breach of EU law in line with the Irish decisions.[921]

561. A range of special and pro rata old-age pensions have been introduced over the years to assist certain people who for various reasons did not satisfy the general contribution requirements, including people whose earnings exceeded the then-earnings threshold for insurability (before this was abolished in 1974) and therefore had gaps in their insurance records,[922] people who were also employed in civil or public service and insured at a 'modified' rate,[923] people who became self-employed contributors for the first time on or after 6 April 1988 and who on or before that date had reached the age of 56,[924] and people who entered insurance prior to 1953.[925] The legislation also contains a number of transitional provisions applying to people who reached pension age at an earlier date.[926]

---

918. This is broadly the approach that was subsequently introduced by way of the homemakers' disregard.
919. Case C-102/88, *Ruzius-Wilbrink v. Bestuur van de Bedrijfsvereniging voor Overheidsdiensten* [1989] ECR 4311.
920. M. Cousins, 'Indirect Discrimination in Social Welfare', ILT 11 (1993): 147–151.
921. Case C-317/1993, *Nolte v. Landesversicherungsanstalt Hannover* [1995] ECR I-4625; Case C-444/1993, *Megner v. Innungskrankenkasse Vorderpfalz* [1995] ECR I-4741. *See* para. 98 above.
922. Section 109(14)–(15) and *see* SW(CCP&C)R, Art. 65.
923. Section 109(16)–(17).
924. Section 109(18)–(19). *See Meagher v. Minister for Social Protection* [2015] IESC 4.
925. Section 113.
926. *See*, for example, s. 109(2)–(6).

§3. Amount of Benefit

562. A contributory pension is payable at a flat rate with increases for qualified adults and qualified children as appropriate.[927] Additional payments are made when the person is over the age of 80 or living alone. 'Household benefits' (such as free electricity, free telephone rental, etc.) are generally payable with the contributory pension subject to a means limit in some cases in which the person has additional income.

§4. Disqualifications

563. A person is disqualified for payment of a contributory pension while undergoing detention in legal custody.[928] An increase for a qualified adult or qualified child can still be paid. A claimant will be disqualified if s/he participates in a Community Employment scheme that commences after 16 January 2012[929] or in a Solas scheme or national internship scheme.[930]

---

927. Sections 111–112.
928. Section 249, *see* Part XII, Ch. 4.
929. Section 247B.
930. Section 247A.

Chapter 2. State Pension (Non-contributory)

§1. Beneficiaries and Conditions

564. In the case of a non-contributory pension, a person must have reached pensionable age (*see* paragraph 545), must satisfy a means test, and must be habitually resident in the State.[931,932]

§2. Means Test

565. The means test[933] includes means from the following:

- most property owned by the person and/or by his or her spouse (but excluding property personally used or enjoyed by the person);
- all income that the person and/or spouse may reasonably expect to receive in the coming year (with certain exceptions);
- the value of any advantage accruing to the person or spouse from the use of property (other than a domestic dwelling or farm building, owned and occupied, furniture, and personal effects) that is personally used or enjoyed by the person or spouse, and the value of any advantage from the leasing of a farm; and
- any property that the person or spouse has deprived him or herself of either directly or indirectly so as to qualify for assistance.

566. The main legal issues that arise in relation to the State non-contributory pension concern the recovery of overpaid pensions after the death of the pensions as a result of non-disclosure of means. These issues are considered in Part XII.

§3. Amount of the Benefit

567. A non-contributory pension is payable at a flat rate with increases for qualified children as appropriate.[934] The normal 'qualified adult' rules do not apply to a non-contributory pension. Increases are payable when the claimant is living with or is wholly or mainly maintaining his or her spouse, civil partner or cohabitant, and

931. Sections 152–160. From the introduction of State pension, persons on blind pension, a WNCP, and OFP over sixty-six no longer receive those payments but receive a State pension instead: s. 16(2)–(4) of the SWLRPA 2006. Section 157 (as substituted by SWLRPA 2006, s. 16) sets out specific provisions as to the rate of pension in such cases.
932. Section 153 as substituted by SWLRPA 2006, s. 16 and amended by s. 11(4) SW&PA 2014. On habitual residence *see* Part XII, Ch. 3.
933. Part 3 of Sch. 3 as substituted by SWLRPA 2006, s. 16. *See* Part XI.
934. Section 156 as substituted by SWLRPA 2006, s. 16.

that person is not in receipt of a payment in his or her own right.[935] However, when the person is over pensionable age, he or she will normally qualify for a non-contributory pension in his or her own right. Additional payments are made when the person is over the age of 80 or living alone. Household benefits are generally payable with a non-contributory pension.

§4. Disqualifications

568. A person is generally disqualified for payment of a non-contributory pension when he or she is receiving a contributory pension or to whom a qualified adult increase of the contributory State pension is payable.[936] A person is also disqualified while undergoing detention in legal custody.[937] Section 249(9) provides that a person is disqualified for pension where he or she is undergoing imprisonment though this provision is legally questionable in light of the Supreme Court decision in *C v. Minister for Social Protection* (*see* paragraphs 782–784). An increase for a qualified child can still be paid. A non-contributory pension is not normally payable outside the State,[938] and, as we have seen, the HRC applies.[939] A claimant will also be disqualified if s/he participates in a Community Employment scheme that commences after 16 January 2012[940] or in a Solas scheme or national internship scheme.[941]

935. Section 157 as amended by SWLRPA 2006, s. 16 and SWPA 2010, s. 26 and Sch. 3. 'Spouse' and 'civil partner' includes a party to a marriage that has been validly dissolved and a civil partner whose partnership has been dissolved, s. 152 as substituted by SWLRPA 2006, s. 37 and SWPA 2010, s. 19.
936. Section 160(1) (as substituted by SWLRPA 2006, s. 16) subject to sub-ss (2) and (3), which allow payment of a non-contributory pension where this would be to the person's advantage and/or continue entitlement to contributory pension.
937. Section 249, *see* Part XII, Ch. 4.
938. Section 249, *see* Part XII, Ch. 3.
939. Section 153(c) as substituted by SWLRPA 2006, s. 16.
940. Section 247B.
941. Section 247A.

Chapter 3. Widow(er)'s and SCP's (Contributory) Pension

§1. Beneficiaries and Conditions

569. To qualify for a widow(er)'s contributory and SCP pension, a person must be a widow or widower or SCP and satisfy the contribution conditions.[942,943] However, in *O'Meara v. Minister for Social Protection* [2024] IESC 1, the Supreme Court took the view that section 124 of the 2005 Act is inconsistent with the Constitution insofar as it does not extend to a parent of children who has been in a long-term cohabiting relationship. A 'widow' is defined as a widow or a woman who would otherwise be a widow but for the fact that her marriage has been dissolved (being a dissolution that is recognized as valid in the State).[944] A 'widower' is defined in the same manner. Thus, to qualify for a widow(er)'s contributory pension, a person must have been validly married, and the spouse must be dead.[945] However, to ensure that 'widows' did not lose out as a result of the introduction of divorce, the legislation provides that a person who would be a widow but for the dissolution of her marriage, when that is recognized as valid by the State, may qualify for the pension.[946] 'Civil partner' means a civil partner within the meaning of the CPCROCA 2010 and, in relation to an SCP who has been party to a civil partnership more than once, refers only to the SCP's last civil partner, which includes a party to a civil partnership that has been dissolved, being a dissolution that is recognized as valid in the State.[947]

570. Section 123 specifically refers to the 'dissolution' of marriage and would thus not appear to apply to a nullity. Therefore, when a marriage is validly annulled, it would appear that the person is not entitled to a widow's pension on the basis of

942. Sections 123–129 and SW(CCP&C)R, Arts 79–83.
943. A pension is also payable where the person's spouse was entitled to a State pension that included an increase with respect to that person at the time of the spouse's death (or would have done so but for receipt of a pension by the person in his or her own right): s. 124(1)(b) & (c).
944. Section 123.
945. On the law relating to marriage, *see* A. Shatter, *Family Law* (Dublin: Butterworths, 1997) and S. Leahy & K. O'Sullivan, 'Changing Conceptions of Marriage in Ireland: Law and Practice', CFLQ 30(3) (2018): 279, Ch. 7; and in relation to death, *see* Shatter, *supra*. Part IX. 'Spouse', in relation to a widow or widower who has been married more than once, refers only to the widow's or widower's last spouse (again including a party to a marriage that has been validly dissolved): s. 123. In *McGovern v. Chief Appeals Officer* [2021] IEHC 202, O'Regan J held that the definition of 'spouse' was exhaustive (at 5.5) and that the use of the term 'including' was not intended to broaden the definition beyond the specific wording of the section. On polygamous marriage, *see H.A.H. v. S.A.A.* [2017] IESC 40 and *I.H. (Afghanistan) v. Minister for Justice and Equality* [2020] IECA 241.
946. On the recognition of valid divorce, *see* Shatter, *ibid.*, Ch. 10. In *McGovern v. Chief Appeals Officer* [2021] IEHC 202, O'Regan J upheld a decision of the Chief Appeals Officer refusing widower's (contributory) pension and the widowed or SCP grant to the applicant on the ground that the residence-based foreign divorce that he obtained from his first spouse was not recognized as legally valid in the State when he married his second partner in 1994. O'Regan J also rejected arguments that the failure to recognise the 1994 divorce was unconstitutional or in breach of the ECHR.
947. *See* ss 2(1) and 123 as amended by SWPA 2010, ss 15 & 17.

that marriage. In a number of cases, issues have arisen as to the granting of widow's pension when a second marriage has been entered into (after the death of the first spouse) and subsequently annulled. In such cases, appeals officers have held that the granting of the annulment means that no marriage ever existed and that, therefore, the person is not debarred from receipt of widow's pension (on the basis of the first marriage) by a subsequent remarriage. However, payment of the pension after the second 'marriage' may well be barred by the fact that the couple is cohabiting – although, exceptionally, cases may arise in which, although persons have gone through a form of marriage, an appeals officer is satisfied that the claimant did not cohabit with the 'spouse'.[948]

571. Issues have also arisen in relation to the period prior to the introduction of divorce in 1996. In a significant number of cases, persons obtained a foreign divorce which would not be recognised in Ireland or a church annulment (which has no legal effect) and subsequently 'remarried' in church. However, the second 'marriage' is not legally valid, and therefore, the second 'spouse' is not entitled to a widow(er)'s pension upon the death of the person, whereas the original spouse may qualify. It might be suggested that the UK case law in this area might be followed to provide assistance in such cases. In *Chief Adjudication Officer v. Bath*,[949] the Court of Appeal held that the presumption of marriage by virtue of a period of long cohabitation would not be rebutted merely because it was preceded by an irregular marriage ceremony. In that case, a woman went through a Sikh marriage ceremony that did not comply with the legal requirements and subsequently lived with the man for forty years until his death. Her claim for widow's pension was allowed by the Court of Appeal following a line of UK cases in relation to the presumption of marriage based on long cohabitation. However, given the constitutional status attached to marriage in Irish law, this line of case law has not been followed in this country, and it would appear unlikely that an Irish court would uphold a claim for widow's pension when a person had contracted into a previous valid marriage that had not been validly dissolved or annulled.[950]

572. The ECtHR has held that failures to provide a 'widow's' benefit to a member of a couple who were not married and to a member of a homosexual couple were not breaches of the ECHR.[951] In the Northern Ireland case of *In the matter of an application by Siobhan McLaughlin for Judicial Review*, this approach was followed in relation to the non-payment of the UK bereavement payment (a once-off payment to the widow(er)s) in the case of a cohabiting couple) and this was not appealed. However, the court ruled that the failure to pay a widowed parent's allowance (a payment to the widow(er)s with dependent children) in the case of a long-standing cohabiting couple *was* in breach of the ECHR, and this was upheld by the

948. *Social Welfare Appeals Office Report 2003*, 23–25 (the case refers to the pre-2011 law on cohabitation).

949. [2000] 1 FLR 8 also reported in R.(G) 1/00.

950. *See McGovern v. Chief Appeals Officer* [2021] IEHC 202 where this point does not even appear to have been argued.

951. *Shackell v. United Kingdom*, App. 45851/99, 27 Apr. 2000; *Mata Estevez v. Spain*, App. 17966/10, 10 May 2001.

UK Supreme Court.[952] The rationale for this ruling was that the widowed parent's allowance was paid where the survivor was responsible for the care of children, and its purpose was, therefore, to benefit the children.[953] Even assuming that the Irish courts would apply a similarly rigorous approach to the ECHR, the rationale adopted in the UK case arguably would not apply to the Irish pension, which is payable whether or not there are dependent children.[954]

573. In the UK, it has been held, on the grounds of public policy, that a widow responsible for the manslaughter of her husband is not entitled to widow's pension.[955] It is not clear whether such an approach would be followed in the Irish jurisdiction.

§2. Contribution Conditions

574. The contribution conditions for the contributory pension are much easier to satisfy than are those in the case of State pension. A person can qualify on the basis of her own or her spouse's or civil partner's contributions (but not a combination of both).[956] The person (or spouse/civil partner) must have at least 260 qualifying contributions and a yearly average of at least thirty-nine paid or credited contributions in the three or five years before the year of the spouse's or civil partner's death or the date when he or she attained pension age or, alternatively, a yearly average of at least forty-eight paid or credited contributions from the entry into insurance to the end of the last complete contribution year. As can be seen, the pension requires a much shorter contribution record for qualification than do State pensions.[957]

§3. Amount of the Benefit

575. A contributory pension is payable at a flat rate with increases for qualified children as appropriate.[958] Additional payments are made when the person is over the age of 80 or living alone. Household benefits are generally payable with a contributory pension to persons over the age of 65 subject to a means limit in some cases in which the person has additional income.

---

952. [2018] UKSC 48. *See also Jackson v. Secretary of State for Work and Pensions* [2020] EWHC 183.
953. [2018] UKSC 48 at para. 27.
954. Indeed in both *McGovern v. Chief Appeals Officer* [2021] IEHC 202 and *O'Meara v. Minister for Social Protection* [2022] IEHC 552, the High Court held that non-payment of a widow's pension in the case of a person who had not been validly divorced and, therefore, had not been validly remarried and to a person who was not married or a surviving partner respectively was not in breach of the Constitution or the ECHR.
955. *R. v. Chief National Insurance Commissioner, ex parte, Connor* [1981] QB 758; *Burns v. Secretary of State for Social Services*, 1985 SLT 351.
956. Section 124(1)(a) as substituted by SWPA 2010, s. 17.
957. Section 125 as substituted by SWPA 2010, s. 17 and amended by SWA 2011, s. 6. A reduced pension is payable where the person has an average of at least twenty-four per year.
958. Sections 126 & 127.

§4. Disqualifications

576. A contributory pension is not payable to a person for any period after remarriage or entry into a civil partnership, and a person is also disqualified for the pension when he or she is a cohabitant.[959] The pension is also not generally payable when the person is undergoing detention in legal custody,[960] and a claimant will also be disqualified if s/he participates in a Community Employment scheme that commences after 16 January 2012[961] or in a Solas scheme or national internship scheme.[962]

959. Section 124(2) & (3) as substituted by SWPA 2010, s. 17. Issues in relation to cohabitation are discussed at paras 326–335. A challenge to a similar rule in relation to the UK widowed parent's allowance on human rights grounds was rejected in *In the matter of an application by Marina Lennon for Judicial Review* [2019] NIQB 68.
960. Section 249.
961. Section 247B.
962. Section 247A.

Chapter 4. Widow(er)'s and SCP's (Non-contributory) Pension

577. To qualify for a widow(er)'s or SCP pension, a person must be a widow(er) or SCP (as defined above though without child dependants),[963][964] must satisfy a means test and must be habitually resident in the State.[965] While a pension was in the past payable at all ages, with the reform of the State non-contributory pension in 2006, a pension is now only payable to persons who have not reached pension age.[966]

578. The means test is broadly the same as that in relation to the State non-contributory pension and is set out in detail in Part XI.[967]

579. A pension is payable at a flat rate with increases though some claimants may also qualify for a Fuel Allowance and/or household benefits.[968]

580. A pension is not payable to a widow(er) or SCP for any period after remarriage or entry into a civil partnership, and a person is also disqualified for the pension when he or she is a cohabitant.[969]

581. A pension is also not generally payable when the person is in detention in legal custody or resident outside the State.[970] Section 249(10) provides that a person is disqualified for pension where he or she is undergoing imprisonment (except where regulations otherwise provide) though this provision is legally questionable in light of the Supreme Court decision in *C v. Minister for Social Protection* (*see* paragraphs 782–784). A claimant will also be disqualified if s/he participates in a Community Employment scheme that commences after 16 January 2012[971] or in a Solas scheme or national internship scheme.[972]

963. Sections 162–171 Arts.
964. A widow, widower or surviving civil partner with child dependants should claim One-Parent Family Payment or Jobseeker's Transitional Payment.
965. Section 163 as amended by SWPA 2010, s. 19.
966. Section 163(1) as amended by SWLRPA 2006, s. 21.
967. Part 5 of Sch. 3.
968. Section 164.
969. Sections 163(2) and 166 as inserted by SWPA 2010, s. 19. Issues in relation to cohabitation are discussed in Part IV, Ch. 7, §5.
970. Section 249(10) and (13).
971. Section 247B.
972. Section 247A.

Part IX. Payments on or after Death

582. This part looks at the two main payments upon or after death: a widowed or SCP's grant and the 'payments after death' arrangements whereby social welfare payments continue in payment for a period after the death of the claimant or beneficiary. A general bereavement grant was abolished with respect to deaths occurring on or after 1 January 2014.[973] It should also be noted that payments with respect to funeral arrangements may be made under the SWA scheme and that the HSE has, in certain circumstances, the power to provide for burials (*see* Part X). In addition, certain death benefits are payable under the occupational injuries scheme when death arises from an occupational accident or disease (*see* Part VI, Chapter 1, §7).

973. Section 8(1) SW&PA 2013.

Chapter 1. Widowed or SCP's Grant

583. A widowed or SCP grant is a one-time payment payable to a widow, widower or SCP on the death of his or her spouse or civil partner (as appropriate). The original objective was to assist with the income support needs of a widow or widower with a dependent child or children immediately following the death of her or his spouse. However, as a result of the 2010 reforms of the grant – primarily intended to include SCPs – it was, until 2014, no longer always necessary that the person have dependent children in order to qualify. Nonetheless, as a result of the abolition of the bereavement grant, it would appear that it is again necessary to have dependent children to qualify. All of which raises the question as to whether there is any coherent rationale for this payment.

§1. Beneficiaries and Conditions

584. Section 137 (as inserted by SWPA 2010) provides that a grant shall be paid to a widow, widower or SCP on the death of his or her spouse or civil partner who is entitled to or in receipt of the death benefit, widow(er)'s or SCP (contributory) pension, OFP, State pension (non-contributory), which includes an increase in respect of a qualified child.[974]

585. As entitlement is based on receipt of one of a range of other social welfare payments, there are no additional contribution conditions or means tests for a grant.

§2. Amount of the Benefit

586. A grant is a one-time lump sum, currently EUR 8,000.[975]

§3. Establishing Death

587. The issue of proof of death rarely gives rise to legal issues in practice. In the case of the above grant, for example, only a copy of the death certificate is required in relation to the death. The legal position is, however, potentially more complicated.

588. At one time, the law, following medical science, treated death as marked by the cessation of breathing or of the heartbeat. At present, the law appears to treat death as meaning brain stem death. In *Airedale NHS Trust v. Bland*, Lord Browne–Wilkinson stated that:

974. Definitions of 'spouse', 'surviving civil partner', 'widow' and 'widower' are set out in s. 137 as inserted by SWPA 2010, s. 18.
975. Section 137(1) as amended by SWA, 2020, s. 9.

> Until recently there was no doubt what was life and what was death. A man was dead if he stopped breathing and his heart stopped beating. There was no artificial means of sustaining these indications of life for more than a short while. Death in the traditional sense was beyond human control. Apart from cases of unlawful homicide, death occurred automatically in the course of nature when the natural functions of the body failed to sustain the lungs and the heart.
>
> Recent developments in medical science have fundamentally affected these previous certainties. In medicine, the cessation of breathing or of heartbeat is no longer death. By the use of a ventilator, lungs which in the unaided course of nature would have stopped breathing can be made to breathe, thereby sustaining the heartbeat. Those, like Anthony Bland, who would previously have died through inability to swallow food can be kept alive by artificial feeding. This has led the medical profession to redefine death in terms of brain stem death, i.e., the death of that part of the brain without which the body cannot function at all without assistance. In some cases it is now apparently possible, with the use of the ventilator, to sustain a beating heart even though the brain stem, and therefore in medical terms the patient, is dead: 'the ventilated corpse'.[976]

589. Under the Civil Law (Presumption of Death) Act 2019, section 5(3), a presumption of death order may be made by the Circuit or High Court where the court is satisfied, in respect of a missing person, that the circumstances in which s/he has gone missing indicate that his or her death is virtually certain or highly probable.

976. [1993] AC 789 at 878. *See*, for example, *Re A (A Child)* [2015] EWHC 443.

Chapter 2. Payments after Death

590. Section 248 (as amended)[977] provides for continued payment of social welfare for a claimant with a qualified adult, spouse, civil partner or a qualified child for a period of six weeks after the death of the claimant, adult, spouse, civil partner or child, as the case may be.

591. The legislative provisions basically provide that:

(a) when a person who is in receipt of a benefit or allowance that includes an increase for a qualified adult, or when the spouse, civil partner or cohabitant[978] is in receipt of any benefit (defined in section 248(1)) in his or her own right, dies, payment of the benefit shall continue to be made for a period of six weeks after the date of death to such person and subject to such conditions as may be prescribed;
(b) when a qualified child to whom an increase of a benefit is being paid dies, the amount of such increase shall continue to be made for a period of six weeks after the date of death; and
(c) when a qualified adult to whom an increase of a benefit is being paid dies, payment of such increase shall continue to be made for a period of six weeks after the date of death.

592. In the case of CA, the extended period is twelve weeks, and in the case of DCA (which is paid monthly), it is three months.[979]

593. Where a person is in receipt of parent's benefit and the child in respect of whom that person is providing or assisting with his or her care dies, payment of the parent's benefit shall continue to be made for the normal duration of entitlement. Where a person in receipt of working family payment or back to work family dividend dies, that payment shall continue to be paid to his or her spouse, civil partner or cohabitant for six weeks (or for the remainder of the fifty-two-week period provided for in accordance with section 230, whichever is the lesser).[980]

977. Most recently by SWA 2020, s. 13.
978. As inserted by s. 26 and Sch. 3 SW&PA 2010.
979. As inserted by s. 9(1)(b) SW&PA 2015 and s. 13(1) SWP&CRA 2018.
980. As inserted by SWA 2020, s. 13.

Part X. Minimum Income Benefit

Chapter 1. Supplementary Welfare Allowance

594. This chapter sets out the details of the Irish minimum income payment, SWA.[981] This is a residual payment payable to persons who do not qualify for one of the other conditional payments in the Social Welfare Code. It is also payable to persons pending decisions on their claims for mainstream payments. The SWA system provides for additional weekly supplements with respect to costs such as housing and diet and for one-time exceptional needs payments.

§1. Beneficiaries and Conditions

595. Section 189 provides that subject to the Act, every person in the State whose means are insufficient to meet his or her needs and the needs of any qualified adult or qualified child of the person shall be entitled to SWA. Thus, subject to specific groups who are disqualified for SWA (*see* below), the only qualification condition to be satisfied is need. The needs of a person are taken to be the rate of SWA appropriate to that person (and dependants).[982] Therefore, if the person has an income less than the current SWA rate, he or she will be entitled to payment. The HRC (*see* Part XII, Chapter 3) applies to SWA payments, but payments under sections 201 (exceptional need) and 202 (urgency) are specifically excluded from this requirement.[983]

596. Section 195 provides that a designated person[984] or a deciding officer *may*, subject to Regulations, determine that a person shall not be entitled to SWA unless: (a) he or she is registered for employment in the manner that the Minister may prescribe;[985] (b) he or she proves unemployment and is capable of, available for, and

981. Sections 187–208 and the Social Welfare (Consolidated Supplementary Welfare Allowance) Regulations 2007 (SW(CSWA)R) [S.I. No. 412 of 2007] as amended.

982. Section 196.

983. Section 192.

984. A 'designated person' is a person designated by the Minister to perform the functions conferred on a designated person by the Social Welfare Acts – *see* s. 18 of the Social Welfare and Pensions Act 2008 and Sch. 1 thereto.

985. SW(CSWA)R, Art. 8(2) prescribes that a person shall be required to prove unemployment in accordance with regulations made under s. 141(1)(b), i.e., as in the case of jobseekers allowance. Quaere whether the enabling provision concerning registration for employment allows a requirement that

genuinely seeking work;[986] and (c) he or she makes application for any statutory or other benefits or assistance to which he or she may be entitled, including such benefits or assistance from countries other than the State.[987] It should be noted that this provision allows but does not require the designated person or deciding officer to require a person to register for employment, prove unemployment, or make an application for benefits. Clearly, the designated person or deciding officer should consider the specific circumstances in coming to a decision as to whether to exercise its discretion in each individual case. In addition, Regulations provide that section 195(a) shall not apply to a person who satisfies the designated person or deciding officer that he or she is incapable of work because of some specific disease or bodily or mental disablement.[988]

§2. Means Test

597. The means test is set out in Part 4 of Schedule *3*. The detailed provisions are set out in Part XI, Chapter 4, of this book. It should be noted that the SWA means test is the strictest of those applying in the area of social welfare and that fewer disregards and concessions apply than those in relation to the other main means tests. In calculating the amount of SWA payable to any person when (i) a husband and wife; or (ii) both civil partners (of the same civil partnership); or (iii) both cohabitants are members of the same household, their needs and means are aggregated and are regarded as the needs and means of the claimant. In the case of a person with a qualified child, his or her needs are taken to include the needs of that child. When the needs of any person are taken into account in determining the entitlement of any other person to SWA, only such other person is entitled to the allowance.[989]

§3. Amount of the Benefit

I. Weekly Payments

598. The amount of basic SWA payable varies in accordance with, among other things, the age of the claimant. The highest rate of EUR 201 per week is payable to claimants aged 25 and older; there is a lower weekly rate of EUR 112.70 for claimants under 25 who are not living independently and who have no child dependants. (This reduced rate does not apply to certain claimants under the age of 25 years who

---

a person 'prove' unemployment, but nothing turns on this in most cases, as the requirement to satisfy s. 141(1)(b) is also in primary legislation: s. 195(b).

986. In accordance with s. 141(1)(b) and (4). *See* Part VII.

987. The use of the word 'entitled' implies that this provision does not extend to requiring persons to seek charitable support.

988. SW(CSWA)R, Art. 8. Although, in terms, this only applies to s. 195(a) (proving unemployment), it would perhaps be unlikely that the deciding officer could reasonably exercise its discretion so as to require such a person to satisfy s. 195(b) (job search).

989. Section 196(2) as amended by SWPA 2010, s. 19.

were in the care of the HSE during the twelve months before reaching the age of 18 years.) Increases for qualified adults and qualified children are payable as appropriate.[990] The general definitions of 'qualified adult' and 'qualified child' do not apply to SWA. For the purposes of the SWA scheme, a 'qualified adult' is defined as:

(a) (i) the spouse of the beneficiary who is being wholly or mainly maintained by him or her;
(ii) the civil partner of the beneficiary who is being wholly or mainly maintained by him or her; or
(iii) the cohabitant of the beneficiary who is being wholly or mainly maintained by him or her;
or
(b) a person who has attained the age of 16 years, is resident in the State, is being wholly or mainly maintained by a beneficiary and has the care of one or more than one qualified child who normally resides with the beneficiary where the beneficiary is a single person, a widow, a widower, a married person not living with, and neither wholly nor mainly maintaining, nor being wholly or mainly maintained by, his or her spouse, an SCP or a civil partner not living with, and neither wholly nor mainly maintaining, nor being wholly or mainly maintained by, his or her civil partner.[991]

No increase is payable in respect of a qualified adult who is resident, whether temporarily or permanently, outside the State or is in prison or otherwise detained in legal custody – section 249(6A) of the 2005 Act, inserted by section 8 of the SWPA 2014.

599. A 'qualified child' is defined as any child who is ordinarily resident in the State, not being a qualified child, who is dependent on that beneficiary for support[992] and (a) is under the age of 18 years or is of or over the age of 18 and is regarded as attending a course of study (within the meaning of section 148(3)(a)), that is, for the period of three months immediately following the completion or the leaving by that person of second-level education or the completion of the Leaving Certificate (whichever is later); or (b) in the case of a beneficiary who has been in receipt of SWA for not less than twenty-six weeks or, subject to prescribed conditions and circumstances, has been entitled to or in receipt of SWA and a relevant payment for not less than 156 days: (i) is under the age of 18 years; (ii) is of or over the age of 18 years and under the age of 22 years and is receiving specified full-time education; or (iii) is of or over the age of 18 years and is regarded as attending a course of study referred to in section 148(3)(a).[993]

990. Section 197.
991. Section 187 as amended by SWPA 2014, s. 8.
992. In *McCormack v. Minister for Social Protection* [2014] IEHC 489, Baker J held that this condition was satisfied where a claimant had transferred the family home into the sole name of his wife, with whom their four children resided.
993. Section 188 as amended by s. 13 of the Social Welfare Act 2016. SW(CSWA)R, Art. 37 provides that periods spent on other social welfare payments may be aggregated for the purposes of calculating the twenty-six weeks' period.

600. As set out above, section 196(2)(c) provides that when the needs of any person are taken into account in determining the entitlement of any other person to SWA, only such other person shall be entitled to an allowance. As section 196(2)(a) provides that when a husband and wife, both civil partners or both cohabitants are members of the same household, their needs are aggregated; this means that – unlike other social welfare payments – only one SWA payment may be paid to a couple.

601. As in the case of jobseeker's allowance, SWPA 2009 introduced a lower rate of SWA for younger claimants, and this was extended by SWPA(No.2)A 2009. There are now two reduced rates that apply: to (a) persons age 18–21; and (b) persons aged 22 and under 25 (who are not entitled to an increase in respect of a qualified child).[994] As in the case of JA, the lower rate does not apply to a person who, during the twelve months before attaining the age of 18 years, was in care (*see* paragraph 514).

602. By virtue of section 14 of the Social Welfare and Pensions (Miscellaneous Provisions) Act 2013, the amount of SWA payable to a claimant may be reduced where s/he refuses: (a) to attend a meeting designed to improve her knowledge of employment, work experience, education, training or development courses available to her, or (b) to have her education, training or development needs assessed, or (c) to participate in prescribed schemes of employment or work experience or courses of education, training or development. Where a claimant persists in this refusal without good cause for more than three weeks, she may be disqualified for receipt of JB for up to nine weeks. If she further persists in this refusal, then the cycle of reduced payment followed by disqualification may commence again.

II. Weekly or Monthly Supplements

603. Section 198 provides that in the case of a person whose means are insufficient to meet his or her needs, Regulations may provide for a weekly or monthly payment to supplement that person's income.[995,996] The Regulations may prescribe the class(es) or person(s) to whom a supplement may be paid and the conditions and circumstances in which a supplement may be paid. Supplements can be paid in relation to rent, mortgage, and diet costs and in 'exceptional circumstances'. It must be stated that the legality of these schemes is now open to question. By law, legislation must set out the general objectives of the policy.[997] Only the details can be set out in Ministerial Regulations. Yet, the level of policy set out in section 198 is minimal, and almost the entire details of, for example, the rent supplement scheme, are set

994. Section 197 as substituted by SWPA 2009, s. 7 and SWPA(No.2)A, s. 13.
995. This category of payment formerly included mortgage interest supplement but this payment was discontinued on 31 Dec. 2017. Claimants in receipt of mortgage interest supplement on that date continue to receive payments under the SWA scheme.
996. As amended with effect from 1 Jan. 1996 replacing the previous s. 179, which arguably provided a direct statutory entitlement to a supplement where a person's needs were insufficient to meet his or her needs, *see State (McLoughlin) v. Eastern Health Board* [1986] IR 416.
997. *Cityview Press Ltd. v. AnCO* [1980] IR 381.

out in Regulations (and amended by Regulations from time to time). It is highly arguable that this is in breach of the constitutional separation of powers.[998]

604. Rent Supplement: In the past, a tenant could apply for assistance with his/her rent, called rent supplement, where s/he satisfied a range of prescribed conditions. However, this has now been significantly affected by the introduction of the Housing Assistance Payment (HAP) scheme operated by local authorities. Pursuant to Part 4 of the Housing (Miscellaneous Provisions) Act 2014, recipients of rent supplement with a long-term housing need now have to apply to their local authority for a HAP. Section 54 of the 2014 Act amends section 198 of the 2005 Act to provide (in conjunction with Article 5 of S.I. No. 411/2014) for the payment of rent supplement now only where the claimant is a bona fide tenant who: (a) was in receipt of a rent supplement in respect of another tenancy immediately before the making of the application or was in receipt of the supplement in the twelve-month period before the application; or (b) had been residing, for not less than 183 days in the twelve months immediately preceding the application, in rented accommodation in respect of which the person was able to pay the rent at the commencement of the tenancy and there was a reasonable expectation that s/he could continue to pay the rent into the future but after the commencement of the tenancy, s/he experienced a substantial change in circumstances not caused by him or her and is now unable to pay the rent; or (c) has been residing for not less than 183 days in the twelve months immediately preceding the application in accommodation for homeless persons or in an institution except where the household of which s/he is a member is determined to be qualified for social housing support pursuant to section 20 of the Housing (Miscellaneous Provisions) Act 2009.[999] 'Rent' is defined as any periodical payment in the nature of rent made in return for a special possession of a dwelling or for the use, occupation, or enjoyment of a dwelling, but it does not include so much of any rent or payment as it: (a) relates to the provision of goods or services; (b) is paid or made to defray the cost of maintenance of, or repairs to, a dwelling for which, in the absence of an agreement to the contrary, the tenant would be liable; or (c) relates to any right or benefit other than the bare right to use, occupy, and enjoy the dwelling as a residence. 'Residence' means residential premises, other than an institution, that is used as the sole or main residence of the claimant when 'residential premises' means a building or part of a building, used or suitable for use, as a dwelling and any land that the occupier of a building or part of a building used as a dwelling has for his or her own occupation and enjoyment

998. However, a successful challenge to the scheme on these grounds would seem likely to lead to the entire scheme being declared void.

999. Rent supplement is not payable to any person not lawfully in the State or who has applied for refugee status under the Refugee Act 1996 (other than a person who has refugee status or is entitled to reside in the State under either s. 17 or s. 18 of the 1996 Act or who has been given permission by the Minister for Justice and Equality to remain in the State) or during any period when that person, his or her spouse, civil partner or cohabitant, is engaged in remunerative full-time employment – s. 198(4).

with the said building or part thereof as its garden.[1000] (By virtue of section 198(3B) and (3C), inserted by section 25(1)(b) of the SWPA 2007, rent supplement is not payable in respect of a residence in an area designated as a regeneration area except where it was already payable to the claimant immediately before the area was designated as a regeneration area or wherein so far as was reasonable in all the circumstances, the person had, at the commencement of the tenancy, an expectation that he or she would continue to be able to pay the amount of the rent, and s/he has experienced a substantial change in his or her circumstances such that he or she is unable to pay the amount of the rent.)

605. An appeals office has held that an EU migrant worker in Ireland is entitled to certain social advantages in the State under the provisions of EU Regulation 492/2011 (formerly Regulation 1612/68), which would include rent supplement. He ruled that the availability or ownership of a place of accommodation in a person's home country in another State within the EU should not be regarded as meeting a person's accommodation needs as prescribed for the purpose of entitlement to rent supplement.[1001]

606. The maximum amount of rent with respect to which a supplement is payable is set by Regulations and varies according to the area of the country and the household type.[1002] The Regulations provide that rent supplement is *not* payable when the rent exceeds these maximum levels.[1003] Thus, it is *not* open for a tenant to pay a higher rent and to seek to fund the extra amount from other sources.[1004]

607. Section 198(4A) inserted by SWPA 2010, section 7 also requires that the landlord provide a tax reference number (although section 198(4B) and 198A allow payment in certain circumstances to avoid 'undue hardship').[1005] By virtue of section 198(3D), inserted by section 25(1)(b) of the SWPA 2007, a designated person may determine that rent supplement is not payable where s/he receives a notification from a housing authority that the statutory standards for rented accommodation prescribed under section 18 of the Housing (Miscellaneous Provisions) Act 1992 are not met.

1000. SW(CSWA)R, Art. 3. An Appeals Officer accepted that a houseboat could be a dwelling (as referred to in the definition of 'rent') but was not a building as required by the definition of 'residence' and so a person living in a houseboat could not normally qualify for rent supplement: *Social Welfare Appeals Office Report 2010*, 22–23. The appeals officer highlighted the lack of alignment of the different definitions set out in the Regulations.

1001. *Social Welfare Appeals Office Annual Report 2012*, 38–39.

1002. Section 198(3E) (as inserted by SWMPA 2008, s. 14) and SW(CSWA)R, Art. 9(2)(i). The current maximum rents are set out in Sch. 1 to the SW(CSWA)R as amended by S.I. No. 340 of 2016. In *McCormack v. Minister for Social Protection* [2014] IEHC 489, Baker J held that that the term 'single person' as used in these Regulations referred to a person who lived alone and was not based on his or her marital or civil status.

1003. SW(CSWA)R, Art. 9(3).

1004. However, SWA may be payable pursuant to SW(CSWA)R, Art. 38 if the designated person or deciding officer concludes that there are exceptional circumstances – *see* para. 619 below and Case 2018/46 – *Social Welfare Appeals Office Annual Report 2018*, 94.

1005. *See also* S.I. No. 462 of 2011.

608. The amount of rent supplement payable is the difference between a person's weekly needs of less than EUR 30 in the case of a single person or EUR 40 in the case of a married person, and his or her weekly means less than the weekly amount of rent or mortgage interest, as the case may be, payable by him or her.[1006]

609. In assessing means for the purpose of a rent supplement, there are a number of specific exemptions set out in Rule 1(2)(b)(v) and Rule 1A of Part 4 of Schedule 3 (*see* paragraphs 684 and 688 in Part XI of this book). Rule 1A also provides for taking into account certain non-cash benefits in assessing rent supplements.

610. However, the amount of a supplement is not to exceed such amount as the designated person or deciding officer considers reasonable to meet the residential needs of the claimant. When a person, other than a qualified adult or child, resides with the claimant other than as a sub-tenant, the designated person or deciding officer is required to reduce the amount of the supplement payable by such amount, which in the opinion of the designated person or deciding officer is reasonably attributable to that other person.[1007]

611. When the tenancy is with an approved body that is in receipt of assistance under the scheme of capital assistance, the maximum supplement payable is currently set at EUR 60 for a couple or EUR 55 in other cases.[1008] This is to take account of the fact that the capital costs of the building have been assisted by the State and that, therefore, the body should be in a position to charge a reduced rent.

612. To provide an incentive for persons in receipt of a rent supplement to take up employment, the means test for SWA provides that a certain amount is to be disregarded from the amount of income derived from net earnings from rehabilitative employment.[1009]

613. A rent supplement payable can continue to be payable for the period in which the beneficiary resides continuously in the same residence. Any period of absence from the residence by virtue of temporary residence for any period that does not exceed thirteen weeks in an institution is to be disregarded.[1010]

614. A person shall be disqualified for receipt of rent supplement where a housing authority notifies the Minister that it is providing social housing support to the

1006. SW(CSWA)R, Art. 12 as amended by S.I. No. 516 of 2013. Lower contributions towards the cost of rent apply in the case of anyone who, by virtue of being aged between 18 and 25 years, is in receipt of reduced rate payments of Jobseeker's Allowance, SWA or Back-to-Education Allowance – *see* S.I. No. 669 of 2016.

1007. SW(CSWA)R, Art. 12(3).

1008. SW(CSWA)R, Art. 13.

1009. Rule 1(2)(v) and SW(CSWA)R, Art. 33.

1010. SW(CSWA)R, Art. 11. Institution is defined as '(a) a hospital, convalescent home or home for persons suffering from physical or mental disability or accommodation ancillary to such hospital or home, (b) any premises providing residence, maintenance or care for the persons therein, (c) a prison or place of detention, or (d) a prescribed institution': s. 187 as inserted by SWP(No.2)A 2009, s. 12.

claimant's household or where the household has done or failed to do anything in consequence of which the household has not taken up housing assistance under Part 4 of the Housing (Miscellaneous Provisions) Act 2014 or where the household refuses a prescribed number of reasonable offers of a specified form of social housing support in any continuous period that is prescribed – section 198(3H) (inserted by section 54(2) of the Housing (Miscellaneous Provisions) Act 2014). By virtue of section 199, a person may be disqualified for receipt of rent supplement or have payment suspended if s/he has had to leave local authority housing because of anti-social behaviour or in the interests of good estate management, or if s/he has been directed to leave a house pursuant to section 20 of the Housing (Miscellaneous Provisions) Act 1997 (because of anti-social behaviour), or if s/he was refused a letting or it was deferred pursuant to section 14 of the 1997 Act (because of anti-social behaviour, good estate management or because the applicant failed to provide information necessary to the application for housing), or if s/he is a respondent to an excluding order or interim excluding order made pursuant to sections 3, 3A or 4 of the 1997 Act (and relating to anti-social behaviour).

615. Diet Supplement: A claimant was entitled to a supplement towards the cost of a specified diet that he or she as a qualified adult or child has been prescribed by virtue of a specified medical condition[1011] (though this payment has been discontinued for new applicants with effect from 1 February 2014).[1012] The following diets are specified:

(i) low lactose, milk-free diet;
(ii) gluten-free diet;
(iii) high-protein, high-calorie diet;
(iv) altered-consistency (liquidized) diet.

616. It is a condition of any claimant's entitlement to a diet supplement: (a) that it is certified by a hospital consultant or registrar that the person or qualified adult or child has been prescribed a specified diet by virtue of a specified medical condition, or, in relation to the diets; (b) that this has been specified by a registered medical practitioner; and (c) that the nature and duration of the diet that has been prescribed is verified by the registered medical practitioner or by a qualified dietician.[1013] A diet supplement is not payable for any period during which the person is in an institution, though it may be paid where a claimant participates in a Community Employment scheme.[1014]

1011. SW(CSWA)R, Art. 15.

1012. *See* Social Welfare (Consolidated Supplementary Welfare Allowance) (Amendment) (No. 1) (Diet Supplement) Regulations 2014 [S.I. No. 36 of 2014]. Quaere whether the Minister's power under s. 198(2) of the 2005 Act to prescribe the class of persons to whom weekly or monthly supplements may be paid and the conditions and circumstances under which such payments may be made extends to excluding certain needs completely from the scope of s. 198(1) which allows for the payment of weekly or monthly supplements to a person whose means are insufficient to meet his or her needs.

1013. SW(CSWA)R, Art. 15(3). 'Qualified dietician', etc., are defined in SW(CSWA)R, Art. 3.

1014. SWPA 2012, s. 7.

617. For the purposes of a diet supplement, a 'qualified child' means any child, not being a qualified adult who is dependent on that claimant for support and who is; (a) under the age of 18 years, or (b) of or over the age of 18 years and under the age of 22 years and is receiving full-time education.[1015]

618. The amount of a supplement payable depends on the diet and is set out in the Regulations less a proportion of the applicant's weekly income.[1016] The amount of any benefit or assistance paid with respect to a qualified child is not assessed as income when calculating a diet supplement with respect to an adult.

619. Exceptional Circumstances: Finally, the designated person or deciding officer may award a supplement in any case in which it appears that the circumstances of the case so warrant.[1017] In particular, a supplement may be paid when: (a) a claimant is living alone or only with a qualified adult or children and has, because of ill-health or infirmity or that of any of the persons living with him or her, exceptional needs by reason of having to maintain a high standard of heating in the residence; or (b) a claimant has exceptional needs other than those already specified in the Regulations.

III. Exceptional Needs Payments

620. Section 201, as amended by section 12 of the Social Welfare, Pensions and Civil Registration Act 2018, provides that a designated person or deciding officer may, in any case in which s/he considers it reasonable, having regard to all the circumstances of the case to do so, determine that SWA shall be paid to a person by way of a single payment to meet an exceptional need which is not necessarily unforeseen. This discretionary provision allows the designated person or deciding officer to make one-time payments to meet exceptional needs. The concept of 'exceptional needs' is not defined in the legislation. Departmental guidelines state that payments would be for such items as special clothing in the case of a person who has a serious illness, bedding or cooking utensils for someone setting up a home for the first time, costs in relation to funerals, and costs for visiting relatives in hospital or prison.

1015. SW(CSWA)R, Art. 15(5).

1016. SW(CSWA)R, Art. 16. Regulations usually provide that the rate of Diet Supplement will not be affected by increases in social welfare payments provided for in the annual budget – *see*, most recently, S.I. No. 717 of 2022.

1017. SW(CSWA)R, Art. 38. In *McDougal v. Secretary of State for Social Services* [1981] SLT 259, the House of Lords held that a high cost of living in a particular area could never by itself amount to exceptional circumstances. In *Vaughan v. United Kingdom*, App. 12639/87, 12 Dec. 1987, the European Commission of Human Rights held that a failure to provide an exceptional circumstances payment under the supplementary benefits scheme to meet the applicant's travel costs to see his children was not in breach of Art. 8 of the ECHR.

IV. Emergency Payments

621. Section 202 provides that the general disqualification of students, full-time workers, or persons affected by trade disputes set out in sections 190, 191, 193, or the imposition of conditions on the grant of SWA pursuant to s, 198 (*see* below) do not prevent the payment of SWA in an urgent case. In addition, in determining whether an allowance is payable in an urgent case and the amount or nature of the allowance, a designated person or deciding officer is allowed to disregard conditions for the grant of SWA set out in sections 195 to 198, which include having regard to means in determining the amount of SWA payable. However, inasmuch as section 202 does not displace section 189, it would seem that determining whether SWA is payable under section 202 involves subjecting the claimant to a means test. However, once section 202 is applicable, it is the case that means do not necessarily have to be taken into account in determining how much SWA is payable. Finally, when SWA is paid pursuant to section 202 to a person who is engaged in remunerative full-time work, the designated person may, if s/he is satisfied that in all the circumstances of the case it would be equitable so to do, determine that the whole or part of the allowance is to be recoverable from that person.[1018]

V. Benefits in Kind

622. Section 200 provides that whenever it appears to a designated person or a deciding officer that by reason of exceptional circumstances, the needs of a person can best be met by the provision of goods or services instead of the payment to which the person would otherwise be entitled, the designated person or deciding officer may determine that such goods or services be provided for him or her under arrangements made by the designated person. In making a determination under this section to meet a sudden and urgent need, the designated person or deciding officer may dispense with an enquiry into means or other circumstances and with compliance to any regulations.

VI. Burials

623. A designated person may provide for the burial of a person who: (a) died in the State and with respect to whose burial suitable arrangements are not otherwise being made, or (b) has been drowned and cast ashore has otherwise perished and been found dead and whose body has not been claimed for burial.[1019] In addition, the designated person may, in any case in which s/he thinks proper, bring into and make arrangements for the burial of the body of a person eligible for SWA who has died outside the State. The designated person may defray all expenses necessarily incurred in the burial of a deceased person under this section of a person and may seek repayment of such expenses from the estate of the deceased person or

1018. Section 202(2).
1019. Section 206 as amended by s. 10 SWP Act 2011.

from any person who was liable to maintain the deceased person immediately before his or her death. These provisions are in addition to the payment of one-time payments with respect to funeral expenses under section 201.

§4. Disqualifications

624. Five groups of people are specifically excluded from entitlement to SWA (other than in exceptional circumstances) *viz.*, students, persons in remunerative full-time work, persons involved in a trade dispute, persons who are not habitually resident in the State and persons in receipt of any benefit or assistance, other than SWA, from which a deduction is being made for the repayment of overpaid social welfare. There is also provision for a temporary disqualification in the case of claimants who do not cooperate with attempts to reintegrate them into the labour force.

625. Section 190 provides that a person shall not be entitled to receive SWA while attending a course of study (within the meaning of section 148) other than in such circumstances and subject to such conditions as may be prescribed. A 'course of study' means a full-time day course of study, instruction, or training at an institution of education.[1020] A person is regarded as attending a course of study for three months immediately following the completion of second-level education or the completion of the Leaving Certificate (whichever is later), for the duration of the academic year (including term vacations), or for the period immediately following the completion of one academic year (other than the final academic year).[1021] This disqualification does not apply to mature students, nor to students on the VTOS, the Back-to-Education Scheme, or such other courses of education as approved by the Minister.[1022] This disqualification is without prejudice to the entitlement of any person to receive SWA with respect to a qualified adult or child.[1023] Notwithstanding subsection (1), SWA may, when there are *exceptional circumstances*, be granted to a person who would be entitled to receive SWA but for that subsection.[1024]

626. Section 191 provides that a person shall not, other than in such circumstances and subject to such conditions as may be prescribed, be entitled to SWA in relation to any period during which he or she is engaged in remunerative full-time

1020. Section 148. 'Institute of education' means a school, university, or college of an university, an institution of higher education designated under the Higher Education Authority Act 1971, any institution to which the Qualifications (Education and Training) Act, 1999, applies, any institution established under the Regional Technical Colleges Act, 1992, any institution incorporated under the Dublin Institute of Technology Act, 1992, any other institution to which the Local Authorities (Higher Education Grants) Acts, 1968–1992, apply, and any other institution as may be prescribed.
1021. Section 148(3).
1022. SW(CSWA)R, Art. 7.
1023. Section 190(2).
1024. Section 190(3). *See Social Welfare Appeals Office Report 2004*, 14–15 for a case where an appeals officer held that such exceptional circumstances existed.

work.[1025] The SWA Regulations state that a person will be regarded as being involved in full-time work when he or she is employed for not less than thirty hours a week.[1026] However, subsection (2) provides that the Minister may, by Regulations, provide for the postponement of the operation of subsection (1) with respect to any class of persons becoming engaged in remunerative full-time work until such period after the commencement of the engagement as may be specified in the Regulations. This power has been exercised to allow persons who take up employment to continue to be eligible for SWA for a thirty-day period after taking up employment or the date on which he or she receives remuneration, whichever is earlier (to allow for possible delays in being paid by an employer).[1027] In addition, persons engaged in remunerative full-time work while participating in the Back-to-Work Allowance (Employees) Scheme, Back-to-Work Enterprise Allowance (Self-Employed) Scheme, Back-to-Work Short-Term Enterprise Allowance Scheme or in Community Employment are also not disqualified for SWA.[1028] Section 191(3) provides that subsection (1) does not apply in the case of any person engaged in remunerative full-time work when the earning power of such person is, by reason of any physical or mental disability, substantially reduced in comparison with the earning power of other persons engaged in similar work. Section 198(4)(a)(iii) – which applies only to a rent supplement – extends this disqualification to the *spouse, civil partner or cohabitant* of a claimant. It provides that a person shall not be entitled to a rent supplement when, during any period, that person, or his or her spouse, civil partner or cohabitant, is engaged in remunerative full-time work. However, where a person is already in receipt of a rent supplement, it may continue to be paid where the person is accepted to be in need of accommodation under the Rental Accommodation Scheme and where s/he is engaged in remunerative full-time work while participating in the Back-to-Work Allowance (Employees) Scheme, Back-to-Work Enterprise Allowance (Self-Employed) Scheme, Back-to-Work Short-Term Enterprise Allowance Scheme or in Community Employment, or where, during the twelve-month period immediately before his or her engagement in such employment, the person was not regarded as being engaged in remunerative full-time employment – section 198(3A).

627. Section 192, as amended by section 11(12) of the SWPA 2014, disqualifies any person not habitually resident in the State for receipt of SWA other than ENPs or in cases of urgency. On the HRC, *see* paragraphs 763–776.

1025. *See also* s. 198(3A) as inserted by SWPA 2007, s. 25. The UK courts have consistently held that in the case of self-employment, 'remunerative' means 'paid' rather than 'profitable': *Perrot v. Supplementary Benefits Commission* [1980] All ER 110; *Smith v. Chief Adjudication Officer*, [1994] UKSSCSC RIS_21_1995; *Chief Adjudication Officer v. Ellis*, [1995] UKSSCSC CIS_815_1992. This approach does not appear to be followed in practice in Ireland.
1026. SW(CSWA)R, Art. 6(3).
1027. SW(CSWA)R, Art. 6(1).
1028. SW(CSWA)R, Art. 6(2) as amended by Art. 4 of S.I. No. 478 of 2012.

628. Section 193 provides that in any case whereby, by reason of a stoppage of work because of a trade dispute at his or her place of employment, a person is without employment for any period during which the stoppage continues, and such person has not, during that stoppage, become bona fide employed elsewhere in the occupation that he or she usually practises, or has not become regularly engaged in some other occupation, his or her needs for that period shall be disregarded for the purpose of ascertaining his or her entitlement to SWA except insofar as such needs include the need to provide for any qualified adults or children. This exclusion is similar to that which applies in relation to jobseeker's benefit.[1029] This disqualification does not apply to any person who is not participating in or directly interested in the trade dispute that caused the stoppage of work.[1030] 'Place of employment' means the factory, workshop, farm, or other premises or place at which the person was employed, but, when separate branches of work that are commonly carried on as separate businesses in separate premises or at separate places are in any case carried on in separate departments on the same premises or at the same place, each of those departments shall, for the purposes of this section, be deemed to be a separate factory, workshop, farm, or separate premises or a separate place, as the case may be.

629. Section 341(7C), as inserted by section 13 of the SWA 2012, provides that a person in receipt of any benefit or assistance, other than SWA, from which a deduction is made for the repayment of overpaid social welfare shall not be entitled to SWA under section 196.

630. Section 198(4) provides that a person shall not be entitled to a rent supplement when: (i) the person is not lawfully in the State; or (ii) the person has made an application for asylum to the Minister for Justice and Equality for a declaration under section 8(1)(a) or (c) of the Refugee Act of 1996 (other than a person who has been declared to be a refugee, or who is entitled under section 18 or 24 of the Refugee Act of 1996 to enter and reside in the State, or who has the permission of the Minister for Justice, Equality and Law Reform to remain in the State under the Aliens Act of 1935 or the Immigration Act of 2004). Thus, a person is disqualified for a rent supplement if he or she is not lawfully present in the State. Given that the definition of 'lawful presence' is much more complex than might be thought, and given the subsequent introduction of the HRC, it is not clear whether this provision has much impact in practice. However, asylum seekers – who are legally present in the State – are also disqualified for a rent supplement (other than in the cases listed above). This measure is intended to and does discriminate against asylum seekers. Its compatibility with the ECHR (specifically, Article 14) may be open to question, given that it is clearly intended to discriminate against a specific group of persons who are, by definition, not of Irish nationality.[1031] However, the ECtHR has tended to give considerable discretion to States in their approach to 'sensitive' issues, such

---

1029. *See* the discussion at para. 496 above.
1030. Section 174(2).
1031. *See* the ECtHR decision in *Niedzwiecki v. Germany*, App. 58453/00, 25 Oct. 2005.

as support for asylum seekers,[1032] and, given that alternative means of accommodation (i.e., direct provision) are provided, it may be that the Court of Human Rights would not find the particular provisions in breach of the Convention.[1033]

631. By virtue of section 14 of the Social Welfare and Pensions (Miscellaneous Provisions) Act 2013, where a claimant persists for more than three weeks in a refusal, without good cause: (a) to attend a meeting designed to improve her knowledge of employment, work experience, education, training or development courses available to her, (b) to have her education, training or development needs assessed, or (c) to participate in prescribed schemes of employment or work experience or courses of education, training or development,[1034] s/he may be disqualified for receipt of JB for up to nine weeks. If s/he further persists in this refusal, then a cycle of reduced payment for three weeks followed by disqualification for up to nine weeks may commence again.

632. In addition, the disqualifications in relation to habitual residence, *temporary or permanent*, outside the State or undergoing detention in legal custody apply to SWA.[1035] Section 249(6) provides that a person is disqualified for SWA where he or she is undergoing imprisonment though this provision is legally questionable in light of the Supreme Court decision in *C v. Minister for Social Protection* (*see* paragraphs 782–784). Finally, a claimant will be disqualified if s/he participates in a Community Employment scheme that commences after 16 January 2012[1036] (except in relation to payments made pursuant to sections 200, 201, 202 or 206) or in a Solas scheme or national internship scheme.[1037]

§5. Reclaiming of Benefits Paid

633. As SWA is often paid as an 'interim' payment while a claim for a main social welfare payment is pending, any SWA paid to or with respect to a person who becomes entitled to a social welfare payment is treated as having been paid 'on account' and is deducted from any arrears of social welfare due to the person.[1038] The same approach applies in relation to persons who become entitled to payments from other EU countries or the UK.[1039]

1032. *See*, e.g., *Muslim v. Turkey*, App. 53566/99, 26 Apr. 2005.
1033. In the absence of such alternative support, the case might raise issues under Art. 3 of the ECHR (inhuman or degrading treatment). *See R v. Secretary of State for the Home Department, ex parte, Limbuela* [2005] UKHL 66 in which their Lordships ruled that denying the respondent's state support when they faced an imminent prospect of homelessness was unlawful having regard to Art. 3.
1034. For the list of prescribed schemes and courses, *see* S.I. No. 258 of 2013 and S.I. No. 441 of 2014.
1035. Sections 192 and 249.
1036. Section 247B.
1037. Section 247A.
1038. Section 204.
1039. Section 205 as amended by WUKEU(CP)A 2020, s. 102(b)(i).

634. SWA may also be reclaimable from a parent or spouse of the person with respect to whom support is paid under the liability to maintain provisions, which are discussed in Part IV.[1040]

1040. Sections 344–359.

Part XI. Means Tests

635. In this part, we examine the four main means tests that apply to Irish social welfare payments.[1041] There is a great deal of commonality in terms of the principles underlying the different tests and significant differences in detail. For that reason, we will first examine some of the main concepts underlying the different means tests and, second, set out the main tests in detail. We also set out here the means test for State support with the costs of nursing home care under the NHSSA 2009.

1041. A fifth means test deals specifically with Working Family Payment and that is examined in paras 532–534.

Chapter 1. General Principles

636. Although there is some variation among them, the main means tests involve an assessment of the following means of a claimant:

- the *property* owned by the person and/or by his or her spouse, civil partner or cohabitant (but excluding property personally used or enjoyed by the person);
- all *income* that the person and/or spouse, civil partner or cohabitant may reasonably expect to receive in the coming year (or has received in the preceding year) with certain exceptions;
- the value of any *advantage* accruing to the person or spouse, civil partner or cohabitant from the use of property (other than a domestic dwelling or farm building, owned and occupied, furniture, and personal effects) that is personally used or enjoyed by the person or spouse and the value of any advantage from the leasing of a farm;
- any property that the person or spouse, civil partner or cohabitant has *deprived* him or herself of either directly or indirectly so as to qualify for assistance.

§1. Property

637. In general, property owned by a person and his or her spouse, civil partner or cohabitant is assessed as means. However, the value of property *personally used or enjoyed* by the person – such as the person's home – is not taken into account.[1042] Exceptionally, also a farm leased by the person is not assessed as property. Instead, the actual rental income is assessed.[1043] After that, the value of property belonging to the person that is invested or is otherwise put to profitable use or that, *though capable of investment or profitable use*, is not so invested or used, is taken into account.[1044] Thus, as long as the property is capable of being invested or

1042. For the purposes of Parts 2, 3 and 5 of Sch. 3 to the 2005 Act, the weekly value of property does not include the weekly value of a house in which the claimant or beneficiary ordinarily resides or resided but has vacated (a) on a temporary basis, or (b) indefinitely, as a consequence of his or her old age or incapacity, or (c) where the house is offered for sale by the claimant or beneficiary, for a period not exceeding two years from the date on which the house was vacated and remains unsold – SW(CCP&C)R, Art. 141.

1043. Appeals officers have suggested that where a farm is no longer let because of poor market conditions, an interim decision to continue to assess it at the former market rent may be taken subject to review after a period of up to two years. If, however, the lands are still idle after the review period 'the position regarding capital value assessment would need to be reconsidered': *Social Welfare Appeals Office Report 2005*, 10. Given the provision in different means tests, that the income to be assessed is that which the person 'may reasonably expect to receive during the year succeeding the date of calculation', or (in the absence of other means of ascertaining it) that received in the year 'immediately preceding' the date of calculation, it may be reasonable to adopt this approach where it appears possible that rental will resume within one year. Where, however, this does not seem likely (or does not occur), in strict law, it would appear that assessment of the capital value should resume as the farm is no longer rented. An alternative approach, such as that suggested above, might better be achieved by amendment of the existing legislation.

1044. Where a claimant proposes to use capital derived from the sale of the family home for the purchase of another home, s/he will be given a period of up to six months to complete such purchase,

put to profitable use, it must be assessed. To avoid assessment, a person must show not only that the property is not so invested or used but also that it is not *capable of* being invested or profitably used (*see* below §3. IV).

638. The means derived from the property is calculated according to a statutory scale whereby a certain set amount of property is disregarded (*see* below). The assessed value of the property increases as the total value of the property rises and is not intended to be an assessment of the actual or likely return from the investment or use (if any) to which the property is put. The actual return on the property – whether greater or lesser than the assessed value – is irrelevant for the purpose of the means test. In practice, it would be administratively impossible to operate a system of assessment of actual income, as this would constantly vary with, for example, varying interest rates on deposit accounts or variation in returns from shares, leading to frequent fluctuations in the level of a pension payable.

639. In the case of a number of payments to older or disabled people, the gross proceeds derived from the sale of a house (up to a certain limit, currently, EUR 190,500) are disregarded when the house is sold to enable the person to move to an alternative accommodation or to a nursing home. 'Gross proceeds derived from the sale of the principal residence' means (a) the agreed-on sale price of the residence, or (b) when the claimant or beneficiary purchases an alternative accommodation, the difference between the agreed-on sale price of the former residence and the agreed-on purchase price of the replacement residence.[1045] To qualify for the exemption, the principal residence must have been sold so that the owner may:

- purchase or rent an alternative accommodation, which he or she occupies as his or her only or main residence;
- move into a private nursing home that has been registered under section 4 of the Health (Nursing Home) Acts of 1990;
- move in with a recipient of CA or benefit, when the recipient is that pensioner's carer; or
- move to sheltered or special housing in the voluntary cooperative, statutory, or private sectors that are funded under the Capital Assistance Scheme operated by the Department of Communications, Climate Action and Environment.

§2. Income

640. The means tests take into account 'all income in cash', including, in certain cases, the value of 'non-cash benefits' and 'benefit and privilege'. There is a lengthy list of statutory exceptions to the income to be taken into account. The

following which if no purchase is made, the capital will then be assessed as means – *see* Case 2016/09, *Social Welfare Appeals Office Annual Report 2016*, 59.

1045. Part 1 of Sch. 4 and Art. 158 of S.I. No. 142 of 2007. Appeals Officers have concluded that, under current legislation, this means disregard does not apply to capital released under equity release schemes: *Social Welfare Appeals Office Report 2006*, 11.

exceptions vary from one means test to another, and even within tests, different exceptions apply to different payments. Many of these are now of a largely historical nature and affect relatively few people. Even the more recent exclusions tend to affect relatively few people.

641. Thus, all income in cash (subject to the various statutory exceptions) is taken into account. Outgoing expenditures (such as the expenditure of loan repayments) are not normally deducted from income for the purposes of means assessment.[1046] This is subject to limited statutory exceptions, such as those whereby, in the case of income from employment and self-employment, certain work-related outgoing expenditures are deductible.[1047]

642. In the case of non-cash income, whether or not this is to be taken into account depends on whether it falls within the categories of prescribed non-cash benefits for the purposes of various benefits or is considered to be 'benefit and privilege' (*see* below).[1048]

643. In most tests, income assessed is, in the absence of other means for ascertaining it, taken to be that actually received during the year immediately preceding the date of calculation. However, when such income is attributable to a period prior to the year immediately preceding the date of calculation but is received in a subsequent year, it is regarded as having been received in the year to which it is attributable.

§3. Defining Income and Capital

644. The terms 'income' and 'property' are not defined in the legislation. While there is no Irish case law on this issue, broadly similar provisions have been considered by the UK courts.

I. Income

645. In *Leeves v. Chief Adjudication Officer*,[1049] the English Court of Appeal held that 'income' should be given its ordinary and natural meaning. In that case,

1046. For example, an appeals officer has held that payments made by a priest to his order were not to be deducted from his annual income for the purposes of the old-age pension means test.
1047. *See*, e.g., Rules 1(5)–(9) of jobseeker's allowance test.
1048. Non-cash benefits are currently taken into account for the purposes of jobseeker's allowance, pre-retirement allowance, disability allowance, farm assist, widow(er)'s and orphan's pensions, and OFP. SW(CCP&C)R, Art. 142 provides that the non-cash benefits prescribed are: (i) the net cash value of annual housing costs paid by a prescribed relative exceeding EUR 4,952 per annum; and (ii) the net cash value to the person of meals, accommodation and related services provided under the 'direct provision' scheme administered by the Department of Justice and Equality. This is to ensure that the value of the direct provision scheme for asylum seekers can be assessed as means. For the purposes of SWA, only the value of direct provision is prescribed: SW(CSWA)R, Art. 35.
1049. [1998] EWCA Civ. 1706.

the claimant was a student who was in receipt of a student grant and a means-tested social security payment. He abandoned his course of studies and was told that he would have to repay the grant. However, the social security authorities continued to take the grant into account as income. The court held that, in principle, the grant was correctly treated as income but that monies that a claimant was under an immediate obligation to repay did not amount to income for the purposes of the relevant means test and that once the educational authority had invoiced the claimant, there was an undisputed and immediate obligation on him to repay it. Accordingly, from that time, the grant could not be considered as income.

646. A question arises as to whether income from illegal sources should be taken into account. There does not appear to be any Irish case law on this point, but it appears to be assumed that income from illegal activities can be assessed.[1050] There does not appear to be any reason, based on the statutory language, why such income should not be assessed.[1051]

II. Benefit and Privilege

647. The SWA test includes 'the value of any benefit and privilege enjoyed by the person'.[1052] 'Benefit and privilege' is not defined in legislation and is potentially a very broad concept. Although dating back to the Old Age Pension Act of 1908, there has been very little judicial consideration of the concept. In *R v. SBC, ex parte Singer*,[1053] the UK courts held that the essential feature of income was an element of recurrence and that ad hoc receipts could not be treated as income as benefit and privilege. However, as noted below, Richards J in *Morrell* expressed some doubts as to whether recurrence is essential.[1054] In the old case of *R (Rooney) v. Local Government Board*,[1055] Gibson J took the view that a casual and temporary benefit did not come within the definition of 'the yearly value of any benefit and privilege'.

1050. *See*, e.g., *McGinley v. Criminal Assets Bureau* [2001] IESC 35 (although the point was not argued).
1051. In the old tax case of *Hays v. Duggan* [1929] IR 406, it was held that illegal earnings were not 'profits or gains' for the purposes of the income tax legislation although this case (subsequently reversed by statute in Ireland) was not followed in the UK, *see*, e.g., *IRC v. Aken* [1990] STC 497. In the US, albeit on entirely different statutory language, it has been held that illegal activity fell within the definition of 'gainful' activity: *Dotson v. Shalala* (1993) 1 F.3d 571; *Jones v. Shalala* (1994) 21 F.3d 191. The latter case, somewhat unusually, also involved a discussion of the capacity for work of a Mr James Joyce, Posner CJ suggesting that Mr Joyce would not have qualified for disability benefits being capable of one gainful activity, *viz.* writing, although unable to engage in other forms of gainful employment.
1052. This rule previously applied also to unemployment assistance (now jobseeker's allowance) but is now confined to very specific circumstances: *see* Rule 1(10) of Part 2 of Sch. 3.
1053. [1973] 1 WLR 713.
1054. [2003] EWCA Civ. 526.
1055. [1920] 2 IR 347.

III. Distinguishing Income from Property

648. In *Lillystone v. SBC*,[1056] the question arose as to whether payment for the sale of a house paid in monthly instalments over a period of ten years was income or capital.[1057] The English Court of Appeal held that the payments must be considered to be capital, as it involved a 'payment of capital by instalments'.[1058] A similar issue arose in *Morrell v. Secretary of State for Work and Pensions*, which also concerned the distinction between income and capital.[1059] In that case, the claimant, who was on a means-tested payment, had been in receipt of regular sums of money from her mother, paid either to the claimant to pay her rent and living expenses or directly to her landlord. The amounts were paid as a loan to be repaid to her mother when the claimant's circumstances improved. She did not disclose this income to the social security authorities, which subsequently decided that there had been an overpayment of benefit. The first issue to be decided was whether the loans were income or capital. The court followed *Leeves* in holding that 'income' should be given its ordinary and natural meaning. It ruled that the sums received had the character of income. As there was no immediate obligation to repay, the fact that the payments were expressed to be loans did not give them a different character. Richards J stated that, while the regular character of the payments seemed to be in favour of their being income, he preferred to leave open the question as to whether an element of regularity or recurrence was essential.[1060] Thorpe LJ, agreeing in the judgment, expressed the view, albeit *obiter*, that 'in the ordinary case sums borrowed will be classified as capital receipts, and perhaps invariably in the case of commercial loans'.[1061]

649. In relation to claims for DA, whereby a trust fund is established for the benefit of a claimant, appeals officers have taken the view that if the applicant owns the trust fund outright, it is assessable as capital, but if he or she has only a life interest (and is entitled to periodic payments only), the income should be assessed as income.[1062]

1056. (1982) 3 FLR 52. *See also Chandler v. Secretary of State for Work and Pensions* [2007] EWCA Civ. 1211 at para. 33 in which the court held that 'a periodic drawdown of capital is not 'income'.
1057. UK legislation uses the term 'capital' rather than 'property'. However, the principles involved in the cases discussed here would appear also to apply to Irish law.
1058. Appeals officers have, clearly correctly, ruled that payment of a lump sum award in respect of a pension from another EU country should be treated as deferred income rather than as capital: *Social Welfare Appeals Office Report 2003*, 10.
1059. [2003] EWCA Civ. 526.
1060. In contrast, in *R. v. SBC, ex parte, Singer* [1973] 1 WLR 713, a case concerning the legal aid means test, the court had held that an essential feature of income was that payments 'display an element of periodic recurrence' and that income could not include ad hoc receipts.
1061. On the classification of lump sum payments as income or capital, *see R v. National Insurance Commissioner ex parte Stratton* [1979] ICR 209 and *Minter v. Kingston Upon Hull City Council* [2011] EWCA Civ 1155. The UK courts have held that the correct approach is to examine the 'true characteristic' of the payment, i.e., whether it is income or capital, rather than the way that it is described or calculated (though whether this assists greatly may be debated).
1062. *Social Welfare Appeals Office Report 2003*, 10.

IV. Property Capable of Being Invested

650. To be assessed, the property must be invested or otherwise put to profitable use or be *capable of* investment or profitable use. Appeals officers have tended to take a flexible approach to the interpretation of when the property is capable of investment or use. For example, in an OFP case in which the claimant's former partner was still living in a house that was jointly owned, the appeals officer ruled that the Department had not shown that taking the property into account was clearly supported by the law. He considered that although there was no legal reason why the claimant could not force a sale to realize her interest, this could lead to adverse consequences for the couple and their child. He noted that when a married couple separate and the person leaving the marital home claims OFP, he or she is not assessed with a beneficial interest in the house. Therefore, the appeals officer suggested that it would be inequitable to do so in the case of cohabitees. On balance, he took the view that the Department had not clearly shown that its approach in taking the property into account was in line with the law and allowed the claimant's appeal.[1063] In other cases, appeals officers have ruled that when there is a doubt or a dispute about the ownership of property, it is clearly not capable of being invested or put to profitable use, and it is, therefore, inappropriate to assess a capital value.[1064] In one case, an appeals officer ruled that property in negative equity was not assessable for the purpose of SWA.[1065]

§4. Advantage

651. The means test includes the yearly value of any *advantage* accruing to a person from: (a) the use or enjoyment of property (other than a domestic dwelling or a farm building owned and occupied, furniture, and personal effects) that is personally used or enjoyed by the person, and (b) a farm leased by the person. There does not appear to be any case law on the meaning of 'advantage' in this context.

§5. Deprivation of Income or Property to Qualify for a Benefit

652. The means tests include provisions whereby if it appears that a person has directly or indirectly deprived him or herself of any income or property *so as to* qualify for receipt of the pension or allowance in question, or to receive a higher rate of pension, that income or the yearly value of that property is taken to be part of the means of that person. However, in the case of the State pension test (and that applies to other long-term benefits), this does not apply to any assignment: (i) that is an assignment to a child or children of the assignor, and (ii) that is an assignment

1063. *Social Welfare Appeals Office Report 2002*, 20–21.
1064. *Social Welfare Appeals Office Report 2003*, 10.
1065. Case 2019/45, *Social Welfare Appeals Office Annual Report 2019*, 85.

of property consisting of a farm (together with or without the stock and chattels thereon) and of which the assignor is the owner and the occupier or the occupier only. 'Assignment' includes any form of conveyance, transfer, or other transaction by which a person parts with the ownership or possession of property. A transfer will generally be accepted by the Department when the farm or business is transferred as a result of advanced age and/or failing health of the claimant or when the transfer is considered to be part of a genuine family settlement.[1066] When the income or the value of the property taken to be part of the person's means has reduced since the date of calculation, the calculation may be revised, subject to such conditions and in such circumstances as may be prescribed, but Regulations shall not cause the income or the yearly value of the property taken to be part of the person's means to be increased.

653. There does not appear to be a recent Irish case law on this issue. Again, however, the interpretation of similar provisions has been featured in UK case law. It appears that the question is a subjective one as to whether the person had the intention of depriving him or herself of the asset 'for the purpose of' qualifying for a pension – although it will often be necessary to look at the factual circumstances surrounding the case in the absence of evidence as to the claimant's intentions.[1067] Deprivation need only be one objective rather than the predominant objective of the transfer.[1068] In *Yule v. South Lanarkshire Council,*[1069] the Scottish Court of Sessions took a rather broad approach to the circumstances in which property transferred would be included as the person's means. In that case, a woman of age 78 transferred her house to her granddaughter for no financial consideration. More than a year later, the woman was admitted to a nursing home. However, the local authority decided that the transfer had been 'for the purpose of' reducing her liability to pay nursing home charges and assessed the value of the property against her. The Court of Sessions held that, as the authority could not look into the mind of the person making the transfer (who was now suffering from dementia), it had to have regard to 'the nature of the disposal within the context of the time at which and the circumstances in which that disposal took place'. To treat the asset as part of her means, it must have material before it from which it could reasonably be inferred that the deprivation of capital took place deliberatively and with the specified purpose. The Court concluded that circumstances, including the fact that there was no other specific reason to transfer the property to her granddaughter at that time and that there was some evidence of declining health, were sufficient to allow the authority to conclude that she had deliberatively deprived herself of the asset for the

1066. *See State (Power) v. Moran* [1976–1977] ILRM 20.

1067. *Yule v. South Lanarkshire Council* [2000] ScotCS 227; *R (Beeson) v. Dorset Co* [2001] EWHC Admin 986.

1068. R(SB) 9/91.

1069. [2000] ScotCS 227. It should be noted that the statutory language is not precisely the same. For example, the British legislation refers to transfer 'for the purpose of' reducing liability rather than 'in order to' as in the Irish law.

specified purpose.[1070] In *R (Beeson) v. Dorset Co.*,[1071] the English High Court followed the approach in *Yule* but quashed the decision of the local authority to take account of transferred assets, as it had not correctly applied the test as to whether the deprivation had taken place 'for the purpose of' avoiding liability for charges.

§6. Whose Means?

654. The means taken into account include, of course, those of the claimant himself or herself. In addition, however, an account is taken of the means of the claimant's spouse, civil partner or cohabitant. 'Cohabitant' is defined in section 2 as 'a cohabitant within the meaning of s. 172(1) of the Civil Partnership and Certain Rights and Obligations of Cohabitants Act 2010', i.e., 'one of 2 adults (whether of the same or the opposite sex) who live together as a couple in an intimate and committed relationship and who are not related to each other within the prohibited degrees of relationship or married to each other or civil partners of each other'. An appeals officer has ruled that the term 'living together' 'is interpreted in an ordinary way as meaning the existence of the state of marriage or of a marriage-like relationship and not that a couple is residing together in one place (although co-residence is ordinarily a feature of a marriage or marriage-like relationship). However, the appeals officer held that 'there could be exceptional circumstances in which that test did not yield a reasonable and defensible result'.[1072] Throughout all the means tests, 'spouse' means each person of a married couple who is living together.[1073] In one case, an appeals officer ruled that where a couple were effectively separated albeit living in the same house, the wife should not have been assessed with means derived from her husband's earnings for the purpose of DA.[1074]

1070. This appears to be a somewhat looser approach than that previously taken by a Social Security Commissioner who ruled that there must be a demonstration of a positive intention to secure benefit rather than that the natural consequence of deprivation was to secure the payment: R.(SB) 9/91.
1071. [2001] EWHC Admin 986.
1072. *Social Welfare Appeals Office Report 1996*, 20 upholding the appeal in that case where the claimant's wife lived with and cared for her mother. Although the marriage relationship was intact, the couple lived apart (because of the care arrangement) and the wife received no support from her spouse. However, this decision appears inconsistent with other decisions in which appeals officers have held that a person is not 'separated' (defined as living apart) for the purposes of OFP while the marriage bond subsists (*see* Part IV, Ch. 7). *See* the New Zealand case of *Director-General of Social Welfare v. W* [1997] 2 NZLR 104.
1073. Part 1 of Sch. 3.
1074. Case 2012/05, *Social Welfare Appeals Office Annual Report 2012*, 21.

Chapter 2. Working Age Schemes Test

655. This test, set out in Part 2 of Schedule 3, applies to jobseeker's allowance, PRETA, DA, and FA. The test provides that in the calculation of the means of a person for the purposes of these payments, account shall be taken of the following.[1075]

656. Rule 1(1), as amended, provides for a system of notional assessment of means from capital:[1076]

> Other than in the circumstances and subject to the conditions and for the periods that may be prescribed, the weekly value of property belonging to the person or to his or her spouse, civil partner or cohabitant (not being property personally used or enjoyed by the person or by his or her spouse, civil partner or cohabitant or a farm of land leased by him or her or by his or her spouse, civil partner or cohabitant) which is invested or is otherwise put to profitable use or which, though capable of investment or profitable use is not invested or put to profitable use and the weekly value, calculated for the purposes of –
>
> (a) jobseeker's allowance, pre-retirement allowance or farm assist in accordance with reference 1 of Table 1 to [Schedule 3], or
> (b) disability allowance in accordance with reference 2 of Table 1 to [Schedule 3]
>
> constitutes the weekly means of a person from that property but, in the case of farm assist, no account shall be taken under any other provision of these Rules of any appropriation of the property for the purpose of current expenditure.

657. It does not matter whether the actual income from capital is greater or lesser than the notional assessment, as the latter is deemed to constitute the weekly means of a person from such capital. In addition, the notional system is designed to favour those with relatively small amounts of capital, as can be seen from the exclusion of the first EUR 20,000 from assessment. In the case of DA, there is a higher allowance of EUR 50,000, and, in addition, a specific exemption for proceeds arising from the sale of the person's house in certain circumstances is set out in Rule 1(2) (below). However, the weekly value of property does not include the weekly value of a house in which the claimant or beneficiary ordinarily resides or resided but has vacated (a) on a temporary basis, (b) indefinitely, as a consequence of his or her old age or incapacity, or (c) where the house is offered for sale by the claimant or beneficiary, for a period not exceeding two years from the date on which the house was vacated and remains unsold.[1077]

1075. The indented text reproduces the actual text of the Act (as amended). Explanatory insertions are in [brackets].
1076. As substituted by SWPA 207, s. 35.
1077. Article 141 of SWCCP&C)R as substituted by S.I. No. 157 of 2010.

658. Rule 1(2), as amended, addresses income in cash and prescribed non-cash benefits:

> All income in cash and any non-cash benefits that may be prescribed[1078] which the person or his or her spouse, civil partner or cohabitant may reasonably expect to receive during the succeeding year, whether as contributions to the expenses of the household or otherwise, but –
>
> (a) *excluding* the amounts at references 1 to 19 in Table 2 to [Schedule 3], and
> (b) *excluding* –
>   (i) in the cases that may be prescribed, any moneys received by way of a maintenance grant,[1079]
>   (ii) any moneys received by way of maintenance payments[1080] (including maintenance payments made to or in respect of a qualified child) in so far as those payments do not exceed the annual housing costs[1081] actually incurred by the person subject to the maximum amount that may be prescribed, together with one-half of any amount of maintenance payment in excess of the amount disregarded in respect of housing costs actually incurred (if any),[1082]
>   (iii) any moneys, subject to the limit that may be prescribed, received by way of repayment of expenses necessarily incurred in relation to travel and meals while undergoing a course of education, training or development approved by the Minister,
>   (iv) in the case of –

1078. SW(CCP&C)R, Art. 142, which prescribes: (a) the net cash value to the person of his or her annual housing costs actually incurred and paid by a liable relative insofar as the cash value exceeds EUR 4,952 per annum and (b) the net cash value to the person of meals, accommodation and related services provided under a scheme administered by the Department of Justice and Equality and known as direct provision, where the costs are met in full by the State. At the time of writing, the taking into account of the value of direct provision arrangements is due to expire on 30 Sep. 2020 – *see* S.I. No. 666 of 2019. In *Bracken v. Minister for Employment Affairs and Social Protection* [2023] IECA 16, the Court of Appeal held that mortgage repayments made by the claimant's ex-partner in respect of the house in which she lived with her child came within the definition of 'housing costs' and within the meaning of 'non-cash benefit' in Art. 142.

1079. 'Maintenance grant' means a grant issued under: (a) a scheme administered by the Minister for Education and Science under the Local Authorities (Higher Education Grants) Acts 1968–1992; or (b) a scheme administered under the aegis of the Minister for Education and Science and known as the: (i) Maintenance Grants Scheme for Students attending Post-Leaving Certificate Courses. (ii) Vocational Education Committees Scholarship Scheme, or (iii) Third-Level Maintenance Grants Scheme for Trainees: Part 1 of Sch. 4.

1080. 'Maintenance payments' means any payments received under or pursuant to any maintenance arrangement that may be prescribed: Part 1 of Sch. 4.

1081. 'Housing costs' means rent or repayment of a loan entered into solely for the purpose of defraying money employed in the purchase, repair or essential improvement of the residence in which the person is, for the time being, residing: Part 1 of Sch. 4.

1082. SW(CCP&C)R, Art. 143 prescribes a maximum amount of EUR 4,952 per annum and states that the payments are to include 'all forms of formal and informal arrangements whether procured by way of Court Order or otherwise'.

(1) jobseeker's allowance and pre-retirement allowance and subject to paragraph (5) all moneys earned by the person in respect of current personal employment under a contract of service,

(2) farm assist and subject to paragraph (8), all moneys earned by the person or by his or her spouse, civil partner or cohabitant in respect of current personal employment under a contract of service,[1083]

(v) in the case of jobseeker's allowance, pre-retirement allowance and farm assist and subject to paragraphs (6), (7) and (8), any moneys earned by the person or by his or her spouse, civil partner or cohabitant from insurable employment of a seasonal nature,[1084]

(vi) the amount that may be prescribed of all moneys earned by the person's spouse from insurable employment,

(vii) …[1085]

(viii) in the case of disability allowance, the amount that may be prescribed of earnings from employment or self-employment,[1086]

(ix) in the case of jobseeker's allowance, pre-retirement allowance and farm assist, all income received under the following schemes except insofar as that income exceeds the sum of (A) EUR 5,000, plus (B) one-half of any amount in excess of EUR 5,000 and (C) any expenses necessarily incurred received under the following:

(1) the Rural Environment Protection Scheme, the Agri-Environment Options Scheme, the Green, Low-Carbon, Agri-Environment Scheme, the Beef Exceptional Aid Measure, the Beef Data and Genomics Programme (2015-20) (2017-22) (2021), the Beef Environmental Efficiency Plan (BEEP-S), the Dairy Beef Calf Programme, the Results Based Environment Agri-Pilot Programme, the Sheep Welfare Scheme, the Afforestation Grant and Premium Scheme (2000-6) (2007-13) (2014-20), the Ash Dieback Replanting Scheme, the Creation of Woodland on Public Lands Scheme, the Deer Tree Shelter and Deer/Hare Fencing Scheme, the Forestry Grants and Premium Scheme (2014-20), the Forest Genetic Resources Reproductive Material Scheme, the Forest Road Scheme, the Forestry Knowledge Transfer Group Scheme, the Innovative Forestry Forest Technology: Central tyre inflation scheme module, the Native Woodland Conservation Scheme, the NeighbourWood Scheme the Reconstitution and Underplanting Scheme (Ash Dieback),

1083. This income is taken into account under Rules 1(5) and (8) below.

1084. This income is taken into account under Rules 1(6)–(8) below.

1085. Deleted by SWPA 2007, s. 35.

1086. SW(CCP&C)R, Art. 147 as substituted by S.I. No. 783 of 2021 and S.I. No. 614 of 2022, prescribes EUR 165 and half the weekly earnings over that amount up to a maximum of EUR 375. Income from a bursary, scholarship or stipend in respect of a doctoral degree is disregarded for the purpose of Disability Allowance by virtue of S.I. No. 109 of 2021 as are ex gratia payments made by the State Claims Agency settling claims made in relation to the Pandemrix vaccine on or after 1 Oct. 2020 – *see* S.I. No. 35 of 2021.

the Woodland Improvement Scheme including Continuous Forestry Cover and such additional schemes administered by the Minister for Agriculture, Food and the Marine relating to agri-environmental schemes as may, following consultation with the Minister be prescribed;[1087]

(2) the National Parks and Wildlife Service Farm Plan Scheme administered by the Minister for Arts, Heritage and the Gaeltacht;[1088]

(x) in the case of jobseeker's allowance and pre-retirement allowance, and subject to paragraph (9), any income derived by a fisherman[1089] from any form of self-employment,

(xi) where the person or his or her spouse, civil partner or cohabitant is engaged on a seasonal basis in the occupation of fishing, one-half of so much of the income derived from that occupation as does not exceed EUR 153 per year and one-third of so much of the income as exceeds EUR 153 per year but does not exceed EUR 381 per year, and

(xii) in the case of farm assist, an amount of EUR 1,270 per annum from the harvesting of seaweed, and

(xiii) any income arising from a grant or allowance in pursuance of a scheme for promoting the welfare of the blind prepared under s. 2 of the Blind Persons Act 1920.

659. Rule 1A provides that in the calculation of the means of a person for the purposes of jobseeker's allowance, PRETA, DA and FA:

> notwithstanding any exclusion under Rule 1(2)(b), account shall be taken of any incentive payments[1090] made to a person or to his or her spouse, civil partner or cohabitant under the special incentive career break scheme and without prejudice to the generality of the foregoing

---

1087. SWA 2021, s. 20, commenced by S.I. No. 284 of 2022. S.I. No. 162 of 2023 prescribes the following additional schemes for this purpose – the Sheep Improvement Scheme; the Agri-Climate Rural Environment Scheme; the Organic Farming Scheme; the Reconstitution of Woodland Scheme (Frost) 2022; the Afforestation Grant and Premium Scheme; and the Forestry Grants and Premium Schemes.

1088. As amended by s. 14 of SWA 2022.

1089. 'Fisherman' means a person engaged in sea fishing as a self-employed person: (a) on a fishing boat entered in the Register of Fishing Boats; or (b) on a fishing boat and in a place in respect of which a fishing license (within the meaning of s. 3 of the Fisheries (Consolidation) Act 1959) for fishing for salmon at sea has been issued: Part 1 of Sch. 4. This income is taken into account under Rule 1(9).

1090. 'Incentive payment' means an incentive payment made under the special incentive career break scheme while 'special incentive career break scheme' means the scheme commonly known by that name announced on the direction of the Minister for Finance on 30 Apr. 2009 entitling civil servants of a certain class to apply for not less than three years special leave without pay and an incentive payment.

(a) the exclusion under Rule 1(2)(b)(iv)(II) of moneys earned by the person or his or her spouse, civil partner or cohabitant shall not apply to any incentive payment made to the person or his or her spouse under such scheme, and
(b) the exclusion under Rule 1(2)(b)(vi) of moneys earned by the spouse, civil partner or cohabitant concerned shall not apply to any incentive payment made to such spouse, civil partner or cohabitant under such scheme.[1091]

660. Rule 1(3) deals with the value of 'advantages'. It assesses the yearly value of any advantage accruing to the person or to his or her spouse, civil partner or cohabitant from (a) the use or enjoyment of property (other than a domestic dwelling or a farm building owned and occupied, furniture, and personal effects) that is personally used or enjoyed by the person or by his or her spouse, civil partner or cohabitant, and (b) a farm leased by the person or by his or her spouse, civil partner or cohabitant.[1092]

661. Rule 1(4) sets out the rule as to deprivation of property to qualify for benefit:

> All income and the value of all property of which the person or his or her spouse, civil partner or cohabitant has directly or indirectly deprived himself or herself in order to qualify for the receipt of jobseeker's allowance, pre-retirement allowance, disability allowance or farm assist, but where the income or the value of the property has reduced since the date of calculation, the calculation may be revised, subject to the conditions and in the circumstances that may be prescribed, but any such regulations shall not cause the income or value of the property taken to be part of the means to be increased.

The interpretation of this provision has been discussed in Chapter 1 of this Part.

662. Rules 1(5)–(9) sets out rules in relation to taking into account income by the person or spouse under a contract of employment:

(5) In the case of a person engaged in employment under a contract of service, the value, ascertained in the prescribed manner of any moneys derived from that employment and the value so calculated constitutes the weekly means of that person from that employment for the purposes of [jobseeker's allowance].[1093]
(6) In the case of a person who makes a claim for jobseeker's allowance during a period in which he or she is engaged in insurable employment of a seasonal nature, the value, ascertained in the prescribed manner, of any

1091. As inserted by SWP(No.2)A 2009, s. 19.
1092. *See* SW(CCP&C), Art. 156.
1093. SW(CCP&C)R, Art. 145 as substituted by S.I. No. 700 of 2007.

moneys derived from that employment and the value so calculated constitutes the weekly means of that person from that employment for the purposes of [jobseeker's allowance].[1094]

(7) In the case of jobseeker's allowance and pre-retirement allowance, the value of all moneys derived by his or her spouse, civil partner or cohabitant from insurable employment of a seasonal nature, ascertained in the prescribed manner, during the period in which his or her spouse, civil partner or cohabitant is engaged in that employment, and the value so calculated constitutes the weekly means of that person from such employment;[1095]

(8) In the case of a farmer or his or her spouse, civil partner or cohabitant engaged in current personal or seasonal employment, the value, ascertained in the prescribed manner, of any moneys derived from that employment and the value so calculated constitutes the weekly means of that person from that employment;[1096]

(9) (a) In the case of a fisherman,[1097] the gross income derived from any form of self-employment, or (b) in the case of a farmer entitled to or in receipt of farm assist, the gross yearly income which the farmer or his or her spouse, civil partner or cohabitant may reasonably be expected to receive from farming or any other form of self-employment,

less –

(i) any expenses necessarily incurred in carrying on any form of self-employment, and

(ii) where the fisherman or farmer has a qualified child, who normally resides with him or her, an amount of (I) EUR 254 per annum in respect of each of the first 2 qualified children, and (II) EUR 381 per annum in respect of each subsequent qualified child, calculated at the rate of 70 per cent.

Thus, the test for FA (and for fishers in receipt of jobseeker's allowance) provides a specific incentive for the claimant to increase his or her earnings, as only 70% of additional earnings (less the disregards for children) are taken into account as means.[1098]

1094. SW(CCP&C)R, Art. 146.
1095. SW(CCP&C)R, Art. 153 as substituted by S.I. No. 700 of 2007 and as amended by S.I. No. 447 of 2012.
1096. SW(CCP&C)R, Arts 145 and 153 as substituted by S.I. No. 700 of 2007 and as amended by S.I. No. 447 of 2012.
1097. 'Fisherman' means a person engaged in sea fishing as a self-employed person: (a) on a fishing boat entered in the Register of Fishing Boats; or (b) on a fishing boat and in a place in respect of which a fishing license (within the meaning of s. 3 of the Fisheries (Consolidation) Act 1959) for fishing for salmon at sea has been issued.
1098. While it might be possible to justify the provision of a difference in approach to a group of claimants (such as farmers) involving the provision of a specific payment for this group, it might be more difficult to justify the application of a specific exemption within jobseekers' allowance to one specific group of claimants. Such an approach might, e.g., be subject to challenge under the provisions of the European Convention on Human Rights, although the Court of Human Rights

663. Rule 1(10) deals with the residual benefit and privilege test:

> In the case of a person entitled to or in receipt of jobseeker's allowance and who has not attained the age that may be prescribed, the yearly value of any benefit or privilege enjoyed by that person by virtue of residing with a parent or step-parent, and the Minister may prescribe by regulations the manner in which the value of the benefit and privilege may be calculated.[1099]

Thus, the benefit and privilege rule, which formerly applied to all claimants, now only applies to persons under 25 and only in relation to the value of any benefit or privilege enjoyed by virtue of residing with a parent or step-parent. Pursuant to this heading, Departmental policy is to take into account 34% of the parents' assessable income. A claimant under the age of 25 who has moved back into the parents' home with his/her partner is exempt from this assessment, while someone who has moved back home after at least three years' independent living is assessed at EUR 7 per week.[1100]

664. Rule 2 – which applies only to DA – exempts the value of proceeds from the sale of the person's house in certain circumstances:

(1) Notwithstanding (Schedule 3) and subject to paragraph (2), for the purposes of DA, the gross proceeds derived from the sale of the principal residence of the claimant or beneficiary or, in the case of a married couple who are living together or both civil partners of the same civil partnership who are living together, the spouse or civil partner of the claimant or beneficiary shall not, subject to the limit and under the conditions and circumstances and for the periods that shall be prescribed, be taken into account in calculating the means of the claimant or beneficiary.[1101]
(2) Paragraph (1) shall not apply to any sums arising from the investment or profitable use of the gross proceeds derived from the sale of the principal residence.

The application of this rule, which also applies to State pensions and other long-term benefits, is discussed above in paragraph 639.

---

has generally granted Member States a broad margin of discretion in relation to the details of social security legislation where discrimination on grounds such as nationality or gender was not in question.

1099. SW(CCP&C)R, Art. 157 prescribes the age of 25 so that the B&P rule now only applies to persons under that age. Rule 3 provides that for the purposes of Rule (10), the income of a person shall, in the absence of other means of ascertaining it, be taken to be the income actually received during the year immediately before the date of calculation.

1100. *See* https://www.gov.ie/en/publication/626ffc-operational-guidelines-jobseekers-allowance-benefit-and-privilege-me/#parental-income (last accessed on 20 Aug. 2020).

1101. As substituted by SWPA 2010, s. 25.

665. Rule 3 provides that for the purposes of Rules 1(2) and (10), the income of a person shall, in the absence of other means of ascertaining it, be taken to be the income actually received during the year immediately before the date of calculation.

666. Rule 4 gives the Minister power by regulations to vary (a) Rule 1(1) and Table 1 to Schedule 3 in relation to the calculation of the weekly value of property belonging to a person, and (b) Rules 1(2)–(10), in the case of FA. However, these apparently broad powers must be interpreted in light of the separation of powers, and the Minister cannot exceed his or her delegated authority. Thus, this provision might, for example, justify up-rating the values in line with increases in prices but would be unlikely to allow the Minister to introduce a different approach to calculation.

Chapter 3. State Pension (Non-contributory)

667. At one time, the old-age (non-contributory) pension test applied to most long-term payments.[1102] With the reform (and renaming) of the pension as the State pension in 2006, separate means tests were introduced for the State pension (Part 3 of Schedule 3) and the other long-term payments (Part 5). The test provides that in calculating the means of a person, account shall be taken of the following.

668. Rule 1(1) provides for a system of notional assessment of means from capital:

> Other than in the circumstances and subject to the conditions and for the periods that may be prescribed, the weekly value of property belonging to the person (not being property personally used or enjoyed by the person or a farm of land leased by him or her) which is invested or is otherwise put to profitable use by the person or which, though capable of investment or profitable use is not invested or put to profitable use and the weekly value, calculated in accordance with reference 1 of Table 1 to [Schedule 3], constitutes the weekly means of a person from that property, but no account shall be taken under any other provision of these Rules of any appropriation of the property for the purpose of current expenditure.

669. It does not matter whether the actual income from capital is greater or lesser than the notional assessment, as the latter is deemed to constitute the weekly means of a person from such capital. In addition, the notional system is designed to favour those with relatively small amounts of capital, as can be seen from the exclusion of the first EUR 20,000 from assessment. However, the weekly value of property does not include the weekly value of a house in which the claimant or beneficiary ordinarily resides or resided but has vacated (a) on a temporary basis, or (b) indefinitely, as a consequence of his or her old age or incapacity, or (c) where the house is offered for sale by the claimant or beneficiary, for a period not exceeding two years from the date on which the house was vacated and remains unsold.[1103]

670. Rule 1(2) addresses income in cash and prescribed non-cash benefits and takes account of:

> All income in cash (including the net cash value of such non-cash benefits as may be prescribed),[1104] and the income received by a qualified child or qualified children that may be prescribed which the person may reasonably expect to receive during the year succeeding the date of calculation, but –

1102. Substituted by SWLRPA 2006, s. 24 and Sch. 4.
1103. Article 141 of SWCCP&C)R as substituted by S.I. No. 157 of 2010.
1104. SW(CCP&C)R, Art. 142, which prescribes: (a) the net cash value to the person of his or her annual housing costs actually incurred and paid by a liable relative insofar as the cash value exceeds EUR 4,952 per annum; and (b) the net cash value to the person of meals, accommodation and related

(a) *excluding* the amounts at references 1 to 19 in Table 2 to [Schedule 3], and
(b) *excluding* –
  (i) any moneys received by way of maintenance payments[1105] (including maintenance payments made to or in respect of a qualified child) in so far as they do not exceed the annual housing costs[1106] actually incurred by the person subject to the maximum amount that may be prescribed, together with one-half of any amount of maintenance payment in excess of the amount disregarded in respect of housing costs actually incurred (if any),[1107]
  (ii) any income arising from a grant or allowance in pursuance of a scheme for promoting the welfare of the blind prepared under Section 2 of the Blind Persons Act 1920,
  (iii) any moneys received under a scheme administered by the Minister for Agriculture and Food and known as the Early Retirement Scheme from Farming operated under Council Regulation (EEC) No. 2079/92 of 30 July 1992,[1108] or Council Regulation (EC) No. 1257/99 of 17 May 1999,[1109]
  (iv) any moneys received in respect of rent from a person who resides with the claimant or beneficiary and but for the residence of the person the claimant or beneficiary would reside alone,
  (v) any sums arising from the investment or profitable use of property (not being property personally used or enjoyed by the person or a farm of land leased by him or her),
  (vi) the prescribed amount of any earnings from employment, subject to the circumstances and conditions that may be prescribed,
  (vii) …
  (viii) …[1110]
  (ix) ….[1111]
  (x) an amount of EUR 5,000 together with one-half of any amount in excess of EUR 5,000 received under the following schemes:

---

services provided under a scheme administered by the Department of Justice and Equality and known as direct provision, where the costs are met in full by the State (though at the time of writing, taking account of the value of direct provision is due to cease on 30 Sep. 2020 – *see* S.I. No. 666 of 2019).

1105. Maintenance payments' means any payment received under or pursuant to any maintenance arrangement that may be prescribed: Part 1 of Sch. 4.

1106. Housing costs' means rent or repayment of a loan entered into solely for the purpose of defraying money employed in the purchase, repair, or essential improvement of the residence in which the person is, for the time being, residing: Part 1 of Sch. 4.

1107. SW(CCP&C)R, Art. 143 prescribes a maximum amount of EUR 4,952 per annum and states that the payments are to include 'all forms of formal and informal arrangements whether procured by way of Court Order or otherwise'.

1108. OJ No. L215, 30.7.92, 91.

1109. OJ No. L160, 26.6.99, 80.

1110. Paragraphs (vii) and (viii) deleted by SWPA 2007, s. 35.

1111. Deleted by SWA 2011, s. 10(1)(b).

(1) the Rural Environment Protection Scheme, the Agri-Environment Options Scheme, the Green, Low-Carbon, Agri-Environment Scheme, the Beef Exceptional Aid Measure, the Beef Data and Genomics Programme (2015-20) (2017-22) (2021), the Beef Environmental Efficiency Plan (BEEP-S), the Dairy Beef Calf Programme, the Results Based Environment Agri-Pilot Programme, the Sheep Welfare Scheme, the Afforestation Grant and Premium Scheme (2000-6) (2007-13) (2014-20), the Ash Dieback Replanting Scheme, the Creation of Woodland on Public Lands Scheme, the Deer Tree Shelter and Deer/Hare Fencing Scheme, the Forestry Grants and Premium Scheme (2014-20), the Forest Genetic Resources Reproductive Material Scheme, the Forest Road Scheme, the Forestry Knowledge Transfer Group Scheme, the Innovative Forestry Forest Technology: Central tyre inflation scheme module, the Native Woodland Conservation Scheme, the NeighbourWood Scheme the Reconstitution and Underplanting Scheme (Ash Dieback), the Woodland Improvement Scheme including Continuous Forestry Cover and such additional schemes administered by the Minister for Agriculture, Food and the Marine relating to agri-environmental schemes as may, following consultation with the Minister be prescribed;[1112]

(2) the National Parks and Wildlife Service Farm Plan Scheme administered by the Minister for Arts, Heritage and the Gaeltacht.

671. As can be seen, income received is subject to a wide range of exceptions, both general exceptions set out in Table 1, which apply to all means tests, and an additional range of specific exemptions applicable only to some or all of the claimants covered by this means test. In the absence of other means for ascertaining it, income is taken to be that actually received during the year *immediately before* the date of calculation. However, when that income is attributable to a period before the year immediately preceding the date of calculation but is received in a subsequent year, it is regarded for the purposes of Rule 1(2) as having been received in the year to which it is attributable.

672. Rule 1(3) deals with the value of 'advantages'. It assesses the yearly value of any advantage accruing to a person from: (a) the use or enjoyment of property (other than a domestic dwelling or a farm building owned and occupied, furniture, and personal effects) that is personally used or enjoyed by the person, and (b) a farm leased by the person.

673. Rule 2 sets out the rule as to deprivation of property to qualify for a benefit:

1112. SWA 2021, s. 20, commenced by S.I. No. 284 of 2022 and amended by s. 14 of SWA 2022.

(1) Subject to paragraph (2), if it appears that any person has, whether before or after the commencement of this Act, directly or indirectly deprived himself or herself of any income or property in order to qualify himself or herself for the receipt of the pension in question, or for the receipt of the pension at a higher rate than that to which he or she would otherwise be entitled, that income or the value of that property shall for the purposes of these Rules be taken to be part of the means of that person.

674. However, Rule 2(2) provides that paragraph (1) does not apply to any assignment (a) that is an assignment to a child or children of the assignor, and (b) that is an assignment of property consisting of a farm (together with or without the stock and chattels thereon) and of which the assignor is the owner and the occupier or the occupier only. An 'assignment' is defined in Rule 2(4) as including any form of conveyance, transfer, or other transaction by which a person parts with the ownership or possession of property. When the income or the value of the property taken to be part of his or her means for the purposes of that paragraph has decreased since the date of calculation, the calculation may be revised, subject to the conditions and in the circumstances that may be prescribed, but Regulations made under this paragraph shall not cause the income or the value of the property taken to be part of the person's means to be increased.[1113] The interpretation of this Rule has been discussed above (paragraphs 652–653). Unlike the jobseeker's allowance test, the State pension Rule has a specific exemption for property assigned to children or that involves a farm.

675. Rule 3 exempts the value of proceeds from the sale of a person's house in certain circumstances:

(1) Notwithstanding (Schedule 3) and subject to paragraph (2), the gross proceeds derived from the sale of the principal residence of the claimant or beneficiary or, in the case of a married couple who are living together or both civil partners of the same civil partnership who are living together, the spouse or civil partner of the claimant or beneficiary where the spouse or civil partner has attained pensionable age, shall not, subject to the limit and under the conditions and circumstances and for the periods that shall be prescribed, be taken into account in calculating the means of the claimant, beneficiary, or pensioner.[1114]

(2) Paragraph (1) shall not apply to any sums arising from the investment or profitable use of the gross proceeds derived from the sale of the principal residence.

This rule is discussed above (paragraph 639).

676. Rule 4 sets out the approach that applies when calculating the means of a person who is one of a couple living together:

1113. Rule 2(3).
1114. As substituted by SWPA 2010, s. 25.

(a) the means of the person shall be taken to be one-half of the total means of the couple;
(b) the person is deemed to be entitled to one-half of all property to which the person or the other member of the couple is entitled or to which the person and the other member of the couple are jointly entitled;
(c) for the purposes of this Rule, the means of each member of the couple shall first be determined in accordance with these Rules (each being regarded as an applicant for a pension or a pension at a higher rate, as the case may be) and the total means shall be the sum of the means of each member as so determined;
(d) where one member of the couple dies, nothing which was reckoned for the purposes of pension, or would (if the deceased member had been entitled to receive any pension) have been so reckoned, as means of the deceased member shall be so reckoned as means of the surviving member for the purpose of reducing the pension of the surviving member if any payment in respect of that pension was made before the death of the deceased member or becomes payable in respect of a period before or part of which was before that death.

677. A 'couple' means a married couple who are living together, both civil partners of the same civil partnership who are living together, or both cohabitants.[1115] In calculating the means of a person who is one of a married couple living apart from his or her spouse, any sum paid by him or her to his or her spouse under a separation order shall be deducted in calculating his or her means.[1116]

678. Rule 5 provides that an increase in another pension (payable to the pensioner or spouse) will not lead to an overall decrease in the combined pension payable. It provides that, notwithstanding the Rules, when:

(a) a State pension (non-contributory) is in the course of payment to or with respect to a person or the spouse, civil partner or cohabitant of the person or both of them; and
(b) a pension or pensions (in this Rule referred to as 'the other pension'), not being a State pension (non-contributory), is in the course of payment to or with respect to the person or the spouse, civil partner or cohabitant of the person or both of them:

In calculating the means of the person or of the spouse, civil partner or cohabitant or of both of them for the purposes of State pension (non-contributory), any portion of the amount of an increase in the other pension or the aggregate increase, where more than one increase in the other pension has occurred, which, if it were reckoned as means, would result in a reduction in the amount

1115. Rule 4(2) as substituted by SWPA 2010, s. 25.
1116. Rule 4(3).

of the pension or combined pensions (as the case may be) which would be greater than the amount by which the other pension has been increased, shall not be reckoned as means.[1117]

679. Rule 6 provides that various military pensions are to be disregarded in the calculation of means for the purposes of a State pension.[1118]

680. Rule 7 provides that the Minister may by Regulations vary Rule 1(1) and Table 1 to Schedule 3 in relation to the calculation of the weekly value of property belonging to a person. However, these apparently broad powers must be interpreted in light of the separation of powers, and the Minister cannot exceed his or her delegated authority. Thus, this provision might, for example, justify up-rating the values in line with increases in prices but would be unlikely to allow the Minister to introduce a different approach to calculation.

1117. For the avoidance of doubt, Rule 5(2) provides that any amount excluded from the calculation of means in accordance with reference 16 in Table 2 is to be subject to Rule 5(1).

1118. Any allowance, special allowance, dependent's allowance, disability pension or wound pension under the Army Pensions Acts 1923–1980, or pension under the Military Service (Pensions) Acts 1924–1964, arising out of service in the period commencing on 23 Apr. 1916 and ending on 30 Sep. 1923, or pension under the Connaught Rangers (Pensions) Acts 1936–1964.

Chapter 4. Supplementary Welfare Allowance

681. A separate means test applies to SWA (set out in Part 4 of Schedule 3), and, as SWA is a safety net payment, it is less 'generous' in terms of many disregards than are other tests. It provides that, in calculating the weekly means of a person for SWA, account shall be taken of the following.

682. Rule 1(1) provides for a system of notional assessment of means from capital:

> Other than in the circumstances and subject to the conditions and for the periods that may be prescribed, the weekly value of property belonging to the person (not being property personally used or enjoyed by the person or a farm of land leased by him or her) which is invested or is otherwise put to profitable use by the person or which, though capable of investment or profitable use is not invested or put to profitable use and the weekly value, calculated in accordance with reference 3 of Table 1 to [Schedule 3], constitutes the weekly means of a person from that property

683. In contrast to other schemes, no amount of property (other than property personally used or enjoyed by the person) is disregarded, and a different system of assessment applies.

684. Rule 1(2) addresses income in cash (including the net cash value of any non-cash earnings derived from personal exertions) and prescribed non-cash benefits:

> All income in cash, including the net cash value of any non-cash earnings derived from personal exertions and the non-cash benefits that may be prescribed[1119] and the actual or estimated amount of any household income, whether as contributions to the expenses of the household or otherwise, but –
>
> (a) *excluding* the amounts at references 2 to 11, 18A and 19[1120] in Table 2 to [Schedule 3], and

1119. SW(SCWA)R, Art. 35, which prescribes the net cash value to the person of meals, accommodation and related services provided under a scheme administered by the Department of Justice and Equality and known as direct provision, where the costs are met in full by the State.

1120. Article 36 of S.I. No. 412 of 2007, as amended by Art. 2 of S.I. No. 156 of 2014, Art. 2 of S.I. No. 14 of 2015, Art. 2 of S.I. No. 60 of 2018, Art. 3 of S.I. No. 292 of 2022, Art. 2(1)(b) of S.I. No. 396 of 2022, Art. 2 of S.I. No. 431 of 2022 and Art. 2 of S.I. No. 160 of 2023, prescribes the following income for the purpose of Reference 19 – (a) income derived from compensation awarded (i) by the Hepatitis C and HIV Compensation Tribunal; (ii) by a court of competent jurisdiction to compensate persons who contracted Hepatitis C or HIV from the use of Human Immunoglobulin Anti-D, whole blood or blood products; (iii) by the Residential Institutions Redress Board; (iv) in relation to disability caused by Thalidomide; (v) under the Provisions of the Health (Repayment Scheme) Act 2006 relating to unlawful health charges imposed on residents of nursing homes; or (vi) a scholarship payment to a maximum of EUR 7,000 p.a. paid by a University under its Higher Education Scholarships for Adult Learners scheme; (b) *ex gratia* payments made

(b) *excluding* –

(i) in the cases that may be prescribed, any moneys received by way of a maintenance grant,[1121]

(ii) any income arising from a grant or allowance in pursuance of a scheme for promoting the welfare of the blind prepared under Section 2 of the Blind Persons Act 1920,

(iii) any sums arising from the investment or profitable use of property (not being property personally used or enjoyed by such person or a farm of land leased by the person),

(iv) in the case of a blind person or a person with another disability, the amount that may be prescribed of earnings from employment or self-employment,[1122]

(iva) any moneys received by way of guardian's payment (contributory), guardian's payment (non-contributory), domiciliary care allowance or respite care grant, and[1123]

(v) in the case of a person in receipt of a supplement under Section 198 towards the amount of mortgage interest or rent payable by him or her in respect of his or her residence,

(I) an amount equal to the sum of the first EUR 75 of any additional income (within the meaning of Rule 2) and 25 per cent of

---

to women who were admitted to and worked in the Magdalene Laundries; (c) *ex gratia* payments under the Lourdes Hospital Redress Scheme 2007, the Lourdes Hospital Payment Scheme and the Surgical Symphysiotomy *ex gratia* Scheme; (d) *ex gratia* payments made by the Stardust Victims' Compensation Tribunal; (e) *ex gratia* payments made on foot of recommendations by the Scoping Inquiry into the CervicalCheck Screening Programme; (f) any payment made by the Residential Institutions Statutory Fund Board; (g) any payments received under the Department of Education and Skills 1916 Bursary Fund; (h) any payments made directly or indirectly by the Minister for Health under the package of support measures for women diagnosed with cervical cancer since 2008; (i) any payments made by Sport Ireland under the International Carding Scheme; (j) any payments made by the Northern Ireland Victim and Survivor Service in accordance with the Victims and Survivors (Northern Ireland) Order 2006; (k) a Special Transport Grant paid by the Minister for Education and Skills in respect of children with special educational needs; l) any payment made under the Tusla Bursary Scheme for Children in Care and Aftercare; (m) any payment made under the Probation Service's KickStart Scholarship scheme; (n) any payment made under the Compensation Scheme for young people who suffered harm while in the care of Kerry Child and Adolescent Mental Health Service; (o) any payment made under the Troubles Permanent Disablement Payment Scheme (Northern Ireland); (p) up until 17 Mar. 2023 or such other date as specified by the Minister, any income, subject to a weekly maximum of EUR 269.23, received by a person for renting out a room in their home to a person who is not an employee or immediate family member; or (q) any financial contribution payment made pursuant to s. 8(1) of the Civil Law (Miscellaneous Provisions) Act 2022 in respect of hosting a refugee from the war in Ukraine.

1121. 'Maintenance grant' means a grant issued under: (a) a scheme administered by the Minister for Education and Science under the Local Authorities (Higher Education Grants) Acts 1968–1992; or (b) a scheme administered under the aegis of the Minister for Education and Science and known as the: (i) Maintenance Grants Scheme for Students attending Post-Leaving Certificate Courses; (ii) Vocational Education Committees Scholarship Scheme; or (iii) Third-Level Maintenance Grants Scheme for Trainees: Part 1 of Sch. 4.

1122. *See* S.I. No. 401 of 2022.

1123. Inserted by SWPA 2007, s. 36 and amended by SWPA 2011, s. 19.

so much of that additional income as exceeds EUR 75, when that additional income has been reduced by the aggregate of

(A) any allowable contribution referred to in Regulations 41 and 42 of the Income Tax (Employments) Consolidated) Regulations 2001, and (B) any amount deducted from reckonable earnings under s. 13 and regulations made under s. 14 and

(II) the amount by which carer's allowance as set out in column (2) at reference 8(*a*) or 8(*b*), as appropriate, of Part 1 of Schedule 4 exceeds –

(A) the amount of supplementary welfare allowance set out in column (3) at reference 10 of Part 1 of Schedule 4, where the person, or the person's spouse, is in receipt of carer's allowance under Part 3; or (B) the amount of supplementary welfare allowance set out in column (2) at reference 10 of Part 1 of Schedule 4, where the person, not being one of a couple, is in receipt of carer's allowance under Part 3;

(III) the amount by which carer's benefit as set out in column (2) at reference 7(*a*) or 7(*b*), as appropriate, of Part 1 of Schedule 2 exceeds (A) the amount of supplementary welfare allowance set out in column (3) at reference 10 of Part 1 of Schedule 4, where the person, or the person's spouse, is in receipt of carer's benefit under Part 2; or (B) the amount of supplementary welfare allowance set out in column (2) at reference 10 of Part 1 of Schedule 4, where the person, not being one of a couple, is in receipt of carer's benefit under Part 2; and

(IV) the amount payable under section 186A.[1124]

(4) ….[1125]

Thus, Rule 1(2)(v) provides a specific exemption in relation to rent and mortgage supplement.

685. Rule 1(3) deals with the value of 'advantages'. It includes the value of any advantage accruing to the person from: (a) the use or enjoyment of property (other than a domestic dwelling or a farm building, owned and occupied, or furniture and personal effects) that is personally used or enjoyed by him or her; and (b) the leasing by the person of a farm.

686. Rule 1(4) sets out the rule as to deprivation of property to qualify for a benefit:

1124. As substituted by SWPA 2008, s. 24.
1125. Amended by SWPA 2007, s. 36.

All income and the value of all property of which the person has directly or indirectly deprived himself or herself in order to qualify himself or herself for the receipt of supplementary welfare allowance.

The interpretation of this provision has been discussed in Chapter 1 of this Part.

687. Rule 1(5) deals with 'benefit and privilege' as:

(a) the weekly value of any benefit or privilege, calculated in the manner that may be prescribed, enjoyed by the person, who has not attained the age that may be prescribed, (currently 25), by virtue of residing with a parent or step-parent,[1126] and (b) the weekly value of any benefit or privilege, other than benefit or privilege under paragraph (a), enjoyed by the person.[1127]

Thus, under Rule 1(5)(b), the broader concept of 'benefit and privilege' (*see* Chapter 1, §3. II) continues to apply (at least in theory) to SWA.

688. The SWPA of 2007 inserted a new Rule 1A concerning rent and mortgage supplement, which provides:

(1) In determining entitlement to rent or mortgage interest supplement payable under section 198, the non-cash benefits referred to in Rule 1(2) shall include the weekly net cash value to the person of his or her annual housing costs actually incurred and paid by a liable relative.[1128]
(2) In assessing the means of a person for the purpose of a rent or mortgage interest supplement payable under section 198, where a claimant has attained the age of 65 years, and his or her combined household income is greater than the rate of SWA appropriate to his or her circumstances, an amount equal to the difference between the maximum rate of State pension (contributory) appropriate to his or her circumstances and the said rate of SWA shall be disregarded.
(3) Where a person or his or her spouse has any additional income to which Rule 1(2)(*b*)(iv), Rule 1(2)(*b*)(v)(I) or Rule 1(A)(1) may apply, only one such Rule shall apply, being whichever is the more favourable.
(4) Subject to paragraph (5), Rules 1(1), 1(2)(b)(iva), 1(2)(b)(v) and 1(A) shall not have the effect of reducing the rate of SWA below the rate payable immediately before the commencement of section 36 of the SWPA of 2007.
(5) Paragraph (4) shall cease to apply to any person where his or her means have increased.

689. Rule 2 now provides for the calculation of 'additional income' for the purposes of Rule 1(2)(b)(v):[1129]

1126. The prescribed age is 25 years: SW(CSWA)R, Art. 34.
1127. Substituted by SWLRPA 2006, s. 34.
1128. As substituted by SWPA 2008, s. 24.
1129. Substituted by SWPA 2008, s. 24.

In Rule 1(2)(b)(v)(I), 'additional income' means the amount by which the aggregate of –

(a) income arising from such employment or training or participation or placement in such scheme or programme as is prescribed,[1130]
(b) income arising from the receipt by the person of working family payment under Part 6, and
(c) the aggregate of –
   (i) any maintenance payments made by a liable relative, and (ii) the net cash value of the non-cash benefits referred to in Rule 1(A)(1), in so far as it exceeds EUR 4,952, which, when aggregated with the assessable weekly means of the person from all other sources under this Part, is in excess of (i) the rate of supplementary welfare allowance set out in column (2) of Part 1 of Schedule 4, increased by (ii) the amount set out in column (3) of that Part, where the person has a spouse, and (iii) the amount set out in column (4) of that Part multiplied by the number of qualified children.

690. Rule 2A(1) provides that in the calculation of the means for the purposes of SWA notwithstanding any exclusion under Rule 1(2)(b), account shall be taken of any incentive payments made to a person or the spouse of such person under the special incentive career break scheme. Without prejudice to the generality of paragraph (1), Rule 2A(2) provides that for the purposes of Rule 2, additional income does not include income arising from any incentive payment under such scheme which is made to a person referred to in Rule 1(2)(b)(v).[1131]

1130. As amended by SWPA 2011, s. 16.
1131. As inserted by SWP(No.2)A 2009, s. 19. 'Incentive payment', etc., is defined above.

Chapter 5. Long-Term Payments Test

691. This test, set out in Part 5 of Schedule 3, applies to BP, widow's (non-contributory) pension, widower's (non-contributory) pension, SCP's (non-contributory) pension, guardian's payment (non-contributory), OFP, and CA. This provides that in calculating the means of a person, an account shall be taken of the following.[1132]

692. Rule 1(1) provides for a system of notional assessment of means from capital:

> Other than in the circumstances and subject to the conditions and for the periods that may be prescribed, the weekly value of property belonging to the person (not being property personally used or enjoyed by the person or a farm of land leased by him or her) which is invested or is otherwise put to profitable use by the person or which, though capable of investment or profitable use is not invested or put to profitable use and the weekly value, calculated in accordance with reference 1 of Table 1 to [Schedule 3], constitutes the weekly means of a person from that property, but no account shall be taken under any other provision of these Rules of any appropriation of the property for the purpose of current expenditure;

693. It does not matter whether the actual income from capital is greater or lesser than the notional assessment, as the latter is deemed to constitute the weekly means of a person from such capital. In addition, the notional system is designed to favour those with relatively small amounts of capital, as can be seen from the exclusion of the first EUR 20,000 from assessment.[1133] In the case of BP, a specific exemption for proceeds arising from the sale of a person's house in certain circumstances is set out in Rule 3 (below). However, the weekly value of property does not include the weekly value of a house in which the claimant or beneficiary ordinarily resides or resided but has vacated (a) on a temporary basis, or (b) indefinitely, as a consequence of his or her old age or incapacity, or (c) where the house is offered for sale by the claimant or beneficiary, for a period not exceeding two years from the date on which the house was vacated and remains unsold.[1134]

694. Rule 1(2) addresses income in cash and prescribed non-cash benefits:

> All income in cash (including, in the case of widow's (non-contributory) pension, widower's (non-contributory) pension, surviving civil partner's (non-contributory) pension, guardian's payment (non-contributory) and one-parent

1132. Inserted by SWLRPA 2006, s. 25 and Sch. 5.
1133. EUR 50,000 in the case of CA – SWA 2021, s. 21.
1134. Article 141 of SWCCP&C)R as substituted by S.I. No. 157 of 2010.

family payment, the net cash value of such non-cash benefits as may be prescribed),[1135] and the income received by a qualified child or qualified children that may be prescribed which the person may reasonably expect to receive during the year succeeding the date of calculation, but –

(a) *excluding* the amounts at references 1 to 19 in Table 2 to [Schedule 3], and
(b) *excluding* –
   (i) in the case of blind pension or one-parent family payment, any moneys received by way of a maintenance grant,[1136]
   (ii) in the case of blind pension, widow's (non-contributory) pension, widower's (non-contributory) pension, surviving civil partner's (non-contributory) pension or one-parent family payment, any moneys received by way of maintenance payments[1137] (including maintenance payments made to or in respect of a qualified child) in so far as they do not exceed the annual housing costs[1138] actually incurred by the person subject to the maximum amount that may be prescribed, together with one-half of any amount of maintenance payment in excess of the amount disregarded in respect of housing costs actually incurred (if any),[1139]
   (iii) any moneys, subject to the limit that may be prescribed, received by way of repayment of expenses necessarily incurred in relation to travel and meals while undergoing a course of education, training or development approved by the Minister,
   (iv) in the case of a blind person, any income arising from a grant or allowance in pursuance of a scheme for promoting the welfare of the blind prepared under Section 2 of the Blind Persons Act 1920,

1135. SW(CCP&C)R, Art. 142, which prescribes: (a) the net cash value to the person of his or her annual housing costs actually incurred and paid by a liable relative insofar as the cash value exceeds EUR 4,952 per annum and (b) the net cash value to the person of meals, accommodation and related services provided under a scheme administered by the Department of Justice and Equality and known as direct provision, where the costs are met in full by the State. At the time of writing, the taking into account of the value of direct provision arrangements is due to expire on 30 Sep. 2020 – *see* S.I. No. 666 of 2019. In *Brennan v. Minister for Employment Affairs and Social Protection* [2020] IEHC 393, Creedon J held that mortgage repayments made by the claimant's ex-partner in respect of the house in which she lived with her two children came within the definition of 'housing costs' and within the meaning of 'non-cash benefit' in Art. 142.

1136. 'Maintenance grant' means a grant issued under: (a) a scheme administered by the Minister for Education and Science under the Local Authorities (Higher Education Grants) Acts 1968–1992; or (b) a scheme administered under the aegis of the Minister for Education and Science and known as the: (i) Maintenance Grants Scheme for Students attending Post-Leaving Certificate Courses; (ii) Vocational Education Committees Scholarship Scheme; or (iii) Third-Level Maintenance Grants Scheme for Trainees: Part 1 of Sch. 4.

1137. 'Maintenance payments' means any payments received under or pursuant to any maintenance arrangement that may be prescribed: Part 1 of Sch. 4.

1138. 'Housing costs' means rent or repayment of a loan entered into solely for the purpose of defraying money employed in the purchase, repair or essential improvement of the residence in which the person is, for the time being, residing: Part 1 of Sch. 4.

1139. SW(CCP&C)R, Art. 143 prescribes a maximum amount of EUR 4,952 and states that the payments are to include 'all forms of formal and informal arrangements whether procured by way of Court Order or otherwise'.

(v) for the purposes of widow's (non-contributory) pension, widower's (non-contributory) pension or surviving civil partner's (non-contributory) pension, any moneys received in respect of rent from a person who resides with the claimant or beneficiary and but for the residence of the person the claimant or beneficiary would reside alone,

(vi) any sums arising from the investment or profitable use of property (not being property personally used or enjoyed by the person or a farm of land leased by him or her),

(vii) in the case of widow's (non-contributory) pension, widower's (non-contributory) pension, surviving civil partner's (non-contributory) pension or [deserted wife's allowance or prisoner's wife's allowance], the prescribed amount of any earnings from employment, subject to the circumstances and conditions that may be prescribed,

(viii) in the case of one-parent family payment, subject to paragraph (4), any moneys received by way of earnings (including wages and profit from any form of self-employment),

(ix) ...[1140]

(x) in the case of a blind person, the amount that may be prescribed of his or her earnings from employment, or self-employment,[1141] or income from a bursary, scholarship or stipend in respect of a doctoral degree.[1142]

(xi) ....[1143]

695. As can be seen, income received is subject to a wide range of exceptions, both general exceptions set out in Table 1, which apply to all means tests, and an additional range of specific exemptions applicable only to some or all of the claimants covered by this means test. In the absence of other means for ascertaining it, income is taken to be that actually received during the year *immediately before* the date of calculation. However, when that income is attributable to a period before the year immediately preceding the date of calculation but is received in a subsequent year, it is regarded for the purposes of Rule 1(2) as having been received in the year to which it is attributable.

696. Rule 1(3) deals with the value of 'advantages'. It assesses the yearly value of any advantage accruing to a person from: (a) the use or enjoyment of property (other than a domestic dwelling or a farm building, owned and occupied, furniture, and personal effects) that is personally used or enjoyed by the person; and (b) a farm leased by the person.

1140. Deleted by SWP&CRA 2018, s. 20(c).

1141. *See* further SW(CCP&C)R, Art. 150 as substituted by Art. 4 of S.I. No. 783 of 2021 and amended by S.I. No. 614 of 2022.

1142. *See* S.I. No. 125 of 2022.

1143. Deleted by SWPA 2007, s. 35.

697. Rules 1(4)(b)–(dd), as amended, prescribe varying amounts of weekly earnings (including wages and profit from any form of self-employment) that are to be discounted for the purpose of determining eligibility for OFP, ranging from EUR 130 and a half of the weekly earnings in excess of that amount to (currently) EUR 165 and a half of the weekly earnings in excess of that amount that is to be disregarded in determining applications for OFP in the periods 1 January 2012–31 December 2012, 1 January 2013–31 December 2013, 1 January 2014–4 January 2017, 5 January 2017–28 March 2018, 28 March 2018–27 March 2019, 28 March 2019–8 January 2020 and on or after 9 January 2020 respectively.

698. Rules 1(5)–(6) – which apply only to *CA* – sets out specific exemptions that apply to that payment:

(5) In the case of carer's allowance, in calculating the weekly means of a carer who is not one of a couple (other than means derived from any benefit, pension, assistance, allowance or supplement under the 2005 Act or a social security payment payable under the legislation of another state), that amount that may be prescribed shall be disregarded.[1144]

(6) In the case of carer's allowance, the amount that the Minister determines that the relevant person (as defined in section 179) could reasonably be expected to contribute to the support of the carer but in determining that amount, no account shall be taken of any sums received by the relevant person [by way of social insurance, social assistance, or child benefit].[1145]

699. Rule 1A relates to disregarding income from foreign social security payments in the case of CA. It provides that, in the case of CA, in calculating the weekly means of a carer who is not one of a couple, the following shall be disregarded: (a) an amount not exceeding the maximum amount set out in column (2) at reference 3 of Part 1 of Schedule 2, of a social security payment payable under the legislation of another state, and (b) an amount not exceeding the maximum amounts set out in columns 4 and 5 at reference 3 of Part 1 of Schedule 2 to the 2005 Act of a social security payment payable under the legislation of another state of respect of each qualified child under the age of 12 and aged 12 and over respectively for whom an increase in CA is payable.[1146]

700. Rule 1B provides that in Rules 1, 1A and 4, 'couple' means: (a) a married couple who are living together, (b) both civil partners who are parties to the same civil partnership and who are living together, or (c) both cohabitants.[1147]

701. Rule 2 sets out the rule as to deprivation of property to qualify for benefit:

1144. SW(CCP&C)R, Art. 144 (as amended by S.I. No. 75 of 2008) prescribes a weekly amount from employment or self-employment of EUR 332.50. The means of a couple are addressed in Rule 4(3).
1145. This provision has never been applied to date.
1146. As inserted by SWP&CRA 2018, s. 17 and Sch. 1.
1147. As inserted by SWPA 2010, s. 10 and substituted by s. 25 of the same Act.

> (1) Subject to paragraph (2), if it appears that any person has, whether before or after the commencement of this Act, directly or indirectly deprived himself or herself of any income or property in order to qualify himself or herself for the receipt of the pension or allowance in question, or for the receipt of the pension or allowance at a higher rate than that to which he or she would otherwise be entitled, that income or the value of that property shall for the purposes of these Rules be taken to be part of the means of that person.

However, Rule 2(2) provides that this does not apply to any assignment (a) that is an assignment to a child or children of the assignor, and (b) that is an assignment of property consisting of a farm (together with or without the stock and chattels thereon) and of which the assignor is the owner and the occupier or the occupier only. An 'assignment' includes any form of conveyance, transfer, or other transaction by which a person parts with the ownership or possession of property.[1148] Rule 2(3) provides that when the income or the value of the property taken to be part of a person's means for the purposes of that paragraph has decreased since the date of calculation, the calculation may be revised, subject to the conditions and in the circumstances that may be prescribed, but Regulations made under this paragraph shall not cause the income or the value of the property taken to be part of his or her means to be increased.

702. Rule 3 – which applies only to BP – exempts the value of proceeds from the sale of a person's house in certain circumstances:

(1) Notwithstanding (Schedule 3) and subject to paragraph (2), for the purposes of BP, the gross proceeds derived from the sale of the principal residence of the claimant or beneficiary or, in the case of a married couple who are living together, both civil partners of the same civil partnership who are living together, the spouse or civil partner of the claimant or beneficiary where the spouse or civil partner has attained pensionable age, shall not, subject to the limit and under the conditions and circumstances and for the periods that shall be prescribed, be taken into account in calculating the means of the claimant, beneficiary, or pensioner.[1149]

(2) Paragraph (1) shall not apply to any sums arising from the investment or profitable use of the gross proceeds derived from the sale of the principal residence.

The application of this Rule, which also applies to a State pension, is discussed above in paragraph 639.

703. Rule 4, which applies only to BP and CA, sets out the approach that applies when calculating the means of a person who is one of a couple living together:

1148. Rule 2(4).
1149. As substituted by SWPA 2010, s. 25.

(1) (a) the means of the person shall be taken to be one-half of the total means of the couple;
(b) the person is deemed to be entitled to one-half of all property to which the person or the other member of the couple is entitled or to which the person and the other member of the couple are jointly entitled;
(c) for the purposes of this Rule, the means of each member of the couple shall first be determined in accordance with these Rules (each being regarded as an applicant for a pension or a pension at a higher rate or CA, as the case may be) and the total means shall be the sum of the means of each member as so determined;
(d) where one member of the couple dies, nothing which was reckoned for the purposes of pension, or would (if the deceased member had been entitled to receive any pension) have been so reckoned, as means of the deceased member shall be so reckoned as means of the surviving member for the purpose of reducing the pension of the surviving member if any payment in respect of that pension was made before the death of the deceased member or becomes payable in respect of a period before or part of which was before that death.

(2) In the case of CA, in calculating the means of the other member of the couple for the purposes of paragraph (1), the following shall be disregarded:
(a) an amount not exceeding the maximum amount set out in column (2), reference 3 of Part 1 of Schedule 2, of a social security payment payable under the legislation of another state and
(b) an amount not exceeding the maximum amounts set out in columns 4 and 5 at reference 3 of Part 1 of Schedule 2 to the 2005 Act of a social security payment payable under the legislation of another state of respect of each qualified child under the age of 12 and aged 12 and over respectively for whom an increase in CA is payable.[1150]

In the case of CA, in calculating the weekly means of the couple (other than means derived from any benefit, pension, assistance, allowance or supplement under the 2005 Act or a social security payment payable under the legislation of another state), the amount that may be prescribed shall be disregarded.[1151]

704. A 'couple' means a married couple who are living together or a man and woman who are not married to each other but are cohabiting as husband and wife.[1152]

705. Rule 4(5) provides a specific rule in relation to calculating the means of one of a married couple living apart from his or her spouse, whereby any sum paid by him or her to his or her spouse under a separation order shall be deducted in calculating his or her means.

1150. As inserted by SWP&CRA 2018, s. 17 and Sch. 1.
1151. SW(CCP&C)R, Art. 144 (as amended by S.I. No. 75 of 2008) prescribes EUR 665 per week in the case of a couple.
1152. Rule 4(4).

706. Rule 5 provides that an increase in another pension (payable to the pensioner or spouse) will not lead to an overall decrease in the combined pension payable. It provides that, notwithstanding these Rules, when:

(a) BP, widow's (non-contributory) pension, widower's (non-contributory) pension, SCP's (non-contributory) pension, guardian's payment (non-contributory), OFP, or CA is in the course of payment to or with respect to a person or the spouse, civil partner or cohabitant of the person or both of them; and
(b) a pension or pensions (in this Rule referred to as 'the other pension'), not being a pension or pensions mentioned in paragraph (a), is in the course of payment to or with respect to the person or the spouse, civil partner or cohabitant of the person or both of them:

> in calculating the means of the person or of the spouse, civil partner or cohabitant or of both of them for the purposes of blind pension, widow's (non-contributory) pension, widower's (non-contributory) pension, surviving civil partner's (non-contributory) pension, guardian's payment (non-contributory), one-parent family payment or carer's allowance (as the case may require), any portion of the amount of an increase in the other pension or the aggregate increase, where more than one increase in the other pension has occurred, which, if it were reckoned as means, would result in a reduction in the amount of the pension or combined pensions (as the case may be) which would be greater than the amount by which the other pension has been increased, shall not be reckoned as means.[1153]

707. Rule 6 provides that the amount of various military pensions is to be disregarded in the calculation of means for the purposes of BP, widow's (non-contributory) pension, widower's (non-contributory) pension, SCP's (non-contributory) pension, guardian's payment (non-contributory), OFP or CA.[1154]

708. Rule 6A(1) provides that in the calculation of the means of a person, notwithstanding any exclusion under Rule 1(2)(b), account shall be taken of any incentive payment made to a person or the spouse of a person under the special incentive career break scheme. Without prejudice to the generality of paragraph (1), Rule 6A(2) provides that for the purposes of Rule 1(2)(b)(viii), the exclusion for OFP, of any money received by way of earnings referred to in that Rule shall not apply to any incentive payment made to a person under the special incentive career break scheme.[1155]

1153. As amended by SW&PA 2010, s. 26 and Sch. 3. Rule 5(2) provides that any amount excluded from the calculation of means in accordance with reference 16 in Table 2 shall be subject to Rule 5(1).

1154. Any allowance, special allowance, dependent's allowance, disability pension or wound pension under the Army Pensions Acts 1923–1980, or pension under the Military Service (Pensions) Acts 1924–1964, arising out of service in the period commencing on 23 Apr. 1916 and ending on 30 Sep. 1923, or pension under the Connaught Rangers (Pensions) Acts 1936–1964.

1155. As inserted by SWP(No.2)A 2009, s. 19. 'Incentive payment', etc., is defined above.

709. Rule 7 allows the Minister to vary by regulations Rule 1(1) and Table 1 to Schedule 3 in relation to the calculation of the weekly value of property belonging to a person. However, these apparently broad powers must be interpreted in light of the separation of powers, and the Minister cannot exceed his or her delegated authority. Thus, this provision might, for example, justify up-rating the values in line with increases in prices but would be unlikely to allow the Minister to introduce a different approach to calculation.

Table 1 Social Welfare (Consolidation) Acts 2005

1. The weekly value of the property referred to in Rule 1(1) of Part 2 (for the purposes of jobseeker's allowance, PRETA and FA), Rule 1(1) of Part 3 and Rule 1(1) of Part 5[1156] shall be calculated as follows:
   (a) the first EUR 20,000 of the capital value of the property shall be excluded;
   (b) the weekly value of so much of the capital value of the property as exceeds EUR 20,000 but does not exceed EUR 30,000 shall be assessed at EUR 1 per each EUR 1,000;
   (c) the weekly value of so much of the capital value of the property as exceeds EUR 30,000 but does not exceed EUR 40,000 shall be assessed at EUR 2 per each EUR 1,000; and
   (d) the weekly value of so much of the capital value of the property as exceeds EUR 40,000 shall be assessed at EUR 4 per each EUR 1,000.
2. The weekly value of the property referred to in Rule 1(1) of Part 2, for the purposes of DA, shall be calculated as follows:
   (a) the first EUR 50,000 of the capital value of the property shall be excluded;
   (b) the weekly value of so much of the capital value of the property as exceeds EUR 50,000 but does not exceed EUR 60,000 shall be assessed at EUR 1 per each EUR 1,000;
   (c) the weekly value of so much of the capital value of the property as exceeds EUR 60,000 but does not exceed EUR 70,000 shall be assessed at EUR 2 per each EUR 1,000; and
   (d) the weekly value of so much of the capital value of the property as exceeds EUR 70,000 shall be assessed at EUR 4 per each EUR 1,000.[1157]
3. The weekly value of the property referred to in Rule 1(1) of Part 4 [SWA] shall be calculated as follows:

1156. Substituted by SWLRPA 2006, s. 17.
1157. Substituted by SWPA 2007, s. 35(d).

(a) the first EUR 5,000 of the capital value of the property shall be excluded;

(b) the weekly value of so much of the capital value of the property as exceeds EUR 5,000 but does not exceed EUR 15,000 shall be assessed at EUR 1 per each EUR 1,000;

(c) the weekly value of so much of the capital value of the property as exceeds EUR 15,000 but does not exceed EUR 40,000 shall be assessed at EUR 2 per each EUR 1,000; and

(d) the weekly value of so much of the capital value of the property as exceeds EUR 40,000 shall be assessed at EUR 4 per each EUR 1,000.

Table 2

Reference No.	*Amount*
1.	any money received by way of benefit, pension, assistance, allowance, supplement or continued payment for qualified children under Parts 2, 3, 4, 5, 6, 7, 7A or 8A;[1158]
2.	any money received by way of CB under Part 4 or a payment corresponding to that benefit from another Member State or the UK;[1159]
3.	any money received from the Health Service Executive by way of a home care grant;[1160]
3A.	Any allowance received under a scheme administered by the Minister for Education and Science and known as the Home Tuition Scheme where that allowance is used towards defraying the cost of home tuition;[1161]
4.	any money received by way of a mobility allowance payable under section 61 of the HA of 1970;
5.	any money received by way of training allowance from an organization while undergoing a course of rehabilitation training provided by the organization (being an organization approved by the Minister for Health for the purposes of the provision of such training);

1158. As substituted by SW(MP)A 2015, s. 14.
1159. Substituted by SWMPA 2010, s. 17 and amended by WUKEU(CP)A 2020, s. 102(d).
1160. *Ibid.*
1161. Inserted by SWLRPA 2006, s. 33(c).

Reference No.	*Amount*
6.	payments by the Health Service Executive pursuant to S.I. No. 260 of 1995 or S.I. No. 261 of 1995 or in accordance with an aftercare plan within the meaning of the Child Care Act 1991 in respect of a child who is boarded out;[1162]
7.	payments by the Health Service Executive in respect of the provision of accommodation for a child under section 5 of the Child Care Act 1991;
8.	payments in respect of not more than 2 persons boarded out under section 10 of the Health (Nursing Homes) Act of 1990 in so far as the aggregate amount of payment received in respect of each person boarded out does not exceed an amount equivalent to the rate set out in column (2) at reference 4 of Part 1 of Schedule 4;[1163]
9.	deleted by SWA 2011, section 10(1)(c);
10.	in the case of a qualified applicant under a scheme administered by the Minister for Community, Rural and Gaeltacht Affairs and known as Scéim na bhFoghlaimeoirí Gaeilge, any income received under that scheme in respect of a person who is temporarily resident with the qualified applicant, together with any other income received in respect of that temporary resident;
11.	any money received from a charitable organization, being a body whose activities are carried on otherwise than for profit (but excluding any public or local authority) and one of whose functions is to assist persons in need by making grants of money to them;
12.	any money received by the person's spouse, civil partner or cohabitant[1164] in respect of participation in a scheme administered by the Minister and known as Back-to-Education Allowance, or Back-to-Work Allowance, or Back-to-Work Enterprise Allowance, Part-Time Job Incentive or national internship scheme;[1165]
13.	any money received by the person's spouse, civil partner or cohabitant[1166] in respect of participation in an approved course of training;[1167]

1162. Amended by SW(No.2)A 2019, s. 21(a).
1163. Amended by SW(No.2)A 2019, s. 21(b).
1164. Amended by SW&PA 2010, s. 26 and Sch. 3.
1165. Amended by SW&PA 2011, s. 16(6).
1166. Amended by SW&PA 2010, s. 26 and Sch. 3.
1167. Amended by SW&P(MP)A 2013, s. 3(4).

Reference No.	*Amount*
14.	any money received by the person's spouse, civil partner or cohabitant[1168] in respect of participation in a scheme administered by the Minister for Education and Science and known as the VTOS;
15.	any income arising from a bonus under a scheme administered by the Minister for Community, Rural and Gaeltacht Affairs for the making of special grants to parents or guardians resident in the Gaeltacht or Breac-Ghaeltacht (as defined in such scheme) of children attending primary schools;
16.	an amount of an allowance, dependant's allowance, disability pension or wounds pension under the Army Pensions Acts of 1923–1980 (including, for the purposes of this subparagraph, a British War Pension), or of a combination of those allowances and pensions, except in so far as the amount exceeds EUR 104 per year;
17.	any expenses necessarily incurred in carrying on any form of self-employment;
18.	deleted by SW&P(MP)A 2013, section 19;
18A.	deleted by SW&P(No.2)A 2013, section 6;
19.	any other income that may be prescribed received by a person or his or her spouse, civil partner or cohabitant[1169] and in the circumstances that may be prescribed.[1170]

1168. Amended by SW&PA 2010, s. 26 and Sch. 3.
1169. Amended by SW&PA 2010, s. 26 and Sch. 3.
1170. This apparently broad power would also have to be interpreted in line with the separation of powers and the practice has been to legislate separately for specific exemptions. However, compensation relating to Hepatitis C awarded by the Compensation Tribunal or a court, compensation awarded by the Residential Institutions Redress Board, compensation relating to thalidomide, compensation under the Health (Repayment Scheme) Act 2006, payments made by the Residential Institutions Statutory Fund Board, payments made to women who worked in the Magdalen Laundries and payments made by the Stardust Victims' Compensation Tribunal or made pursuant to recommendations proposed by the Scoping Inquiry into the CervicalCheck Screening Programme, payments made under a package of support measures for women diagnosed with cervical cancer since 2008, payments made under the Lourdes Hospital Redress Scheme, the Lourdes Hospital Payment Scheme and the Surgical Symphysiotomy Scheme bursaries from the Department of Education and Skills 1916 Bursary Fund, University Higher Educational Scholarships for adult learners to a maximum value of EUR 7,000, payments made by Sports Ireland under the International Carding Scheme, payments made by the N. Ireland Victims and Survivors' Service in accordance with the Victims and Survivors (N. Ireland) Order 2006, Special Transport Grants made as part of the School Transport Scheme for Children with Special Educational Needs; payments made under the Tusla Bursary Scheme for Children in Care and Aftercare; payments made

Chapter 6. Nursing Home Support Scheme Test

710. This test, set out in Schedule 1 of the NHSSA 2009 as amended,[1171] applies to the NHSS administered by the HSE under the auspices of the Department of Health. Given that the legislation is entirely different, the test adopts a different structure to that of the main social welfare tests. However, unless otherwise required by the context and statutory language, judicial consideration of general concepts such as income and capital (here described as 'assets') may also be relevant.

711. The NHSSA means test provides for the assessment of (i) income; (ii) cash assets; and (iii) 'relevant' assets (defined below). It is presumed, unless the Executive is satisfied that it is not the case, that where there is more than one person with an interest in an asset, each owner has an equal interest in the asset concerned.[1172] In such a case, the onus is on the applicant to show that, under the general law relating to the relevant property, he or she has a different interest in the property.

§1. Means of a Single Person

712. Part 1A of Schedule 1 to the 2009 Act deals with the assessment of the means of a person who is not a member of a couple. Paragraph 2 of Part 1A in relation to *income* provides that this assessment should follow the directions at steps A–E:

A. Establish the annual income of the person using the definition of 'income'.
B. Deduct allowable deductions (*see* below).
C. Divide amount produced by step B by 52 to establish net weekly income.
D. Take 80% of amount produced by step C (net weekly income), which amount, unless step E applies, is the weekly assessed income.
E. Where applying the rule in step C produces a result whereby 20% of net weekly income is less than the minimum retained income threshold, the weekly assessed income is the amount established by step C less the minimum retained income threshold.

---

under the Probation Service's KickStart Scholarship scheme; payments made under the Compensation Scheme for young people who suffered harm while in the care of Kerry Child and Adolescent Mental Health Service; and payments made under the Troubles Permanent Disablement Payment Scheme (Northern Ireland) are excluded from assessment as means: SW(CCP&C)R, Art. 155 as amended.

1171. By virtue of s. 7 of the Health (Amendment) Act 2013, an amended means test set out in Part 1A of Sch. 1 to the 2009 Act applies to applications for State support made on or after 25 Jul. 2013 by a person who is not a member of a couple. The original means test set out in Part 1 to Sch. 1 to the 2009 Act applies to such applications made before that date.

1172. Paragraph 5 of Part 3 of Sch. 1 of the NHSSA 2009.

713. 'Income' means:

(a) income from an employment, trade, profession or vocation;
(b) rental income whether arising in the State or otherwise;
(c) income from holding of an office or directorship;
(d) income from a pension (whether under the social welfare code or otherwise);
(e) income whether in the nature of a benefit or allowance arising from social welfare, social insurance or other sources of a similar character;
(f) income from fees, commissions, dividends, interest, or income of a similar character;
(g) payments under a settlement, covenant, estate or payment in respect of maintenance;
(h) income from royalties and annuities;
(i) transferred income of a character described in paragraphs (a)–(h);[1173] and
(j) such other forms of benefit as may be prescribed, under regulations made under section 36, for the purposes of this paragraph, whether in money or monies worth and arising within the State or otherwise.[1174]

714. 'Minimum retained income threshold' means (a) for the purposes of the assessment of a person who is not a member of a couple, 20% of the maximum weekly amount of State pension (Non-Contributory) at the date of the application for State support; (b) for the purposes of the assessment of a couple, in a case where the partner of the person assessed is receiving financial support, the weekly assessed income of the partner, or where the partner is habitually resident in a relevant facility or nursing home, the amount of any contribution required to be paid by the partner pursuant to section 67C(1) of the HA 1970, together with, in both cases, 40% of the maximum weekly amount of State pension (non-contributory) at the date of the application for State support, and in all other cases the maximum weekly amount of State pension (non-contributory) together with 20% of the maximum amount of State pension (non-contributory) at the date of the application for State support.[1175]

715. 'Transferred income' means any income which the person whose means is being assessed would have been entitled to receive in the assessable period, but which by reason of a particular action having been taken by or on behalf of that person, a person other than the person whose means are being assessed has received, is receiving or will receive an amount of money or monies worth (whether by way of a single payment or a series of payments) and which action by the person whose means are being assessed occurred within five years of the date of the first application for State support but does not include payments made in respect of the maintenance of a child, a spouse or a former spouse under a maintenance agreement, a separation agreement or pursuant to an order of a court of competent jurisdiction.

1173. Thus, unlike the SW Acts, the NHSSA 2009 test also includes concept of 'income disposed of' – although how enforceable this provision will be may be questionable.
1174. Paragraph 1 of Part 3 of Sch. 1 of the NHSSA 2009.
1175. Paragraph 1 of Part 3 of Sch. 1 to the 2009 Act as amended by s. 17(b)(ii) of the HMPA 1010 and s. 7(e)(ii) of the Health (Amendment) Act 2013.

716. Paragraph 3 of Part 1A provides for the assessment of the weekly value of the *cash assets* by following the directions at steps A–F:

A. Establish all the cash assets of the person being assessed using the definition of 'cash assets' and value each cash asset on the basis of the estimated market value.[1176]
B. Deduct from the estimated market value of each cash asset the amount of allowable deductions relating to that cash asset to produce the net value of each cash asset.
C. Aggregate all net values of cash assets established under step B.
D. Deduct general assets deductible amount from the amount produced by step C to produce annual assessed cash assets.
E. Take 5% of the amount produced by step D to establish the amount of the annual assessed cash assets.
F. Divide amount produced by step E by 52 to produce weekly assessed cash assets.

717. 'Cash assets' means (a) monies, whether held as currency or in an account with a financial institution; (b) monies lent to another person which are repayable; (c) shares, stocks, bonds, securities, and other financial instruments; and (d) a transferred asset which is a cash asset, in which in the case of an asset referred to in paragraphs (a)–(c) the person concerned has a beneficial interest and in the case of an asset referred to in paragraph (d), the person concerned had a beneficial interest.[1177]

1176. 'Estimated market value' means:

(a) subject to paragraphs (b) and (c), the price the asset concerned would fetch on the open market on the date on which the application for State support is made subject to such conditions as might reasonably be calculated to obtain for the vendor of the asset the best price of the asset;
(b) in the case of a cash asset which comprises monies, the amount of such monies, converted to the currency of the State in the case where such monies are not held in the currency of the State, at the official conversion rate specified by the Central Bank of Ireland on the date the application for State support is made, and
(c) in the case of an asset not situated in a place the currency of which place is the currency of the State, by converting the value of such asset in the currency of the place where the asset is situated into the currency of the State at the official conversion rate specified by the Central Bank of Ireland on the date the application for State support is made. *Ibid.*, s. 10(4)–(5) provide that the HSE may ascertain the estimated market value in such manner and by such means as it thinks appropriate and may authorize a suitable person to value the item (with the costs of such valuation defrayed by the Executive).

1177. *Ibid.* The concept of 'transferred asset' is discussed below.

'General assets deductible amount' means (a) in the case of a person who is not a member of a couple, means (i) EUR 36,000, or (ii) the amount prescribed, under regulations …, whichever is the greater, and (b) in the case of a couple, (i) EUR 72,000, or (ii) the amount prescribed, under regulations …, whichever is the greater;

718. Paragraph 4 of Part 1A provides for the assessment of *relevant assets* by following the directions in steps A–F:

A. Establish all assets which are relevant assets using the definition of 'relevant assets' of the person being assessed and value each relevant asset on the basis of the estimated market value.
B. Deduct from the estimated market value of each relevant asset the amount of allowable deductions relating to that relevant asset to produce the net value of each relevant asset.
C. Aggregate all net values of relevant assets to produce total net value of relevant assets.
D. If the general assets deductible amount has not been fully used in connection with the cash assets assessment, apply unused balance by deducting the unused amount from total net value of relevant assets produced by step C.
E. Take 7.5% of the amount produced by step D or, if step D does not apply, by Step C to produce the annual assessed relevant assets amount.
F. To establish assessed weekly value of relevant assets, divide result of step E by 52.

719. 'Relevant assets' means all forms of property, whether situated in the State or not, other than cash assets, including options and incorporeal property generally in which the relevant person has a beneficial interest including transferred assets which would have been relevant assets if not transferred.[1178]

720. 'Transferred asset' means an interest of the person in an asset (whether a cash asset or a relevant asset) which has been transferred at any time in the period of five years prior to the date on which an application for State support is first made by or on behalf of that person which transfer is made (a) for no consideration, (b) for nominal consideration, or (c) for consideration which is less than 75% of the estimated market value of the interest of the person in the asset at the time of the transfer but does not include the transfer of an asset made in respect of the settlement of any claim made in respect of the maintenance of a child or other matrimonial proceedings, and that the Executive is satisfied that such transfer was made for that purpose, and the estimated market value of a transferred asset shall be determined on the basis of the value of the asset at the time of the transfer, and where the asset comprises monies not being in the currency of the State, or other assets held in a place outside the State, the currency of which is not the currency of the State,

1178. Paragraph 1 of Part 3 of Sch. 1 of the NHSSA 2009.

converted into the currency of the State at the date of the transfer of the asset concerned. Although the term does not actually appear in the Act, a definition of 'transferred asset value' is provided, which is presumably to be used in calculating the value of transferred assets: 'transferred asset value', in relation to a transferred asset, means the amount calculated by the application of the following formula: MV – CR where MV is the estimated market value of the asset concerned at the time of the transfer, CR is the amount of the consideration received by the person or the estimated market amount of the consideration received by the person (whichever is the higher). Thus, the concept of 'transferred assets' is functionally similar to that of 'property disposed of' discussed in paragraphs 652–653. However, unlike the social welfare equivalent, it does not explicitly include any intentional element. In addition, paragraph 11 of Part 3 provides that a transferred asset shall not cease to be a transferred asset where (a) the person makes a subsequent application for State support, or (b) a review is carried out under this Act of the means of the person or his or her partner, by reason of the date of such subsequent application or review being more than five years after the transfer of the asset occurred. However, section 31 provides that where a transferred item is taken into account by the HSE in determining the means of the person and the transfer of the transferred item was effected prior to 9 October 2008; the person may apply to the HSE to recalculate the means of the person by excluding one or more than one of the transferred items on the ground that it is necessary to do so in order to avoid 'undue financial hardship'.

721. Paragraph 6 of Part 3 of Schedule 3 provides that the interest of a person in a principal residence,[1179] or in a transferred asset which qualifies as a principal residence, shall not be or shall cease to be a relevant asset where the person concerned is receiving or has received:

(a) care services;
(b) transitional care services within the meaning of section 13;
(c) services in a nursing home which services would, if they had been provided after the coming into operation of the definition of 'approved nursing home', have come within the meaning of the definition of 'long-term residential care services', or
(d) any combination of the services referred to in paragraphs (a)–(c), for a period of 3 years (which period need not be continuous).

722. Paragraph 10 of Part 3 provides that in a case where the person ('relevant person') was a member of a couple, and:

(i) the other member of the couple ('other member') received both services of any kind referred to in paragraph 6 and financial support, and
(ii) the principal residence concerned is the same principal residence as the principal residence assessed under the financial assessment of the other member,

1179. 'Principal residence' means the principal private residence of a person and includes land which the person has for his or her own occupation and enjoyment with that residence as its garden or grounds up to an area (exclusive of the dwelling house) not exceeding one acre. *Ibid.*

the total of the amounts of the weekly assessed means under the NHSSA which relate to the principal residence, arising pursuant to the financial assessment relating to the other member and the financial assessment relating to the relevant person, when aggregated, subject to subparagraph (c), shall not exceed the amount which is 22.5% of the estimated market value of that residence at the date of valuation of the asset in connection with the first financial assessment of the relevant person less allowable deductions applicable to that asset, and on that threshold being reached, notwithstanding any other provision of this Schedule the asset shall cease to be a relevant asset.[1180]

723. Paragraph 7 of Part 3 similarly provides that, subject to paragraphs 8 and 9, the interest of a person in a farm[1181] or relevant business[1182] shall not be or shall cease to be a relevant asset where the person concerned is receiving or has received:

(a) care services;
(b) transitional care services within the meaning of section 13 of the 2009 Act;
(c) services in a nursing home which services would, if they had been provided after the coming into operation of the definition of 'approved nursing home', have come within the meaning of the definition of 'LTRCS', or
(d) any combination of the services referred to in subparagraphs (a)–(c), for a period of three years (which period need not be continuous).

724. However, paragraph 8 limits the circumstances in which this concession applies and states that paragraph 7 shall not apply unless:

(a) the person receiving care services has suffered a sudden illness or disability which caused that person to require care services, and

---

1180. Paragraph 10 as amended by s. 7(h)(i) of the Health (Amendment) Act 2013. By virtue of subparagraph (c), inserted by s. 7(h)(ii) of the 2013 Act, the cap on the assessed means under this heading is 15% of the estimated market value of the residence where the other member and the relevant person both applied for State support on or after 17 Oct. 2009 and prior to 25 Jul. 2013 and 18.75% of that value where the other member applied for State support on or after 27 Oct. 2009 and prior to 25 Jul. 2013 and the relevant person applied for State support on or after 25 Jul. 2013.

1181. 'Farm' means agricultural land, pasture and woodland, crops, trees and underwood growing thereon, farm buildings appropriate to the property and farm machinery, livestock and bloodstock thereon but excluding all residential property while 'farming' includes dairy farming, livestock production, and the cultivation of grass, tillage, and other crops, including horticultural crops whether under protected cropping conditions or in the open. Para. 1 of Part 3 of Sch. 1 of the NHSSA 2009.

1182. 'Relevant business' means (a) the business or an interest in a business carried on by a sole trader or by a partnership, including any land, building, machinery or plant used wholly or mainly for the purpose of the business, or (b) the unquoted shares [not quoted on a recognized stock exchange] in or securities of a company carrying on a business in which the applicant or his or her partner has until the onset of the sudden illness or disability which caused that person to require care services been actively involved in carrying on the business. 'Business' means a business carried on in the exercise of a trade, profession or vocation, but does not include a business carried on otherwise than for gain. *Ibid.*

(b) a substantial part of the working day of the person requiring care services or his or her partner was regularly and consistently applied to the farming of the farm or carrying on of the relevant business until the onset of the sudden illness or disability, and
(c) a family successor[1183] certifies in writing that he or she will, on a consistent and regular basis, apply a substantial part of his or her working day to the farming of the farm or carrying on of the relevant business.

725. Finally, paragraph 9 provides that paragraph 7 shall apply to a relevant asset, which is a transferred asset and which is a farm or relevant business.

§2. Means of a Couple

726. Part 2A[1184] deals with the assessment of the means of a person who is a member of a couple. 'Couple' means:

(a) two persons married to each other;
(b) a man and woman who are not married to each other but are cohabiting as husband and wife, or
(c) two persons of the same sex who are cohabiting in domestic circumstances comparable to that of a man and woman who are not married to each other but are cohabiting as husband and wife,

who are habitually living together at the date of the making of an application for State support by either or both of them or at the date of the commencement of the provision of care services to either or both of them.[1185] Unmarried couples (of whatever sexual preference) are not be considered as habitually living together unless they have been cohabiting for a period of not less than three years immediately preceding the date of the making of an application for State support by either or both of them or of the commencement of the provision of care services to either or both of them.[1186] However, notwithstanding subsection (2), a person will be considered as habitually living together with the other member of the couple where:

1183. 'Family successor' means a partner or relative of the person applying for State support, which person, at the time of the application for State support (*a*) in the case of a farm, regularly and consistently applies a portion of his or her working day in farming the farm, or (*b*) in the case of a business, regularly and consistently applies a portion of his or her working day in the carrying on of the relevant business. *Ibid.*

1184. By virtue of s. 7 of the Health (Amendment) Act 2013, an amended means test set out in Part 2A of Sch. 1 to the 2009 Act applies to applications for State support made on or after 25 Jul. 2013 by a person who is a member of a couple. The original means test set out in Part 2 to Sch. 1 to the 2009 Act applies to such applications made before that date.

1185. Section 4(1) of the 2009 Act. For the law on cohabitation, *see* above paras 326 et seq. This provision extends the cohabitation rule to same-sex couples but is different to the new approach adopted under the Social Welfare Acts. There would appear to be an absence of case law both in Ireland and elsewhere as to how this is to be assessed (in the UK only civil partners are subject to the cohabitation rule).

1186. Section 4(2).

(a) either of them resides in or enters a relevant facility or approved nursing home for the purposes of being provided with care services;
(b) both of them reside in or enter a relevant facility or approved nursing home for the purposes of being provided with care services;
(c) either of them resides in or enters an institution (of whatever kind) for purposes related to:
    (i) a physical or mental condition of the person concerned; or
    (ii) the imprisonment, or the taking into lawful custody, of the person concerned; or
(d) both of them reside in or enter an institution (of whatever kind) for purposes related to:
    (i) a physical or mental condition of the person concerned; or
    (ii) the imprisonment, or the taking into lawful custody, of the person concerned.[1187]

Thus, in order for an unmarried couple to be treated as a couple, they have to be habitually living together at the relevant time (date of application or of commencement of care) and to be considered habitually living together, they must have been cohabiting for three years immediately prior to the relevant date. However, they will be considered as habitually living together (even though they are not) in the circumstances outlined above. The area of cohabitation is inevitably an already complex one, but one could not describe these provisions as a model of legislative clarity.

727. Paragraph 2 of Part 2A provides for the assessment of weekly *income* by following the directions at steps A–F:

A. Establish the annual income of the person and his or her partner using the definition of 'income'.
B. From the annual income of each of those persons deduct allowable deductions applicable to that person's income to establish net annual income of each member of the couple.
C. Aggregate the two net annual incomes established under step B.
D. Divide amount produced by step C by 52 to establish net weekly income.
E. Take 40% of amount produced by step D and the amount established following that calculation is, unless step F applies, the weekly assessed income.
F. Where applying the rule in step E produces a result whereby 60% of net weekly income is less than the minimum retained income threshold, the weekly assessed income is the amount established by step D less the amount which is the minimum retained income threshold.

For the definition of income, *see* above (paragraph 713).

1187. Section 4(3).

728. Paragraph 3 provides that for the assessment of *cash assets* by following the directions at steps A–G:

A. Establish all the cash assets of the person to whom the assessment relates and his or her partner using the definition of 'cash assets' and value each cash asset on the basis of the estimated market value.
B. Deduct from the estimated market value of each cash asset the amount of allowable deductions relating to that cash asset to produce net value of each cash asset.
C. Aggregate all net values of cash assets established under step B.
D. Deduct general assets deductible amount from the amount produced by step C to establish total assessed cash assets.
E. Take 7.5% of the amount produced by step D to establish the amount of the annual assessed cash assets of the couple.
F. Divide amount established by step E by 2 to establish the amount of the annual assessed cash assets of the person in respect of whom the financial assessment is being carried out.
G. Divide amount established by step F by 52 to produce the assessed weekly cash assets of the person in respect of whom the financial assessment is being carried out.

For the definition of cash assets, *see* above (paragraph 717).

729. Paragraph 4 provides for the assessment of *relevant assets* by following the directions at steps A–G:

A. Establish all assets which are relevant assets of the person in respect of whom the financial assessment is being carried out and his or her partner using the definition of 'relevant assets' and value each relevant asset on the basis of estimated market value.
B. Deduct from the estimated market value of each relevant asset the amount of allowable deductions relating to that relevant asset to produce the net value of each relevant asset.
C. Aggregate all net values of relevant assets established under step B.
D. If the general assets deductible amount has not been fully used in connection with the cash assets assessment, then apply the unused balance by deducting the unused amount from the amount established by step C.
E. Take 5% of the amount established by step D or, if step D does not apply, by Step C to establish the annual assessed relevant assets amount.
F. Divide amount established by step E by 2 to establish the amount of the annual assessed relevant assets of the person in respect of whom the financial assessment is being carried out.
G. Divide the amount established by step F by 52 to produce the assessed weekly value of relevant assets of the person in respect of whom the financial assessment is being carried out.

For the definition of relevant assets, *see* above (paragraph 719). The provisions in relation to assets excluded from or taken into account under this rule (paragraphs 6–9 of Part 3 of Schedule 1) set out above in relation to a single person also apply to couples.

§3. ALLOWABLE DEDUCTIONS

730. 'Allowable deduction'[1188] means:

(a) subject to paragraph 2, in relation to income:
   (i) income tax required by law to be deducted or paid from the income and in respect of which (other than as respects payments or expenses to which clauses (iv), (v) or (vi) refer) the applicant or any other person is not entitled to claim an exemption, relief or allowance or the repayment of tax already paid;
   (ii) social insurance contributions;
   (iii) levies required by law to be paid;
   (iv) payments which – (I) are paid in respect of interest on monies borrowed for the purchase, repair or improvement of the principal residence of the person, or (II) are paid in respect of rent on the principal residence of the person concerned under an agreement entered into at arm's length if, and only for so long as, there resides therein the person's partner or a child under the age of 21 years of the person or the person's partner, less the amount of any relief from income tax which may be claimed in respect of such payments;
   (v) health expenses to which section 469 of the Taxes Consolidation Act 1997 applies, less the amount of any relief from income tax which may be claimed by the applicant, the spouse of the applicant or a relative, but for the purposes of this subparagraph, any payments made by a person in respect of care services shall not be included;
   (vi) payments made in respect of the maintenance of a child, a spouse or a former spouse under a separation agreement or pursuant to an order of a court of competent jurisdiction, less the amount of any relief from income tax which may be claimed in respect of such payments;
   (vii) such other deduction as may be prescribed, under regulations made under section 36, for the purposes of this paragraph.[1189]

1188. *Ibid.*

1189. The Nursing Home Support Scheme (Allowable Deductions) Regulations 2010 [S.I. No. 631 of 2010] prescribe payments in respect of borrowings incurred specifically for the purchase, repair or improvement of the principal residence of the person or the person's partner to the extent that such amount has not been repaid, and in respect of which borrowings the HSE is satisfied that the purpose of incurring the borrowings was for the purpose of the purchase, repair or improvement of the principal residence. Where a person avails of this deduction, he or she cannot also seek to offset the same mortgage against the value of the asset concerned and vice versa: *Ibid.*, Arts 3–4. S.I. No. 311 of 2014 expands the definition of 'allowable deduction' to include payments made in

(b) subject to paragraphs 3 and 4, in relation to cash assets, means borrowings incurred specifically for the purchase of the asset concerned to the extent that such amount has not been repaid and in respect of which borrowings the Executive is satisfied that the purpose of incurring the borrowings was for the purpose of acquiring the asset concerned; and
(c) subject to paragraphs 3 and 4, in relation to relevant assets, means borrowings incurred specifically for the purchase, repair or improvement of the relevant asset concerned to the extent that such amount has not been repaid, and in respect of which borrowings the Executive is satisfied that the purpose of incurring the borrowings was for the purpose of the purchase, repair or improvement of the relevant asset concerned.

731. In relation to the definition of 'allowable deduction', with respect to income, a deduction is allowed in respect of either paragraph (a)(iv)(I) or paragraph (a)(iv)(II) of that definition, but not both.[1190]

Where in relation to a cash asset or a relevant asset, a deduction is claimed as an allowable deduction by reason of borrowings relating to such asset as permitted by paragraphs 3 and 4 of Part 1 or Part 2, an allowance in respect of such borrowings may not be given where to do so would permit a deduction in relation to the same indebtedness more than once.[1191] Where in relation to a cash asset or a relevant asset, a deduction is claimed as an allowable deduction by reason of borrowings relating to such asset as permitted by paragraphs 3 and 4 of Part 1 or Part 2, and such indebtedness applies to more than one person whether jointly or severally, the amount of such indebtedness which may be allowed as an allowable deduction shall be proportionate to the proportion of the value of the interest of the person in respect of whom the financial assessment is being carried out bears to the estimated market value of the entire asset concerned.[1192]

§4. Disregards

732. Finally, the Redress for Women Resident in Certain Institutions Act 2015, as amended, provides for the disregard of certain payments for the purpose of the NHSS means test.[1193] The relevant payments are:

(a) an ex gratia payment or payments made to the person under the Scheme established by the 2015 Act, including any benefit provided under that Scheme;
(b) an ex gratia payment or payments made to the person under the terms of the Scheme referred to as the Lourdes Hospital Redress Scheme 2007;

---

respect of the maintenance of a dependent child, though the payments cannot exceed, in a calendar month, the amount of Child Benefit plus the full rate of the increase for a qualified child and, where relevant, childcare costs.

1190. Paragraph 2 of Part 3 of Sch. 1, NHSSA 2009.
1191. Paragraph 3 of Part 3.
1192. Paragraph 4 of Sch. 3.
1193. *See* s. 4.

(c) an ex gratia payment or payments made to the person under the terms of the Scheme established by the Minister and referred to as the Lourdes Hospital Payment Scheme;
(d) a payment or payments made to the person under the terms of the Surgical Symphysiotomy ex gratia Scheme referred to as the Symphysiotomy Payment Scheme;
(e) an ex gratia payment or payments made to the person by the Minister for Health or the *Conterganstiftung für behinderte Menschen* in respect of a disability caused to that person by Thalidomide, or
(f) such other ex gratia payment or payments as may be prescribed under section 36(5A) (inserted by section 7 of the Health (Miscellaneous Provisions) Act (HMPA) 2017) for the purposes of paragraph 1 of Part 3 of Schedule 1 to the 2009 Act.[1194]

1194. *See* HMPA 2017, s. 8 and Redress for Women Resident in Certain Institutions (Amendment) Act 2019, s. 4.

Part XII. Claims, General Provisions and Adjudication

Chapter 1. Claims

§1. Introduction of Claims

I. Making a Claim

733. Section 241(1) provides that it shall be a condition of any person's right to any benefit (i.e., any social insurance benefit listed in section 39(1), the cost of OIB medical care under section 86, assistance listed in section 139(1), CB, CSG, WFP, continued payment for qualified children, BTWFD or EU payments within the meaning of Part 8)[1195] that he or she makes a claim therefore in the prescribed manner and satisfies the Minister as to his or her identity.[1196] Section 241(2) provides that when a person fails to make a claim for benefit within the prescribed time, he or she shall be disqualified for payment for specific periods (*see* below). The detailed provisions in relation to claims are set out in the Social Welfare (Consolidated Claims, Payments and Control) Regulations of 2007 as amended. The usual requirement is that the claimant must complete and sign the appropriate application form and ensure that it is submitted to the Department within the prescribed time.

734. Article 179 allows the Minister discretion in regard to what may be accepted as constituting a valid claim.[1197] The Minister may accept a letter, or other suitable form of notification, as satisfying the requirement of making a claim within the prescribed time. In practice, this discretion is applied administratively by officers within each scheme. Such a decision is not subject to appeal to an appeals officer, as it is a Ministerial rather than a deciding officer function. A dissatisfied claimant may, however, request the decision to be reviewed, and the review will be

---

1195. Section 240 as substituted by s. 29 SWLR&PA 2006 and amended by s. 10(c) SW&PA 2007, s. 5(1) SW&PA 2015, Schedule to SW(MP)A 2015 and s. 8(1) and Sch. 1 SWA 2017.

1196. As substituted by SWLRPA 2006, s. 29 and amended by s. 15 SW&PA 2012. Thus, it is clear that a claim is a necessary precondition for entitlement, unlike the position in the UK, where the House of Lords held that a valid claim was not a precondition of entitlement as opposed to the right to payment: *Insurance Officer v. McCaffrey* [1985] 1 All ER 5. The UK legislation was subsequently amended.

1197. For a discussion of what constitutes a claim, albeit under somewhat different statutory provisions *see Novitskaya v. London Borough of Brent* [2009] EWCA Civ 1260.

carried out by an officer of higher rank. In practice, a claim for any social welfare payment will normally bc accepted as a claim for a related social welfare payment, and a claim for a non-contributory payment will be accepted as a claim for the equivalent contributory benefit. In addition to making a claim, the person is required by Article 181 to provide necessary certificates, documents or information for the purpose of deciding the claim,[1198] and he or she may be required to attend an office or other place so as to establish eligibility.[1199]

735. Section 241(9) provides that any claim or notice made or sent by post or by any other method shall be deemed to have been made or given on the date of receipt of such claim or notice by an officer of the Minister.

II. Time for Claiming and Late Claims

736. The 'prescribed time' for making a claim is specified in Article 182. When a claim is made after the prescribed time, a statutory disqualification is incurred, and payment cannot be made for the period of disqualification. The period of disqualification is prescribed in section 241. The prescribed time for making a claim and the period of disqualification for late claims are set out below.

Table 3 Prescribed Time for Making a Claim and Period of Disqualification for Late Claims

Type of Claim	*Prescribed Time for Making Claim*	*Disqualification for Periods Prior To*
Adoptive Benefit	First date of entitlement	Date of claim
BP	First date of entitlement	Date of claim
CA	First date of entitlement	Date of claim

1198. In *Kozinceva v. Minister for Social Protection* [2020] IECA 7, the Court of Appeal, *per* Haughton J, held that requiring a homeless person to provide evidence that she was currently residing in a particular catchment area for the purpose of claiming Jobseeker's Allowance was *ultra vires* the Minister as this was not provided for by legislation and had the effect of unlawfully denying the applicant access to the administrative process for determining her claim for this allowance. The Court did accept that in normal circumstances it might be reasonable to require an applicant to provide a current residential address but it also stated that this could not justify the imposition of a further residential requirement in respect of an applicant known to be homeless and who could not comply with the requirement.

1199. As amended by S.I. No. 201 of 2022. Appeals officers have held that a deciding officer cannot 'withdraw' a claim when such information is not provided: *Social Welfare Appeals Office Reports 2004*, 18; *Social Welfare Appeals Office Reports 2010*, 34. While the legislation does not specify precisely what should be done in such circumstances, it would seem that a deciding officer should reject the claim on the basis that there is insufficient evidence to support it (when efforts to obtain the necessary information have proved unsuccessful). This would allow the claimant to appeal against the decision.

Type of Claim	*Prescribed Time for Making Claim*	*Disqualification for Periods Prior To*
Carer's Benefit	Eight weeks before the first day of entitlement	Date of claim
CB	Within twelve months of the first date of entitlement	Date of claim
Constant Attendance Allowance (OIB)	Within three months of the first date of entitlement	Three months before the date of claim
Death Benefit (OIB)	Within three months of the death of deceased	Three months before the date of claim
DA	Within seven days of first entitlement	Seven days before the date of claim
Disablement Benefit (OIB)	Within three months of the first date of entitlement	Three months before the date of claim
DCA	First date of entitlement	Date of claim
FA	First date of entitlement	Date of claim
Guardian's Payment (Contributory)	Within three months of first entitlement	Six months before the date of claim
Guardian's Payment (Non-Contributory)	Within three months of first entitlement	Date of claim
Health and Safety Benefit	First date of entitlement	Date of claim
IB	Within six weeks of becoming incapable of work	Six weeks before the date of claim
Incapacity Supplement (OIB)	Within three months of first entitlement	Three months before the date of claim
IP	Within three months of first entitlement	Six months before the date of claim
Jobseeker's Allowance	First date of entitlement	Date of claim
JB	First date of entitlement	Date of claim
Maternity Benefit	First date of entitlement	Date of claim
Occupational Injury Benefit (OIB)	Within six weeks of becoming incapable of work	Six weeks before the date of claim
OFP	Within three months of first entitlement	Date of claim

Type of Claim	*Prescribed Time for Making Claim*	*Disqualification for Periods Prior To*
Parents Benefit	First date of entitlement	Date of claim
Paternity Benefit	First date of entitlement	Date of claim
State Pension (Contributory)	Within three months of first entitlement	Six months before the date of claim
State Pension (Non-Contributory)	First date of entitlement	Date of claim
Widow(er)'s and SCP (Contributory) Pension	Within three months of first entitlement	Six months before the date of claim
Widow(er)'s (Non-Contributory) Pension (WNCP)	Within three months of first entitlement	Date of claim
Widowed and SCP Grant	Within twelve months of first entitlement	Date of claim
WFP	Within three months of first entitlement	Date of claim

737. However, these time periods may be extended in certain circumstances, either where there is 'good cause' for the delay (section 241(3)–(4A)) or for a range of broader reasons (section 241(7)).

A. *'Good Cause'*

738. Section 241(3) specifically provides that with respect to a number of benefits (those listed in section 241(2)(c)–(f)), when a claimant proves to the satisfaction of a deciding officer or appeals officer that, on a date earlier than the claim, the claimant was entitled to a benefit (apart from satisfying the condition of making a claim) and that there is 'good cause' for the delay 'throughout the period', the claimant is not disqualified for receiving payment for *up to six months* before the claim was made.[1200] Thus, the legislation limits to six months prior to the date the claim is actually made, the period for which payments may be backdated under this clause.[1201]

739. Formerly, Article 105 of S.I. No. 417 of 1994 provided for the backdating of claims in the case of most payments when the delay can be shown to be for 'good

1200. *See also* s. 241(4) in relation to child benefit and 241 (4A) (inserted by SWPA 2008, s. 16) in relation to domiciliary care allowance.

1201. Other than in the case of child benefit, when the claim may be backdated to the date when entitlement would have first existed.

cause'. For reasons that are unclear, this provision is not included in the 2007 consolidation of the Regulations, and the 2007 Regulations now make no specific reference to 'good cause'.[1202] However, there has been no change in the primary legislation, and it is not clear that the change in the wording of the regulations has led to any change in the law or practice. 'Good cause' is not generally defined in legislation,[1203] and the Departmental Guidelines state that 'good cause' must be assessed by deciding officers by applying common sense principles to the contentions put forward by the claimant and by the evaluation of the evidence available to support those contentions.[1204]

740. Departmental Guidelines state that lack of knowledge by itself is not regarded as a sufficient reason for not submitting claims in time. It is stated that:

> The Deciding Officer must consider what is a reasonable level of knowledge to be expected in the particular case. If, for example, legislation extends entitlement to a particular scheme a plea of ignorance of the change may be reasonable. Similarly particular circumstances may arise where the Deciding Officer is satisfied that it was reasonable for the person to believe that s/he had no entitlement, or that there was nothing to enquire about.

741. The Guidelines also state that the receipt of incorrect advice or information from any person other than a person employed by the Department is not normally regarded as a good cause for failure to claim at the correct time. However, the deciding officer should have regard to whether the person believed that the source of advice was authorized by the Department and therefore whether it was reasonable for the person to rely on this advice rather than make further enquiries of the Department. This may apply in relation to the state or semi-state offices where claim forms and information leaflets are officially made available to the public on behalf of the Department. Entitlement throughout the period must also be proven to the satisfaction of the deciding or appeals officer.

742. Article 186 sets out further specific provisions concerning backdating. When a delay in making a claim resulted from information given by an officer of the Minister to the person concerned or to a person appointed to act on his or her behalf, the claim may be backdated to the date of commencement of entitlement if this is subsequent to the date on which the information was given or (if entitlement already existed) the date on which that information was given plus any period with respect to which a disqualification would not have been imposed if the claim had been made on that date.[1205]

1202. Other than in Art. 199, re extinguishment of the right to benefit.

1203. On the extensive UK case law, *see* M. Partington, *Claim in Time* (Legal Action Group, 1994), and the older editions of *Ogus & Barendt*. However, amendments to the law have altered the UK law in this area.

1204. *Operational Guidelines: Claims and Late Claims*, 2019.

1205. Article 186(2). In *Social Welfare Appeals Office Report 2004*, 16–17, an appeals officer applied this provision by analogy where a person had been advised by a citizen's information centre funded by the Minister and allowed the claim to be backdated by about nine months. The correct

743. When the delay arose because the person was incapacitated to such an extent that he or she was unable to make a claim or appoint a person to act on his or her behalf, backdating of the claim may be considered.[1206] The Guidelines state that an illness, though disabling, which by its nature would not cause the claimant's mental faculties to diminish significantly, will not be regarded as sufficient reason for the failure to make a claim in time. In these circumstances, the claim may be backdated to the date of initial entitlement when such incapacity existed at that time, or in other cases, to the date the person became so incapacitated, plus any period with respect to which a disqualification would not have been imposed if the claim had been made on that date, provided that the claim must be made within twelve months of the person ceasing to be so incapacitated.

744. In addition, section 241(7) provides that the period specified in section 241(2), with respect to which a payment may be made before the date on which the claim is made, may be extended by a deciding officer or appeals officer in prescribed circumstances and conditions (*see* Article 186).

B. Departmental Delay and Compensation

745. When a person makes a claim under section 241 and payment is delayed for a period exceeding twelve months as a result of solely or mainly circumstances within the control of the Department and the person has not contributed to such delay, additional payment will be with respect to the loss of purchasing power and the prescribed costs actually and necessarily incurred by the person.[1207]

§2. Protection Against Seizure and Transfer

746. Section 277 makes void and of no effect any alienation of every book, card, payable order, voucher, or other document issued to a person on the basis of which a benefit is payable.[1208] Any person who buys, takes in exchange or takes in pawn such a document is guilty of a criminal offence (section 276). Failure to deliver such an alienated document on demand to the owner (or his or her duly authorized agent) or a social welfare inspector is a criminal offence.[1209] The intention is to prevent the alienation of such documents as security for loans and to prevent the abuse of low-income persons by unscrupulous lenders.

---

basis for the decision to allow backdating would appear to be that the provision of incorrect advice by such persons might reasonably be considered to constitute 'good cause' for the delay in claiming (but subject to a six-month limit).

1206. Article 186(3).

1207. Section 243 and Art. 212.

1208. *See also* s. 283.

1209. Section 278.

§3. Legal Capacity to Receive Benefits

747. The Act itself does not contain any rules concerning legal capacity to receive benefits. The general rules in relation to personal legal capacity would apply. However, Irish law does not contain a clear statement of capacity.[1210] In practice, issues do arise when, for one reason or another, a person is not capable of or best placed to manage his or her benefits (or those with respect to a qualified adult or child). Section 244 provides that Regulations may provide:

(a) for enabling a person to whom benefit is payable to nominate another person to receive that benefit on his or her behalf;[1211]
(b) for enabling a person to be appointed to exercise, on behalf of a claimant or beneficiary who is under 16 years of age or who is certified by a medical practitioner to be a person who is or is likely soon to become unable for the time being to manage his or her own financial affairs, any right or power which the claimant or beneficiary may be entitled to exercise under this Act and for authorizing a person so appointed to receive and deal with any sum payable by way of benefit on behalf of the claimant or beneficiary;
(c) when it appears to the Minister that the circumstances so warrant, for enabling a person to be appointed to receive and deal with on behalf of a claimant or beneficiary the amount of the increase in respect of a qualified adult or child (as applicable) or in the case of disablement pension, CB, or WFP, so much of the pension, benefit, or supplement as the Minister considers reasonable in the circumstances;
(d) in connection with the death of any person, for enabling a claim for benefit to be made or proceeded with in the person's name, subject to the conditions that may be prescribed.

748. Regulations may also provide that probate or other proof of title may be dispensed with in the case of payment of any benefit, and that in any such case, the sum may be paid to or distributed among the persons appearing (as provided by the Regulations) to be entitled to receive payment either as persons beneficially entitled to that sum under any testamentary instrument or as next of kin or as being creditors of the deceased person.[1212]

1210. *See* Law Reform Commission *Consultation Paper on Law and the Elderly*, LRC, 2003. *See* now the Assisted Decision-Making (Capacity) Act 2015 as amended by the Assisted Decision-Making (Capacity) (Amendment) Act 2022. Section 2(1) of this Act provides that 'making an application for … social welfare or other benefits or otherwise protecting or advancing the interests of the relevant person in relation to those matters' falls within the concept of a person's 'property and affairs' which fall within the scope of the Act.

1211. *See* Arts 201–202A of SW(CCP&C)R as amended by S.I. No. 378 of 2009 and S.I. No. 13 of 2017.

1212. As amended by SWPA 2008, s. 20. The relevant regulations are SW(CCP&C)R, Arts 205 et seq.

Chapter 2. Accumulation Rules (Overlapping Provisions)

749. Section 247(1)[1213] provides that when more than one benefit (other than a death benefit by way of a grant with respect to funeral expenses, or a widowed or SCP grant), any assistance (other than DCA, SWA or a widowed or SCP grant) would be payable, only one benefit or allowance shall be payable. In addition, when a benefit, assistance, IQA, or IQC would be payable to or with respect to a qualified child, only one shall be payable (subject again to the exceptions as in section 247(1).[1214] Notwithstanding these provisions, the Minister may make regulations enabling more than one payment to be made to a person.[1215] Thus, the legislation sets out a general ban on double payment, which may be relaxed by regulation.[1216] In general terms, only one social welfare income maintenance payment is payable at a time, although it is, of course, possible to receive an income maintenance payment (such as JB) and a child support payment, such as CB.

750. The SW Acts and Regulations provide, *inter alia*, that a person shall receive concurrently:

(1) Disablement benefit and any social assistance or social insurance payment.[1217]
(2) Guardian's payment (contributory), guardian's payment (non-contributory), or death benefit by way of orphan's pension and IB; maternity benefit; health and safety benefit; adoptive benefit; paternity benefit, parent's benefit, JB; injury benefit; incapacity supplement; death benefit by way of widow's pension, widower's or SCP pension, deserted wife's benefit, and OFP.[1218]
(3) Maternity, health and safety or adoptive benefit, which is payable at a reduced rate with limited other social welfare payments.[1219]
(4) BP and (a) any benefit other than carer's benefit, State pension (contributory), State pension (transition), or IP, and (b) any assistance other than jobseeker's allowance, PRETA, State pension (non-contributory), CA, DA, or FA.[1220]
(5) WFP, for a period of up to six weeks, and IB, when a person, who is working and claiming WFP, becomes incapable of work.[1221]

1213. Substituted by s. 19 SW&P(MP)A 2013.
1214. Section 247(2).
1215. Section 247(4).
1216. The legislation now allows the Minister to specify those situations in which double payment is allowed. This replaces the previous arrangements whereby the Minister *disallowed* double payment by regulation, a procedure that was found to be *ultra vires* the Act by the Supreme Court in *McHugh v. Minister for Social Welfare* [1994] 2 IR 139. McCarthy J stated that it would seem more desirable that restrictions on entitlement, itself determined by primary legislation, should be provided for in similar fashion, [1994] 2 IR 139 at 156. *See* M. Cousins, 'Note', DULJ 14 (1992):193.
1217. Section 247(3A) as inserted by SWPA 2007, s. 24(g).
1218. SW(CCP&C)R, Art. 222 as amended.
1219. SW(CCP&C)R, Art. 223A as inserted by S.I. No. 38 of 2012 as amended.
1220. SW(CCP&C)R, Art. 224.
1221. Section 247(7).

751. Section 247A and 247B also provide that a person is disqualified for benefit and assistance (with limited exceptions) while participating in the work placement programme, the national internship scheme (or any variation, extension or replacement thereof), or community employment.[1222]

1222. Section 247A inserted by Inserted by s. 27 SW&PA 2010 and amended by s. 16(2) SW&PA 2011 and s. 19 SW&P(MP)A 2013. And *see* s. 298A as substituted by s. 16(3) SW&PA 2011. Section 247B as inserted by s. 12 SWA 2011 and amended by s. 7 SW&PA 2012 and s. 19 SW&P(MP)A 2013.

Chapter 3. Residence and Absence

752. Until relatively recently, residence was not a central issue concerning qualification for most benefits (other than healthcare). In a small number of cases, persons were required to be 'ordinarily resident' in the State to qualify, and 'absence from the State' generally acted to disqualify persons for receipt of benefits. However, in 2004, a 'habitual residence' condition was introduced for a wide range of non-contributory benefits. The 2009 Act made it a requirement that, in order to be habitually resident, a person must have a right to reside in Ireland.

§1. Ordinary Residence

753. A person is required to be 'ordinarily resident in the State' to qualify for certain benefits – such as CB.[1223] This issue is also relevant in terms of access to healthcare as, to be eligible for public healthcare, a person is required to be 'ordinarily resident' in the State. The concept of 'ordinarily residence' has recently been reviewed by the Court of Appeal which, having considered UK and Irish case law, set out a series of factors to be considered:

(i) The critical inquiry is directed to whether the subject has a settled and usual place of abode in the place in question. To that end, his or her residence there must be neither casual nor uncertain.
(ii) In determining whether the subject has established such a residence, the focus is properly on the question of whether the person has adopted an abode in the jurisdiction for settled purposes and as part of the regular order of his or her life for the time being, whether of short or long duration.
(iii) That purpose, while settled, may be for a limited period, it may be a limited purpose and it may be contingent. All that is required is that there be a sufficient degree of continuity to be properly described as settled.
(iv) Absent legislative provision to the contrary, it is possible to be ordinarily resident in more than one place at the same time.
(v) In a legislative context where public bodies have to reach determinations based upon where a person is ordinarily resident, the Court should incline towards a test which is objective and readily capable of application without a detailed inquiry into whether the subject has established a permanent home in the jurisdiction.
(vi) Proof of ordinary residence will depend more upon the evidence of matters susceptible of objective proof than upon evidence as to state of mind or subjective intention.

1223. Section 219(1)(c). Such provisions are, of course, frequently overruled by EU law on freedom of movement.

(vii) It is not correct to frame this test by reference to where a person has their 'real home' in the sense of where they have, on a long-term basis, the centre of their social, economic or familial interests.[1224]

754. In that case, the Court upheld a ruling that students undertaking a course of more than one year's duration are ordinarily resident in the State. Given the absence of case law in the social protection field (and the lack of clarity about how ordinary residence is interpreted by the relevant agencies), it is difficult to know how (if at all) these factors may affect the approach adopted in practice.

755. As discussed in Part III, the HSE interprets ordinary residence, for the purposes of access to healthcare, as requiring an intention to reside in the State for at least one year but it is not clear that persons who reside for a shorter period cannot be ordinarily resident.[1225]

§2. Absence from the State

756. Section 249(1) and (2) provides that a person is disqualified for receiving any benefit (and increase thereof) under Part 2 (i.e., social insurance benefits) while that person is absent from the State and from receiving any increase of benefits with respect to the person's spouse for any period during which that spouse is absent from the State.[1226] However, the Minister is enabled to make regulations allowing such payments in prescribed circumstances. In addition, section 249 is subject to the overriding provisions of EU law when these are relevant.

757. Regulations provide that, notwithstanding section 249, a person who is absent from the State shall not be disqualified for receiving the following benefits (including increases):

(a) State pension (contributory), widow(er)'s and SCP (contributory) pension, guardian's payment (contributory).
(b) IB: (i) during such period as the Minister may allow, having regard to the circumstances of the case, if the absence is temporary and for the specific purpose of receiving treatment for incapacity which commenced before the person left the State; (ii) while he or she is 'posted' abroad under Article 98 of the SW(C-CI)R of 1996.
(c) Maternity benefit: (i) during such period as the Minister may allow, having regard to the circumstances of the case, if the absence is temporary and for the specific purpose of receiving treatment for incapacity which commenced before

1224. *Chubb European Group v. Health Insurance Authority* [2020] IECA 91 at [98]. The case concerned ordinary residence in the context of health insurance.
1225. *See*, for example, *Chubb* at 141. In *Chubb* Murray J described the DoH circular as not 'a binding interpretation' of the legislation (at 107).
1226. The definition of 'qualified child' set out in s. 2(3) provides that the child must be 'ordinarily resident in the state'.

the person left the State; (ii) while he or she is 'posted' abroad under Article 98 of thc SW(CCI)R of 1996; or (iii) while that person is on holiday for a period or periods not exceeding six weeks in total during the period of entitlement to the benefit.[1227]

(d) JB and JB (self-employed) for any period during which that person, or his or her qualified adult, (i) in respect of the first two weeks of any such absence in a calendar year, provided that during the period of his or her absence from the State the person does not engage in gainful employment, or (ii) while representing Ireland in an amateur capacity at an international sporting event, or (iii) during such period as the Minister may allow, having regard to the circumstances of the case, if the absence is temporary and due to force majeure or where the person (who has attained the age of 65 years) is temporarily absent from the State provided that during the period of his or her absence from the State the person does not engage in gainful employment.[1228]

(e) CA or benefit for any period during which the carer is absent from the State: (i) on holiday with respect to the first three weeks of any such absence in a calendar year; or (ii) during such period as the Minister may allow, having regard to the circumstances of the case, if the absence is temporary and for the specific purpose of accompanying a relevant person while that person is receiving treatment for a disability which commenced before the person left the State.

(f) State pension (transition) provided that during the period of his or her absence from the State, the person does not engage in gainful employment of any nature, and he or she submits such evidence to that effect as the Minister may require.

(g) IP for such period as the Minister may allow, having regard to the circumstances of the case, provided that the person furnishes such medical evidence of incapacity as the Minister may require.[1229]

(h) Parents benefit or paternity benefit for a period not exceeding two weeks while that person is on holiday during the period of entitlement to the benefit.[1230]

(i) Adoptive benefit for a period or periods not exceeding six weeks in total while that person is on holiday during the period of entitlement to the benefit.[1231]

758. As can be seen, long-term contributory benefits such as a State pension (contributory) are payable abroad without any restriction, while short-term benefits are only payable in more restricted circumstances.

759. Section 249(2) provides that, except when regulations otherwise provide, when social insurance benefits include an increase for a qualified adult, the increase shall not be payable for any period during which the qualified adult is absent from

---

1227. As amended by S.I. No. 12 of 2017.
1228. As amended by S.I. No. 495 of 2022. On 'temporary absence', *see Chief Adjudication Officer v. Balmer* [1994] UKSSCSC CS_140_1991.
1229. SW(CCP&C)R, Art. 217.
1230. As amended by S.I. No. 12 of 2017 and S.I. No. 554 of 2019.
1231. As inserted by S.I. No. 12 of 2017.

the State.[1232] The current Social Welfare (Consolidated Claims, Payments and Control) Regulations of 2007 (SW(CCP&C) Regulations) do not appear to provide for an exception from this rule.

760. There are a number of specific provisions in relation to social assistance payments to persons 'absent from' or 'resident outside the State'. This appears to be the result of an incomplete consolidation of earlier provisions.[1233] The specific provisions provide that:

(1) A person is disqualified for receiving jobseeker's allowance, SWA, DA or FA (including any increases) while he or she is resident, whether temporarily or permanently outside the State and no increase in payable in respect of a qualified adult where that person is resident whether temporarily or permanently outside the State.[1234]
(2) State pension (non-contributory) and BP are not payable to any person absent from the State except when a person takes up residence in Northern Ireland, where payment may continue for a period of five years or until the person receives a payment from the Northern Ireland Authorities.[1235]
(3) Widow(er)'s and SCP (non-contributory) pension and guardian's payment (non-contributory) pension are not to be granted to or with respect to a person resident outside the State.[1236]
(4) A person is disqualified for receiving OFP, deserted wife's allowance, and prisoner's wife's allowance while he or she is resident, whether temporarily or permanently outside the State.[1237]
(5) A person is disqualified for DCA, except where regulations otherwise provide, while the person is resident, whether temporarily or permanently, outside the State.[1238]

1232. Substituted by s. 16 SW&PA 2015.
1233. A consolidating provision was passed in 1995 but never commenced for reasons that are unclear.
1234. Section 249(6) as amended by s. 18/Sch. 1 SW&PA 2008 and s. 8(2) SW&PA 2014. On 'temporary absence', *see Chief Adjudication Officer v. Balmer* [1994] UKSSCSC CS_140_1991 in which the Court held that an absence may be 'temporary' even though no date is fixed for the claimant's return but the absence must be for a limited period only. There is no Irish case law on the meaning of the terms 'absent from the state' or 'temporary residence outside the State'. It would appear that DSP has tended to treat these as synonymous but it is not clear that this is a correct view.
1235. Section 249(7) & (8). In an appeal before an Appeals Officer, it was stated that, on an administrative basis, DSP allowed up to thirteen weeks' absence from the State at that time. The Appeals Officer pointed out that the law did not allow for payment where a person was absent from the State and that the exercise of Departmental discretion fell outside the remit of the Appeals Office. The Chief Appeals Officer, on review under s. 318, did not consider that the Appeals Officer had erred in fact and/or law: *Social Welfare Appeals Office Annual Report 2018*, 137–138.
1236. Section 249(13).
1237. Section 249(14).
1238. Section 249(17) as inserted by s. 16(h) SW & PA 2008.

761. Finally, section 249(15) provides that CB shall only be paid in the State.[1239] However, this provision is frequently overruled by EU Regulations on social security law.[1240] In addition, as the Chief Appeals Officer has pointed out, there is no legislative prohibition in relation to a child being absent from the State for the purposes of CB.[1241]

762. The EU Regulations on social security only apply to those payments within their scope. It is arguable that some of the 'absence from the State' provisions may fall afoul of EU law on a person's right to travel and to avail him or herself of services. At present, Irish law would, in theory, disqualify claimants of several social assistance schemes for receipt of payment if the claimant is outside the State. Thus, such a person could be disqualified if, for example, he or she went on holiday to another Member State, although he or she would be entitled to go on holidays anywhere in Ireland. Such persons can be within the scope of EU law.[1242] Under EU law, Member States must allow persons wishing to go to another Member State as recipients of services to leave their territory. It is arguable that the disqualification of a social welfare claimant for receipt of his or her only income is an effective denial of the right to leave the territory and that it is therefore in breach of EU law.[1243] In practice, however, under administrative arrangements, most social assistance claimants are allowed to take holidays abroad for two to three weeks without affecting their right to payment.

§3. Habitual Residence and Right to Reside

763. Prior to 1 May 2004, there was no long-term 'residence' requirement in most areas of Irish social welfare law. As outlined above, persons who were not in the country were disqualified for certain benefits, in particular means-tested payments, but persons moving from another country qualified for a benefit more or less immediately (subject to satisfying the other relevant conditions). In the run-up to the accession of the eight new Member States from Central and Eastern Europe (in addition to Malta and Cyprus), a number of EU countries exercised their rights under the accession treaties to impose restrictions on the immigration of workers from the new Member States for a period of up to seven years. Ireland did not do so and remains one of the few old Member States that allow full free movement to workers from the new Member States (although the same approach was not initially

1239. *See also* s. 192, which defines 'qualified child' as for the purposes of child benefit as being a child 'ordinarily resident in the state' expect in the case of children of members of the Defence Forces or the civil service working outside the state for the Government, the State, or an international organization.

1240. F. Pennings, *European Social Security Law*, 7th ed. (Antwerp: Intersentia, 2021), Ch. 14.

1241. *Social Welfare Appeals Office Annual Report 2013*, 23.

1242. Joined Cases 286/82 and 26/83, *Luisi & Carbone* [1984] ECR 377 and Case 186/87, *Cowan* [1989] ECR 195.

1243. Marc van der Woude & Philip Meade, 'Free Movement of the Tourist in Community Law', CMLR 25 (1988): 117; Stephen Weatherill, 'Case Note on *Cowan v. Tresor Public*', CMLR 26 (1989): 563.

applied to persons from Romania and Bulgaria). However, in the Social Welfare (Miscellaneous Provisions) Act of 2004, Ireland introduced a new HRC in relation to all means-tested allowances and CBs. The 2009 Act made it a requirement that, in order to be habitually resident, a person must have a right to reside in Ireland. Social insurance benefits remain payable without any such restrictions.[1244] In addition, CB and other family benefits under EU law (in particular, OFP) are payable to persons when Ireland is the competent state for family benefits under Regulation 883/2004.

764. The relevant provisions are now contained in section 246 of the Act and in each of the relevant chapters concerning the payments affected. The provisions require that to be entitled to the various allowances, a person must be 'habitually resident in the State'. The payments affected are:

- jobseeker's allowance;[1245]
- State pension (non-contributory);[1246]
- BP;[1247]
- widow(er)s and SCP pension and guardians payment (non-contributory);[1248]
- OFP;[1249]
- CA;[1250]
- DA;[1251]
- SWA (except exceptional needs payments and urgent needs payments);[1252] and
- CB.[1253]

765. Section 246(1) provides that the requirement that a person be habitually resident in the State means that:

(a) the person must be habitually resident in the State at the date of the making of the application, and the person must remain habitually resident in the State thereafter; or
(b) the person is a worker or a self-employed person, residing in the State pursuant to Article 7 of Directive 2004/38/EC from (i) a Member State, or (ii) a Member State of the EEA; or
(c) the person is a family member of a person referred to in paragraph (b); or

1244. The requirement of a certain minimum number of contributions to qualify for insurance benefits may mean that migrants will not immediately qualify for benefits, although persons covered by EU Regulation 883/2004 may be able to aggregate contributions paid in other states so as to qualify.
1245. Section 141(9).
1246. Section 153(c) as substituted by SWLRPA 2006.
1247. Section 161A(d) as inserted by SWLRPA 2006.
1248. Sections 163(3) and 168(5).
1249. Section 173(6).
1250. Sections 180(2) and 186A(2) as inserted by SWPA 2008.
1251. Section 210(9).
1252. Section 192, which specifically excludes payments under s. 201 (exceptional needs) and s. 202 (urgency).
1253. Section 220(3).

(d) where a person referred to in paragraph (b) ceases to be such a worker or self-employed person, the person must be habitually resident in the State immediately after the date of such cessation, and must remain habitually resident in the State; or
(e) where a person referred to in paragraph (b) ceases to be such a worker or self-employed person, a family member of such a person must be habitually resident in the State immediately after the date of such cessation, and the family member must remain habitually resident in the State.[1254]

766. Habitual residence' is a term used in EU law, in particular, in Regulation 883/2004. Regulation 883/2004 defines 'residence' as 'the place where a person habitually resides'.[1255] The Court of Justice has interpreted this concept in a number of rulings which are now reflected in section 246(4) which provides that, in assessing habitual residence, a deciding officer shall take into consideration all the circumstances of the case including, in particular:

(a) the length and continuity of residence in the State or in any other particular country;
(b) the length and purpose of any absence from the State;
(c) the nature and pattern of the person's employment;
(d) the person's main centre of interest, and
(e) the future intentions of the person concerned as they appear from all the circumstances.[1256]

767. The Court of Justice has ruled that for the purposes of that assessment, the length of residence in the Member State in which payment of the benefit is sought cannot be regarded as an *intrinsic* element of the concept of residence.[1257] The Court of Justice has also ruled that, for the purposes of Regulation 883/2004, a person cannot simultaneously have two habitual residences in two different Member States.[1258]

768. There has been little judicial consideration of *how* the habitual residence test should be applied. In *Douglas v. Minister for Social Protection,* the High Court (in an *ex tempore* judgment) ruled that an appeals officer's decision that a woman, who had lived for 49 years in the UK, who had recently moved to Ireland to study law and who was, at the time of her claim, living in bed and breakfast accommodation, was not habitually resident in Ireland, did not constitute an error of law.[1259] There are many appeals to officer's decisions on the issue in the annual SWAO Reports, although these tend to focus on the facts rather than the law.

1254. As substituted by s. 11(1)(a) SW&PA 2014.
1255. Article 1(j) of Regulation 883/2004.
1256. Inserted by SWPA 2007 s. 30.
1257. Case C-90/97 *Swaddling v. Adjudication Officer* [1999] ECR I-1075.
1258. Case C589/10, *Wencel v. Zakład Ubezpieczeń Społecznych w Białymstoku* [2013] ECR I-303. As noted above, this is unlike the position in relation to ordinary residence: *AA v. Secretary of State for Work and Pensions* [2013] UKUT 406.
1259. [2012] IEHC 27, paras 11–15.

769. Section 15 of the SWP(No.2)A 2009 added a requirement that a person must have a legal right to reside in Ireland in order to be habitually resident. In *Munteanu v. Minister for Social Protection,* the Court of Appeal ruled that the 'right to reside' test is not inconsistent with EU law.[1260] Section 246(5) now states that 'a person who does not have a right to reside in the State shall not, for the purposes of [the] Act, be regarded as being habitually resident in the State'.[1261]

770. Section 246(6) goes on to list various categories of persons who are to be taken to have a right to reside in the State.[1262] These are:

- (a) an Irish citizen under the Irish Nationality and Citizenship Acts 1956–2004;
- (b) a person who has the right under the European Communities (Free Movement of Persons) Regulations 2015 (S.I. No. 548 of 2015) to enter and reside in the State or is deemed under those Regulations to be lawfully resident in the State;
- (c) a person in relation to whom a refugee declaration within the meaning of the International Protection Act 2015 is in force, or is deemed under that Act to be in force;
- (ca) a person in relation to whom a subsidiary protection declaration within the meaning of International Protection Act 2015 is in force, or is deemed under that Act to be in force;
- (d) a person who has been given, or is deemed under the International Protection Act 2015 to have been given, a permission to enter and reside in the State under section 56 of that Act, where the permission concerned is in force;
- (da) This is also a list and not continuing with (d).--> a person who has been given, or is deemed under the International Protection Act 2015 to have been given, a permission to reside in the State under section 57 of that Act, where the permission concerned is in force;
- (e) a person who is a programme refugee within the meaning of section 59 of the International Protection Act 2015 or is deemed to be a programme refugee under subsection (4) of that section;
- (f) a person who has been given, or is deemed under the International Protection Act 2015 to have been given, a permission to reside in the State under section 54 of that Act, where the permission concerned is in force;
- (g) (has been repealed);
- (h) a person whose presence in the State is in accordance with permission to be in the State given by or on behalf of the Minister for Justice, Equality and Law Reform under and in accordance with section 4 or 5 of the Immigration Act 2004;

1260. [2019] IECA 236 upholding the High Court ruling in *Munteanu v. Minister for Social Protection* [2017] IEHC 161.
1261. In *Razneas v. Chief Appeals Officer* [2022] IECA 227, the Court of Appeal upheld the constitutionality of this condition and also held that it did not violate the provisions of the European Convention on Human Rights Act 2003.
1262. As amended by SWPA 2014 and SWA 2016.

(i) a person who has been given permission to reside in the State under section 60(6) of the International Protection Act 2015, where the permission concerned is in force.

The wording of section 246(6) suggests that this is not an exclusive list and, in particular, the Court of Justice has established that persons have a right to reside under EU law in a number of situations not listed in section 246(6).[1263] However, as long as such persons have a right to reside, they should not be excluded by section 246(5). It is submitted that the view taken by the English Court of Appeal that 'lawful presence' in the State is not sufficient to constitute a 'right to reside' is correct.[1264]

771. Given the lack of a comprehensive system of registration of residence, deciding officers and appeals officers increasingly have to decide complex issues of law concerning rights to reside.[1265] An appeals officer has commented that where a person's claim is disallowed with reference to the HRC on the grounds that they no longer retain a right to reside, the case should be examined on all available facts, prior to appeal, for any indication that the person may have a right to reside on alternative grounds or in a different capacity.[1266]

772. Conversely, section 246(7)[1267] provides that various persons shall not be regarded as being habitually resident in the State for the purpose of the Act. Note that this applies to habitual residence in general and does not relate only to rights of residence. These include:

(a) a person who has made an application (for asylum) under section 8 of the Refugee Act 1996 and where the Minister for Justice, Equality and Law

1263. The scope of the right to reside under EU law has been developed through the case law of the CJEU and is not always easy to define. *See*, for example Case C-34/0 *Ruiz Zambrano v. Office National de l'Emploi (ONEm)* [2011] ECR I-1177 and subsequent case law. *See also* Case C507/12, *St. Prix v. Secretary of State for Work and Pensions* [2015] 1 CMLR 5 EU:C:2014:2007 in which the CJEU ruled that a woman who gives up work, or seeking work, because of the physical constraints of the late stages of pregnancy and the aftermath of childbirth retains the status of 'worker', and, therefore a right to reside, provided she returns to work or finds another job within a reasonable period after the birth of her child.

1264. *Abdirahman v. Secretary of State for Work and Pensions* [2007] EWCA Civ 657.

1265. The complexities of EU law concerning the scope of the right to reside are well illustrated in a number of recent rulings concerning the Irish social welfare system including Case C-442/16, *Gusa v. Minister for Social Protection,* Case C-442/16, [2018] 2 CMLR 23; EU:C:2017:1004; Case C-483/17 *Tarola,* EU:C:2019:309; *Griga v. Chief Appeals Officer* [2017] IEHC 602 and *Voican v. Chief Appeals Office* [2020] IEHC 258 (this case is currently before the Court of Justice of the EU having been referred by the Court of Appeal). *See also* the cases discussed in *Social Welfare Appeals Office Report 2021,* p. 118 et seq. We do not discuss here the extent of the right to reside under EU and national law as this is not primarily a matter of social welfare law.

1266. *Social Welfare Appeals Office Report, 2016*, 83–85.

1267. As amended by SWPA 2014 and SWA 2016.

Reform has not yet made a decision as to whether a declaration under section 17 of that Act will be given in respect of such application:[1268]

(aa) an applicant within the meaning of section 16 of International Protection Act 2015, or a person deemed to have made an application under that Act;

(b) an applicant within the meaning of European Union (Subsidiary Protection) Regulations of 2013, or any other person awaiting a grant of permission to reside in the State under Regulation 23, 25 or 26 of the Regulations of 2013;

(c) a person who has been notified under section 3(3)(a) of the Immigration Act 1999 that the Minister for Justice, Equality and Law Reform proposes to make a deportation order, whether or not that person has made representations under section 3(3)(b) of that Act, and where the Minister for Justice, Equality and Law Reform has not yet made a decision as to whether a deportation order is to be made in respect of such person;

(d) a person who has made an application under section 8 of the Refugee Act 1996 which has been refused by the Minister for Justice, Equality and Law Reform;

(da) a person who has made, or is deemed under the International Protection Act 2015 to have made, an application under section 15 of that Act which has been refused by the Minister for Justice and Equality;

(e) a person (i) whose application for subsidiary protection under Regulation 4 or 16 of European Communities (Eligibility for Protection) Regulations of 2006 has been refused, or whose permission under Regulation 4 or 16 of the Regulations of 2006 has been revoked, (ii) whose application under Regulation 3 of European Union (Subsidiary Protection) Regulations of 2013 for a subsidiary protection declaration has been refused, or whose subsidiary protection declaration has been revoked, under the Regulations of 2013, or (iii) whose application under Regulation 25 or 26 of the Regulations of 2013 has been refused, or whose permission under Regulation 25 or 26 of the Regulations of 2013 has been revoked;

(f) a person in relation to whom a deportation order has been made, or has been deemed under section 51 of the International Protection Act 2015 to have been made, under section 3(1) of the Immigration Act 1999.

773. Finally, section 246(8) provides that, in a number of circumstances, persons are not to be considered as habitually resident prior to certain dates on which declarations of status and permissions to enter and/or reside in the State were issued. In particular, a person who:

(a) is given, or deemed under the International Protection Act 2015 to be given, a refugee declaration under that Act,

1268. This reverses a decision by the Chief Appeals Officer to the effect that an asylum seeker could be considered to be habitually resident. *See* the discussion in Bob Clark's note on the SWP(No.2)A 2009 in the *Irish Current Law Statutes Annotated.*

(b) is given, or deemed under the International Protection Act 2015 to be given, a permission to enter and reside in the State under section 56 of that Act,

(ba) is given, or deemed under the International Protection Act 2015 to be given, a permission to reside in the State under section 57 of that Act,

(c) is given, or deemed under the International Protection Act 2015 to be given, a subsidiary protection declaration under that Act, or

[(d) deleted]

(e) is granted permission to remain in the State under and in accordance with the Immigration Act 2004

is, nonetheless, not to be regarded as being habitually resident in the State for any period *before* the date on which the declaration or permission was given.[1269]

774. This is despite the fact that it is well established in law that a person is a refugee within the meaning of the 1951 Convention as soon as he or she fulfils the criteria contained in the definition. This would necessarily occur prior to the time at which the refugee status is formally determined. Recognition of refugee status does not, therefore, make him or her a refugee but declares him or her to be one. He or she does not become a refugee because of recognition but is recognized because he or she is a refugee.[1270] This position has been confirmed by the Irish High Court where Cooke J stated that:

> The determination of an asylum application does not have as its purpose or outcome the discretionary grant or refusal of refugee status .... An asylum seeker is a refugee as and when the circumstances defined in the Geneva Convention arise and apply. The determination of the asylum application is purely declaratory of a pre-existing status.[1271]

775. Nonetheless, the Supreme Court ruled in *Michael (a minor) v. Minister for Social Protection* that the refusal, in line with section 246(8), to backdate CB in respect of a child because of the immigration status of his or her mother was not in breach of Article 40.1 of the Constitution nor in breach of EU law.[1272]

776. In practice, the Department applies a two-stage process which involves establishing, in the first instance, whether a person may be held to have a right to reside and, second, determining whether the person may be deemed to be habitually resident with reference to the factors outlined in section 246(1).

1269. As amended by SWPA 2014 and SWA 2016.
1270. UN High Commission on Refugees.
1271. *D. (a minor) v. Refugee Applications Commissioner* [2011] IEHC 33 at 58.
1272. [2019] IESC 82.

§4. Directive 2004/38/EC and Disqualification for Social Assistance

777. Directive 2004/38/EC sets out the right of citizens of the Union and their family members to move and reside freely within the territory of the Member States. Given that the Member States were concerned that such rights might create rights to social benefits where none existed under national law, Article 24(2) of the Directive provides that:

> the host Member State shall not be obliged to confer entitlement to social assistance during the first three months of residence or, where appropriate, the longer period provided for in Article 14(4)(b) [jobseekers] ... .[1273]

778. The Directive is implemented in Irish law by the European Communities (Free Movement of Persons) Regulations 2015 [S.I. No. 548 of 2015]. These Regulations apply to (a) Union citizens entering or remaining in the State in accordance with these Regulations, and (b) a family member of such a Union citizen who: (i) enters the State in the company of the Union citizen, (ii) enters the State for the purpose of joining the Union citizen, or (iii) becomes a family member while in the State and seeks to remain with the Union citizen in the State.[1274]

779. Regulation 17(2)(a) provides that:

> a person to whom Regulation 6(1) [first three months of residence] or 6(2) [jobseeker] applies shall not be entitled to receive assistance under the Social Welfare Acts.

However, it goes on to say that this does not apply in relation to a payment of SWA under sections 201 [exceptional needs] and 202 [urgency] of the Social Welfare Consolidation Act 2005.

780. It is unusual that direct reference is made to entitlement to social welfare in non-social welfare legislation, and the effect of this provision is rather unclear.[1275] If taken as a general disqualification for social assistance, it is probably unnecessary in many cases as most persons would not be considered to be habitually resident (including the right to reside aspect) in the first three months of residence. However, since there is no general disqualification for persons in the first three months of residence in Irish law, the Regulation could (at least in theory) give rise to reverse discrimination whereby all EU citizens (other than Irish nationals) were disqualified for assistance, but some non-EU citizens (who, on the facts, satisfied the habitual residence requirement) were not disqualified. The provision is perhaps better read as simply meaning that no entitlement to assistance is created by the

1273. Article 14(4)(b) refers to the period during which persons may not be expelled from a Member State 'for as long as the Union citizens can provide evidence that they are continuing to seek employment and that they have a genuine chance of being engaged'.

1274. Regulation 3 of S.I. No. 548 of 2015.

1275. It is not clear that it is used in practice by deciding officers.

2015 Regulation, as this appears to be the intention of Article 24 of the Directive itself, rather than as creating a new disqualification. Thus, a person whose right to reside was based only on Regulation 6(1) or (2) would not, thereby, acquire a right to reside so as to be entitled to welfare but a person during their first three months of residence or a jobseeker would not, per se, be disqualified for benefit if they could show a right to reside on another basis or an alternative right to benefits under EU law.

781. This approach, in broad terms, seems to have been adopted in a recent case where an appeals officer concluded that a person was a jobseeker within the meaning of Regulation 6(2) but that such status as a jobseeker did not confer any entitlement to access to the social assistance system. This decision was upheld by the Chief Appeals Officer.[1276] However, it would be preferable if the position was clarified in law given that section 246(6) (set out above) provides that a person with a right to reside under the 2015 Regulations has a right to reside for the purposes of the SW Acts and this would appear somewhat in conflict with this reading of Regulation 17(2).

1276. *Social Welfare Appeals Office Report 2018*, 121–125.

Chapter 4. Imprisonment, Detention in Legal Custody & Institutions

§1. Imprisonment & Detention in Legal Custody

782. The rules in relation to imprisonment have been thrown into some confusion by the recent Supreme Court decisions in *C. v. Minister for Social Protection,* where the Court found that aspects of the current legislation (section 249(1)) were unconstitutional.[1277] The implications of the ruling are that a number of other subsections are also unconstitutional (*see* below). The Oireachtas has now legislated to a limited extent in relation to certain illness and disability benefits, but, at the time of writing, legislation in relation to long-term benefits, such as pensions, is still awaited.

783. Section 249(1) provides that:

> Except where regulations otherwise provide, a person shall be disqualified for receiving any benefit under Part 2 (including any increase of benefit) for any period during which that person … (b) is undergoing imprisonment or detention in legal custody.

784. However, as noted above, the Supreme Court made a declaration of constitutional invalidity in respect of:

> that portion of s. 249(1)(b) of the 2005 Act which disqualifies the appellant and persons in the same position from benefits while serving a lawful term of imprisonment in respect of a sentence imposed upon them.[1278]

O'Donnell J's formulation of the extent of the holding of invalidity would seem to leave section 249(1)(b) intact insofar as it applies to detention in legal custody occurring other than pursuant to a sentence of imprisonment following the conviction for an offence. Though O'Donnell J. does not explicitly identify the portion of section 249(1)(b) that disqualifies convicted prisoners for receipt of benefits, it is arguable that this consequence flows from the use of the word 'imprisonment', which carries with it connotations of punishment and that section 249(1)(b) should now simply read 'is undergoing detention in legal custody'. However, it would also seem to follow from this litigation that subsections 6, 9 and 10 of section 249 are unconstitutional insofar as they disqualify convicted prisoners for receipt of welfare

1277. [2017] IESC 63; [2017] 2 ILRM 369 and [2018] IESC 57. Note that in *P.C v. Ireland*, 26922/19, 1 Sep. 2022 the European Court of Human Rights held that the disqualification of a person for old age pension while serving a sentence of imprisonment was not in breach of Art. 14 of the Convention taken in conjunction with Art. 1 of Protocol No. 1.

1278. *C v. Minister for Social Protection* [2018] IESC 57, O'Donnell J. at para. 23 of his judgment. In line with this ruling, we have deleted references to imprisonment as a disqualification although these formally remain in the legislation at the time of writing.

in circumstances where such prisoners would otherwise be entitled to specific welfare payments notwithstanding the fact of their detention, a point that appears to have been accepted, *obiter*, by O'Donnell J. at paragraph 4 of his judgment.

785. The term 'detention in legal custody' is not statutorily defined, but, as a result of the *C.* case, detention in respect of a sentence imposed following a criminal conviction is clearly excluded. Section 249(1A) provides that a person shall *not* be regarded as undergoing detention in legal custody for the purposes of entitlement to DA while the person is detained for treatment pursuant to:

(a) an admission order or renewal order made under the Mental Health Act of 2001;[1279]
(b) an order made under section 38 of the HA of 1947;[1280]
(c) an order made under section 4 or section 5 of the Criminal Law (Insanity) Act of 2006;[1281]
(d) an order made under section 17 of the Lunacy (Ireland) Act of 1821;[1282] or
(e) an order made under section 2 of the Trial of Lunatics Act of 1883.[1283]

786. The Social Welfare (Consolidated Claims, Payments and Control) Regulations of 2007 (SW(CCP&C)R) provide for exceptions from the general rules as to disqualification (as allowed by section 249). First, Article 218(1)(a) provides that section 249 shall not operate so as to disqualify a person for receiving a range of social insurance benefits[1284] with respect to any period during which the person is detained in any institution for the treatment of mental illness or infectious disease (other than in the case of a person found not guilty by reason of insanity under the provisions of the Criminal Law (Insanity) Act of 2006).[1285]

1279. This concerns an involuntary admission order with respect to a person suffering from a mental disorder.
1280. This concerns the detention of a person who is a probable source of infection.
1281. Section 4 concerns the detention in the central mental hospital of a person who is unfit to be tried by reason of mental disorder, while s. 5 covers a person found not guilty by reason of insanity.
1282. Section 17 of the 1821 Act provides that persons found unfit to plead are detained at the Central Mental Hospital until the Executive decides whether they should be released or, in the event that they become fit to plead, stand trial, while s. 2 of the 1883 provides for the verdict of guilty but insane. Both are now repealed by the Criminal Law (Insanity) Act, 2006.
1283. Inserted by s. 10(1)(b) SWPA 2008. The fact that the exemption applies only to DA is an (unfortunately typical) example of the rather inconsistent nature of the provisions in this area.
1284. Illness benefit, maternity benefit, jobseeker's benefit, jobseeker's benefit (self-employed), State pension (contributory), State pension (transition), invalidity pension, widow's (contributory) pension, widower's (contributory) pension, bereavement grant or guardian's payment (contributory), (including in each case, subject to Art. 218(1)(b)), any increase thereof. Art. 218(1)(b) provides that no IQC under s. 43, 66, 112, 117, 122, or 127 shall be payable to a person to whom para. (a) applies.
1285. Thus, persons found not guilty by reason of insanity are not disqualified for a social welfare payment while detained in any institution for the treatment of mental illness if they are in receipt of disability allowance but are so disqualified if they are in receipt of other payments. It would appear that such persons are the only group so disqualified while detained in any institution for the treatment of mental illness (other than in the case of DA). The rationale for this difference in

787. Second, Article 218(4)(a) provides that notwithstanding that a person, by reason of undergoing a period of detention in legal custody is disqualified by virtue of section 249 for receiving IB, IP, State pension (transition), widow's (contributory) pension, widower's (contributory) pension, OFP, a payment by virtue of section 178, State pension (contributory), widow's (non-contributory) pension, or widower's (non-contributory) pension (including, in each case, any IQA or qualified child), the increase shall be paid to any person appointed by the Minister. However, in the case of IB, paragraph (a) only applies when the person is detained in an institution for the treatment of mental illness or is a person who was entitled to such benefit immediately before the commencement of any such period, or would, but for section 40(2) have been so entitled.

788. Specific rules are also set out in relation to OIB in the Social Welfare (Consolidated Occupational Injuries) Regulations of 2007 (SW(COI)R) (Articles 72–73). These, *inter alia*, provide an exemption from disqualification for OIB for persons detained in an institution for the treatment of mental illness – other than in the case of a person found not guilty by reason of insanity.

789. There are a number of additional provisions in relation to social assistance payments payable to a person in legal detention, but, as noted above, the Supreme Court ruling in *C.* would appear to suggest that these also may be unconstitutional, at least in part. The specific provisions provide that:

(1) A person is disqualified for receiving jobseeker's allowance, PRETA, DA, or FA while he or she is undergoing imprisonment or detention in legal custody.[1286]
(2) A person is disqualified for a State pension (non-contributory) and BP when he or she has been convicted of any offence and ordered to be imprisoned without the option of a fine or to suffer any greater punishment while he or she is detained in prison in consequence of the order.[1287]
(3) A person is disqualified for receiving OFP, widow's (non-contributory) pension, deserted wife's allowance, and prisoner's wife's allowance for any period during which she is undergoing imprisonment or detention in legal custody (except where regulations provide otherwise).[1288]

790. It is important to note that, in general, even when a person is excepted from disqualification, payment of a benefit or allowance is normally suspended while the person is detained and is paid at the end of the period of detention. Alternatively, it

---

treatment is very unclear and it would appear so arbitrary that there must be some doubts about its legal validity (either on the basis that it is void for unreasonableness or that it is in breach of the equality provisions of the Constitution).

1286. Section 249(6).
1287. Section 249(9).
1288. Section 249(10).

may be paid during the period of detention to a person appointed by the Minister to deal with the money on behalf of the person or dependent.[1289]

791. Finally, section 219 defines 'qualified child' for the purposes of CB in such a way as to exclude a child detained in a children's detention centre[1290] or undergoing imprisonment or detention in legal custody.

792. Section 4 of the Social Welfare (No. 2) Act 2019 effects a number of changes to the eligibility conditions for IB, DA, PCB, IP and BP in response to the decisions of the Supreme Court in *C*. Explaining these changes in the Dáil, the then Minister, Regina Doherty, T.D., pointed out that core eligibility for these payments is that unavailability for work is a direct result of illness and the effect of the changes is to provide that where a person becomes unavailable for work for a secondary reason such as incarceration, s/he will not be eligible for the payments.[1291] In relation to IB, which may be claimed in respect of a day of incapacity that forms part of a period of interruption of employment, it must be shown that the period of interruption of employment is due to the claimant being incapable of work and for no other reason – section 4(a). In order to qualify for PCB, a claimant must show, *inter alia*, that s/he has a profound restriction on his or her capacity for work. Now section 4(b) requires that a claimant must also show that the reason for the restriction is a direct result of the claimant being incapable of work and for no other reason. In relation to IP, section 4(c) now requires a claimant to show that the reason for his permanent incapacity to work is a direct result of the claimant being incapable of work and for no other reason and also that s/he would be available to work in insurable employment or insurable self-employment were it not for this incapacity. Similarly, in relation to BP, a claimant must now show that his/her incapacity to perform any insurable employment or insurable self-employment for which eyesight is essential or to continue his/her ordinary occupation is a direct result of his/her blindness and for no other reason and that, were it not for this incapacity, s/he would be available to work in insurable employment or insurable self-employment – section 4(d). The same provision is made, *mutatis mutandis,* in relation to the condition of eligibility for DA that a claimant must be substantially restricted in relation to undertaking employment of a kind which, if the claimant was not suffering from that disability, would be suited to his/her age, experience and qualifications –section 4(e). This provision also provides that a person shall not be disqualified for receipt of DA while engaged in a prescribed course of education, training or development.

793. While subsection 249(6) and (9) of the 2005 Act disqualifying convicted prisoners for receipt of DA and BP respectively are arguably unconstitutional in

1289. SW(CCP&C)R, Art. 219.

1290. The term 'children detention centre' is introduced under the Children Act, 2001 and the wording of the Social Welfare Acts is amended by the SWMPA 2008. although, *see*, in any case, s. 159(4) of the Children Act 2001.

1291. Dáil Debates, Wednesday, 27 Nov. 2019.

light of the *C.* decisions, the introduction of a new condition of eligibility in relation to each of these schemes that a claimant would have to be available to work but for his/her blindness or disability respectively means that any claimant of these payments who is imprisoned or detained in legal custody for reasons unconnected to his or her disability will no longer be eligible for either of these two payments. (In the case of a person detained under, e.g., the Mental Health Act 2001, it would at least be arguable that the ultimate reason why s/he was unavailable for work was still related to his/her disability.) While section 4 appears to be in response to the decisions in the two *C* cases, it may have consequences in other contexts as well. In relation to IP and BP, claimants who had been detained in legal custody but where the criminal charge had been withdrawn or the claimant had been acquitted of the offence were still entitled to receive welfare during the period of their detention. This also applied where such claimants underwent imprisonment as an alternative to paying a fine. In light of the changes effected by section 4, however, it would appear that these two welfare payments are no longer payable in such circumstances as now the claimants are unable to show that the only reason why they are unavailable for work is because of their incapacity or disability. In relation to IB, previously days of unemployment could have been taken into account in establishing a period of interruption of employment, and the change effected by section 4(a) may mean that a claimant of IB may no longer be able to rely on a day of unemployment to establish a period of interruption of employment.

794. The EU Court of Justice has held that a Member State is not necessarily required under EU law to treat imprisonment in another EU Member State as equivalent to imprisonment in the competent state.[1292] In that case, an Irish national resided in the UK. On a visit to Ireland, he was imprisoned and, while in prison, became ill. On his return to the UK, he claimed a sickness benefit. UK law provides that imprisonment is a bar to entitlement to a benefit, but it appeared that judicial interpretation confined this to imprisonment in the UK. The Court of Justice was asked whether Regulation 1408/71 allowed imprisonment in another EU country to be treated as equivalent to imprisonment in the competent state. While this might appear to lead to a more coordinated application of national provisions, it was argued that there was considerable variation among the rules in relation to detention in legal custody in the Member States. The Court held that the prohibition on discrimination in Regulation 1408/71 did not apply to possible differences in treatment resulting from the differences among the laws of Member States provided that these laws are based on objective criteria and do not take into account the nationality of the person concerned. Thus, whether or not detention in legal custody in another EU Member State (or indeed, in any foreign country) operates as a disqualification would depend on whether or not, as a matter of legal interpretation, such detention

1292. *Kenny v. Insurance Officer* [1978] ECR 1489.

falls within the definition of 'undergoing detention in legal custody' set out in section 249 (having regard to the non-discrimination principle in cases covered by EU law).[1293]

§2. Institutions

795. Disqualifications for persons in institutions have been gradually removed from many areas of the social welfare code. However, there are a small number of remaining disqualifications, including:

> Section 78(2) which provides that an increase of disablement pension where constant attendance is needed shall not be payable in respect of any period during which the beneficiary is receiving medical treatment as an in-patient in a hospital or similar institution.
>
> Section 147(1) which provides that JA is not payable to an inmate of an institution maintained wholly or partly out of public moneys or by a local authority.[1294]
>
> Article 132 of the SW (CCP&C) Regulations provides that the carer's allowance is not payable if the carer is resident in an institution.[1295]
>
> Section 186E provides that domiciliary care allowance is not payable for any period during which a child is resident in an institution (although there are exceptions set out in section 183E(2) and (3) where the child spends some of the week at home).[1296]

796. Section 225(2) provides that the carer's support grant is not payable if the person to be cared for is resident of an institution.[1297]

797. In a number of cases, ECHR arguments concerning non-payment of benefits to persons in civil institutions (such as hospital patients) have been considered by the courts in Ireland and the UK. In two UK cases, the claimant argued that a reduction in retirement pension while they were in hospital was in breach of Article

1293. In the UK, it was eventually held after protracted litigation that the disqualification provision in UK law did apply to periods of detention abroad, Ogus & Barendt, *The Law of Social Security*, 2nd ed. (London: Butterworths, 1982), 401.
1294. It is not clear whether such a person would satisfy the qualification conditions for JA in the first place.
1295. Although there is not a specific disqualification, the terms of the carer's benefit legislation would seem to lead to the same outcome, *see* Art. 56 of the SW(CCP&C) Regs.
1296. *See Donnelly v. Minister for Social Protection* [2022] IESC 31. Now where a child is admitted to an institution on a full-time basis for the purpose of receiving medical or other treatment of a temporary nature or where a child born on or after 1 January 2023 remains in hospital immediately after birth for the purpose of receiving medical or other treatment, the allowance is payable for not more than twenty-six weeks in a twelve-month period – S.I. No. 129 of 2023.
1297. Article 166 of the SW(CCP&C) Regulations provides that carer's support grant is not payable if the carer is resident in an institution (except where s/he is undergoing medical or other treatment of a temporary nature in an institution for a period or periods amounting to not more than thirteen weeks (Art. 167(a)). However, it is not clear that this is allowed by the primary legislation.

1 of Protocol 1 and Article 14.[1298] The Social Security Commissioner held that the reduction did not involve a 'deprivation' of a benefit but rather a provision defining and quantifying benefit. Thus, the claimant was not being deprived of an acquired right, and if she was, the reduction was 'in the public interest'. The Commissioner accepted that the claimant was treated differently from persons in hospital who did not receive a state benefit and/or a pensioner not in hospital but held that such persons were not in an analogous situation and, alternatively, that there was an objective and reasonable justification for the difference in treatment. More recently, the UK Supreme Court upheld a challenge to the suspension of payment of disability living allowance to a child who has been in the hospital for more than eighty-four days. The Court took the view that there was a violation of Article 14 of the Convention.[1299] However, this should be seen as a rather exceptional case, and the UK lower courts have continued to uphold other 'institutional' bars to payment, distinguishing *Mathieson*.[1300] In *Donnelly v. Minister for Social Protection* the Irish Supreme Court held that a disqualification for DCA where the child was in hospital was not contrary to the guarantees of equality in Article 40.1 of the Constitution or Article 14 of the European Convention on Human Rights.[1301]

1298. CP/5084/2001 (8 Aug. 2002); and CP/518/2003 (18 Nov. 2005).
1299. *Mathieson v. Secretary of State for Work and Pensions* [2015] UKSC 47.
1300. *See, e.g.*, *MH v. SSWP (PIP)* [2017] UKUT 424.
1301. [2022] IESC 31.

Chapter 5. Overpayments and Repayments

798. The law in relation to overpayment of social welfare and the recovery thereof is set out in Part 11 of the Act.[1302] However, as liability to repay is in many cases determined by the revision of a deciding officer's decision, regard must also be given to sections 301 and 302.[1303]

799. Section 301 provides that a deciding officer may, at any time, revise any decision of a deciding officer if it appears that the original decision was erroneous in light of new evidence or of new facts that have been brought to his or her notice since the original decision, or by reason of some mistake having been made in relation to the law or the facts, or (was to entitle a person to any benefit) if it appears that there was a relevant change of circumstances.[1304] Section 302 provides that:

> A revised decision … shall take effect as follows –
>
> (a) where … the revised decision is given owing to the original decision having been given, or having continued in effect, by reason of any statement or representation (whether written or verbal) which was to the knowledge of the person making it false or misleading in a material respect or by reason of the wilful concealment of any material fact, it shall take effect from the date on which the original decision took effect but the original decision may, in the discretion of the deciding officer, continue to apply in any period covered by the original decision to which such false or misleading statement or representation or such wilful concealment of any material fact does not relate;
>
> (b) where … the revised decision is given in the light of new evidence of new facts (relating to periods prior to and subsequent to the commencement of this Act) which have been brought to the notice of the deciding officer since the original decision was made, it shall take effect from such date as the deciding officer shall determine having regard to the new facts or new evidence,

---

1302. Sections 334–343.

1303. The position concerning pre-termination procedures is discussed in para. 849 below.

1304. In *Iarnród Éireann v. Social Welfare Tribunal* [2007] IEHC 406 Murphy J stated that 'If new evidence is to be construed as 'fresh evidence' then such a reference in an enactment imports the usual legal meaning of this phrase as evidence which is not merely additional to that adduced on the former occasion but could not be [sic.] reasonably have been expected to be produced then'. In a social welfare context, the Canadian Federal Court of Appeal has pointed out that 'new' facts must be 'new', i.e., if the fact has been raised previously in relation to the claim it cannot be 'new'. Second, it has defined 'new facts' as 'facts that either happened after the decision was rendered or had happened prior to the decision but could not have been discovered by a claimant acting diligently and in both cases the facts alleged must have been decisive of the issue put to the umpire': *Canada (Attorney General) v. Chan* (1994), 178 N.R. 372; *Mansour v. Canada (Attorney General)*, 2001 FCA 328. In *Cooke v. Secretary of State for Social Security* [2001] EWCA Civ 734, the English Court of Appeal ruled that whether there has been a change of circumstances is a question of fact (so that it can be challenged only if irrational) and, second, that it is necessary to compare the circumstances as they were at the time of the original decision with those at the time of the review.

(c) in any other case, it shall take effect as from the date considered appropriate by the deciding officer having regard to the circumstances of the case.[1305]

800. Thus, in summary, when the original decision arose from any statement or representation (whether written or verbal) that was to the knowledge of the person making it false or misleading in a material respect or by reason of the wilful concealment of any material fact, the revised decision will apply *ab initio,* and an overpayment will be incurred, to be dealt with in accordance with section 335.[1306] Canadian unemployment legislation uses very similar wording, *viz.* when a claimant makes 'a statement or representation that he knew to be false or misleading'.[1307] The Canadian Federal Court of Appeal has interpreted this as requiring 'a subjective test in determining whether the requisite knowledge is present'. The claimant must actually know the statement to be false. However, this does not mean that the claimant can simply profess a lack of knowledge, and the adjudicating authorities may take into account common sense and objective factors.[1308] In any other case, the decision will apply from such date as the deciding officer shall determine or consider appropriate, and an overpayment may or may not arise.[1309]

801. The legislation does not provide any guidance as to how this discretion should be applied. However, Departmental Guidelines suggest that section 302(b) should be applied with retrospective effect if:

– new facts have occurred since the person claimed the social welfare payment in question, or if new evidence has come to light which was not available at the

1305. As amended by SWLRPA 2006, s. 29. Section 319 (as amended by SWLRPA 2006, s. 29) applies the same wording to appeals officers' decisions. *See also* s. 325 in relation to decisions in relation to SWA.

1306. In *State (Hoolahan) v. Minister for Social Welfare* Unreported, High Court, 23 Jul. 1986, the Court held that prior to a finding of fraud, the rules of natural justice required that this allegation be put to the claimant to allow him or her the opportunity to respond. The US Supreme Court has held that under US law, there is no constitutional requirement that an oral hearing be held in relation to the assessment of an overpayment of social security benefits per se. However, the Court held that the legislation required that an oral hearing be held where a claimant requested a waiver of the overpayment on the basis that the overpayment arose without any fault of their part or that it would be, *inter alia,* inequitable to recover the money. While the latter decision was on the basis of a purposive reading of the legislation, the strong implication was that the Court would have, if necessary, found that this was also a Constitutional requirement: *Califano v. Yamaski* 442 US 682.

1307. Although the statutory context is somewhat different, in that a finding that such a statement or representation has occurred is grounds for the imposition of an administrative penalty, overpayments being generally repayable.

1308. *Canada (AG) v. Gates* [1995] 3 FC 17; *Canada (AG) v. Purcell* [1996] FC 644; *Mootoo v. Canada (Minister of Human Resources Development)* [2003] FCJ 724. For the application of this test, *see Canada (Attorney General) v. Bellil*, 2017 FCA 104.

1309. However, SW(CCP&C)R, Art. 200 provides for an obligation to repay child benefit and early childcare supplement which are not due as a result of a change in the claimant's circumstances. Quaere whether this provision is *ultra vires* as it appears to conflict with the statutory provisions as to overpayments.

claim stage and the person was aware of the new facts or evidence but failed to report this information to the Department; or
- it is not possible for the deciding officer to establish that the person wilfully concealed the facts on a previous interview or enquiry, but the deciding officer is satisfied that the person could reasonably have been expected to be aware of the new facts (or evidence) and their relevance.[1310]

802. Circumstances, when it suggested it would be appropriate to revise a decision under 302(b) with effect from a current date, include cases in which the deciding officer is satisfied that:

- the person could not reasonably have been expected to know the relevance of the new fact; or
- the person was not aware of the undisclosed evidence at the point when he or she made a claim or subsequently.

803. It would appear that (in a case in which the claimant is deceased) when an overpayment does arise, in assessing the amount of the overpayment, the Department will have regard to funeral and legal expenses to which the estate is liable.[1311]

804. Issues concerning overpayments frequently arise before appeals officers. Although it is somewhat difficult to identify the precise legal principles involved, it would appear that appeals officers take the view that the need to show fraud imposes a high onus of proof[1312] on the Department and are generally not prepared to apply a decision retrospectively in the absence of clear culpability on the part of the claimant. For example, appeals officers have decided not to make retrospective decisions when the claimants have made some efforts to notify the Department and/or had not been notified of the introduction of an earnings limit or of the amount of such limit.[1313]

805. Section 335[1314] provides that:

> Where in accordance with the provisions of Sections 302, 319 [revised decision by appeals officer] or 325 [revised determination concerning SWA], a decision or determination is varied or revised by a deciding officer, an appeals officer or a designated officer in the case of SWA (as the case may be) so as to

1310. Operational Guidelines: Revised Decisions and their Date of Effect, 2019.
1311. *Social Welfare Appeals Office Report 2005*, 15–16.
1312. *See* the Chief Appeals Officer's decision at *Social Welfare Appeals Office Report 2017,* 114–116.
1313. *Social Welfare Appeals Office Report* 2003, 25–26; *Social Welfare Appeals Office Report 2004*, 9, 21–22; *Social Welfare Appeals Office Report 2005*, 16–18; and *see also Social Welfare Appeals Office Report 2005*, 21–22; *Social Welfare Appeals Office Report 2012*, 43–45; *Social Welfare Appeals Office Report 2015,* 75–77; 85–86; *Social Welfare Appeals Office Report 2016*, 72–74; 88–90; *Social Welfare Appeals Office Report 2017*, 55–56; 94; *Social Welfare Appeals Office Report 2018*, 102.
1314. As amended by SWLRPA 2006, s. 29.

disallow or reduce any benefit, assistance, CB, WFP, continued payment for qualified children or BTWFD paid or payable to a person –

(a) any benefit paid in pursuance of the original decision shall be repayable to the Social Insurance Fund to the extent to which it would not have been payable if the decision on the appeal or revision had been given in the first instance and such person and any other person to whom the benefit was paid on behalf of such person, or the personal representative of such person, shall be liable to pay to the said Fund, on demand made in that behalf by an officer of the Minister, the sum so repayable.
(b) any assistance (other than supplementary welfare allowance under Part III), CB, or WFP, continued payment for qualified children or BTWFD paid in pursuance of the original decision shall be repayable to the Minister to the extent to which it would not have been payable if the decision on the appeal or revision had been given in the first instance and such person and any other person to whom the said assistance, CB or WFP, continued payment for qualified children or BTWFD (as the case may be) was paid on behalf of such person, or the personal representative of such person, shall be liable to pay to the said Fund, on demand made in that behalf by an officer of the Minister, the sum so repayable,
(c) any supplementary welfare allowance paid in pursuance of the original decision shall be repayable to the Minister to the extent to which it would not have been payable if the revised determination had been given in the first instance and such person and any other person to whom the supplementary welfare allowance was paid on behalf of such person, or the personal representative of such person, shall be liable to pay to the said Fund, on demand made in that behalf by the Minister, the sum so repayable.

806. Further, section 336 provides that when, in any case *other than a case* involving a revised decision or determination, a person has been in receipt of any benefit, assistance, CB, WFP, continued payment for qualified children or BTWFD for any period during which he or she was not entitled to it or was in receipt of a higher rate than that to which he or she was entitled, that person (and any other person to whom it was paid on behalf of such person or his or her personal representative) is liable to pay to the Fund, or the Minister (as the case may be), on demand, the amount of the overpayment. This section establishes a right to recover a repayment made resulting from an administrative error.[1315]

807. Section 337 provides that when a person is convicted of an offence under section 32 of the Larceny Act of 1916 or Part 2 of the Criminal Justice (Theft and Fraud Offences) Act of 2001, by virtue of having received any benefit, assistance, CB, WFP, continued payment for qualified children or BTWFD that he or she was

1315. *See* Operational Guidelines: Management of Customer Overpayments and Recovery of Customer Debt, 2019.

not entitled to receive, that person shall be liable to pay a sum not exceeding the amount of such payment to which the conviction applies to the Fund, or the Minster (as the case may be).

808. Finally, section 338 makes binding sections 336 and 337 by providing that when a person has received money from the Department to which he or she was not entitled, the person shall be liable to repay that money on demand. The intention of this section is to cover situations such as impersonation when a person other than the person entitled to the payment receives money from the Department.

809. Section 341[1316] provides that all sums due to the Social Insurance Fund or the Minister other than in accordance with section 336 (i.e., resulting from an administrative overpayment) shall be recoverable as debts due to the State and, without prejudice to any other remedy, may be recovered by the Minister as a debt under statute or a simple contract debt in any court of competent jurisdiction, that is, the District Court for sums up to EUR 6,350 and the Circuit Court for sums up to EUR 38,092. Proceedings for the recovery of any sum due to the Fund by way of employment contributions under section 10(1) or self-employment contributions under section 18(1) may be brought at any time, so the normal limitation periods do not apply.

810. Section 341(7) further provides that any benefit, assistance, supplement or payment supplement, payment or dividend repayable in accordance with sections 335, 336, 337 or 338 may, without prejudice to any other method of recovery, be recovered by deduction from any benefit, assistance, supplement or payment supplement, payment or dividend to which the person concerned is or becomes entitled.[1317] However, section 341(7A) provides that the weekly amount to be deducted for the purposes shall not, without the prior written consent of the person liable to repay the overpayment, exceed 15% of the weekly rate of benefit or assistance to which the person concerned is entitled.[1318] Any CB repayable under sections 335–338 shall be recoverable from any payment of CB to which the person is or becomes entitled.[1319] Thus, general benefit or assistance overpayments may be recovered from any benefit or assistance entitlement other than CB. CB overpayments may only be recovered from CB entitlements (without prejudice, obviously, to a civil action to recover the debt).

811. Section 342 provides that, notwithstanding anything to the contrary and subject to section 342A, an authorized officer of the Minister or an officer of the HSE may, in accordance with prescribed circumstances and conditions, suspend,

1316. As amended by s. 6(8) SW&P(MP)A 2013.
1317. *See also* s. 341(9) (as substituted by SWPA 2014) which allows overpayments to be deducted from certain lump sum payments made by the Minister for Social Protection to that person, i.e., refunds of PRSI contributions, lump sum payments made under the Redundancy Payments Act 1967 and under the Protection of Employees (Employers' Insolvency) Act 1984.
1318. Section 341(7) as amended by s. 6(8) SW&P(MP)A 2013. Section 347(7A) inserted by s. 13(1)(b) SWA 2012.
1319. Section 341(8) as amended by SWLRPA 2006, s. 29.

reduce or cancel repayment of any amount due to be repaid.[1320] The prescribed circumstances and conditions referred to in section 342 are contained in Part 9 of the Social Welfare (Consolidated Claims, Payments and Control) Regulations (S.I. No. 142 of 2007). However, section 342A provides that where a person is required to repay an amount by virtue of a revised decision arising from a statement or representation (whether written or verbal) which was to the knowledge of the person making it false or misleading in a material respect or by reason of the wilful concealment of any material fact, the amount to be repaid shall *not* be reduced by the amount of any other social welfare payment to which the person would otherwise have been entitled in the period to which the overpayment relates.[1321]

812. In accordance with natural justice, the Regulation requires that, when an overpayment has been assessed against a person, he or she shall be:

(a) informed of the factors that gave rise to the overpayment;
(b) informed of the amount of overpayment involved;
(c) advised of the proposed method of recovery; and
(d) afforded an opportunity to bring to the notice of the Department or HSE:
    (1) any views he or she wishes to offer on the assessment of the overpayment;
    (2) his or her views on the proposed method of repayment; and
    (3) any facts or circumstances that he or she considers relevant to the repayment of the overpayment[1322] before any decision is made regarding the recovery of the overpayment.[1323]

813. Having considered the person's response (if any), the authorized officer will make a determination in relation to the recovery of the overpayment (e.g., the weekly amount to be repaid). There is no appeal from this determination, as it is not a deciding officer's function. It can, however, be reviewed. The Regulation states that every effort should be made to recover payments in full. However, it also provides that the amount of repayment shall not cause, without the prior written agreement of the person liable to repay the overpayment, that person's weekly payment of benefit or assistance, as the case may be, to fall below the weekly rate of SWA appropriate to his or her family circumstances.[1324] As noted above (paragraph 736), section 342 provides that repayment may be deferred, suspended, reduced, or cancelled in prescribed circumstances and subject to prescribed conditions. It does not appear that any such conditions and circumstances are currently prescribed for deferral or suspension.

814. However, Article 246 first provides that an overpayment to be repaid may be reduced or cancelled when the overpayment arose because of a failure by the Department to act within a reasonable period on information that was provided by

1320. As amended by SWPA 2011, s. 17.
1321. As inserted by SWPA 2011, s. 18.
1322. *See State (Hoolahan) v. Minister for Social Welfare*, Unreported, High Court, 23 Jul. 1986.
1323. SW(CCP&C)R, Art. 242.
1324. SW(CCP&C)R, Art. 245.

or on behalf of the person concerned, or an error by the Department, and the person concerned could not reasonably have been expected to be aware that a failure or error had occurred.[1325] Second, the amount to be repaid shall, when the facts or circumstances warrant, be reduced to an amount accepted in settlement. Third, where the overpayment has not arisen due to fraud, the amount to be repaid may be reduced by the amount of any other benefit, assistance, or supplement to which the person would have been entitled in the period to which the overpayment is related.[1326] Fourth, any omission made by or on behalf of the person concerned that contributed in whole or in part to the overpayment being made is to be taken into account in determining whether repayment of an overpayment is to be reduced or cancelled. Finally, the repayment of an overpayment may be cancelled when there is no reasonable prospect of securing repayment in whole or in part.

815. In conclusion, section 340 provides that when sums are due, the Minister or the Fund, in accordance with section 336 or 338, because the payment that was intended for a person was paid to his or her account in a financial institution and the person died before the payment was made, the payment may be recovered directly from the institution on written notice being given to the institution by the Minister.[1327] Given the increasing use of electronic fund transfer by social welfare claimants, there is also an increasing incidence of payments being made in the period between the death of a person and notification of the death reached the Department. The intention of this section is to allow the Minister to recover such money directly from the financial institution without having to seek recovery from the estate.

816. The overpayment provisions have been considered by the Supreme Court in *Minister for Social, Community and Family Affairs v. Scanlon.*[1328] In that case, the defendant had been in receipt of a disability benefit from 1985 to 1994. In 1994, the decision as to the claimant's entitlement was revised by a deciding officer and, subsequently, by an appeals officer, on the basis that the defendant had worked between those dates and was not, therefore, entitled to a disability benefit. The appeals officer, unlike the deciding officer, was 'not fully satisfied' that Mr Scanlon knowingly made false or misleading statements, but based on the new evidence that he was working, he was satisfied that the benefit was not payable and should be refunded. The Minister sought to recover a sum of IEP 43,000 from the defendant.

817. The Supreme Court, in a judgment delivered by Fennelly J, held that the provisions, which originally came into force between 1991 and 1993, had a retrospective effect and that the Minister was entitled to recover a payment made in the period 1985–1991, even though they would not have been recoverable at the time, as no false or misleading statement had been found by the appeals officer. The Court, which took a different view on this issue from that of Laffoy J in the High

1325. The Child Appeals Officer held that the provisions of Art. 246(1) could not be applied, by analogy, to the provision of information by Tusla: *Social Welfare Appeals Office Report 2016*, 104.
1326. Article 246(3) as substituted by S.I. No. 511 of 2014. *See also* s. 342A as inserted by SWPA 2011.
1327. As amended by SWLRPA 2006, s. 36.
1328. [2001] IESC 1; [2001] 1 IR 64.

Court, held that the rule against retrospective legislation was designed to guard against injustice, in the sense that new burdens should not be imposed with respect to past actions. However, as a rule of construction and not of law, it amounted to a presumption that might be displaced by the clear words of a statute and, perhaps surprisingly, held that the wording of (what is now) section 301(1)(b) was sufficiently clear to require retrospective effect.

818. In addition, the Court held that, while a formal demand was required by (what is now) section 335, the letter conveying the decision of the deciding officer constituted a demand. The Act did not envisage that any new demand be made after the confirmation of the decision of the deciding officer by an appeals officer, and the claim could proceed on foot of the claim based on the original decision, including the demand made on foot thereof. Thus, the Court has given a broad, purposive interpretation of the overpayment provisions.

Chapter 6. Distribution of Assets

819. The SW Acts impose various obligations on the personal representative of a person who was in receipt of a social assistance payment (and, by implication, on the lawyers acting on behalf of such personal representatives). This has particular relevance to older persons in receipt of a State pension (non-contributory) or widow's (non-contributory) pension. The purpose of the legislation is to establish the means of a person at the time of his or her death, to compare this with the means as disclosed to the Department, and to recover any overpayment from the estate. This is a provision that is commonly applied.

820. Section 339(1) requires a personal representative of a person 'who was at any time in receipt of assistance', not less than three months before commencing to distribute the assets of that person, to inform the Minister in writing of his or her intention to distribute the assets and to provide the Minister with a schedule of the assets of the estate. The wording of this section is extremely broad, and it would, in practice, be difficult for a personal representative to know if a deceased person had been in receipt of any social assistance payment at any time. In practice, the provision is applied mainly in the case of State and widow(er)'s and SCP (non-contributory) pensions, as these are the groups of claimants for whom deaths mostly occur. On receipt of the relevant information, the Department will compare the schedule of assets with its own record of the claimant's means. If there is no discrepancy, the personal representative will be notified that he or she may proceed to distribute the assets. If, however, there is a discrepancy, the personal representative will be notified of this. If requested by the Minister within three months of providing the information, the personal representative must ensure that sufficient assets are retained to repay any sum that may be determined to be due to the Minister or the State with respect to payment of assistance to the person when the person was not entitled thereto, or payment in excess of the amount to which the person was entitled. For the purposes of determining the sum due to the Minister, the means of the deceased person for the period with respect to which assistance was paid to him or her, shall, in the absence of evidence to the contrary, be calculated on the basis that his or her assets at the time of death belonged to him or her for that entire period.

821. A personal representative who contravenes section 339(1) and distributes the assets without payment of the sum due to the Minister shall be personally liable to repay this amount to the Minister.[1329] Finally, any proceedings to recover assistance due to the Minister as a debt due to the State under section 341(3) must be brought against the estate of a deceased person within six years commencing on the date on which the notice and schedule of assets are received by the Minister.[1330]

1329. Section 339(3).
1330. Section 339(4).

Chapter 7. Recovery and Deductibility of Benefits in Personal Injury and Fatal Accident Claims

§1. PERSONAL INJURY CLAIMS

822. Section 2(1) of the Civil Liability (Amendment) Act of 1964 provides that in assessing damages in an action in respect of a wrongful act (including a crime) resulting in personal injury not causing death, account shall not be taken of, *inter alia*, 'any pension, gratuity or other like benefit payable under statute or otherwise in consequence of the injury'.[1331] This provision was amended to a certain extent by social welfare law.

823. Prior to August 2014, certain social welfare benefits could be taken into account in the calculation of damages for personal injury.[1332] However, the SWPA 2013 introduced a new approach whereby once a specified illness or disability payment is paid by the DSP to a person who is unable to work as a result of an accident, injury or disease, and that social welfare recipient has been compensated for that accident, injury or disease, whether by way of court settlement or otherwise, the amount of such illness-related social welfare payments that have also been paid as a consequence of that personal injury is to be repaid to the Minister by the person liable to pay compensation, which in most cases will be insurance companies. Depending on the circumstances, this amount can be partially or fully offset by the compensator against any compensation for loss of earnings or profits.

824. Section 13 of the SWPA 2013 inserts a new Part 11B (section 343L–343W), which provides that where a compensator (as defined in section 343M) intends to make a compensation payment to a person as a consequence of a non-fatal personal injury, the compensator must pay the Minister for Social Protection an amount equal to the illness and disability-related social welfare payments that have also been paid as a consequence of that personal injury. This applies notwithstanding section 2 of the Civil Liability (Amendment) Act 1964.[1333]

825. Section 343M provides that the provisions of Part 11B apply where: (a) a compensation payment is made by a compensator in respect of a non-fatal personal injury (on or after 1 August 2014), and (b) the injured person has received an illness-related social welfare payment as a result of that personal injury. However, section 343M(2) provides that recovery does not apply where compensation payments are made to an injured person:

(a) by the Hepatitis C and HIV Compensation Tribunal;

1331. As amended by the Civil Liability and Courts Act of 2004, s. 27.
1332. *See* the earlier editions of this book.
1333. Section 343M(4).

(b) by a court of competent jurisdiction to compensate certain persons who have contracted Hepatitis C or Human Immunodeficiency Virus within the State from the use of Human Immunoglobulin Anti-D, whole blood or other blood products;
(c) by the Residential Institutions Redress Board;
(d) by the Residential Institutions Statutory Fund Board;
(e) under the provisions of the Health (Repayment Scheme) Act 2006;
(f) by the Criminal Injuries Compensation Tribunal;
(g) in relation to disability caused by Thalidomide;
(h) in accordance with the Garda Síochána (Compensation) Acts 1941–2003; or
(i) by a tribunal, redress board or under a prescribed scheme of compensation.

826. The specified benefits are:

(a) IB;
(b) PCB;
(c) injury benefit (OIB);
(d) an increase of disablement pension (OIB), where the person is incapable of work and likely to remain permanently so incapable;
(e) IP; and
(f) DA.[1334]

827. Benefits are recoverable for the period beginning on the date on which the injured person first becomes entitled to a specified benefit as a result of the personal injury and ending on the earliest of the following: (a) five years from that date, (b) the date on which a compensator makes a compensation payment in final discharge of any claim in respect of the personal injury, or (c) the date on which an agreement is made whereby an earlier payment is treated as having been made in final discharge of the claim.[1335]

828. Section 343R(1) provides that a compensator (as defined by s. 343M) shall pay to the Minister the amount of recoverable benefits specified in the statement of recoverable benefits before making any compensation payment to, or in respect of, an injured person. S. 343(2) further provides that where the specified recoverable benefits exceed the amount of the relevant compensation payment and that relevant compensation payment was the subject of *an order of a court* or assessment by the Personal Injuries Assessment Board, the compensator is liable only to the extent of that amount so ordered or assessed. It appears that the practice had developed of insurance companies (the de facto compensator) seeking a consent order in relation to settlements with the result that the company was arguably not liable to repay sums which would have otherwise been due to the Minister (in effect the taxpayer).

1334. Section 343O.
1335. Section 343N.

High Court judges had taken different views as to whether or not this was consistent with the Act.[1336] Most recently, however, it appears that the Minister for Social Protection agrees with the interpretation that a 'consent settlement order' is not an 'order of a court' for the purposes of s. 343R(2) of the Social Welfare Consolidation Act, 2005.[1337]

§2. Fatal Injuries

829. In relation to fatal injuries, section 50(1) of the Civil Liability Act of 1961 provides that in assessing damages for fatal injuries:

> account shall not be taken of –
>
> (a) any sum payable on the death of the deceased under any contract of insurance;
>
> (b) any pension, gratuity or other like benefit payable under statute or otherwise in consequence of the death of the deceased.[1338]

830. The wording of this section is the same as that of section 2. In *State (Hayes) v. The Criminal Injuries Compensation Tribunal*,[1339] Finlay P said that section 50 clearly excluded the deduction of 'any social welfare benefit payable to a dependant' from an award of damages.[1340]

831. Section 96(3) provides that, notwithstanding section 50 of the 1961 Act, in assessing damages with respect to a person's death under Part IV of that Act, account may be taken of any death benefit (by way of a grant under section 84 with respect to funeral expenses) resulting from the person's death.

832. Section 285 provides that in assessing damages in any action under the Fatal Injuries Act of 1956 or Part IV of the Civil Liability Act of 1961, the following shall not be taken into account: CB, widow(er)'s or SCP (contributory) pension, guardian's payment (contributory and non-contributory), OFP in the case of a widow(er), and widow's or SCP (non-contributory) pension.[1341] White has argued that this section is otiose, as these payments would not be deductible in any case having regard to section 50.[1342]

1336. *See* against the practice, *Condon v. HSE; Szwarc v. Hanford Commercial Ltd. T/A Maldron Hotel Wexford* [2021] IEHC 474; *Fahy v. Padraic Fahy Tiling Contractors* [2021] IEHC 682; *Kuczak v. Treacy Tyres* [2022] IEHC 181 (Twomey J), *See contra Matthews v. Eircom* [2021] IEHC 456 where Cross J was prepared to allow the practice.

1337. *Kuczak v. Treacy Tyres [Portumna] Ltd (No. 2)* [2022] IEHC 619.

1338. As amended by the Civil Liability and Courts Act of 2004, s. 27.

1339. [1982] ILRM 210.

1340. At 212, albeit that the statement was *obiter*.

1341. Amended by SWLR&PA 2006, SW(MP)A 2010, and SW&PA 2010.

1342. At para. 9.4.09.

Chapter 8. Adjudication

833. This chapter looks at the social welfare decision and appeals system.[1343] Over one million new claims for social welfare benefits (in addition to review decisions) are adjudicated by deciding officers (and, in the case of SWA, designated persons) of the Department whose decisions may be appealed to appeals officers in the SWAO.[1344] The SWAO dealt with 18,507 appeals in 2018. This chapter outlines the operation of the social welfare decision and appeals system. It goes on to look at the operation of the SWA appeal system. We begin with a brief look at the rules of fair procedures as they apply to welfare appeals.

§1. Decisions, Appeals, and Fair Procedures

834. The constitutional right to fair procedures applies in relation to all appeals, whether there is a formal appeals system or not.[1345,1346] Broadly similar procedural entitlements are derived from Article 6 of the ECHR.[1347] The right to fair procedures means that the claimant is entitled to know the information upon which a decision has been made in relation to his or her case,[1348] he or she is entitled to see and comment on any reports or other documentation that may be relied on in coming to a decision on the case,[1349] and he or she is entitled to know the reasons for a decision to refuse the claim under appeal.[1350] In coming to a decision on an appeal, the adjudicating officer must come to a decision based on the evidence before him or her.[1351] The officer must not take into account irrelevant matters,[1352] nor must the officer allow a set rule or policy, or another office or organization, to dictate the outcome of the appeal.[1353] It is also clear that in some cases in which there is a direct conflict of evidence, the claimant should be entitled to an oral hearing of the case so that the claimant can present the evidence in person and so that he or she can

1343. There is no comprehensive appeal system in relation to healthcare. Such systems as do exist are discussed in Part III.

1344. On the historical development of these systems, *see* M. Cousins, 'Social Welfare Adjudication, 1847–1995', Ir. Jur. 27–30 (1993–1995): 361.

1345. *See generally* Hogan, Morgan & Daly, *Administrative Law in Ireland*, 5th ed. (Dublin: Round Hall, 2019).

1346. *Kiely v. Minister for Social Welfare* (No. 2) [1977] IR 267; *Duffy v. Eastern Health Board* unreported, High Court 14 Mar. 1988, *see* G. Whyte, 'Social Welfare Law 1987/88: The Year in Review', JISLL 7 (1988): 82, 103.

1347. *See generally* M. Cousins, 'The Implications of the European Convention on Human Rights for Social Security Appeals', EJSS 7 (2005): 180.

1348. *Kiely v. Minister for Social Welfare* (No. 2) [1977] IR 267; *State (Williams) v. Army Pension Board* [1983] IR 308.

1349. *Kiely v. Minister for Social Welfare* (No. 2) [1977] IR 267; *National Museum of Ireland v. Minister for Social Protection* [2016] IEHC 135; *Feldbrugge v. Netherlands* (1986) 8 EHRR 425; *HAL v. Finland*, Case 38267/97, 27 Jan. 2004.

1350. *State (Creedon) v. Criminal Injuries Compensation Tribunal* [1988] IR 51.

1351. And not material of which the claimant has no notice, *Kiely (No. 2)* [1977] IR 267.

1352. *State (Keller) v. Galway Co* [1958] IR 142.

1353. *State (Kershaw) v. Eastern Health Board* [1985] ILRM 235; *State (McLoughlin) v. Eastern Health Board* [1986] IR 416; *Galvin v. Chief Appeals Officer* [1997] 3 IR 240.

question any person who is giving evidence that is contrary to the claimant's case.[1354] The Irish courts have held that where the conflict of fact is a stark one and the resolution of this conflict is central to the fair disposition of the complaint, then it is impossible to avoid the conclusion that some form of an oral hearing is objectively necessary in order to give effect to (the constitutional guarantee of basic fairness of procedures).[1355] It also appears that appeals officers are, as a matter of fair procedures, required to give reasons for their decisions, at least when those decisions are being challenged.[1356]

835. The ECtHR has held that the provisions of Article 6(1) of the ECHR also apply to social welfare payments – both in relation to contributory and occupational injury benefits and also to non-contributory schemes when there is a legal right to payment – and to the payment of social insurance contributions.[1357] However, the provisions of the ECHR do not apply to initial decisions.

836. Article 6(1) provides that:

> In the determination of his civil rights and obligations … everyone is entitled to a fair and public hearing within a reasonable time by the independent and impartial tribunal established by law.

837. The Court has, for example, held that failure to allow an appellant to submit her views nor to afford her or her representative to consult medical reports in relation to her case was in breach of the Convention.[1358] The Court's case law in relation to failure to hold an oral hearing in a social welfare appeal has been somewhat inconsistent. In 2002, the Court held in a number of cases involving medical issues that an oral hearing was required to comply with the requirements of the Convention.[1359] In the subsequent *Miller* case, the Court again 'clarified' its approach. While holding (by the narrowest of majorities) that an oral hearing was required in that case, the Court stated that:

1354. *See Goldberg v. Kelly* 397 US 254.
1355. *See O'Neill v. Financial Services Ombudsman* [2014] IEHC 282 at [21], *see also Lyons v. Financial Services Ombudsman* [2011] IEHC 454, *Hyde v. Financial Services Ombudsman* [2011] IEHC 422 and *Smith v. Financial Services Ombudsman* [2014] IEHC 40. In relation to many appeals to the Social Welfare Appeals Office, the appellant will be entitled to an oral hearing in accordance with the statutory provisions (*see* below).
1356. *State (Creedon) v. Criminal Injuries Compensation Tribunal* [1988] IR 51; *M.D. v. Minister for Social Protection* [2016] IEHC 70; *National Museum of Ireland v. Minister for Social Protection* [2016] IEHC 135; *Brennan v. Minister for Employment Affairs and Social Protection* [2020] IEHC 393. Again, there are specific legislative provisions under the social welfare code (*see* below). Under the ECHR, *see Hirvisaari v. Finland* Case 49684/99, 27 Sep. 2001.
1357. *Feldbrugge v. Netherlands* (1986) 8 425; *Deumeland v. Germany* (1986) 8 EHRR 425, 448; *Salesi v. Italy* (1993) 26 EHRR 187; *Schuler-Zgraggen v. Switzerland* (1993) 16 EHRR 405; *Mennitto v. Italy* App. 33804/96, 5 Oct. 2000; *Schoulen v. Netherlands* (1994) 19 EHRR 432. *See* S. Jones, 'The Human Rights Act 1998 and the Appeals Service', JSSL 7 (2000): 134 at 146–152 and S. Jones, 'Case Digest', JSSL 7 (2000): 117.
1358. *Feldbrugge* at para. 44.
1359. *Lundevall v. Sweden*, App. No. 38629/97, and *Salmonson v. Sweden*, App. 38978/97, 12 Nov. 2002.

> The exceptional character of the circumstances that may justify dispensing with an oral hearing essentially comes down to the nature of the issues to be decided by the competent national court, not to the frequency of such situations. It does not mean that refusing to hold an oral hearing may be justified only in rare cases. For example, the Court has recognized that disputes concerning benefits under social-security schemes are generally rather technical, often involving numerous figures, and their outcome usually depends on the written opinions given by medical doctors. Many such disputes may accordingly be better dealt with in writing than in oral argument. Moreover, it is understandable that in this sphere, the national authorities should have regard to the demands of efficiency and economy. Systematically holding hearings could be an obstacle to the particular diligence required in social-security cases.[1360]

In *Miller*, the Court found that an oral hearing was necessary as it had been requested, the evidence as to the appellant's degree of disability and consequent extra costs was not straightforward, and oral evidence might have helped to clarify this situation.[1361]

838. It would appear that the Court will require an oral hearing unless (i) this is 'waived', that is, not requested; or (ii) when the case raises no question of fact or law that cannot adequately be resolved on the basis of written submissions (although the precise scope of this latter exception is far from clear). It should be noted that it is not necessary, under the Convention, for an oral hearing to be public in all cases, as Article 6(1) specifically provides that the press and public may be excluded when necessary on grounds, *inter alia*, of privacy.

839. As the provisions of the ECHR are taken into account in interpreting EU law, it is arguable that this guarantee of a fair hearing applies in all appeals involving claims under EU law, that is, in relation to the EU Regulation on the social security rights of migrant workers and the directive of equal treatment in social security.[1362]

§2. Social Welfare Decisions and Appeals

I. Decisions

840. Decisions relating to entitlement to social welfare payments and to the insurability of employment are made by 'deciding officers' appointed by the Minister.[1363] Section 300 provides that every question to which it applies, save when the context otherwise requires, shall be decided by a deciding officer. Section 300(2) specifies that this involves every question arising under:

1360. *Miller v. Sweden,* App. 55853/00, 8 Feb. 2005 at para. 29. The Court found a breach of Art. 6(1) by a 4–3 majority with one of the four doing so 'grudgingly'.
1361. *Miller v. Sweden,* at para. 34.
1362. Case 222/84, *Johnston v. Chief Constable of the R.U.C.* [1986] ECR 555, Case 222/86, *UNECTEF v. Heylens* [1987] ECR 4097.
1363. Sections 299 and 300.

(a) Part 2 (social insurance) being a question:
  (i) in relation to a claim for benefit;
  (ii) as to whether a person is or was disqualified for benefit;
  (iii) as to the period of any disqualification for benefit;
  (iv) as to whether an employment is or was insurable employment or insurable (occupational injuries) employment;
  (v) as to whether a person is or was employed in an insurable employment or insurable (occupational injuries) employment;
  (vi) as to what rate of employment contribution is or was payable by an employer in respect of an employed contributor;
  (vii) as to who is or was the employer of an employed contributor;
  (viii) as to whether a person is or was entitled to become a voluntary contributor;
  (ix) on any such other matter relating to Part 2 as may be prescribed;
  (x) as to whether an employment is or was an insurable self-employment;
  (xi) as to whether a person is or was in insurable self-employment; or
  (xii) as to what rate of self-employment contribution is or was payable by a self-employed contributor;
  (xiii) as to whether a contribution is or was payable in accordance with Chapter 5A or 5B of Part 2; or
  (xiv) as to the rate of contribution which is or was payable in accordance with Chapter 5A or 5B of Part 2.

(b) Part 3 (social assistance) other than Chapter 9 (SWA) except claims in respect of rent allowance or mortgage interest supplement or claims for SWA where the claimant is awaiting a decision on an application for a social insurance or social assistance payment or where such decision is under appeal.
(c) Part 4 (CB).
(d) Part 5 (CSG).
(e) Part 6 (WFP).
(f) Part 7 (continued payment for qualified children):[1364]
  (i) Part 7A (BTWFD).
(g) Part 8 (payments to persons in receipt of certain EU benefits living on certain islands).
(h) Part 9 (general provisions relating to social insurance, social assistance and insurability):
  (i) Part 11B (questions as to whether benefit or assistance paid to a claimant is a recoverable benefit within the meaning of Part 11B where the claimant is entitled to compensation in respect of a non-fatal personal injury.
(i) Part 12 (liability to maintain family).

Section 108(2A)[1365] also provides that the question of whether a person satisfies the criteria set out in the definitions of ‘homemaker’ and ‘home caring period’ in section 108(2) is a question that may be decided by a deciding officer.

1364. Note that by virtue of s. 234(1A), inserted by SW(MP)A 2015, s. 7, this payment ceased to be payable following the enactment of SW(MP)A 2015.
1365. Substituted by SW&PA 2008, s. 11(b).

841. Thus, deciding officers make all decisions concerning claims for and disqualification for all social insurance benefits and also decide all questions concerning entitlement to social assistance payments (except certain types of claims for SWA) and CB. They also decide questions relating to whether employment (including self-employment) is insurable under the SW Acts (i.e., whether a social insurance contribution is payable or not), what rate of contribution is payable, who is the insured person's employer, and whether a person is entitled to become a voluntary contributor. A deciding officer may refer a question to an appeals officer rather than deciding the question him or herself.[1366] Deciding officers are 'required to be free and unrestricted in discharging their functions'.[1367]

842. In a very limited number of cases involving decisions concerning persons who are the subject of investigation by the Criminal Assets Bureau, for security reasons, decisions are made by deciding officers who are members of the Bureau.[1368]

843. Administrative decisions are not decided by deciding officers but by other social welfare officials.[1369] Decisions relating to social welfare schemes that are not provided for in the SW Acts are also not made by deciding officers, for example, the household benefits and the fuel allowance. In addition, legislation has provided for administrative (in practice, computerized) decision-making in certain circumstances. Initially, provision was made for some specific claims. First, when a person is already in receipt of CB, section 300(5) provides for an administrative decision to award CB with respect to a second or subsequent child. Second, section 300(6) allows a bereavement grant or payment after death to be awarded administratively. Third, the intention of sections 113A and 113B appears to be to allow automatic payment of State pensions to persons in receipt of invalidity and State pensions (transition) immediately before reaching pension age.[1370] However, when any question arises subsequently as to whether any of the preceding payments are or are not payable or as to who is entitled to receive the payment, it is to be referred to a deciding officer for a decision.[1371] More recently, provision has been made for the wider use of computerized decision-making by section 15 of the SWP&CRA 2018, which inserts subsection 2A–2C into section 330 of the 2005 Act. Subsection 2A provides that the Minister may provide for an application to be made by electronic means in respect of a matter specified in section 300(2), while subsection 2B provides that the Minister may provide for the award of a payment in relation to any matter

1366. Section 303.
1367. *McLoughlin v. Minister for Social Welfare* [1958] IR 1.
1368. Criminal Assets Bureau Act of 1996. In such cases, an appeal goes to the Circuit Court rather than an appeals officer: s. 307(1A) as inserted by s. 7 SWA 2019.
1369. On the implications of the European Convention of Human Rights for decisions not covered by an appeals system, *see R. (Beeson) v. Dorset Co* [2001] EWHC Admin 986 and CIS 540/02.
1370. Section 113A & B (as inserted by SWLRPA 2006, s. 11) provide that 'pension shall be payable … in the case of a person … ' rather than the usual wording of 'a person shall be entitled'. Arguably, this does not give rise to any issue for a deciding officer under s. 300, although a specific clause ousting the deciding officer's jurisdiction might be preferable in terms of legal clarity.
1371. Section 300(7)–(10).

referred to in section 300(2) pursuant to an electronic application. However, subsection 2C provides that where pursuant to the making of an electronic application referred to in subsection 2A or the award of a payment referred to in subsection 2B, any question arises in respect of the electronic application or the payment, such question shall be decided in accordance with subsection 1, i.e., by a deciding officer.

844. Other exclusions from the remit of the deciding officer are questions concerning the granting of credited contributions and decisions to suspend payments. Such decisions, therefore, are not subject to appeal to an appeals officer.

845. When the deciding officer makes a decision, it must be given in writing and, when the decision is not in favour of the claimant, the deciding officer must set out the reasons for the decision, and a memorandum of this must be issued to the person as soon as is possible after the making of the decision.[1372] Decisions in relation to the insurability of employment and the reasons, therefore, are given to all parties who are subject to the decisions. Deciding officers are told that, while not legally necessary, it may be appropriate to give reasons for favourable decisions in certain circumstances.

846. In *Murphy v. Minister for Social Welfare*,[1373] a case involving a dispute as to the insurability of the applicant, Blayney J held that the deciding officer only had jurisdiction in relation to the question specifically before him, in that case as to the appropriate rate of contribution payable by the applicant. Blayney J held that the deciding officer did not have jurisdiction to decide that the applicant was not in insurable employment at all. It is submitted that this interpretation is excessively legalistic and is not justified by the broad terms of section 300.[1374]

847. In determining a person's entitlement to any benefit, assistance or CSG, a deciding officer or designated person may seek the opinion of a medical assessor in

1372. SW(CCP&C)R, Art. 191. In *A.M. v. Minister for Social Protection* [2013] IEHC 524 the High Court ruled that 'There is not an obligation on the Department to explain its decisions in detail but rather to inform applicants of the grounds for the decision so that the appeal is not impaired. Decision makers should not have to provide reasons that are extremely detailed explaining every step of the decision as this would render the process unworkable.' However, in *MD v. Minister for Social Protection* [2016] IEHC 70, Baker J indicated that an applicant is entitled to know whether the decision maker had directed his or her mind adequately to the issues before him or her. She held that reports from departmental medical assessors that were devoid of factual content or analysis, and followed almost exactly the statutory formula when indicating that the legislative test for qualifying for domiciliary care allowance was not met, did not provide the deciding officer with a factual basis on which the officer could compare or evaluate the cases for and against eligibility. Accordingly, the applicant had established that the deciding officer had failed properly to consider all the evidence furnished by her and was therefore in breach of fair procedures. In *National Museum of Ireland v. Minister for Social Protection* [2016] IEHC 135, Murphy J held that appeals officers must set out clearly the facts upon which the decision is based. *See also M.D. v. Minister for Social Protection* [2023] IEHC 88.

1373. [1987] 1 IR 295.

1374. *See* G. Whyte, *Social Inclusion and the Legal System: Public Interest Law in Ireland,* 2nd ed. (Dublin: IPA, 2015), 226–227.

respect of a non-exhaustive list of questions of a medical nature set out in subsection – section 300A(1) (inserted by section 10 SWMPA 2015. Section 300A(3) provides that where a medical assessor has provided an opinion in response to such a request, a deciding officer or designated person[1375] shall have regard to that opinion in deciding the question in respect of which the opinion was sought.[1376]

848. In *B. v. Minister for Social Protection,*[1377] Barrett J. held that a deciding officer had abdicated his statutory duty to decide an application for DCA in circumstances in which it was shown that the officer had not once departed from the opinion offered by a medical assessor in 3,806 cases. However, on appeal, this decision was overturned by the Court of Appeal, which held that the former section 186C(3) of the 2005 Act required the deciding officer to 'have regard' to the opinion of the medical assessor in such cases (*B v. Minister for Social Protection* [2016] IECA 116.) Hogan J. held, at 13, that the statement by a departmental official that the department does not, in fact, operate a fixed policy was entitled to evidential weight, and that Barrett J. had been incorrect to conclude that the department statement that it would be 'highly unusual' for a deciding officer not to follow the opinion of a medical assessor 'indicated that the deciding officer would or should just simply follow the opinion of the medical assessor' (at 22). Hogan J. also disagreed with the High Court's conclusion that 'a situation in which it is "highly unusual" for [deciding officers] to depart from [the views of medical assessors] suggests there to be a fettering of their role'. He stated, at 30, that:

> If it were indeed the case that the deciding officer regarded himself or herself as *bound* by the medical assessor's opinion, this would clearly amount to an unlawful fettering of discretion in the light of cases such as *McLoughlin.* While the deciding officer is required by statute to have regard to that opinion, he or she is nonetheless required to make his or her own independent decision. But short of that, the fact that the deciding officer invariably follows the views of the medical assessor is not in point. (emphasis in original).

He suggested at 31 that the analysis might 'be different if, for example, the statistical evidence had shown that a particular deciding officer had always (or almost always) decided in favour of the Minister'.

849. A deciding officer may revise a decision at any time if the original decision was erroneous in light of new evidence or new facts that came to light since the original decision; or by reason of some mistake having been made in relation to the law or the facts; or where the effect of the decision was to entitle a person to any benefit within the meaning of section 240, it appears to the deciding officer that

1375. Though s. 300A(3) does not explicitly refer to designated persons, s. 321, as amended by s. 18 SW&PA 2008, provides that, for the purpose of SWA, any reference to a decision in Part 10 of the 2005 Act shall be read as a reference to a determination by a designated person.

1376. By implication, this provision does not apply to appeals officers and so this leaves unaffected the ruling of the Supreme Court in *Kiely v. Minister for Social Welfare* (No. 2) [1977] IR 267 on the limited role of medical assessors in social welfare appeals.

1377. [2014] IEHC 186.

there has been a relevant change of circumstances which has come to notice since the decision was made.[1378] Section 302(a), as amended, provides that where the revised decision discontinues or reduces any benefit, assistance, WFP, continued payment for qualified children or BTWFD and the original decision or determination was given or continued in effect by reason of a false or misleading representation knowingly made or by reason of the wilful concealment of any material fact, the revised decision will take effect from the date on which the original decision or determination took effect, though the original decisions or determination may, at the discretion of the deciding officer, continue to apply to any period covered by it to which the false or misleading representation or the wilful concealment of any material fact does not relate. Section 302(b), as amended, provides that where any of the above payments are disallowed or reduced in a revised decision by virtue of new evidence or new facts coming to the attention of the deciding officer, the revised decision shall take effect from such date as the deciding officer shall determine, having regard to the new facts or new evidence and the circumstances of the case. In any other case, a revised decision shall take effect from the date considered appropriate by the deciding officer having regard to the circumstances of the case – section 302(c). An appeal can be made against a revision of a decision in the same way as an appeal against the original decision. A deciding officer cannot revise a decision that is under appeal unless the revision would be favourable to the claimant.[1379] In any other case, however, a deciding officer can revise a decision in a way that will be unfavourable to the claimant, for example, if he or she feels that the claimant is no longer entitled to the payment. However, before a deciding officer comes to a decision that the claimant who has been in receipt of a social welfare payment should have a continuing payment disallowed, the courts have held that the rules of natural justice require a pre-termination procedure.[1380] In particular, the deciding officer 'should inform the person concerned that the position is being reviewed by him, the grounds upon which he is considering disallowing further-payment and the person should be given the opportunity to answer the case made

1378. Section 301 as amended by s. 3(1)(a) SW&P(No.2)A 2013. In *Browning v. National Insurance Commissioner* [1984] 3 CMLR 192, the English Court of Appeal held that a change in benefits declared under EC Regulation 1408/71 was a 'relevant change of circumstances'. Following this decision, the Court in *Chief Adjudication Officer v. McKiernon* (reported in R(I) 2/94) held that a retrospective change in law was also a relevant change of circumstances – although expressing the view, *obiter*, that a change in the interpretation of the law by an appellate court would not because the court would be merely declaring the law as it has always been. The view that a change in the interpretation of the law by an appellate court does not amount to a change in the law was followed in the Scottish case of *In the petition of Sodagar Chowdry* [2000] ScotCS 86. This is a somewhat artificial approach, and it would appear that the Irish authorities would, in practice, revise a decision where a court indicated that the previous interpretation was incorrect (on the basis that a mistake had been made in relation to the law). It would appear that the relevant UK legislation differed from the Irish legislation in that it did not specifically provide for revision in the case of mistake of law in all circumstances.

1379. Section 301(3).

1380. *Thomson v. Minister for Social Welfare* [1989] IR 618. In *State (Hoolahan) v. Minister for Social Welfare* unreported High Court 23 Jul. 1986, Barron J stated that the claimant 'should know fully the extent of the case being made against her and that no decision should be made until she has been given proper opportunity to deal fully with a case'.

against him'.[1381] This need not involve an oral hearing, and the deciding officer may inform the person either in person or by letter.[1382]

850. Decisions may be revised on receipt of notification that the claimant has submitted an appeal, although there is no statutory framework for such a process. Deciding officers are advised that the arguments put forward by the appellant should be carefully examined to see whether the decision should be revised, wholly or in part, or whether it should stand. In practice, almost all appeals in which there is a dispute about medical incapacity or disablement are referred by the Department for a further medical opinion from the Department's Medical Assessors. If a more favourable medical decision is given, the deciding officer will revise the decision in favour of the claimant. In an appeal in which there is a dispute about means, the Department may arrange for a further investigation by a social welfare inspector. If the deciding officer decides to revise the decision by allowing the case *in part only*, the person will be asked whether he or she is satisfied with the revised decision or whether he or she wishes to pursue the appeal.

851. In *McDonagh v. Chief Appeals Officer,*[1383] the Supreme Court held that a refusal on the part of a deciding officer to revise an earlier decision of another deciding officer was itself a decision against which an appeal could be taken.

852. In some cases, a deciding officer will have access to a report from a Departmental inspector[1384] when deciding a case. The powers of social welfare inspectors are set out in section 250 of the 2005 Act as amended. Essentially an inspector may investigate and report on any claim for payment of social welfare or any application for, or use of, a Personal Public Service number referred to the inspector by the Minister and for that purpose may require certain designated persons, such as the claimant, spouse, civil partner, employer, personal representative of the deceased, to furnish, within prescribed time limits, such information and documentation as the inspector may reasonably require.[1385] An inspector may enter any premises liable to inspection under the Act – premises where persons were or are employed, where

1381. *Thomson* at 621.

1382. In the United States, the Supreme Court held that the constitutional guarantee of due process required that an oral hearing be held prior to termination of 'welfare' payments: *Goldberg v. Kelly* 397 US 254. However, the Court subsequently distinguished *Kelly* (arguably on somewhat unconvincing grounds) to hold that an oral hearing was not required prior to termination of disability benefits: *Mathews v. Eldridge*, 424 US 319. And *see Richardson v. Wright* 405 US 208.

1383. [2021] IESC 33.

1384. Section 15 of the Social Welfare and Pensions Act 2014 now provides, among other things, for members of the Gardaí seconded to the Minister to exercise the powers and duties of a social welfare inspector. Such Gardaí remain under the general direction and control of the Commissioner of the Garda Síochána and retain all the powers and duties of a member of the Garda Síochána – s. 250(1C)–(1D).

1385. Section 250(2). In the context of a claim for rent supplement pursuant to s. 198(3), a landlord may be required to provide a written statement confirming that the claimant is his/her tenant, indicating whether the landlord is receiving rent solely from the claimant or from any other person under the tenancy, specifying the period of the tenancy and confirming that the claimant resides at the residency for the period for which supplement has been, or is to be, paid – s. 250(2A)(a), inserted by SW&PA 2012, s. 14. A landlord may also be required to provide such other information, in

there are or have been self-employed persons or where documents relating to employees or self-employed persons are kept[1386] – at all reasonable times and carry out such examination or enquiry, inspect and take copies of any records found there and remove and retain those records for such period as may be reasonable for further examination where any such action is necessary to ascertain whether the 2005 Act is being complied with.[1387] S/he may also secure records for later inspection and may question every person found on the premises, or whom s/he has reasonable cause to believe to be or to have been an insured person and to require every such person to sign a declaration of the truth of the matters in respect of which the person is examined.[1388] An inspector may also require certain specified persons to attend departmental offices to answer questions[1389] or to hand over specified documents either at such office or at the person's residence.[1390] An inspector may be accompanied by a member of the Garda Síochána when exercising any power under section 250.[1391] In order to ensure compliance with the 2005 Act, inspectors accompanied by Gardaí or customs officials may also stop vehicles in order to question the driver and/or passengers.[1392] While attending any port or airport for the purpose of ensuring compliance with the 2005 Act, an inspector who has reasonable grounds to believe that there has been a contravention of the Act and who is accompanied by a member of the Garda Síochána, an officer of Customs and Excise or immigration, may, on the production of his/her certificate of appointment, question any passenger in relation to any matter concerning compliance with the Act and may request such person to produce any document or other information that the inspector may reasonably require for the purposes of establishing the identity and, where appropriate, habitual residence of the person.[1393] Wilfully obstructing or delaying an inspector in the exercise of any duty or power under section 250 or refusing or neglecting to answer any question or give any information or produce any record when required to do so under section 250 or concealing or preventing or attempting to conceal or prevent any person from appearing before or being examined by a social welfare inspector is an offence.[1394]

---

writing, relating to the tenancy of the claimant as the inspector may reasonably require for the purpose of his/her investigation – s. 250(2A)(b), inserted by SW&PA 2012, s. 14.

1386. Section 250(8).

1387. Section 250(3)(a)–(b). In carrying out an enquiry in relation to Ch. 2 of Part 2 of the 2005 Act relating to employed contributors and employment contributions, an inspector may also enquire as to whether s. 121(1)(a) of the Pensions Board is being complied with and to report, if necessary, to the Pensions Board.

1388. Section 250(3)(c)–(d).

1389. Section 250(3)(e).

1390. Section 250(4)–(4A), inserted by SWA 2011, s. 13(7). In the case of records required under regulations made under s. 17(5) of the 2005 Act, an inspector may also require that these be produced at the person's principal place of business – s. 250(11).

1391. Section 250(15).

1392. Section 250(16).

1393. Section 250(16B) inserted by SW&PA 2012, s. 17.

1394. Section 250(6).

853. Authorized officers appointed by the Minister pursuant to section 250B may require a financial institution to produce records that contain or, in the officer's reasonable opinion, may contain information relevant to a possible contravention of the social welfare code.[1395]

II. Appeals

854. The SWAO was established in 1990 as an independent office with its own separate premises and staff.[1396] The Chief Appeals Officer is responsible for the distribution of appeals to the appeals officer and, ultimately, for the overall operation of the SWAO.[1397] All appeals officers are appointed by the Minister.[1398] Appeals officers are quasi-judicial officers and are 'required to be free and unrestricted in discharging their functions'.[1399] However, the Supreme Court has also held that decisions by appeals officers (and deciding officers) are 'inherently administrative' and that the fact that such officers are bound to act judicially does not alter the character of their functions.[1400]

855. Any person who is dissatisfied with a decision given by the deciding officer[1401] may appeal to an appeals officer[1402] by giving notice of appeal to the

1395. Section 250A, inserted by SW&P(No.2)A 2009, s. 17.
1396. The provisions concerning appeals are set out in Ch. 2 of Part 10 of the Act and in the Social Welfare (Appeals) Regulations, 1998 [S.I. No. 108 of 1998].
1397. By virtue of s. 305(1)(b) as amended by SWA 2021, s. 17, the Minister may designate one or more of the other appeals officers to act as deputies for the Chief Appeals Officer when the latter is not available.
1398. It is submitted that this is not necessarily inconsistent with the appeals officers constituting an 'independent and impartial' tribunal for the purposes of Art. 6(1) of the ECHR. *See Ettl v. Austria* [1988] 10 EHRR 255 and the UK case of *R. (Hamid Ali Hussain) v. Secretary of State for the Home Department* [2001] EWHC Admin 852. SWMPA, s. 22 removed the requirement that appeals officers (other than the chief and deputy chief appeals officers) be 'officers of the Minister'.
1399. *McLoughlin v. Minister for Social Welfare* [1958] IR 1.
1400. *Minister for Social, Community and Family Affairs v. Scanlon* [2001] 1 IR 64 at 87.
1401. However, no appeal may be taken against a decision of a deciding officer that where a claimant is entitled to compensation in respect of a non-fatal personal injury, the party paying the compensation must pay to the Minister an amount equal to the illness-related social welfare payments made to the claimant, subject to a maximum of five years' payments, unless this sum has already been paid to the Minister – s. 311(4) as amended by s. 12(1)(b) SW(MP)A 2015.
1402. Where a person appeals a decision of a deciding officer, (other than a bureau officer) and the Chief Appeals Officer certifies that the ordinary appeals procedures are inadequate to secure the effective processing of an appeal, the appeal is submitted to the Circuit Court – s. 307(1) as amended by s. 7 SWA 2019. In the case of an appeal against a decision of a bureau officer concerning a Criminal Assets Bureau case, the Chief Appeal Officer must issue a direction to the appellant directing him or her to submit the appeal within twenty-one days of receipt of the direction to the Circuit Court – s. 307(1A) as inserted by s. 7 SWA 2019. No appeal lies from a decision of the Circuit Court on an appeal in either of these two types of cases – s. 307(3). On the operation of these provisions *see Hoey v. Chief Appeals Officer*, unreported, High Court, Barrett J., 21 Dec. 2016.

Chief Appeals Officer within the time laid down.[1403] Therefore, any claimant who is dissatisfied with a decision can appeal against that decision. An employer who is dissatisfied with a decision regarding, for example, insurability or rate of contributions can also appeal against a decision. To appeal, the claimant must give notice, in writing, to the Chief Appeals Officer within twenty-one days from the date on which the claimant received notification of the decision.[1404] However, a notice of appeal given outside this time can be accepted with the consent of the Chief Appeals Officer.[1405] The notice of appeal should contain a statement of the facts and the contentions upon which the claimant intends to rely, that is, the grounds of the appeal. Any written evidence, for example, medical reports, etc., should be submitted with the notice of appeal.[1406] If written evidence is not available when the appeal is being submitted, it can be submitted at a later date. The appeals officer may require the appellant, the deciding officer or the designated officer, as the case may be, or any other person appearing to the appeals officer to be concerned, to furnish to him or her, in writing, further particulars regarding the appeal.[1407] The appeals officer also has the power to allow the claimant to raise matters at the appeal that were not mentioned in the appeal notice. Any person who wishes to withdraw an appeal can do so by sending a notice of withdrawal to the Chief Appeals Officer.[1408]

856. When the Chief Appeals Officer receives a notice of appeal, he or she must send it to the Department, which is required to return (i) a statement from the deciding officer setting out to what extent the claimant's facts or arguments are admitted or disputed, and (ii) any information, document, or item that the deciding officer has that is relevant to the appeal.[1409]

857. Hearings: The Social Welfare (Appeals) Regulations provide (in Article 3) that 'hearing' means 'an oral hearing', but Article 13 provides that where the appeals officer is of the opinion that the case is of such a nature that it can properly be determined without a hearing, he or she may determine the appeal summarily. About one-third of appeals are now heard orally, mainly in relation to issues such as illness, disability, occupational injury, care, and unemployment appeals. Questions concerning the means test are more often dealt with summarily. Oral hearings are held in private.[1410] Under the relevant Regulations, an appeals officer has discretion as to whether to grant an oral hearing or not, but this is not an unlimited

1403. Section 311. In *O'Connor v. Chief Appeals Officer* [2021] IEHC 155, Heslin J refused to set aside a decision of the Chief Appeals Officer refusing to hear an appeal because it had been lodged out of time. The application in this case had been lodged 138 days after the original decision, which Heslin J characterised as a significant delay, and no explanation had been provided for the failure to bring the appeal in time.
1404. Article 9.
1405. Article 9(2).
1406. Article 9(4).
1407. Article 12.
1408. Article 9(5).
1409. Article 10.
1410. Quaere whether this position in light of Art. 6(1) of the European Convention on Human Rights although, as noted above, Art. 6(1) allows non-public hearings where necessary on grounds of privacy.

discretion.[1411] The basic rule is that the claimant should be given an oral hearing unless the case can properly be determined without one. The Supreme Court, in interpreting the relevant provisions, has stated that:

> An oral hearing is mandatory unless the case is of such a nature that it can be determined without an oral hearing, that is, summarily. An appeal is of such a nature that it can be determined summarily if a determination of the claim can fairly be made on a consideration of the documentary evidence. If, however, there are unresolved conflicts in the documentary evidence, as to any matter essential to a ruling of the claim, the intention of the Regulations is that those conflicts shall be resolved by an oral hearing.[1412]

858. In *Galvin v. Chief Appeals Officer*,[1413] a case concerning a dispute as to whether social insurance contributions had been paid in the past by the applicant, Costello P held that:

> There are no hard and fast rules to guide an Appeals Officer … as to when the dictates of fairness require the holding of an oral hearing. The case (like others) must be decided on the circumstances pertaining, the nature of the inquiry being undertaken by the decision-maker, the rules under which the decision-maker is acting, and the subject matter with which he is dealing and account should also be taken as to whether an oral hearing was requested.

In that case, the Court came to the conclusion that an oral hearing had been necessary as otherwise, it would have been extremely difficult, if not impossible, to arrive at a true judgment on the issues because of a range of factors, including the distant time period to which the dispute referred (between thirty-six and fifty years previously) and departmental errors in relation to the contribution record.

859. In *L.D. v. Chief Appeals Office*,[1414] Peart J held that an appeals officer revising an existing decision of an appeals officer pursuant to section 317 of the 2005 Act may do so by way of an oral hearing. In the companion case of *Smith v. Chief Appeals Officer*,[1415] the same judge held that the Chief Appeals Officer could proceed likewise when revising the decision of an appeals officer pursuant to section 318 of the 2005 Act. A difficulty with the decision in *L.D.*, however, is that section 317 only applies where there are new facts or new evidence. Peart J suggested that

1411. Articles 13 & 14. Section 326 gives the Minister the power to direct that an oral hearing be held in a particular case. The policy objective of this section is unclear and it does not appear to be used in practice.
1412. *Kiely v. Minister for Social Welfare* (No. 2) [1977] IR 267 at 278. The onus of identifying the unresolved conflicts in the documentary evidence lies on the appellant and simply asserting a state of affairs, without providing any further detail, does not establish a conflict requiring an oral hearing – *see FD v. Chief Appeals Officer* [2022] IEHC 454. For the right to an oral hearing under the Irish Constitution and the European Convention on Human Rights, *see* above paras 834–838.
1413. [1997] 3 IR 240.
1414. [2014] IEHC 641.
1415. [2014] IEHC 633.

it was arguable that a request for an oral hearing could itself constitute a new fact, even if it could not constitute new evidence, thereby enabling an appeals officer to decide *proprio moto* to hold an oral hearing once asked to do so and to hold it for the purpose of a section 317 revision. However, this is questionable. The new facts or evidence must relate to the original claim for benefit, and a request for an oral hearing has nothing to do with this.[1416]

860. Assessors: Assessors are appointed by the Chief Appeals Officer on the nomination of the trade unions and employer organizations.[1417] They are asked to serve on a *rota* basis and do so about twice a year. Two assessors are called to oral hearings involving JB or allowance claims, one from the employers' panel and the other from the trade union panel.[1418] If either or both assessors are not present, the appeals officer must get the claimant's consent before the appeal can go ahead. If the claimant does not wish to consent to this, the appeal cannot go ahead and must be adjourned.[1419] It is quite usual for either or both of the assessors to be absent. The assessors do not decide on the appeal and do not have any say in the appeals officer's decision. Their function is simply to assist the appeals officer with their local knowledge of the employment situation. The Supreme Court has interpreted the role of the assessor very narrowly and has held, in the case of a medical assessor, that the assessor should not take an active part in the appeal or ask questions

1416. Peart J. commented *obiter*, at para. 32, that the new facts or new evidence referred to in s. 317(1)(a) of the Act:

> are not confined to matters that may have happened or been generated since the decision, but may consist of material or evidence which, though it existed before the appeal decision was made, was not before the appeals officer at the time the appeal decision was made.

He did not consider whether there were any restrictions on what could be considered to be 'new'. However, in *R. v. Medical Appeal Tribunal (North Midland Region), ex parte Hubble* [1959] 2 QB 408, [1959] 3 All ER 40, where the English Court of Appeal considered the meaning of 'fresh evidence' in light of which a decision could be revised, Morris LJ stated, at pp. 424 and 47 respectively, that this meant:

> some evidence which the claimant was unable to produce before the decision was given or which he could not reasonably be expected to have produced in the circumstances of the case.

The court rejected the argument that 'fresh evidence' simply meant some further or additional evidence not presented at the original hearing. In *Iarnród Éireann v. Social Welfare Tribunal* [2007] IEHC 406, Murphy J. (again *obiter*) took a similar approach stating, at para. 8.2, that:

> If new evidence is to be construed as 'fresh evidence' then such a reference in an enactment imports the usual legal meaning of this phrase as evidence which is not merely additional to that adduced on the former occasion but could not be [sic.] reasonably have been expected to be produced then.

1417. Section 309.
1418. A number of types of appeal are excluded: (a) means test; (b) dependency and cohabitation; (c) concurrent working and claiming; (c) the couple limitation; (e) late claims and backdating of payments; and (f) the HRC: *Social Welfare Appeals Office Report 2004*, 8.
1419. Section 315 and *see Thomson v. Minister for Social Welfare* [1989] IR 618.

directly of the claimant.[1420] This decision, based on case law under the Workman's Compensation Act,[1421] is arguably not appropriate to the much different role that an assessor should play in unemployment appeals. Such assessors should, and frequently do in practice, take a sufficiently active part in the appeal to allow them to properly assist the appeals officer with their expert knowledge.[1422]

861. Representation: If an oral hearing is granted, the claimant may appear in person. The appeals officer can award the claimant travelling expenses. The appeals officer may also award any other expenses that the claimant incurs in attending the appeal, for example, if the claimant has to take time off work.[1423] A claimant may, with the permission of the appeals officer, be represented by a member of the family or by any other person.[1424] In practice, the appeals officer will almost always give this permission.[1425] The Government-funded Legal Aid Board cannot represent the claimant at a social welfare appeal because such appeals do not fall within the scope of civil legal aid. In *Corcoran v. Minister for Social Welfare*,[1426] Murphy J held that there was no authority for the proposition that a lay tribunal exercising a quasi-judicial function must afford to the parties an opportunity to procure legal advice and be represented by lawyers or that the State should be bound to pay for such assistance. If a solicitor or other representative appears at the appeal, the appeals officer can award expenses only with respect to that person's actual attendance.[1427] The deciding officer may appear at the appeal, although it is less usual for this to happen, or he or she may be represented by another officer of the Department or any other person appointed by the Minister. Any other person who, in the opinion of the appeals officer, should be heard may also appear at the hearing, for example, an employer in a question involving dismissal from work.

862. Evidence, Witnesses and Procedure: In dealing with an appeal, the appeals officer is not confined to the grounds on which the deciding officer decided the case

1420. *Kiely*. For decisions in other jurisdictions, *see R. v. Deputy Industrial Injuries Commissioner, ex parte, Jones* [1962] 2 All ER 430 and *Richardson v. Perales* 402 US 389.
1421. *Delaney v. Valentine* [1945] IR 1.
1422. On the role of medical assessors in relation to the making of decisions by deciding officers, *see* above, paras 847–848.
1423. Section 316.
1424. Article 15.
1425. However, in *Corcoran v. Minister for Social Welfare* [1991] 1 IR 175, Murphy J expressed the view that a solicitor could not, as a matter of right, attend a hearing although it would have been 'churlish' if the appeals officer had refused to hear a solicitor.
1426. [1991] 1 IR 175. However, the case law of the European Court of Human Rights would suggest that where legal aid was essential to allow access to the courts, e.g., in a case of great legal complexity, legal aid would be required under Art. 6(1) of the ECHR.
1427. Section 316 provides that in relation to appeals, an appeals officer may make an award to a person appearing before the officer towards the person's expenses. 'Expenses' means: (i) expenses necessarily incurred by the appellant or a witness in respect of his or her travel and subsistence or loss of remuneration; and (ii) in the case of a person appearing before an appeals officer in a representative capacity, an amount only in respect of that person's actual attendance. This is a legislative reversal of *O'Sullivan v. Minister for Social Welfare*, unreported, High Court, 9 May 1995, Barron J.

but may decide the question as if it were being decided for the first time.[1428] The procedure at the hearing is determined by the appeals officer. In practice, the procedure is informal, and the appeal usually takes the form of a question and answer session between the appeals officer and the claimant. Thus, given the frequent absence of any Departmental representative, the hearing normally assumes an investigative rather than an adversarial approach, with the appeals officer explaining the background of the case and the reasons for the Department's decision and then clarifying the claimant's case by questioning him or her and any relevant witnesses.[1429] The appeals officer can hear evidence from any person concerned in the appeal or any person whom the appeals officer feels should be heard. The appeals officer may also admit any duly authenticated written statement as prima facie evidence if he or she thinks that it is appropriate to do so.[1430] However, it appears that written evidence should be outweighed if a witness can give credible oral evidence contradicting the written statement.[1431] For example, the appeals officer can admit a report from the Department's medical referee stating that, in the medical referee's opinion, the appellant is capable of work as evidence of that fact. However, if the appellant's doctor attends the appeal and gives credible evidence that contradicts the written report, this should outweigh the medical referee's evidence.[1432] Therefore, it is important for the claimant to make sure that any necessary witnesses attend the appeal. In the case of a medical appeal, the appeals officer can award expenses to the claimant's doctor if he or she attends as a witness.[1433]

863. The appeals officer has the power to take evidence under oath and may administer oaths to people who attend as witnesses at the hearing.[1434] The appeals

1428. Section 311(3).
1429. Article 18. In *O'B v. Chief Appeals Officer* [2014] IEHC 48, Baker J held, *inter alia*, that a claimant pursuing a social welfare appeal is not entitled to insist on the attendance of the deciding officer at the appeal as the function of a deciding officer at an appeal is not to give evidence but, rather, to defend the original decision. While Art. 15(3) of S.I. No. 108 of 1998 allows a deciding officer or designated person to appear at the hearing of an appeal, Baker J held that the word 'appear' in this provision meant 'attend', not 'give evidence'.
1430. The Supreme Court in *Kiely* seemed to be of the opinion that appeals were intended to operate on an adversarial basis with a representative of the Department attending to argue its case. This certainly does not happen in practice and, in the author's opinion, it is questionable if such an approach would be in the claimant's best interests.
1431. Article 18(3).
1432. *Kiely*. This is contrary to the position at common law: *Williamson v. Secretary of State for Work & Pensions* [2010] ScotCS CSIH 4.
1433. In practice, a rigid interpretation of *Kiely* might require the Department to have its medical referees available to give evidence in each appeal in case conflicting oral evidence was given. This could give rise to great practical difficulties. *See* the very similar US case of *Richardson v. Perales* 402 US 389, in which the Supreme Court held that written reports by doctors which had examined a claimant for disability benefits did constitute 'substantial evidence' supporting a finding of non-disability despite the absence of cross-examination and the opposing testimony of the claimant and his medical witness. *See also Passmore v. Astrue* 533 F.3d 658 (8th. Circuit 2008); B.S. Dixon, 'There but for the Grace of God Go I: The Right of Cross-Examination in Social Security Disability Hearings', MLR 74 (2009): 823 and V.G. Rosenblum, 'The Right to Cross-Examine Physicians in Social Security Disability Cases', FSULR 26 (1999): 1049.
1434. Section 313.

officer also has the power to require any person to attend to give evidence or to produce any documents relating to the appeal.[1435] A notice requiring a person's attendance must be either given to him or her in person or by sending by registered post to the address at which the person ordinarily resides or at his or her place of business.[1436] A person who has received such a notice and who refuses or wilfully neglects to attend or to give evidence or to produce documents is guilty of an offence and will be liable, on summary conviction, to a fine not exceeding EUR 1,500.[1437] When a person required to attend to give evidence or to produce documents fails to do so, the appeals officer may, on serving notice on that person, apply to the District Court for an order directing the person to attend or to produce the documents.[1438] If, once notice of the hearing has been given, the claimant or any other party fails to attend, the appeals officer may take such steps as he or she thinks appropriate, including deciding the appeal in the claimant's absence.[1439] The appeals officer may postpone or adjourn the appeal from time to time.[1440] If the claimant is unable to attend the appeal, an adjournment may be requested by contacting the appeals office. This will normally be allowed if there is a legitimate reason for asking for an adjournment.

864. Appeal Decision: If an oral hearing is held, the appeals officer normally does not give a decision there and then. The appeals officer sends the decision as soon as possible to the Chief Appeals Officer, who then notifies the claimant of the decision. When the decision is not in the claimant's favour, the appeals officer must give a note of the reasons for the decision, and this will also be sent to the claimant.[1441] The reasons should make clear to the unsuccessful appellant in 'general and broad terms' the grounds of the decision.[1442] Unlike the position in the UK, appeals officers' decisions are not publicly available, but in recent years, sample case studies have been reported in the annual report of the Chief Appeals Officer and are now reported on the Website of the office.[1443]

865. The question of the publication of decisions by administrative tribunals was considered by the Supreme Court in *Atanasov v. Refugee Appeals Tribunal.*[1444] Geoghegan J (for the Court) said that:

> fair procedures require some reasonable mechanisms for achieving consistency in both the interpretation and the application of the law in cases … of a similar category. Yet, if relevant previous decisions are not available to an

1435. Section 314.
1436. Section 314(2).
1437. Section 314(3).
1438. Section 314(4).
1439. Article 16.
1440. Article 18(2).
1441. Article 18.
1442. *See State (Creedon) v. Criminal Injuries Compensation Tribunal* [1988] IR 5; *Crake v. Supplementary Benefits Commission* [1982] 1 All ER 498.
1443. www.socialwelfareappeals.ie.
1444. [2006] IESC 53.

> appellant, he or she has no way of knowing whether there is such consistency. It is not that a member of a tribunal is actually bound by a previous decision but consistency of decisions based on the same objective facts may, in appropriate circumstances, be a significant element in ensuring that a decision is objectively fair rather than arbitrary.

Accordingly, the Court ruled that an appellant's rights to fair procedures and natural and constitutional justice under Article 40.3 of the Constitution meant that he or she was entitled to obtain relevant tribunal decisions (where so requested). The position of the SWAO is not on all fours with the Refugee Appeals Tribunal in that some decisions are published (albeit in 'case study' format), and a system of precedent does not generally apply; that is, one appeals officer is not bound by the decision of another. However, the *Atanasov* case does suggest that a social welfare appellant would also be entitled to request copies of relevant and material decisions that might be of importance (when such exist) and, more generally, suggests the need for a greater focus on publishing in full all important decisions of the appeals officers on an ongoing basis.

866. In the decision of *Jama v. Minister for Social Protection*, the High Court distinguished *Atanasov* and held that there was no duty on the DSP to maintain a database or open library of decisions to which the public may have access and, therefore, no question of a right of access thereto arose.[1445] Indeed, there was no evidence that any relevant decisions existed in that case. However, the analysis of the legal issues in *Jama* may be open to question, and it is not clear that this is the final word on the matter.[1446]

III. Further Appeal

867. An appeals officer's decision is stated to be final and conclusive,[1447] but there are several ways in which such a decision can be challenged.

868. Revision by an Appeals Officer: An appeals officer may, at any time and from time to time, revise any decision of an appeals officer if the original decision appears to be wrong in light of new evidence or new facts that came to light since the original decision was made or, where the effect of the decision was to entitle a person to any benefit within the meaning of section 240, there has been a relevant change of circumstances which has come to notice since that decision was given.[1448] There is no set procedure for asking for a revision of a decision, and a

1445. [2011] IEHC 379 at para. 6.9.
1446. *See* now *Doyle v. Criminal Injuries Tribunal* [2020] IECA 342 where the Court of Appeal held that the inability of the appellants to access any information as to how the Tribunal applied specific provisions in the past was in breach of their constitutional right to fair procedures.
1447. Section 320, as amended by s. 13 SW&PA 2014.
1448. Section 317 as amended by s. 4(1) SW&P(No.2)A 2013. The amendment was in response to the decision in *C.P. v. Chief Appeals* Officer [2013] IEHC 512 where the High Court ruled that the original s. 317 of the 2005 Act, empowering an appeals officer to review an earlier decision of an

claimant should simply write to the appeals office asking that the decision be revised and setting out the new facts, new evidence, or change of circumstances that would justify a revised decision. By virtue of section 319, as amended, the revised decision of an appeals officer takes effect on the same basis as the revised decision of a deciding officer, discussed above in paragraph 799.

869. Revision by the Chief Appeals Officer: The Chief Appeals Officer may, at any time and from time to time, revise the decision of an appeals officer if it appears that the decision was wrong because of a mistake in relation to the law or to the facts.[1449] Therefore, the claimant does not need to show new facts or new evidence to have a decision revised. In *Castleisland v. Minister for Social and Family Affairs,* the Supreme Court commented that this provision did not confer a 'double appeal'.[1450] Rather, what is envisaged is that the Chief Appeals Officer would review the materials before the appeals officer to establish whether there was any error of fact or law. It is essentially 'a revising rather than an appellate procedure'.[1451] Again, there are no set procedures for seeking such a review.[1452] The Chief Appeals Officer may refuse to revise the decision, he or she may allow the appeal, or he or she may set aside the appeals officer's decision and arrange a new hearing before a different appeals officer. The Chief Appeals Officer will normally only revise an appeals officer's decision if it is clearly wrong and one that no reasonable appeals officer would have come to or if a serious mistake was made in hearing the appeal.

870. Revision by a Deciding Officer: A deciding officer may revise a decision of an appeals officer where the effect of the decision entitles a person to any benefit within the meaning of section 240, and it appears that there has been a relevant change of circumstances that have come to notice since the decision was made.[1453] This provision reverses the High Court decisions in *Lundy v. Minister for Social Welfare* and *O'Connor v. Minister for Social Welfare*, in which the Court held that there was no such power of revision under the legislation as it stood at that time.[1454]

---

appeals officer in light of new evidence, applied to cases in which a claim for a welfare payment had been rejected at the first appeal. On the meaning of 'new evidence' *see* para. 802 above. In *LL v. Chief Appeals Officer* [2021] IEHC 191, Owens J held that a claimant must be entitled to benefit or assistance at the time the claim is made and that, for the purpose of a review of a decision to refuse payment, it is not enough to establish that the conditions of entitlement were satisfied at some point after the claim was lodged. However, he also held that an appeals officer erred in law in deciding that, when reviewing an earlier decision, the only matter to be looked at was whether the evidence available at the time of that earlier decision showed it to be correct. In *F.D. v. Chief Appeals Officer* [2023] IECA 123, the Court of Appeal described the breadth of the revision provisions as 'possibly, unique in the field of the administration of public law'.

1449. Section 318.

1450. [2004] IESC 40.

1451. Insofar as anything in the judgment in *Maher v. Minister for Social Welfare* [2008] IESC 15 might appear inconsistent with this, it is submitted that the fully reasoned decision in *Castleisland* is to be preferred.

1452. The criticism of this approach by the High Court in *Castleisland Cattle Breeding Society Ltd v. Minister for Social and Family Affairs* [2003] IEHC 133 was not adopted by the Supreme Court.

1453. Section 301(1)(b) as substituted by s. 3(1)(a) SW&P(No.2)A 2013.

1454. [1993] 1 IR 406; High Court, unreported, 30 Apr. 1993.

The purpose is to clarify that deciding officers can revise a decision when there has been a change of circumstances and to avoid the administrative burden that would otherwise be imposed on appeals officers.

871. Appeal to the High Court: Section 320 provides that:

> The decision of an appeals officer on any question shall, subject to sections 301(1)(*b*), 317, 318, 324(1)(*c*), and 327, be final and conclusive.[1455]

This is subject to a specific right of appeal to the High Court on the point of law from an appeals officer's decision set out in the SW Acts.[1456] Section 327 provides that any person who is dissatisfied with (a) the decision of an appeals officer, or (b) the revised decision of the Chief Appeals Officer on any question may appeal that decision or revised decision to the High Court on any question of law.[1457] Although the reference to 'person' might have encompassed the Minister, section 327A specifically provides that where the Chief Appeals Officer revises (or does not revise), under section 318, a decision of an appeals officer, the Minister may appeal that decision to the High Court on any question of law.[1458] However, section 327(2) provides that such an appeal by the Minister shall not operate as a stay on the payment of benefit or assistance to a person arising from a decision of an appeals officer or the Chief Appeals Officer.

872. In addition, the Chief Appeals Officer may, when he or she considers it appropriate, refer a question, other than one to which s. 320 applies, to the High Court for a decision.[1459] By virtue of Ord.84C, r.2(5) of the Rules of the Superior Courts, any statutory appeal to the High Court must be taken within twenty-one days of receipt of the decision by the appellant or within such further period as the Court may allow where there was good and sufficient reason for extending that period and where the extension will not result in an injustice being done to any other person concerned in the matter.[1460]

873. In *Henry Denny*, a case brought under (the predecessor of) section 327, Hamilton CJ expressed the view that:

1455. As amended by SWMPA 2010, s. 15. Presumably, s. 327A (*see* below) should also be referred to here.
1456. Section 327 as amended by SWMPA 2010, s. 16. The amendment reflected the position in practice in light of the decision in *Kingham v. Minister for Social Welfare,* unreported High Court 25 Nov. 1985 in which Lynch J took a broad view of the High Court's jurisdiction in hearing such appeals, stating that legislation excluding the right of appeal should be construed narrowly so as not to oust the jurisdiction of the High Court save when such ouster was clear.
1457. In *Castleisland*, the Court suggested that the Act does not give a right of appeal where the Chief Appeals Officer decides not to revise a decision and here, the appeal lies from the original (unrevised) decision of the appeals officer.
1458. As inserted by SWMPA 2010, s. 16.
1459. Section 306.
1460. In *Mocanu v. Chief Appeals Officer* [2023] IECA 176, the Court of Appeal held, on the facts, that there were no grounds to justify an extension of the period within which to bring an appeal against a decision of an appeals officer to the High Court.

> The courts should be slow to interfere with the decisions of expert administrative tribunals. Where conclusions are based upon an identifiable error of law or an unsustainable finding of fact by a tribunal such conclusions must be corrected. Otherwise, it should be recognized that tribunals which have been given statutory tasks to perform and exercise their functions, as is now usually the case, with a high degree of expertise and provide coherent and balanced judgments on the evidence and arguments heard by them it should not be necessary for the courts to review their decisions by way of appeal or judicial review.[1461]

874. Keane J, in the same case, approved the Supreme Court decision in *Mara (Inspector of Taxes) v. Hummingbird Ltd*,[1462] a case concerning income tax appeals, in which Kenny J, speaking for the Court, said:

> A case stated consists in part of findings on questions of primary fact … These findings on primary facts should not be set aside by the courts unless there is no evidence whatever to support them. The commissioner then goes on in the case stated to give his conclusions or inferences from these primary facts. These are mixed questions of fact and law and the court should approach these in a different way. If they are based on the interpretation of documents, the court should reverse them if they are incorrect for it is in as good a position to determine the meaning of documents as is the commissioner. If the conclusions from the primary facts are ones which no reasonable commissioner could draw, the court should set aside his findings on the ground that he must be assumed to have misdirected himself as to the law or made a mistake in reasoning. Finally, if his conclusions show that he has adopted a wrong view of the law, they should be set aside. If, however, they are not based on a mistaken view of the law or a wrong interpretation of documents, they should not be set aside unless the inferences which he made from the primary facts were ones that no reasonable commissioner could draw.

875. In *Douglas v. Minister for Social Protection*, Charleton J stated that in hearing a section 327 appeal:

> the appeal jurisdiction which I am exercising is one which is limited to the High Court examining the original decision and deciding whether or not it is undermined by a serious and significant error or a series of errors which together amount to such an error.[1463]

876. The learned judge was applying his own ruling in *Manorcastle Ltd v. Commission for Aviation Regulation*[1464] which, in turn, adopted the approach of the

1461. *Henry Denny & Sons (Ireland) Ltd v. Minister for Social Welfare* [1998] 1 IR 37. For a case in which the courts actually applied this approach, *see ESB v. Minister for Social, Community and Family Affairs* [2006] IEHC 59.

1462. [1982] 2 ILRM 421.

1463. [2012] IEHC 27 at para. 2.

1464. [2008] IEHC 386.

Supreme Court in *Orange Communications v. Director of Telecommunications.*[1465] However, the statutory language involved in those cases was quite different from that of section 327 and did not specifically confine the appeal to a question of law. It is submitted that the approach adopted by Charleton J is not applicable to section 327 appeals and that, instead, the well-established law concerning appeals on a question of law should apply (as set out in *Henry Denny*).[1466]

877. In *Petecel v. Minister for Social Welfare,*[1467] the Supreme Court said that in an appeal under section 327, the High Court is asked to determine whether or not the task of interpreting and applying the provisions of the relevant legislation has been carried out correctly, by reference to the legislation and the evidence supporting the decision under appeal. The Court cannot take into account issues such as jurisdiction, whether the decision maker had acted in an *ultra vires* manner or whether the legislation might be unconstitutional.

878. Judicial review – The deciding officers and appeals officers are also subject to the general power of the High Court to judicially review any administrative decision.[1468] However, the question arises as to whether (and to what extent) it is necessary to exhaust the internal remedies available under the social welfare code before seeking judicial review.

879. In State (Abenglen Properties Ltd.) v. Dublin Corporation, Henchy J. stated:

> where Parliament has provided a self-contained administrative and quasi-judicial scheme, postulating only a limited use of the Courts, certiorari should not be issued when, as in the instant case, use of the statutory procedure for the correction of error was adequate (and, indeed, more suitable) to meet the complaints on which the application for certiorari is grounded.[1469]

880. However, in a number of subsequent cases, the Supreme Court approved Barron J's statement in a subsequent High Court case that:

> The real question to be determined where an appeal lies is the relative merits of an appeal against granting relief by way of judicial review. It is not just a question of whether an alternative remedy exists or whether the applicant has

1465. [2000] IESC 22.
1466. For a recent discussion of the authorities *see M.D. v. Minister for Social Protection* [2023] IEHC 88. *Orange* has been followed in relation to appeals from decisions of the Financial Services Ombudsman in *Ulster Bank Investment Funds Limited v. Financial Services Ombudsman* [2006] IEHC 323; but again, the statutory wording was not confined to questions of law. *See also M & J. Gleeson v. The Competition Authority* [1999] 1 ILRM 401 and *Carrigdale Hotel Limited v. The Comptroller of Patent Designs and Trade Marks* [2004] 3 I.R. 410.
1467. [2020] IESC 25.
1468. *See* generally Hogan, Morgan & Daly, *Administrative Law in Ireland*, 5th ed. (Dublin: Round Hall, 2019), Chs 10 and 11.
1469. [1984] IR 381.

> taken steps to pursue such a remedy. The true question is which is the more appropriate remedy considered in the context of common sense, the ability to deal with the questions raised and principles of fairness; provided, of course, that the applicant has not gone too far down one road to be estopped from changing his or her mind.[1470]

Applying this approach, for example, in *O'Donnell v. Tipperary South Riding,* which involved an employment claim where the Oireachtas had clearly provided an alternative quasi-judicial remedy (the EAT), the Supreme Court ultimately ruled that the appropriate remedy was that of the appeal to the Tribunal but only on a consideration of all the facts of the case.[1471] Denham J (as she then was) stated that in deciding between judicial review and an alternative remedy:

> the true question is as to which is the more appropriate in the context of common sense, the ability to deal with the questions raised and the principles of fairness.[1472]

However, in a number of cases, *Abenglen* continues to be relied on.[1473]

881. As Hogan J. said:

> not all of the case-law on this topic since the Supreme Court's first comprehensive examination of this question [in *Abenglen*] has been perfectly consistent. Indeed, it may justly be observed that few topics have proved to be more vexed and uncertain that the question of whether the availability of a statutory appeal ought to deprive an applicant of the right – whether as a matter of jurisdiction or discretion – to seek judicial review of a decision which he contends is *ultra vires*. It is clear from the Supreme Court's decision in *Tomlinson* (and, for that matter, *O'Donnell*) that irrespective of what either O'Higgins C.J. or Henchy J. said or intended in *Abenglen Properties* on this topic, there is no such jurisdictional bar. The question is, therefore, one of discretion, to be applied on a case by case basis.[1474]

1470. *McGoldrick v. An Bord Pleanála* [1997] 1 I.R. 497 at p. 509. Approved by the Supreme Court in *Buckley v. Kirby and another* [2000] 3 IR 431; *Stefan v. Minister for Justice* [2001] 4 IR 203; *Tomlinson v. Criminal Injuries Compensation Tribunal* [2005] IESC 1 and *O'Donnell v. Tipperary South Riding* [2005] IESC 18. *See* the discussion by Denham J (as she then was) in *Tomlinson v. Criminal Injuries Compensation Tribunal* [2005] IESC 1, although the learned judge does not explain where the more recent approach leaves the earlier view.
1471. [2005] IESC 18.
1472. At para. 22.
1473. In *N. v. MJELR* [2008] IEHC 308, for example, Hedigan J relied on *Abenglen* in refusing to grant judicial review of a refugee decision and stated that it was only 'only in very rare and limited circumstances indeed' that judicial review would be available in respect of such decisions. In *AM v. Minister for Social Protection* [2013] IEHC 524, Hanna J indicated that the applicant should have taken an appeal under the 2005 Act rather than seeking to have a decision refusing payment of domiciliary care allowance quashed by way of judicial review.
1474. *Ho v. Minister for Justice* [2012] IEHC 231.

882. The circumstances in which a court may, in its discretion, allow judicial review even where an alternative remedy (e.g., appeal) exists were summarized by MacMenamin J in *Sheehan v. Minister for Social and Family Affairs*:

> It is a well-established precept of judicial review that in general where the law provides for a code, or appeal mechanism prior to resorting to judicial review an applicant should exhaust his rights of appeal, unless want of jurisdiction or breach of fair procedures or error of law can be shown.[1475]

In the *Sheehan* case, the judge ruled that the applicant had not exhausted his remedies and refused the reliefs sought. However, the exceptions outlined in *Sheehan* would appear to be quite broad and capable of covering many (if not most) circumstances under which judicial review might be sought. Nonetheless, when one examines more closely the cases cited by MacMenamin J, it would appear that it is not all errors of law which attract judicial review but only where errors of law were made 'in excess of jurisdiction' or 'appear on the face of the record of the decision'. O'Higgins CJ in *Abenglen* specifically stated that:

> If the decision impugned is made without jurisdiction or in breach of natural justice then, normally, the existence of a right of appeal or of a failure to avail of such, should be immaterial. Again, if an appeal can only deal with the merits and not with the question of the jurisdiction involved, the existence of such ought not to be a ground for refusing relief. Other than these, there may be cases where the decision exhibits an error of law and a perfectly simple appeal can rectify the complaint, or where administrative legislation provides adequate appeal machinery which is particularly suitable for dealing with errors in the application of the code in question. In such cases, while retaining always the power to quash, a court should be slow to do so unless satisfied that, for some particular reason, the appeal or alternative remedy is not adequate.[1476]

It is submitted that in most social welfare cases, any errors of law will be within the jurisdiction, and the appeals system generally provides an adequate mechanism to reconsider such errors. Indeed, given that appeals effectively involve a rehearing of the case, it is arguable that even any breach of fair procedures below will normally be capable of being addressed through the appeals system.

883. In *F.D. v. Chief Appeals Officer*, the Court of Appeal recently stated that common sense dictates

> applicants for social benefits/allowances ought to use the very wide [revision] provisions in the Act which are intended to ensure that potentially qualifying applicants would not be excluded on narrow or technical grounds.[1477]

1475. [2010] IEHC 4 at 19. *See also FD v. Chief Appeals Officer* [2022] IEHC 454.
1476. [1984] IR at 393.
1477. [2023] IECA 123 at 44.

884. In that case, the Court held that there was an alternative remedy available to the appellant which she failed to exhaust.

885. However, in a number of cases, the High Court has allowed judicial review claims to proceed, although there was no attempt to exhaust the available appeal procedures.[1478] In *Hrisca v. Minister for Social Protection*, White J (at p. 3) held that the applicants did not, in that case, have to exhaust other remedies including a right to appeal to the SWAO and held that judicial review was the 'more appropriate remedy' given the complex issues of European law involved in that case. It may be that the judges in the other cases were adopting a similar approach. White J referred to the *O'Donnell* line of jurisprudence. In *Petecel v. Minister for Social Protection,*[1479] the Supreme Court, per O'Malley J, held that where the appellant challenged the validity of an EU instrument, he did not have to have recourse to the appeal process as that process could not provide the remedy he sought and so he could proceed by way of judicial review. The Court indicated that this was an exception to the normal rule requiring recourse to the statutory appeal process. Barrett J in *B. v. Minister for Social Protection* suggested a further category of the case not required to exhaust remedies, *viz.* where the process whereby that decision was formulated is challenged, and there is no provision in the social welfare code whereby the applicants can challenge the process, as opposed to the outcome, of decision-making.[1480]

886. Applications for judicial review should normally be brought within three months of the decision being challenged but in *Murphy v. Chief Appeals Officer* [2021] IEHC 455, Simons J granted an extension of this time limit because social welfare legislation may impact on people who are vulnerable and with little formal education and because the system of social welfare appeals and reviews is labyrinthian. In light of these factors, he considered it would be unduly harsh to shut out an individual from a remedy because s/he failed to comply with a time-limit that was not obvious.

887. Ombudsman: The Ombudsman may review the decisions of appeals officers.[1481]

888. Reference to the Court of Justice of the European Union: In accordance with Article 267 of the EU Treaty, when any question concerning the interpretation of EU law is raised before any court or tribunal of a Member State, the court or tribunal may, if it considers that a decision on the question is necessary to enable it to

1478. *Solovastru v. Minister* for Social Protection [2011] IEHC 532; *Hrisca v. Minister for Social Protection*, High Court, unreported 16 Feb. 2012; *Genov and Gusa v. Minister for Social Protection* [2013] IEHC 340.

1479. [2020] IESC 25.

1480. [2014] IEHC 186. This issue was not considered by the Court of Appeal in its subsequent decision in this case – [2016] IECA 116.

1481. *See* Hogan, Morgan & Daly, *Administrative Law in Ireland*, 5th ed. (Dublin: Round Hall, 2019), Ch. 9. Given the quasi-judicial functions and increased independence of the Social Welfare Appeals Office, this jurisdiction is arguably now somewhat inappropriate.

give judgment, request the Court of Justice to give a ruling on that question. The Court of Justice has considered the question as to which national bodies are to be considered to be tribunals for this purpose and, therefore, to have the power to refer a question to the Court. The Court has taken a broad interpretation of the concept of what constitutes a tribunal for this purpose.[1482] The Court decided that a tribunal of a Dutch social security fund was entitled to refer a question to the Court. The Court of Justice noted that the tribunal was set up under public law, its rules had to be approved by a Dutch Minister of State, the members of the tribunal were appointed by the responsible Minister, and the tribunal was bound to apply the rule of law in disputes coming before it. Similarly, the position of appeals officer is set up under the SW Acts, the Regulations relating to appeals are made by the Minister who also appoints the appeals officers, and an appeals officer must apply the law in coming to a decision on an appeal. The decision of an appeals officer is legally binding. Therefore, it is arguable that the position of an appeals officer comes within the definition of a tribunal for the purpose of Article 267 of the EU Treaty (TFEU) and that an appeals officer has the power to refer a question involving an interpretation of EU law in relation to an appeal to the Court of Justice.[1483] References to the Court of Justice are frequently made by the social security appeals bodies in the other Member States, including the Upper Tribunal in the UK.

§3. The SWA Determination and Appeal System

889. Section 299(2), as amended by section 34 SW&PA 2007 and section 15(b)(i) SW&PA 2014, authorizes the Minister to appoint designated persons for the purposes of determining the entitlement of any person to SWA and the amount of any such allowance[1484] (though by virtue of section 300(3A),[1485] deciding officers determine claims for SWA where the claimant is (i) awaiting a decision on a claim for another social welfare payment, or appealing against a decision made in respect of such claim or (ii) where the claim is in respect of rent supplement in prescribed cases). A designated person may revise a determination of another designated person in relation to entitlement to SWA where (i) it appears that the original determination was erroneous in light of new evidence or new facts brought to his or her attention or because of some mistake having been made in relation to the law or the facts, or (ii) where there has been a relevant change of circumstances since the original determination to grant SWA to the claim – section 324(1) as substituted by

1482. Case 61/65, *Vaassen-Gobbels v. Beambtenfonds voor het Mijnbedrijf* [1966] ECR 261.

1483. Note, however, that in *Petecel v. Minister for Social Protection* [2020] IESC 25, the Supreme Court, per O'Malley J, stated *obiter*, at para. 55, that the Chief Appeals Officer and appeals officers did not constitute a tribunal for the purpose of referring questions of EU law to the Court of Justice for preliminary ruling under Art. 267 TFEU. However, no reference was made to the *Vaassen-Gobbels* case.

1484. Section 321, as amended by s. 18 SW&PA 2008, further provides that, for the purpose of SWA, any reference to a decision in Part 10 of the 2005 Act shall be read as a reference to a determination by a designated person.

1485. As inserted by s. 18 SW&PA 2008.

section 5(1) SW&P(No.2)A 2013.[1486] This second situation does not apply where the original determination was to refuse to grant SWA, and there has been a subsequent change of circumstances. In this scenario, the claimant must make a fresh application for SWA. A designated person may also revise the decision of an appeals officer to grant SWA where there has been a relevant change of circumstances – *ibid.*[1487] Section 325(a), as amended by section 18 SW&PA 2008, provides that where the revised decision discontinues or reduces SWA and the original determination was given or continued in effect by reason of a false or misleading representation knowingly made or by reason of the wilful concealment of any material fact, the revised decision will take effect from the date on which the original determination took effect, though the original determination may, at the discretion of the designated person, continue to apply to any period covered by it to which the false or misleading representation or the wilful concealment of any material fact does not relate. Section 325(b), as amended by section 18 SW&PA 2008, provides that where SWA is disallowed or reduced in a revised determination by virtue of new evidence or new facts coming to the attention of the designated person, the revised determination shall take effect from such date as the designated person shall determine, having regard to the new facts or new evidence and the circumstances of the case. In any other case, a revised determination shall take effect from the date considered appropriate by the designated person having regard to the circumstances of the case – section 325(c), as amended by section 18 SW&PA 2008. A bureau officer may also revise a determination of a designated person in relation to entitlement to SWA where it appears to the bureau officer that the determination ought to be revised having regard to the facts as they are established to the satisfaction of the bureau officer – section 301(2) as amended by section 18 SW&P(No.2)A 2013. However, this power cannot be exercised in a case where the matter is on appeal under section 311 unless the revised determination is in favour of the claimant – section 301(4) as amended by section 18 SW&PA 2008.

890. By virtue of section 311(1) as amended by section 13(c) SW&PA 2013 and section 18 SW&PA 2008, any person dissatisfied with any decision of a deciding officer or with the determination of a designated person under sections 196 (relating to the calculation of SWA), 197 (relating to the weekly amount of SWA payable), or 198 (relating to the payment of weekly or monthly supplements) may appeal against the decision or determination to an appeals officer. Section 323 provides that when a person is dissatisfied with the determination by a designated person of a claim for SWA made under sections 200, 201 or 202, (relating to allowances in kind, ENPs and urgent cases, respectively), an appeal shall lie against such determination to

1486. By virtue of s. 301(2A) as inserted by s. 3(1)(b) SW&P(No.2)A 2013, a deciding officer may revise the determination of a designated person on the same grounds, though not in a case where the matter is on appeal under s. 311 unless the revised determination is in favour of the claimant – s. 301(4) as amended by s. 18 SW&PA 2008.

1487. A designated person may not revise a determination of another designated person or a decision of an appeals officer where the matter is on appeal under s. 311 or s. 323 unless the revised determination is in favour of the claimant – s. 324(2) as amended by s. 18 SW&PA 2008.

another person appointed or designated by the Minister.[1488] Appeals in relation to SWA are dealt with in the same manner as general social welfare appeals (as outlined above) once submitted to the SWAO.[1489]

891. Section 330 provides that the Minister may by regulations specify the procedures to be followed in, *inter alia*, making determinations on SWA. Part 7 of the Social Welfare (Consolidated SWA) Regulations of 2007 (as substituted by Article 6 of S.I. No. 514 of 2011) set out the rules in this regard.

892. Article 40 of the Regulations provides that a determination by any designated person on a claim to SWA is to be in writing and that a determination that is not in favour of the person must include a note of the reasons for the determination. Article 41 provides that any person who is dissatisfied with the determination by of a designated person of a claim for SWA and wishes to appeal against such determination must give notice in that regard, in writing, to an officer appointed or designated by the Minister under section 323 of the Principal Act to determine such appeal and known as a Review Officer. An appeal must be made within twenty-one days from the date of the notification of the determination to the appellant, but notice of appeal given after the end of that period may, with the approval of the Review Officer, be accepted. The notice of appeal should contain a statement of the facts and contentions upon which the appellant intends to rely, and the appellant should include with the notice of appeal any documentary evidence in support of the appeal. The Review Officer then sends the notice of appeal to the Minister, who returns to the Review Officer (a) a statement showing the extent to which the facts and contentions advanced by the appellant in relation to his or her appeal are admitted or disputed, and (b) any information, document, or item in the power and control of the designated officer that is relevant to the appeal.[1490] The Review Officer may seek further details on the appeal from the appellant or the designated officer. He or she may allow the amendment of any notice of appeal, statement, or particulars at any stage of the proceedings.[1491]

893. The SWA Appeal Regulations do not make any reference to oral hearings, and it is rare for an oral hearing to be given under the SWA scheme. Article 44 provides that the appeal determination must be in writing and that in any case in which the determination is not in favour of the appellant, it must include a note of the reasons for the decision. The Review Officer then notifies the appellant of the determination and (when relevant) of the reasons therefor.

894. All decisions regarding eligibility for SWA are subject to judicial review by the High Court, and they can also be investigated by the Ombudsman.

1488. This person is known as a Review Officer – *see* Art. 41 of S.I. No. 412 of 2007 as substituted by Art. 7 of S.I. No. 514 of 2011.
1489. The provisions of the Social Welfare (Appeals) Regulations, 1998 apply to these SWA appeals.
1490. SW(CSWA)R, Art. 42.
1491. Article 43.

Selected Bibliography

Legislation

Clark, R., *Annotated Guide to Social Welfare Law*, London: Sweet & Maxwell, 1995.

Clark, R., *Irish Current Law Statutes Annotated*, Dublin: Round Hall, Various.

Monographs

Whyte, G. *Social Inclusion and the Legal System* (2nd ed.) Dublin: IPA, 2015.

Selected Bibliography

Table of Cases

Table of Legislation

Table of Sections of the Social Welfare (Consolidation) Act 2005

Table of Sections of the Health Act 1970

Index

The numbers here refer to paragraph numbers.

Index

www.ingramcontent.com/pod-product-compliance
Lightning Source LLC
Chambersburg PA
CBHW071411230926
51846CB00001B/55
* 9 7 8 9 4 0 3 5 1 8 1 8 3 *